TITANIC

THE SHIP THAT NEVER SANK?

ROBIN GARDINER

Ian Allan

PUBLISHING

First published 1998 in hardback
Reprinted 1998
First paperback impression 2001
Reprinted 2003 and 2004
Second paperback impression 2009

ISBN 978 0 7110 3486 0

Published by Ian Allan Publishing

an imprint of Ian Allan Publishing Ltd, Hersham, Surrey KT12 4RG.
Printed and bound in the UK by CPI Mackays, Chatham ME5 8TD.

Code: 0910/C2

Contents

Acknowledgements

I would like to express my gratitude to all those authors whose published works provided such a welter of invaluable information, far too many to name here but who are listed in the Bibliography. It was these books, some of them written many years ago, that first aroused my interest in the loss of the *Titanic*. Another huge source of information was a transcript of the Board of Trade inquiry, taken by a Chamber of Commerce reporter in 1912, which was hunted down at the Bodleian Library by a most determined librarian, despite it being misfiled. Unfortunately I do not know the lady's name.

Many thanks to the people who have provided me with ideas or additional information: Arthur (Jack) Kimberley, Graham Barton, Rev Pat Thomas, Mrs Ann Robinson, Steve Hall, Robert McDougall, Miss J. Petrie, Patricia Meikle, Frank Sinclair, William Fong, Ian Church, Midori Brawn, to name but a few.

Although he was not involved in the writing of this book, my thanks to Dan van der Vat who, in the past, has given freely of his advice on style and presentation. I learned a lot from Dan. My thanks to Dinah Wiener for her continuing support.

Thanks to my friends who over the years have listened to my opinions, expressed their own views when they could get a word in, and kept me informed of newspaper articles, television programmes etc, particularly Roger, John, Derrick, Alan, Eric, Mick and Lis. And, of course, my wife Lynn and son Bill who have put up with the *Titanic* for longer than most people could stand.

Finally I would like to thank all those at Ian Allan's who have made the publication of this book seem so easy.

Prologue

Even a cursory examination of the available evidence is enough to show that the story of the loss of the White Star liner *Titanic*, as we have been told it through the years, must be untrue. Just about all accounts tell of passengers and crew members being swept off the ship as she foundered, swimming about for up to a couple of hours and then spending up to another four hours standing on an upturned lifeboat. Nobody could have survived in the icy waters of the North Atlantic for as long as this group of *Titanic's* survivors claimed. Maximum survival time in water as cold as that surrounding *Titanic* (-2ºC) is a very few minutes at best. It was this simple absurdity that first set me thinking that I might be looking at a cover-up.

As I delved deeper into the story, more and more inconsistencies became apparent. Inconsistencies that individually meant little but collectively pointed to a grimmer reality than that depicted in the usual heroic legend. Gone was the calm orderly evacuation of the sinking liner. Instead, a scene of chaos and discrimination emerged. It was no accident that a far higher percentage of first class passengers was saved than second class. Nor then did it come as any surprise to find that an even bigger discrepancy existed between those saved from second and third class.

Officers who were later acclaimed as heroes were exposed as anything but. One in particular removed a boy from a lifeboat, at gunpoint, before escaping in that same boat himself. Another told how he and his superior left the ship after being told by the captain to abandon their post. The timing of a wireless message received aboard another vessel in the general area proves without a doubt that this officer was lying. Yet another, ordered when he left in a lifeboat to stand close by the ship in order to pick people from the water after the ship foundered, promptly rowed away as fast as he could.

Descriptions of the collision and damage supposedly sustained by *Titanic* do not agree. The slight scrape with the ice that was hardly noticed by most aboard contradicts solid evidence of structural damage at least 5½ft within the outer hull of the vessel.

Titanic carried a total of 20 lifeboats, four of them collapsibles which looked more like life-rafts. Three independent witnesses all described an extra lifeboat close to where the ship sank, one of them seeing this boat fairly soon after the collision. An extra lifeboat on the scene must have meant another ship was very close by.

Then came evidence to show that the ice the ship encountered was seen first not 500yd ahead but more like 11 miles. I began to wonder if perhaps the sinking of the *Titanic* might not have been an accident at all.

Preface

Many of you coming to this book will already have read *The Riddle of the Titanic*. However, for the benefit of those who haven't, the basic arguments of that book are:

- That the collision between HMS *Hawke* and RMS *Olympic* may have caused more serious damage to the liner than its owners were prepared to admit at the time.
- That the inquiry, which automatically followed any collision involving a naval vessel, was not entirely unbiased.
- That, as a result of the inquiry, the White Star line could not recover the cost of repairs to its ship from the insurance companies.
- That, given the immense initial outlay in constructing *Olympic* and *Titanic*, and the amount of income lost by the former's two-month lay up following the *Hawke* incident, the owners and builders were left with serious financial problems.
- That the owners, with the help of the builders, might have decided to switch the brand new *Titanic* with her slightly older sister in order to get at least one vessel back to sea and earning money.
- That the owners, deciding that repair of the *Olympic* was uneconomic, might have resolved to dispose of the ship in such a way as to be able, this time, to collect on their insurance.

Although *The Riddle of the Titanic* is a serious and accurate account of events surrounding the loss of the *Titanic*, the theory of there having been a possible insurance fraud linked to the switching of the *Titanic* with her sister ship *Olympic* is to a great extent swallowed up by the sheer weight of other material in the book and has been deemed unlikely in light of what has become known as the '401 Test'. However, since publication of *The Riddle* further research has shown that the '401 Test' — 401 being the *Titanic's* build number — is not the acid test it was once considered to be by some.

Since details of my hypothesis have been made public, I have been asked time and again, by readers, for more details of the switch theory and for another book on the same subject. With the benefit of new information, some of which came to light as a direct result of *The Riddle of the Titanic*, and further research, it is now time, I believe, for that book. This is it …

1

'Paddy the Pig'

The passenger and crew lists for the White Star liner RMS *Titanic* are notoriously unreliable. For example, two men gave evidence at the British Inquiry whose names do not appear on the crew list — Thomas Ranger and Samuel James Rule. The second of these witnesses not only fails to appear on the crew list but is also absent from the lists of survivors. However, there can be no doubt that both were aboard the vessel at the time of the disaster.

Nine more crew members whose names are absent from the crew list appear on the lists of survivors saved by the Cunard vessel *Carpathia*. In total the number of crew aboard the White Star ship, arrived at by adding the number of names on the official crew list to the 11 extra known survivors, is 884. The minimum number of crew aboard was estimated by the Board of Trade at 885. More realistically, the White Star Company and emigration officers, having examined every crew member aboard, put the figure at 892. How many more there might have been is anybody's guess. To learn the names of crew members who did not appear on the signing-on list we would have to find them as survivors whose names were recorded aboard *Carpathia*, or those called to give evidence before one of the official inquiries.

Which brings me to Paddy Fenton, whose story appeared in an Australian newspaper, the *Northern Star*, on 31 July 1996.

Paddy Fenton, also known as 'Paddy the Pig', was well known amongst the sea-going fraternity off the Australian coast, of which he was a long standing member. Over a period of many years Paddy told any number of times the story that follows. In 1971 he happened to recount it to Dennis Finch, one of four seafaring brothers. (Dennis Finch recalled being told the story in 1968 but Australian Maritime Safety Authority records show that the only period he and Fenton were together in the *Kooliga* was from 9 July 1971 to 6 September 1971. After 25 years, he might be forgiven for getting his dates confused.) In the fullness of time the tale reached Dennis's father, F. B. Finch who passed it on to the *Northern Star* in the form of a letter.

'Paddy Fenton first went to sea in 1898 as an eight-year old cabin boy aboard a sailing ship called the *Red Rock* and they went missing for 180 days in the Indian Ocean; the vessel was "becalmed". In 1912 Paddy was a 22 year old Bucko [Ordinary Seaman] aboard the *Titanic*.

'He always maintained that the iceberg alone did not sink the *Titanic*, that it had a fire burning in the coal bunkers for a week and that the Captain and the company knew about it. Paddy also said that when the crew joined the *Titanic* there were rumours that the company had switched ships at lay up and that an insurance scam was going on.

'They sailed in a great hurry from Belfast and said that when they hit the iceberg it did not do serious damage but when the cold water hit the coal fire, it exploded and caused the fatal damage.

'The chief mate put Paddy in charge of a lifeboat, keeping older hands on deck for lowering boats.

'When the surviving crew got to port they were all taken aside and met by two men, one in a high position in the company, the other man was in a very high position in the Government. The Government man read the crew the Official Secrets Act, explaining that if they told of the real reason of the sinking, or the rumours of an insurance scam, they would serve a minimum of 20 years in jail and would never get a job when they got out.

'The Government man told them that if the truth got out it would finish the shipping Company and "Bankrupt the Government".

'Paddy said that the guilt of keeping quiet all those years had taken a great toll on his health and the sanity of the surviving crew.

'This story was told to Dennis Finch either on the *Kooyong* or the *Kooliga* and when the ship was laid up in 1969–70, Paddy was put in a old people's home. The ship picked a crew up six months later and the seaman's Union convinced the company to take Paddy back as Bosun as he and the ship did not have long to go. Paddy Fenton died in 1971.'

Was Paddy Fenton fantasising, or is the story nothing less than the truth, with perhaps an allowance to be made for slight lapses of memory over the 56 years between the events he spoke of and his telling what he knew? In essence, many of his assertions, as far as they can be checked, are correct.

Titanic did leave Belfast in a great hurry, but not to start her maiden voyage. She was bound for Southampton to provision and take aboard linen, cutlery and all that would be required at sea, that the builders could not provide. There was no time to be lost and the activity aboard would have been feverish as a short-handed crew prepared the ship for her maiden voyage.

There was a fire burning in the ship's bunkers. This would not have been widely known at the time. The White Star line would hardly have advertised the fact that they were sending luxury liners to sea, on fire.

When the surviving crew members did eventually return to England they were met by persons occupying a high position in the company, most notably Harold Sanderson, a manager and director of White Star and another director, E. C. Grenfell (later to be elevated to the peerage). Representing the Government was a Board of Trade official with four assistants, names unknown, and Mr W. Woolven, Receiver of Wrecks — imposing enough figures to strike fear into the stoutest hearted ordinary seaman.

Paddy Fenton's claim that if the truth got out, it would 'Bankrupt the Government', at first seemed ridiculous, but even a little simple research soon showed that the owner of the White Star line was indeed in a position to embarrass governments. He was John Pierpont Morgan, an American financier who owned the giant International Mercantile Marine Company (IMM), which in turn owned the Oceanic Steam Navigation Co, which owned the White Star line. He was a close friend of Alfred de Rothschild and Rothschild money had supported the British Government throughout the Crimean War of 1854–56. Early in the 20th century Morgan, in company with Rothschild's and Baring's banks, subscribed half of a £32 million British Government issue of consols (Government securities). Even as questions were being asked in the House of Commons about Morgan's attempt to buy the British shipping companies (IMM was also acquiring control through share purchases of other British shipping companies such as the Atlantic Transport, Leyland and Dominion Lines), Mr Balfour, Lord Salisbury's successor as Prime Minister, praised his long record in Anglo-American finance.

As controller of a substantial amount of American steel production, Morgan was able to enforce harsh price agreements with foreign governments. With war in Europe looming, the British Government would be needing the magnate's goodwill. To be on the safe side, the Government employed Morgan's London office to procure war materials from the United States.

It would be all too easy to write off Mr Finch's letter about the story told to his son, except that some of the details mentioned were not widely known in 1971; indeed, they are not widely known today. Outside the ever-growing army of people who study the great ship and the disaster which befell her, how many people know that the surviving crew members were kept incommunicado on their return to England? How many know of the bunker fire in a forward boiler room? More to the point, how many know of the existence of a large hole in the starboard side of the wreck's hull, forward of the bridge? This hole has all the hallmarks of having been caused by an internal explosion.

The wreck of the *Titanic* was not discovered until 1985 when Dr Robert Ballard first filmed the remains of the ship. Even then the hole in the hull escaped his attention and was not mentioned by anyone until some years later. How could Paddy Fenton have known about an explosion aboard the vessel in 1968, or 1971, unless he was a witness to that explosion and its results more than half a century earlier?

'The iceberg did not do serious damage,' said Paddy. This remarkable comment is supported by the descriptions of the collision given by the majority of the survivors. Most of those aboard felt nothing more than a slight vibration consistent with the engines being put 'Full Astern'; they didn't notice a collision at all.

'They sailed in a great hurry from Belfast,' says the letter, implying that Paddy Fenton joined the ship there and not in Southampton. This could explain why his, and other names fail to appear in the list of crewmen who signed aboard in the Hampshire port on the south coast of England.

We know from the letter that Paddy went to sea at the tender age of eight years old, and we can fairly assume from his name that he came from Ireland. The sea has long been the poor man's escape from poverty and unemployment ashore; both conditions were commonplace in Ireland at the end of the 19th century. After serving for 72 years Fenton had still only risen to the rank of Bosun, a subordinate officer who directs working parties aboard ship. On land he would be known as a foreman. The most likely cause of Paddy Fenton's excruciatingly slow rise in his chosen service is the lack of a formal education. It is a fact of life that people like doing what they are good at or, conversely, are good at what they like doing. That he remained at sea for so long is ample evidence that Paddy liked his job, so much so that he chose to spend the last few months of his life afloat, coming out of retirement to do so.

If Paddy Fenton was lacking what is today regarded as a normal education, then is it likely that he would have read the daily transcripts of the British Inquiry? Unless he was aboard the *Titanic*, or knew somebody that was, then that is one of the very few ways that he could have known about the bunker fire.

What Paddy had to say about his experience of the *Red Rock* also withstood scrutiny, with the usual allowances for uncertain memory so long after the event. On 20 February 1899, with a crew of 24, *Red Rock* sailed from Townsville in Queensland, Australia, for Noumea in New Caledonia. The voyage was only of about a thousand miles and should, even allowing for unfavourable conditions, have been completed in a couple of weeks. On 16 June 1899 Lloyd's posted the ship as missing; she had been gone for more than 16 weeks. Six days later the *Red Rock* reached her destination. To date she is the only vessel declared as 'missing' by Lloyd's that has ever reappeared.[1]

Fenton's story has the ring of truth in as much as, if he told it in 1971, he had to be aboard the *Titanic* to know as much as he apparently did. He is unique, as far as I am aware, in being the only person, other than myself, to suggest that the *Titanic* had been switched with her slightly older sister *Olympic*. He also advances a fascinating explanation of how such a huge and seemingly outlandish fraud could have been kept secret – with the connivance of the British Government. He does not explain why the Government should be a party to such a cover-up.

Did the British Government conspire with the White Star line to suppress the real reasons for the *Titanic* disaster? Regrettably, to my mind the answer appears to be yes.

Ample evidence was introduced at the inquiry to make it plain that witnesses were not telling all that they knew, if not actually lying. Feats of endurance were accepted by Lord Mersey's committee that were absolutely impossible to believe. Ships' positions, worked out by competent navigators, were disregarded. Witnesses who tried to tell how they had been approached by interested parties, before the inquiry began, were ignored. Signals sent up by the doomed liner were misrepresented, to the extent that attention was diverted from what had really happened, to focus on the hapless captain of the *Californian*.

It remains focused on Captain Lord to this day, even though the discovery of the wreck established, beyond all reasonable doubt, that his ship was too far from *Titanic* to have seen her signals. The smokescreen thrown up by Lord Mersey, and to a lesser extent by William Alden Smith, at the American Inquiry still obscures the facts.

Nevertheless, a close examination of the available evidence — what was said at the inquiries, and what was said by witnesses before and after those inquiries — reveals a very different sequence of events from those suggested by both official investigations.

Already we have established that:

- There were a number of crew members aboard *Titanic* who do not appear on the official lists;
- Amongst the hitherto unnamed mariners was, quite possibly, James A. Fenton, alias 'Paddy the Pig', who in the early 1970s hinted at how the loss of that vessel was not entirely accidental.

2

A Potted History of White Star
and another 'Atlantic' Crossing

During the 50 years between 1875 and 1925 Harland & Wolff was probably the greatest shipyard in the world.[1] The company built the finest ships possible and, in its efforts to attain perfection, constructed what is probably the most famous ship ever built. However, this did not mean that the yard showed a profit and for the first few years of the new century it was in serious financial difficulties. This was brought about by a price war between the major transatlantic shipping lines of the day. The whole dilemma had been caused by the machinations of one man in his efforts to buy up all the passenger lines engaged in the normally lucrative emigrant trade.

As a result of the fierce competition for the North Atlantic passenger trade, fares had fallen to an all-time low. Most ship owners were in difficulties and in no financial position to order new vessels. Nevertheless, even when most other North Atlantic steamship lines didn't pay their shareholders a dividend, one company always did. Despite the hard times, the Oceanic Steam Navigation Co always managed to repay the confidence of its shareholders to the tune of at least 7% per annum.[2]

In 1893 the world's most powerful financier was making an Atlantic crossing. Sometime during this voyage a fellow traveller asked J. P. Morgan if it might be possible to buy up all the passenger shipping then on that route. The idea was to eliminate any competition and so allow the cartel owners to charge realistic fares. As things were, in order to attract passengers, owners were offering lower and lower rates. The inevitable consequence of this fare slashing was lower profits and therefore lower standards.

'Ought to be,' was Morgan's laconic reply.[3]

At that time Mr Morgan was fully occupied. He was buying up as much of America's steel-producing capacity as was available and putting together a consortium known as 'Big Steel'. Even while the steel cartel was being assembled, the financier was also swallowing up railroads until he controlled every piece of rolling stock on America's eastern seaboard. Nevertheless, he did not forget the suggestion and just before the turn of the century he acted by buying the American Inman and Red Star lines.[4]

Then this financial colossus, with the power to control governments, turned his acquisitive gaze toward Europe. (In 1896, to halt a run on the dollar, Morgan had made up the US treasury reserves from $38,000,000 to the necessary $100,000,000. At that time Morgan had one and a half times as much gold in Fort Knox as the government of the embryonic superpower.) He approached the German Hamburg-Amerika Company. The Germans at first seemed receptive to his advances, but even in 1900 they were planning their own domination of the maritime market. Morgan therefore switched direction and focused on Britain. His primary targets were the leading British companies, White Star and Cunard.[5] Before making a move against either, he snapped up two smaller British lines, Leyland and Dominion.

Because of fierce competition from the Germans and Cunard, White Star had been experiencing financial difficulties for some time and was vulnerable to a Morgan takeover.[6] Never one to haggle, Morgan invariably offered more than the face value of a company when he made a takeover bid. His offer for White Star was no exception to that rule. He offered 10 times the line's earnings for 1900, an exceptionally good year[7] due to troop transportation during the Boer War.

J. Bruce Ismay, chairman and managing director of the line, resisted the takeover so Morgan escalated the price war mentioned above. Third class fares for an Atlantic crossing fell as low as £2,[8] which was, of course, uneconomic. The independent shipping lines were forced into financial trouble and even though White Star and Cunard were supported by the British Government, they still felt the pinch. White Star could not even afford to have any new ships built by close partner Harland & Wolff,[9] and so Morgan's economic tactics were felt by both the builders and owners.

At the outset both companies had been funded by the same Liverpool financier, Gustav Schwabe. Schwabe had first invested heavily in the Bibby Line. He then financed Edward Harland when Harland initially, in 1859, took over Hickson's Queen's Island yard, on the River Lagan. The financier gave all Bibby's construction and repair work to Harland and, in return, the shipbuilder took on Schwabe's nephew Gustav Wolff as a partner in the business. Wolff was placed in charge of the drawing office, but he was also an engineer and so brought more than mere money into the partnership.[10]

In an age of wooden ships, Harland's ambition was to build entirely in iron and steel. This aspiration was realised with his first contract for three 270ft long steamers for the Bibby Line.[11]

The White Star line was founded in 1845 by John Pilkington and Henry Threlfall Wilson and originally operated wooden sailing ships carrying immigrants to the new world. In the early 1850s the company did very well transporting prospective miners headed for the Californian gold fields.[12] When Pilkington retired in 1857, Wilson took on James Chambers and the company name was changed to Wilson & Chambers, although it was still popularly known as White Star. By this time the gold rush in California had fizzled out and another in Australia had begun, so the line carried hopeful prospectors there instead.[13] In December 1865 Chambers left the company and was replaced by John Cunningham. In 1867 Wilson & Cunningham owed the Royal Bank of Liverpool £527,000 and the company was dissolved and went into liquidation.[14]

In the same year Thomas Henry Ismay bought the White Star flag and goodwill for £1,000.[15] Two years later he was invited to dine with that prominent merchant Gustav Schwabe. Schwabe told him that his nephew Gustav Wolff had entered into partnership with Edward Harland in a shipbuilding yard at Belfast and that the shipbuilder had lately designed and constructed some iron ships for the Bibby Line.

Schwabe had already invested as much money as he possibly could in Harland & Wolff and there were no more shares available. However, he wanted to invest more money in shipping and he suggested that Ismay might be the man to start a new North Atlantic steamship company. If Ismay were prepared to have all of the new line's steamships built by Harland & Wolff on a 'cost plus 4%' basis then Schwabe would back the line to the limit and use his influence with other Liverpool business men to do the same.[16] Ismay agreed, and on 6 September 1869 the Oceanic Steam Navigation Co, more generally known as the White Star line, was formed with £400,000 capital in £1,000 shares. The earliest list of shareholders includes the names T. H. Ismay, E. J. Harland and Gustavus W. Wolff.[17]

As a consequence of Schwabe's interest, White Star and Harland & Wolff were closely connected right from the beginning. As the shipping line prospered, so must the builders. Indeed, over the years Harland & Wolff would build more than 75 ships for the White Star line, most on the 'cost plus' basis.

No sooner was the company formed than an order was placed with Harland & Wolff for four iron ships, this was soon increased to six.[18] Edward Harland designed the new ships in such a way that the superstructure was a continuation of the hull. This was a revolutionary new concept and rendered all existing steamers obsolete.[19] Until then the usual practice had been to build a hull, fit the decks and then build on deckhouses as required. From these earliest days all White Star steamers had a gold band round the hull immediately below the white painted superstructure,[20] making them distinctive.

No other shipbuilder ever received an order from White Star. Harland & Wolff were given carte blanche to construct the finest possible ships, which they did, all on the 'cost plus' basis. The only vessel not built on this basis was the *Laurentic II*[21] of 1927, by which time both companies were mere shadows of their former selves.

The first of the initial order constructed was given the company name *Oceanic* and launched on 27 August 1870, at a cost of £120,000. Three months later, on 26 November 1870, a second vessel was launched and named *Atlantic*. Within a year the sister ships *Baltic* and *Republic* and the somewhat larger *Adriatic* and *Celtic* were added to the White Star fleet.

Although almost identical in outward appearance, *Atlantic's* passenger accommodation was even more magnificent than that of the already lavish *Oceanic*.[22] It was described at the time thus:

'The interior decorations are on a most magnificent scale ... The lounges and fixed seats are upholstered in crimson velvet; the panels are damasked with white and pink and the pilasters, brackets and cornices are of teak, picked out with gold. The bed hangings of the staterooms and sleeping berths, which are large and commodious, are of green rep (similar to corduroy), and the apartments are in all respects elegant and complete.'[23]

Atlantic left Liverpool on her maiden voyage on 6 June 1871.[24]

In a curious parallel with the *Titanic*, 41 years later, *Atlantic* was designed to carry up to 1,166 passengers but carried only 10 lifeboats. These few lifeboats had a total capacity of 600 people and even this exceeded the then Board of Trade regulations by 50%.[25] Another parallel with *Titanic* was that the shortage of lifeboat accommodation would make absolutely no difference to the numbers saved or lost in the event of the vessel foundering.

On All Fools' Day 1873 the White Star line first became the

holders of a dubious record: for the worst shipping disaster in history. Twelve days before, on Thursday, 20 March, *Atlantic* left Liverpool on her 19th and last voyage with about 967 tons of coal in her bunkers. Bestriding the bridge was Captain James Agnew Williams, aged 33.[26] She stopped at Queenstown to pick up a few more passengers and then set out to cross the North Atlantic.[27] Aboard the vessel officially were 35 first class and 776 steerage passengers, 141 crew members and 14 stowaways, making 966 in all. Of these, almost 200 were children.

As the ship sailed steadily westward at about 12.5kts, the weather deteriorated. By Tuesday, 25 March, a full southwesterly gale battered the liner, slowing her to about 8kts. By the following day the storm had worsened considerably, the waves demolishing lifeboat number four, damaging number 10 and smashing a wheelhouse window. Then the steering gear was damaged and the emergency hand gear had to be used until repairs could be made. This slowed the vessel even further until she was making no more than 5kts. At noon on Monday, 31 March, after 11 days at sea, the *Atlantic* was still 460 miles east of Sandy Hook, the entrance to New York harbour. The chief engineer, Foxley, reported that only 128 tons of coal remained in the bunkers, just enough to get them to within 80 miles of Sandy Hook.[28] Captain Agnew altered course for Halifax, Nova Scotia, some 170 miles away — at the Canadian port the ship could obtain additional coal and provisions to assure a safe, if somewhat overdue, arrival in New York.[29]

Taking full advantage of the smoother passage afforded by the ship running before the wind, the firemen decided to clean the fires. Although this was a normal maintenance job, the stokehold men neglected to inform the bridge of what they were doing. The cleaned out furnaces produced more heat and, as a result, the ship gained a little speed. Normally this would not have mattered to any great extent. The officers of the watch would ordinarily notice the increase in speed when they next took a sighting and worked out the vessel's position. This time they did not notice.

At close to midnight, shortly before retiring, Captain Williams ordered Second Officer Henry Ismay Metcalf to keep a sharp lookout for ice. At the same time the captain ordered the officer to keep a special watch for the Sambro Light. If the light, which was situated on an island to the south of the harbour entrance, was sighted or visibility deteriorated, Williams was to be called immediately. The captain ordered that he was to be wakened at 3am at the latest and asked that his steward bring him a hot cocoa at 2.40am.[30]

Unfortunately, the steward, instead of taking the cocoa directly to the captain, first visited the bridge. While he was there Metcalf remembered that Williams had asked to be awakened at 3am. Believing that the steward was 20min early, the second officer said, 'Never mind calling him. I will call him myself in a moment.'[31] At this time there was nothing in sight, even though visibility was good and the lookouts should have been able to see the Sambro Light.

At 3.12am, contrary to regulations, Metcalf left the bridge unattended and went to call the captain.[32] Even as the second officer shook the captain awake, Joseph Carroll, a forward lookout, cried 'Breakers ahead!' Metcalf rushed from the chart room to the bridge and pulled the telegraph handle to full astern. The helmsman, Quartermaster Robert Thomas, put the wheel hard a-starboard.[33] It was all to no avail; before the engines could be reversed the vessel struck Marr's Rock, about 50yd from Meagher's Island, Newfoundland. The *Atlantic* was 12 to 13 miles west of where the officers thought she was.[34] In seconds, five great holes were torn in *Atlantic's* iron plating and the vessel settled more firmly onto the rocks. The only warning the passengers received that anything was amiss was the noise and shock of the ship grinding on the rock. Within seconds all was pandemonium as panic set in.

Heavy seas pushed the ship's stern round until the port side was exposed to the full fury of the elements. One by one the port side lifeboats were smashed to splinters or washed away by the waves. On the starboard side, things were a little better as the officers and crew struggled to lower the boats from that side. Boat three left the ship with no plug in the drainage hole below the waterline. Boat seven was swept away and lost.[35]

Eight minutes after the collision the vessel began to list to starboard. As the list increased, dozens of people were swept off the deck by the merciless waves. Boat number five with Second Officer Metcalf and between 30 and 40 others aboard was crushed under the ship's hull as the list increased to 50°. Water poured into the hull through every opening, drowning those persons who were still below decks. The survivors aboard were obliged to climb the rigging to escape the raging seas. Then, with a huge roar, the boilers exploded.[36]

At 6.30am the first local fishing boats arrived on the scene to take survivors from both the wreck and the rocks that the ship had struck.

Once ashore, Third Officer Brady commandeered a boat and returned to the wreck in an attempt to save some of the people who were still clinging to the rigging. These included Captain Williams, whose hair had, overnight, begun to turn white. Steadily, the fishermen and crew rescued those who remained on the wreck and all but two were safely away from the ship by 8.45am. The two people who remained were rescued by a volunteer crew in a boat commanded by a 36-year old cleric, Rev William J. Ancient. One of these last two was the only child to survive the disaster, of the 200 aboard. Of the unknown number of women who had taken passage on the vessel, not a single one survived.[37] In the worst merchant shipwreck up to that time 565 men, women and children had perished.[38]

In an inquiry into the causes of the disaster beginning on 5 April of that year E. M. MacDonald, Collector of Customs, heard four days of testimony from 22 witnesses. At the end of that inquiry he was in no doubt about the cause of the accident.

Captain Williams' defence, that his decision to alter course for Halifax was 'prudent and justifiable', was accepted, as was his statement that he was asleep in the chart-room, fully dressed, within easy call of the bridge. Captain Williams also pointed out that he had left instructions he was to be wakened at 3am and that he had every confidence in his second officer. As far as it went, Williams' defence was upheld by the inquiry.

However, in his report MacDonald says:

'It seems impossible to account for the error in estimating the ship's speed except on the grounds of incompetence or carelessness ... It seems to have been culpable rashness for [Captain Williams] to order the ship to be run towards the land for three hours at her then full speed, without taking precautions to guard against any possible error in his estimate of his position. The greatest ... and fatal error is ... that the lead was never used although the ship was within soundings for eight hours before she struck; this is a neglect of duty for which there can be positively no excuse.'

MacDonald also said that White Star had insufficiently provisioned the ship with coal. He went on to say that Fourth Officer Brown and the late Second Officer Metcalf had 'improperly' prevented the steward from waking Captain Williams at 2.40am.

In a display of charity rarely seen at such inquiries, MacDonald said that, although revocation of Williams' master's certificate was justified, he would show leniency. In view of the captain's heroic behaviour subsequent to the collision the certificate would merely be suspended for two years.[39]

Five years later, in 1878, the Oceanic Steam Navigation Co had recovered from the blow of the Atlantic tragedy. John Burns, the head of Cunard, no doubt realising that Ismay's star was in the ascendant, suggested that the two companies should merge.[40] Although this merger would indeed take place, it would not happen for another 50 years.

By 1880 the White Star line had become one of the most prominent steamship lines operating a transatlantic service. White Star's first steel ship, the *Ionic*, was delivered on 26 March 1883. This ship and her sister, the *Doric*, were equipped with engines built at Harland & Wolff, the first engines built at the yard.[41]

T.H. Ismay died in 1899 and was succeeded by his 36-year-old son Joseph Bruce.[42] Ismay junior was to remain as chairman of the company until shortly after the loss of the *Titanic*. J. Bruce Ismay (as he is commonly known) was of a shy and sensitive nature, not the ideal disposition for the chairman of a shipping line in a highly competitive marketplace. To hide his real nature, he habitually adopted a defensive façade that made him appear short-tempered and irascible. This often caused people to dislike him until they got to know him better and realised that this was mere bluff.[43] In reality, the young Ismay was a shrewd and capable business man.

While all this was going on at White Star, things had also been happening at Harland & Wolff. In 1862 the Belfast shipyard took on a 15-year old Canadian as an apprentice. Twelve years later, William James Pirrie became a partner in the ever-growing business. Twenty years later, following Edward Harland's death in 1895, Pirrie became chief executive, turning the yard into a public company.

When Gustav Wolff retired in 1906, the ambitious Pirrie was made chairman as well as managing director. One of the first major changes he already had in hand was modernising the yard to enable construction of ever larger vessels. This was accomplished by dispensing with three slipways and establishing two in their place. Over the new slipways he had a huge gantry built of steel girders,[44] 840ft long, 270ft wide and 185ft high. Obviously Pirrie had something special in mind.

As the battle between Morgan and Ismay for control of the White Star line developed, Pirrie backed Morgan rather than support his friend and best customer.[45] Pirrie realised that his yard would have a much larger assured market if Morgan took over White Star.[46] Three years after the death of his father, J. Bruce Ismay was persuaded by Pirrie and Morgan to sell out.[47] The White Star line passed into the hands of J.P. Morgan in 1902, following the purchase of the Oceanic Steam Navigation Co for £10 million.[48]

As the International Navigation Company of Philadelphia, and with the assistance of the Pennsylvania Railroad Company, the Morgan combine had acquired the Inman and Red Star lines in 1893.[49] Now, in 1902 the company changed its name to the International Mercantile Marine Company (IMM) and raised its capital from $15 million to $120 million. IMM began to buy up shares in the Atlantic Transport, Leyland and Dominion lines, rapidly gaining control of those companies.[50]

Morgan was not so fortunate in his attempt to gain control of Cunard, which was thwarted by the British Government's offer of a low interest loan to that company. A condition of this loan was that Cunard would not sell out to the Americans for at least 20 years. The advance of £2.6 million was to finance the construction of two new super-liners, which were to be bigger, faster and more luxurious than anything previously built. In addition, the Government would provide Cunard with a mail subsidy of £150,000 a year.

The Germans, in the shape of the Hamburg-Amerika and North German Lloyd lines, never had any intention of selling out to the acquisitive financier.[51] Mendaciously, they had led him to believe that his plans would be unopposed while secretly securing their own position.

So Morgan had lost his gamble to gain control of all the passenger shipping on the North Atlantic. Characteristically, however, he made do with the one third share which IMM now owned.[52] In total, the company possessed over 100 ships and more were under construction.

Initially, the huge unwieldy combine did not prosper, possibly the only Morgan enterprise to suffer that fate until that time.[53] Morgan realised that he needed an experienced operator to run the new cartel. He believed that there was only one man capable of resolving the problems that beset IMM. That man was the former chief executive of the White Star line, J. Bruce Ismay.[54] At first Ismay resisted Morgan's advances, but by late 1903, one year after its formation, the whole combine was in an unstable financial position[55] and so Morgan redoubled his endeavours. In his efforts to induce Ismay to become president and managing director, Morgan told him that he would give him 'entire control over everything to do with the shipping lines in the combine, except finance'. Privately he assured the ex-Chairman of White Star that money would not be a problem. Morgan said that he would 'make available a private line of cash, which would be greatly to the advantage of both White Star and Harland & Wolff'.[56] Morgan was, in effect, offering Ismay absolute control of the company.[57]

By 9 February 1904, J. P. Morgan had invested $2–3 million of his own fortune in IMM. He was beginning to get a little anxious about investing any more. The total invested in IMM by stockholders was somewhere about $50 million.[58] Morgan decided to limit his investment over the next three years.

Ismay was given a letter explaining just what Morgan intended:

'Mr Morgan is prepared, in the event of the earnings of the International Mercantile Marine Company and subsidiary companies not being sufficient to meet the fixed charges of the International Mercantile Marine Company and subsidiary companies, to advance the monies necessary to make good any deficiencies for a term of three years after the 1st January 1904.'[59]

The financial limitations that J. P. Morgan was setting were thus fully explained to Ismay.[60]

In February 1904 Ismay accepted Morgan's offer and became Chairman and Managing Director of IMM. He was also a director of the Asiatic Steamship Company, the Sea Insurance Company, the Liverpool & London Steamship Protection Association, the Pacific Loan & Investment Company, the Liverpool London & Globe Insurance Company and the London & North Western Railway.[61] His starting salary with IMM was £20,000 a year.[62]

The retiring boss of IMM, Clement Griscom, was ill[63] but he stayed on until Ismay could take the reins, helping the new man settle into the job. Between them they decided, on 7 February 1904, that something needed to be done to clarify the position of the Leyland Line within the organisation. They believed that the situation was, 'at present, impossible'.[64] Mr Wilding, the manager of the Leyland Line, was running it as an independent company, which the other heads of the combine found, understandably, annoying.[65] Slowly but surely Ismay whipped the giant combine into shape until, at last, IMM was an efficient concern[66]—but not quickly enough to suit the rapacious Pirrie, who then had not received the influx of cash that he had anticipated. On 5 March 1904 he wrote to Ismay saying that IMM's greatest stumbling block was 'Want of Capital'. In the same letter, Pirrie admitted that he and Harland & Wolff were in serious financial difficulties. The shipbuilders were unable to find the money to complete the construction of the *Baltic* for White Star.[67] Somehow the money was found, probably from the private line of cash promised by Morgan, and *Baltic* was completed in 1904. She survived to rescue the passengers and crew of the *Republic* after that ship was rammed by the Italian liner *Florida* in January 1909.[68] In Pirrie's pecuniary predicament we find a root cause of much that was to come later. Pirrie's shortage of cash, though, is only one of a number of reasons for suspecting that the loss of the *Titanic* was not the accident it has always been represented as being.

At about the same time as Pirrie was complaining to Ismay about his inadequate funds, Morgan told Ismay that he thought Pirrie was on the verge of bankruptcy. In fact, Morgan thought that if the combination which made up IMM had not been formed, then Pirrie would have been bankrupt in six months.[69]

During the early part of the 20th century, German lines had captured a large part of the North Atlantic trade from their British counterparts. Their liners were noted for their speed and the grandeur of their furnishings and decor. They were also notable for the constant vibration from which they suffered.[70]

The year 1906 saw the advent of a new era in transatlantic travel. Cunard launched the first two liners of an entirely new generation, *Lusitania* and *Mauretania*, the result of the earlier Government loan. These new, turbine-driven, super-liners were impressive, weighing well over 30,000 tons apiece. They were as ornate as the best of the German ships and free of the vibration problems that beset them. The new Cunarders were also to be much faster than any other liners in the world, with a top speed significantly more than 26kts. These vessels made all earlier ocean liners obsolete at a single stroke. Passengers flocked to the new leviathans to the chagrin of other ship owners. Something had to be done to entice disloyal passengers back to White Star ships.

At a dinner party at Downshire House, Pirrie's Belgrave Square, London mansion, he first suggested to Ismay the idea of building two fabulous new liners. It was also suggested that a third be built soon after completion of the first two. Initially Ismay liked the idea and the two men discussed the possibilities. The original concept was for three funnels and four masts[71] but this layout could and would be altered to suit the requirements of the owners and builders. Three-funnelled liners were not to become fashionable until almost the eve of World War 2. The 'Olympic' class liners were still only an idea, but they were destined soon to become a reality.

Harland & Wolff started work in earnest preparing detailed drawings of the new ships. On 29 July 1908, a group of distinguished senior management members from White Star arrived at the Belfast shipyard. They had come to examine the plans of the proposed liners. The scale drawings, prepared under the watchful eye of Pirrie and his nephew Thomas Andrews, the manager of the drafting department, bore the legend:

'400 Plan — 29 July 1908 (Proposed General Arrangement)
S S No 400
850 × 92 × 64ft 6in
Design "D" '

The outline for the new ships included a great glass dome over the first class dining saloon, as in the new Cunarders. There would be electric lifts even in second class, a gymnasium, Turkish baths and a swimming pool.[72] Unlike the Cunard vessels, the new 'Olympics' were planned with two reciprocating engines instead of the relatively novel turbines. They were expected to return a speed of 21kts on these engines alone. This was done despite the turbine's proven superiority in both economy and power. Initially the management of White Star simply would not believe in the supremacy of turbines until they had proven it for themselves. With this end in sight, they commissioned Harland & Wolff to build *Megantic* and *Laurentic*. *Megantic* was fitted with traditional reciprocating engines while *Laurentic* had a combination of turbine and reciprocating. The turbine-powered *Laurentic* would not be ready for her trials until well after construction of the first of the new 'Olympics' had begun.[73]

As well as being more opulent than either the *Lusitania* or the *Mauretania*, the new liners were to be half as large again as the Cunard flagships. They were planned to be the largest man-made moving objects on earth.

The party from White Star, which included among others Harold Sanderson and J. Bruce Ismay, was more than happy with the initial design. Two days later the contract letter (subsequently described as 'a sheet of quarto paper') was signed.[74]

Harland & Wolff's next step was to prepare working drawings from which the tradesmen in the shipyard would actually construct the ships. White Star didn't lay down any specification for the 'Olympic' class vessels, leaving the design almost entirely in the hands of James Pirrie and his team. Strange as it may seem, there were not even any firm instructions about the number of lifeboats that were to be placed aboard; this was left to the discretion of the builders, as long as they stayed within the bounds of the Board of Trade (BoT) regulations.[75]

The BoT regulations, which were set down in 1894, only allowed for vessels up to 10,000 tons and were hopelessly out of date by 1907.[76]

The nominal chief designer at Harland & Wolff was the Honourable Alexander Carlisle, Pirrie's brother-in-law. He was nearing retirement and, as a result, the main design work was carried out by the chairman himself. Carlisle contented himself with most of the detail work such as decoration, fixtures and fittings and the life-saving equipment.[77] Originally Carlisle wanted 64 lifeboats, but this was considered extravagant and the numbers were reduced, against Carlisle's better judgement, first to 48, then 32 and finally to 16. (As with *Atlantic*, this number was far too small to accommodate the number of people that the ship could carry.) The decision to reduce to 16 was made sometime in the week of 9–16 March 1910.[78]

Eventually the plans for the first two of the new class of vessels were finalised. There only needed to be one complete set of drawings as both ships were to be identical and would be built from the same plans.[79]

To raise some of the money to build the first of the new super-ships (*Olympic*), in 1908, White Star issued £1.5 million worth of new shares.[80] This sum, as it turned out, proved to be precisely how much each of these monsters cost to build.

The time for the *Olympic* and *Titanic* was at hand.

Now we know that:

- The White Star line and Harland & Wolff were so closely allied that they were in many respects one company;
- White Star had already held the record for the worst shipping disaster in history with the *Atlantic*;

- Early in the 20th century the new owner of the White Star line, J. P. Morgan, had the power to influence governments.

Identical Twins

To understand later events fully, it is worthwhile here to include a brief description of the 'Olympic' class ships, of which there were three, *Titanic* being the second. As planned they were to be 882ft 6in long and 92ft 6in wide. Weighing 45,324grt but displacing (actual all-up weight) about 66,000 tons,[1] they would be, by a comfortable margin, the largest vessels in the world. The White Star line undoubtedly expected the sheer size of the new ships to attract trade.[2]

The keel of the first of these ships, *Olympic*, was laid on 16 December 1908. It was fabricated from a single thickness of 1.5in steel plating and a flat steel bar 19.5in wide and 3in thick. The ribs of the vessel were of 10in steel channel spaced 2ft apart forward, 2ft 3in at the stern and 3ft apart amidships. The outer plating was of steel plates 6ft wide, 1in thick and usually 30ft long, each weighing 2.5 to 3 tons. A double bottom was incorporated, which extended right out to the sides of the ship. The distance between the inner and outer skins was 63in over most of its length, but this was increased to 75in beneath the main engine rooms, two-thirds of the way back from the bow. This double bottom was divided into 73 separate compartments to provide water storage for the boilers etc, and trimming tanks.[3]

The main part of the hull was subdivided into 16 separate compartments by 15 half-inch thick transverse bulkheads[4] which reached, in most cases, to well above the waterline. However, forward bulkhead A was closer to the bow than was deemed advisable,[5] effectively reducing the useful number of compartments to 15. The bulkheads were stronger than were required by Lloyd's.[6] Many of the main compartments were subdivided yet again, the hull containing no fewer than 29 supposedly watertight boxes.[7] The bulkhead between boiler rooms four and five was exceptional in that it reached only 2.5ft above the waterline (see Fig 1 in illustrative section). It had been suggested to Harland & Wolff, while the ships were still at the planning stage, that all the bulkheads should be extended up as far as the Saloon Deck. (For an explanation of *Titanic's* deck arrangements see below.) The suggestion was not adopted and, in any case, would not have helped *Titanic* if she really had suffered the sort of damage that is normally said to have been caused by the iceberg.[8]

The bulkheads were fitted with watertight doors on the lower decks to allow communication between the boiler and engine rooms. These watertight doors would close automatically if the lower part of the ship was flooded. They could also be closed by simply flicking a switch on the bridge. The vessel was so subdivided as to be able to remain afloat with any two major compartments flooded. When one considers that an average boiler room on this class of ship was 57ft long and 90ft wide, one realises what an achievement this was. The ship would probably also remain afloat in good weather conditions with any four forward compartments flooded, which was only likely to happen as far as the designers were concerned in the event of the vessel ramming another ship or hard object, or going hard aground. If the vessel was itself rammed, the worst that could be expected was the opening of two compartments to the sea. The bulkheads between the boiler rooms were backed by coal bunkers which again ran the full width of the ship. Bulkheads two, three and four, numbering from the bow, were pierced by a watertight passageway on the lowest deck of the vessel (Tank Top). This passageway was protected at each end by watertight doors. At its nearest point to the outer skin of the ship it came within 5ft 3in of the bottom plating and 16ft of the plating of the hull side. This firemen's passage, as it was known, presents a major problem when dealing with the collision which supposedly sank *Titanic* (see Fig 2).

The 'Olympic' class ships had 10 steel decks. The uppermost or Boat Deck had no passenger accommodation, but the senior officers' cabins were situated at the forward end, immediately behind the bridge. The wireless room was about 20yd back on the port side of this block of cabins, known to the crew as the 'officers' house',[9] abaft the forward funnel casing. Marconi, the company which supplied the wireless, guaranteed a range of 350 miles[10] from the 1.5kW apparatus.[11]

As can be gathered from the name, most of the ships' boats were kept on the Boat Deck: 16 wooden lifeboats under davits and two collapsible boats, C and D, resting on the deck just inboard of forward boats 1 and 2. Two more collapsible boats, A and B, were kept on top of the officers' cabins on either side of the forward funnel, where they would be all but useless in an emergency. Boats 1 and 2, only 25ft long compared to the 30ft of the other wooden lifeboats, were emergency boats, which were kept swung out while the ship was at sea. They were not true lifeboats in the strictest sense in as much as they were not fitted with buoyancy tanks.

After going to the expense of fitting the very latest, specially made davits, capable of handling as many as 10 boats, only one lifeboat was suspended from each pair. In total the first two 'Olympic' class vessels had lifeboats for 1,178 persons each, while American regulations of the period called for 2,142 places.[12]

As well as the lifeboats, the ships carried 3,560 life-jackets, a mere 13 more than the total number of persons who could legitimately be transported, as well as 48 lifebuoys.[13] These were of the traditional variety, comprising a red and white painted ring of cork with rope hand-holds attached. At least six of these lifebuoys were fitted with an electric light which illuminated automatically when the lifebuoy entered the water.[14]

Besides devices intended to increase the chances of survival for those already in the water, the ships were equipped with a variety of apparatus to summon assistance, hopefully before the vessel sank. Pyrotechnic signalling arrangements included 36 socket signals, in lieu of guns, manufactured by the Cotton Powder Company Ltd, with a firing socket on either side of the bridge. Besides these there were 12 ordinary rockets, two Manwell Holmes deck flares, 12 blue lights and six lifebuoy lights. If these precautions proved insufficient, then there was always the rotary spark wireless installation, the most powerful set then available from the Marconi Company.[15]

The open areas of the 500ft-long Boat Deck[16] were devoted to promenade space for officers forward, and first class passengers on the largest part of the deck, amidships. Immediately aft of the first class promenade was a short section of deck for the use of the engineers, while the aft part was for second class passenger usage, all separated by iron railings.

The next deck, descending, was A Deck. This was exclusively for the use of first class passengers. Here were both first class entrances with their grand staircases and lifts. The verandah and Palm Court restaurants, the first class smoking room and the lounge were all here. There were also about 30 staterooms at this level, but A Deck was predominantly a first class promenade deck, with public rooms.

B Deck supposedly differed on *Titanic* from that originally fitted to *Olympic* (a point which we shall contest when the time comes; see Fig 3). Common to both ships was the entirely first class cabin space, second class smoking room and restaurant. On *Olympic* the outer edges of B Deck were promenade areas. The forward section with glazed windows was for first class passengers and the aft part, which was open to the elements, was for the use of second class.

On *Titanic*, B Deck was ostensibly not a promenade deck but had cabins and suites reaching right out to the sides of the ship. Where the starboard side second class promenade was sited on *Olympic*, *Titanic* had the sidewalk cafe, the Café 'Parisien'.

C Deck was again entirely devoted to first class cabin space amidships, with the second class library just aft. The aft well deck was promenade space for third class and on the aft part of the deck, beneath the Poop Deck, were the third class public rooms. At the extreme forward end of this deck in the forecastle were situated the crew's galley and messes, the crew hospital and carpenter's shop. The rest of the forecastle at this level was machinery space.

D Deck amidships was yet again first class with the dining saloon, reception rooms and cabins. Further aft were the first and second class galley (the same galley served both classes), sculleries, hospital, pantries, butchers and bakers. Next came the second class dining saloon and then second class cabins. The extreme rear of the deck was third class accommodation. The forward end of the deck immediately in front of and below the bridge was the third class open space. In the bow were firemen's quarters and stores.

E Deck was mixed accommodation with trimmers and seamen forward, third class aft of them. Then came first class in the forward part of its midships section, followed by second class. Bringing up the rear, as usual, came third class.

F Deck, deep within the ship, was mostly third class. At the extreme front end came firemen's quarters, then a large number of third class cabins. The midships areas of F Deck contained one of the first swimming baths afloat,[17] third class dining saloon and engineers' accommodation. Further aft were second class cabins and right in the extreme stern came third class, again.

G Deck had crew quarters forward followed by third class open berths (hammock space); first class baggage rooms, then the post office and squash court. The whole midships section of this deck was taken up by coal bunkers, boiler casings, engine casings and store rooms. Aft of this area came second class cabins and, bringing up the rear, more third class, in this case not even permanent. This third class area could be made to double as cargo space.

On the next deck down, the Orlop Deck, forward was found cargo and the mail room space. The centre section was again devoted to boiler casings, coal bunkers and the tops of the huge engines. Aft of these came the refrigerated cargo rooms, store rooms and the aft cargo hold.

On the lowest deck, the Tank Top, were the main engine rooms (these actually reached up three decks) containing the largest reciprocating marine steam engines built up to that time. The motors which powered the refrigeration plant were also in the main engine room. Then there was the turbine engine room (as tall as the main engine room). Aft of the turbine were the four electric dynamos which produced the power to drive all the cranes and winches, the lights, the heaters, the gymnasium machinery, first and second class lifts and all the other electrical equipment aboard. In addition to the main dynamos there were two emergency generators situated on D Deck, adjacent to the after boiler casing.[18]

Forward of the main engine room were the six huge boiler rooms, numbering forward from the engine room. Number 1 contained five single-ended boilers each with three furnaces. Numbers 2, 3, 4 and 5 each contained five double-ended boilers with three furnaces at each end. Number 6 boiler room, sited where the vessel's hull began to narrow towards the bow, only held four of the double-ended boilers; making a total of 29 boilers and 159 furnaces. At the forward end of Number 1 boiler room, and at both ends of all the others, were the coal bunkers, containing the fuel for the hungry fires.

On the 17th day of the British Inquiry, Harold Sanderson said, 'The pumping arrangements were also exceptional, each boiler compartment having its own equipment, which is quite unusual.'

From the forward end of Number 6 boiler room to the aft end of the forward cargo hold, through two more holds, ran the watertight firemen's passage. It will be remembered that this passageway was 5ft 3in from the bottom of the ship and more than 16ft from the outer plating of the hull sides.

The main engines were capable of producing 15,000hp apiece and the turbine, only added as an afterthought, turned out a further 16,000. In the original concept only the main engines were included and it was estimated that these alone would give the ship a top speed in excess of 20kts.[19] The decision to fit the extra turbine was taken only after the construction of the ships had begun and would have necessitated structural changes to the rear part of Olympic's hull to accommodate the extra 22ton propeller and its shaft. The new propeller was situated between and astern of the two mighty 38ton wing propellers. What the top speed with the extra engine might have been has never been disclosed.

The structural steel of the ship was, in the main, hydraulically riveted together for extra strength, a relatively new process at the time. This was about the only new procedure or idea employed in the construction of this class of ship.

Contrary to popular belief, *Olympic* and *Titanic* were not at the cutting edge of technology: they were traditionally designed and constructed; only in the comprehensive use of electricity and in their impressive size did they break new ground.

On 31 March 1909, three months from the time the keel of *Olympic* was laid, the keel of what was intended to be an identical sister, *Titanic*, was begun on slipway Number 3 of the Belfast yard. Side by side the monsters grew until they towered over the homes of those who laboured to build them. In October 1910, the *Olympic* was ready for launching and on the 20th of that month the enormous hull, especially painted white for the benefit of photographers, slid rear end first into the River Lagan; its passage was eased by 23 tons of grease and soap, the vessel attaining a speed of 12.5kts before being brought to a halt by the braking effect of six anchors, drags and 80tons of cable.[20] Shortly after launching, while being towed to the fitting out basin, *Olympic* suffered her first minor accident. A gust of wind caught her and as a result she crashed into the dry-dock wall, denting some hull plates.[21]

Fitting out was to take just over seven months. In that time the boilers were installed, along with the masts, which towered 200ft above the waterline,[22] and four enormous funnels, only 55ft shorter.

The ornate first class cabins were fitted out with all the care normally reserved for stately homes. The interiors of the public rooms were panelled and painted, carpets were laid and machinery installed. The installation of more than 200 miles of cable was required to feed power to all the electrical fixtures and fittings, including more than 10,000 light bulbs. During the construction of the ship she was visited more than 2,000 times by Board of Trade inspectors, ensuring that the work met their requirements.

At the end of this seven months, on 29 May 1911, *Olympic* began her two days of sea trials, which went off without any serious problems. She was handed over to her owners, with full ceremony, in a brilliant example of Edwardian media management, on the 31st. That self-same day the second leviathan was launched. The two ships represented an investment of £3,000,000 by J. P. Morgan in the White Star line's name.

At about 4.30pm, *Olympic* left Belfast for Liverpool where she was to be opened for public inspection for one day. She departed that port on the evening of 1 June for Southampton to prepare for her maiden voyage under the Commodore of the White Star fleet, Captain Edward John Smith.

With the extra workers available from *Olympic* one would have expected *Titanic's* fitting out to proceed apace but, as we shall see, this is not quite what happened.

On 14 June 1911, *Olympic* left Southampton for New York, via Queenstown (now Cobh) in Ireland, on her maiden voyage. Contrary to a widely-held belief, fostered by erroneous accounts of the occasion, *Olympic's* departure on her maiden voyage is far less well documented than that of *Titanic*.[23] She completed the journey at an average speed of 21.17kts, entering New York harbour at 7.45am on 21 June, after an uneventful passage. Overseeing the well-being of the vessel's engines and other machinery was Chief Engineer Joseph Bell,[24] later, supposedly to enter into a private agreement with Ismay concerning the speed trials of *Titanic*. Her owners confidently expected the second ship in the class to do a little better with regard to speed. During the last few moments of docking, *Olympic* had her second minor accident, backing into and almost sinking the tug *O. L. Hallenbeck*. It was not an auspicious beginning.

Nor was it Captain Smith's first accident. On 27 January 1889, only two years after gaining his first command, he ran the *Republic* aground off Sandy Hook at the entrance to New York harbour. She remained fast for five hours before being floated off. She entered port and off-loaded her passengers before a second calamity struck the vessel. A furnace flue above a forward boiler fractured, killing three crewmen and injuring seven more. The unflappable Captain Smith commented only that the damage was 'slight' and that the injured were able to walk from the ship to the ambulance.[25] (This was the first *Republic* which was sold off in 1889, not the 1903 ship which was lost after a collision in January 1909.)

Almost two years later, Smith's propensity for running ships aground struck again when he stranded the *Coptic* off Rio de Janeiro in December 1890.[26]

Things appear to have gone well for the accident-prone skipper for the next 11 years until 1901. At 5am on 7 August of that year, aboard *Majestic* (1890), an electrical fire broke out in a linen closet. A hole was cut in the deck above the closet and water was poured in. For a time it seemed as if the fire was out, but at 10am it restarted, choking fumes and smoke filling adjacent cabins. The fire was finally extinguished by injecting steam into the blazing closet. Captain Smith denied any knowledge of this fire,[27] which is curious. As any seaman knows, there is nothing so dangerous at sea as fire.

Smith became Commodore of the White Star fleet in 1904 and from then onwards captained the newest and largest ships in that fleet, beginning with the second *Baltic*. He was still master of that vessel on 3 November 1906 when, in Liverpool docks, fire broke out in Number 5 hold. The hold was flooded and the fire put out, but 640 bales of wool were destroyed by fire or water. On this occasion it appears that Smith was not above using a port's fire-fighting facilities, although he was to be a little more reticent six years later.

Barely a year later, on 4 November 1909, running true to form, Captain Smith approaching New York yet again, ran *Adriatic* hard aground at the entrance to the Ambrose channel. The ship was stuck for five hours.

On 31 May 1911, Captain E. J. Smith took command of RMS *Olympic*.

In essence, *Titanic* and *Olympic* were very similar. Initially they were constructed from the same plans and at the times of their respective launchings were as close to identical as the technology of the times allowed. What changes were made took place only after *Olympic's* first voyage and were not of a major structural nature. To the casual observer the two ships would have appeared indistinguishable from one another. This similarity was made good use of by the owners who freely advertised one as the other. Even after the disaster, many commemorative postcards, sweet tins, cups and sheet music covers displayed pictures of *Olympic* masquerading as her sister.

We see how:

- The 'Olympic' class vessels were designed in such a way that they were almost unsinkable in the event of a collision;
- The subdivision of the hull was set out in such a way as to ensure that the ship remained on an even keel if it was seriously damaged;
- Captain Smith's record as a commander was not without incident.

4

Hawke's Legacy

To my mind, any story of events surrounding the loss of the *Titanic* must really begin at about lunchtime on 20 September 1911. *Olympic* had just left Southampton harbour to begin her fifth voyage across the Atlantic and back. Aboard were about 1,313 passengers and 885 crew.[1] To reach the open sea from the White Star dock, the liner had first to perform a tricky left turn at the mouth of the dock into the River Test. From there she would proceed toward the southeast until reaching the mouth of the River Itchen and then Southampton Water. Still heading southeasterly, she would continue down Southampton Water until gaining the Solent on her right or the wider waterway of Spithead to her left. Although the Solent offered the more direct route to the English Channel, and thence to Cherbourg, Captain Smith invariably chose the more open Spithead[2] route, and this time was no exception.[3] Directly ahead of the vessel at this point would be Ryde on the Isle of Wight; to the northeast lay Portsmouth, home of the Royal Navy. Both the Solent and Spithead have seen more than their fair share of shipwrecks and are still notorious for shoals and sand-spits. The Brambles, as they are still known, formed as infamous a sandbank as any and, even though marked by buoys, continue to present a danger to shipping, sitting as they do at the convergence of these three bodies of water.[4] To avoid this sand bar the liner would have to make a long S-turn as she entered the wider waterway of Spithead.[5]

Even in 1912 merchant vessels were obliged to utilise the services of a Southampton river pilot. On this occasion the pilot actually commanding *Olympic* was Captain William George Bowyer, a man with 30 years' experience and who regularly supervised the initial stages of a voyage by White Star vessels. The pilot's services would be required until the ship reached the Nab Lightship.

At 12.30pm, *Olympic* reached Black Jack buoy which marked the end of Southampton Water. Bowyer ordered the liner's speed reduced from 17.5kts in preparation for the turn to port into Spithead. Four buoys marked the channel around the western edge of the shoal.[6] At 12.34pm *Olympic* passed Calshot Spit buoy and then, three minutes later, she passed North Thorn buoy. By this time her speed was down to 12kts. The next buoy, Thorn Knoll, marked the most complicated part of the vessel's turn. The order for the port engine to go 'full astern' was given at 12.40pm, then came 'slow ahead', when the central turbine engine was stopped. When the ship was about two-thirds of the way from the Thorn Knoll buoy to the West Bramble buoy, the helm was put hard a-starboard, the port engine was stopped and then reversed. At this point, *Olympic's* speed was down to 11kts. The liner gave two blasts on the whistle, a signal to other ships in the vicinity that announced she was going to turn to port.

The turn was completed by 12.43pm and, one minute later, all engines (turbine included) were put 'full ahead'. Two minutes after that the ship had accelerated up to 16kts.

While all of these manoeuvres were going on, *Olympic's* second officer, Robert Hune, was keeping lookout from the crow's-nest high on the foremast.[7] At about the time the ship was passing Calshot Spit buoy, Hune spotted a vessel rounding Egypt Point, about four miles away, and rapidly closing on *Olympic's* course. HMS *Hawke*, a Royal Navy armoured cruiser was only about two miles from *Olympic* when the liner's two blasts on the whistle boomed out.[8]

HMS *Hawke*, captained by Cdr William Frederick Blunt RN, had been undergoing speed tests in the Solent and was returning to Portsmouth at about 15kts.[9] Under ideal conditions, it had been found, the cruiser could still manage her design speed of 19.5kts despite a dirty bottom and the passage of 23 years.

By the time *Olympic* had completed the turn around the West Bramble buoy and began to gather speed, the gap between the two ships had closed to about 1.5 miles.

HMS *Hawke* was one of six 'Edgar' class cruisers. The 360ft-long 7,350ton warship was long since outdated in a rapidly changing world. With her backwards raked bow, seen in profile, she looked as if the extreme forward end of the vessel had been fitted upside down. Even by the most generously minded observer she could not in honesty be described as a handsome ship.

Beneath the waterline, the 5in thick armour of the cruiser's hull was pierced by two underwater torpedo tubes. An important design feature of this class of ship was a steel beak projecting forward beneath the water, from the bow.[10] The purpose of the beak was to inflict the maximum amount of damage on opponents should the opportunity arise to ram them. This armoured ram was about to prove how effective it could be.

As the vessels drew closer to one another, the cruiser was, for a while, moving the faster and for a moment or two it looked as if the ageing warship would manage to overtake. Then the speed of the accelerating ocean liner matched and finally surpassed that of the cruiser.[11]

According to contemporary accounts, the Royal Navy ship's bow was just about level with the larger vessel's bridge and about 200yd off her starboard side, before the liner's gathering speed made her fall back.[12] The *Olympic* began to draw away from the warship until the latter's bow was about level with her compass platform (between the second and third funnels) when *Hawke* suddenly began to swing to port, towards the *Olympic*.[13]

Aboard *Olympic*, Captains Smith and Bowyer were watching the warship anxiously. Captain Smith, as the cruiser swung to port (left), said to the pilot, 'I don't believe he will get under our stern, Bowyer.' The River Pilot replied, 'If she is going to strike sir, let me know in time so I can put the helm hard over to port.' Bowyer's composure slipped a little and he shouted 'Is she going to strike, sir?'

Captain Smith, obviously also becoming agitated, shouted back, 'Yes, she is going to strike us in the stern.'

On the bridge of the *Hawke*, all was pandemonium. Events here, though more dramatic than those on *Olympic's* bridge, are equally well recorded. Cdr Blunt had already said to his navigating officer, Lt Reginald Aylen, 'If she is going east she will not have much room to turn; we will give her as much room as possible.' He then ordered port helm, which meant a turn to starboard, away from *Olympic*. It should be mentioned here that until 1928 helm orders were reversed as if vessels were still steered by an oar or tiller rather than a wheel. To port the helm meant move the helm, or tiller, to port, thus turning the rudder and the vessel to starboard.

Instead of turning to starboard in response to Blunt's order the cruiser suddenly swung between four and five points (between 45° and 56°) in the opposite direction, toward the liner. Cdr Blunt, no doubt fearing that the helmsman had turned the wheel the wrong way, shouted, 'What are you doing? Port, port, hard a-port ... stop port (engine), full astern starboard!' Petty Officer first class Ernest Hunt, the quartermaster on the wheel, shouted out, 'Helm jammed!'.

The officer of the watch, Lt Geoffrey Bashford, and Leading Seaman Henry Yeates, another helmsman, leapt to Hunt's assistance and the three men threw their combined weight onto the wheel as they tried to force it round.

After turning to indicate a mere 15° of port rudder applied, the wheel jammed again. The strain on the gearing had caused it to lock up completely. When the pressure was relaxed the helm responded perfectly, but by then it was too late. Cdr Blunt had himself bounded down the ladder from the bridge to the wheelhouse and used the engine room telegraph to ring down for 'full astern both'.

On the liner, Bowyer ordered the helm 'hard a-port' in an effort to swing the liner's stern clear of the rapidly approaching warship but there was no time.[14]

Olympic's bow had swung about 7° to starboard when the cruiser's hardened ram struck with a noise 'like a howitzer going off'. The effect of an explosion was reinforced by the clouds of paint dust which were stripped from *Olympic's* starboard after quarter by the impact.[15]

The *Hawke's* bow only remained wedged in the liner's side for seconds before the race of water along the side caused by *Olympic's* momentum slewed the cruiser's hull through an ear-shattering arc. The tremendous twisting movement sheared off *Hawke's* damaged underwater ram[16] as she reeled away 'like a top'.[17]

A large hourglass-shaped hole had been punched in the side of *Olympic*, supposedly about 8ft deep and extending from D Deck down through E, F and G Decks, well below the waterline, about 86ft from the stern.[18] However, there is some reason to doubt the accuracy of the published assessments of damage sustained by *Olympic* in the *Hawke* incident. It now appears that following the collision hull plating required replacement over more than a third of the vessel's overall length.[19]

Watertight doors were closed on both ships and, although *Olympic's* two aftermost compartments were flooded, she was in no danger of sinking. The same could not be said of HMS *Hawke*, which took an enormous roll to port. The people watching from the liner thought the cruiser was about to capsize, but she recovered and moved clear of the larger vessel.[20]

Hawke's steel ram had done more than merely punch a hole in the outer plating of *Olympic*. The liner's starboard main propeller was damaged, 18ft of the outer steel propeller shaft covering was crushed and torn, the starboard propeller shaft was bent and the crankshaft of the starboard engine was badly damaged.[21] The impact must have given the starboard engine quite a jolt, which might well have caused further structural damage that was not apparent on initial inspection.

Proceeding at very slow speed the *Hawke* crept away towards Portsmouth. Luckily her collision bulkhead was undamaged and she was able to make the short journey unaided.[22]

Olympic was unable to return to Southampton until the tide turned and so dropped anchor for the night in Osborne Bay off Cowes, Isle of Wight. She was joined by the Red Funnel Line tug, *Vulcan*, which would figure in the departure of her sister on her maiden voyage some months later.[23]

It was painfully obvious that *Olympic's* voyage could not be continued and so passengers were disembarked into tenders and had to find alternative means of reaching their respective destinations.[24]

The following morning, Thursday 21 September, *Olympic* was towed slowly back to Southampton harbour where her cargo was discharged.[25] Fortuitously, Harland & Wolff had a repair and maintenance facility at Southampton and it was to here that *Olympic* was moved.[26] Company officials, divers and the ship's carpenters, along with inspectors from Harland & Wolff, appraised the damage and quickly determined that the vessel was beyond the capabilities of the Southampton yard to repair. She would need to return to Belfast, to the only dry dock in the world large enough to receive her.

Before she could even attempt the 570-mile voyage, the extensive damage to her hull would have to be temporarily patched up. Steel plates were fixed across the gaping hole in the plates below the waterline and heavy timbers above. Such was the extent of the damage that it was two weeks before the ship was in any condition to attempt the short run to Belfast. Relieved of her cargo, much of her coal and with only a skeleton crew aboard, she departed Southampton on Wednesday, 4 October. With her cruising speed reduced to less than 13kts and able to steam on just her port main engine, *Olympic* crept into Belfast Lough and dropped anchor at 11am on the 6th.[27] Here a new problem presented itself. Although the dry dock was long and wide enough to take the crippled liner, it wasn't deep enough. Even at high tide there was only 35ft 3in of water at the entrance. With her two aft compartments flooded, *Olympic* could not pass over the sill of the dock, so she had to be lightened. One weighty item removed from the after part of the ship was the damaged starboard propeller and crankshaft (to be replaced later with an identical part which was awaiting installation in her sister *Titanic*).[28]

Thus began a curious game of musical chairs, which would be

repeated with confusing efficiency during *Olympic's* next visit to the yard. *Titanic*, which occupied the dry dock at the time of *Olympic's* arrival, had to be removed to make room for her damaged sister. Once in the dry dock, the water was pumped out and the true extent of the damage could be ascertained accurately.

At this time, I suspect, the realisation that the hull of *Olympic* was damaged beyond economic repair dawned on senior management and engineers of Harland & Wolff. The ship could be patched up well enough to get her back to sea for a reasonable sum, but she would never again pass the Board of Trade inspections which were required before a new certificate of seaworthiness would be issued.

It was also round about this time that J. Bruce Ismay decided to retire from IMM on 31 December 1912. At the end of January of that year, he changed his mind and moved the retirement date back by six months.[29]

On 20 November, *Olympic* left the builders' yard, after six and a half weeks of repair work, to resume the transatlantic service interrupted by HMS *Hawke* two months before. Repairs and lost fares from three cancelled voyages had left White Star (and IMM) more than £250,000 out of pocket.[30]

Only two days after the collision between *Hawke* and *Olympic*, a Royal Navy Court of Inquiry (obligatory after any collision involving a navy ship), under the presidency of Capt Henry W. Grant, assisted by Capt Edward L. Booty RN, unsurprisingly found that all blame for the accident lay with the White Star vessel.

Cdr Blunt's claim that *Olympic* had taken far more room than necessary for the turn into Spithead and had forced *Hawke* into the southern edge of the safe channel formed the basis of the navy's case. As a result of this crowding, the ships were too close together for safety and the water displaced by the speeding liner had simply pulled the smaller cruiser into her side.[31]

The partiality of the Admiralty Inquiry is forcefully demonstrated by the simple fact that all of the witnesses were naval personnel, of one sort or another, while the *Olympic*, White Star line and the owners were not represented. In modern parlance, it was a stitch-up.

White Star understandably refused to accept the Admiralty verdict and sued Cdr Blunt for damages. The Admiralty cross-petitioned for damages to their cruiser. On 16 November a hearing began aboard the Portsmouth guard ship *Duke of Wellington* that was to last for nine days.

Capt John Pritchard of the *Mauretania* testified that he had never encountered suction of any kind with the big Cunard ship.

Sir Samuel Adams, President of the Admiralty Division, announced his verdict on 19 December. He found that the *Olympic* had made an over-wide swing around the Brambles and had almost crowded *Hawke* out of the safe channel. This negligent navigation, allied to the effects of suction, was responsible for the collision.[32]

The White Star claim that the liner had been under the mandatory command of George Bowyer the pilot was upheld. As the pilot was in the enviable position of being immune from prosecution, the Admiralty claim was dismissed as well. White Star was left to foot the bill for the repairs to *Olympic* and to stand the loss occasioned by the cancelled voyages, so once again they appealed to a higher court.

The appeal court found against *Olympic* and awarded costs against them to boot. Still unable to accept the verdict, White Star — urged on by Captain E. J. Smith — took the matter to the House of Lords. The Lord Chancellor took the case, supported by Lords Atkinson, Shaw and Sumner. Predictably at this stage, the appeal failed and on 9 November 1914 the Court unanimously dismissed the final appeal with costs. Despite all of the legal verdicts against them, the White Star line always maintained that they were morally in the right.[33]

White Star certainly seem to have a strong case. The fact that the cruiser's helmsman had clearly turned the wheel the wrong way following Cdr Blunt's initial command to port the helm in order to make more sea room for the liner, was obviously deemed irrelevant! This helmsman's blunder is shown by the *Hawke's* sudden swing to port and the commander shouting at the helmsman, 'What are you doing? Port, port, hard a-port!' It was this gaffe which brought the cruiser within the 'zone of pull-in' in the first place. Nor was the fact that the cruiser's helm had jammed, compounding the original error and making the collision unavoidable, considered of any importance. So obvious was the travesty of justice which labelled the pilot, George Bowyer, incompetent, that both his employer, Trinity House, and the White Star line continued to use his services.

Capt Smith continued to enjoy the confidence of his employers and remained in command of RMS *Olympic*. Cdr Blunt was promoted to the rank of captain and given command of HMS *Cressy*, another ageing cruiser, half as big again as *Hawke*.

By the time the House of Lords' verdict was brought in on

9 November 1914, its relevance to those involved in the *Hawke/Olympic* incident is questionable. Captain E. J. Smith lost his life on the morning of 15 April 1912 when, in his capacity as captain, he went down with his ship, RMS *Titanic*.

On the morning of 22 September 1914, while patrolling off the Dutch coast in company with two more obsolete cruisers, HMS *Aboukir* and HMS *Hogue*, the *Cressy* was torpedoed by *U9* commanded by Otto Weddigen. All three cruisers were sunk in rapid succession by the U-boat, with the loss of 1,460 lives. Twenty-three days later, Weddigen in U9 pushed his tally of British cruisers up by sinking HMS *Hawke*, again in the North Sea. She went down in 6min with the loss of most of her 550 sailors.

After her repairs, which — as we know — took over a month and a half, *Olympic* returned to service. Shortly after the middle of November she left the builders' yard and made her way back to Southampton. Ten days later she sailed on her first transatlantic voyage since her encounter with the Royal Navy.

On the fourth two-way crossing after her repair, shortly after leaving New York, *Olympic* struck what appeared to be a submerged wreck and lost a blade from her port main propeller. The shock was felt throughout the ship, but the passengers remained calm and there appeared to be no other damage.[34]

Losing a propeller blade was not that unusual, but it was not a common occurrence either, and for *Olympic* to lose a blade was a minor catastrophe. It would necessitate yet another return to Belfast, to the only dry dock large enough to handle her. On top of this, here was the world's largest ship shedding one of the world's largest propeller blades, while the ship was making better than 20kts (her usual cruising speed). No matter how quickly the port engine was stopped, the heavy vibration must have given the — supposedly — recently repaired hull a quite dramatic shaking up before the horribly unbalanced propeller ceased revolving. Yet no damage was reported. This, it seems to me, is very surprising, particularly when the quality of the steel hull of the ship is examined.

At the time of this propeller break-up, *Olympic* was about 750 miles to the east and slightly south of Newfoundland, steaming across the Grand Banks.[35] It was the dead of winter and in an area affected not only by icebergs, but also by the cold Labrador current. It would be surprising to find that the water temperature was very much higher than 31°F. In 1993 a paper, delivered to the United States Society of

Naval Architects & Marine Engineers, offered another reason to suspect that the damage done to *Olympic* might be more serious than had hitherto been admitted. In this paper the authors say:

'Tests done on steel recovered from the wreck site [of Titanic] by IFREMER [the French National Institute of Oceanography] and the Bedford Institute of Oceanography have indicated that the type of steel used in the Titanic became brittle when exposed to the water temperature of 31º.'

As *Titanic* and *Olympic* were built alongside one another, it is reasonable to assume that the same quality of steel was used in both ships.

Of *Olympic's* encounter with HMS *Hawke*, the paper goes on to say:

'She was struck on her starboard side abreast of the main mast and the opening was mainly below the waterline. The plate tears in the area of impact exhibited a brittle fracture type of failure. There were some failures in the riveted joints and plate ripping adjacent to the hole made by the Hawke, but many of the plate tears were unusually sharp in their extent and had the appearance of brittle fracture.'

The *Olympic/Hawke* collision had occurred in the relatively warm coastal waters of the English south coast where the steel of the vessel's hull would not be subjected to a temperature anything like as low as 31º. However, at the time *Olympic* shed her port propeller blade in the North Atlantic, the steel she was built from would have been at its weakest.

After shedding a propeller blade *Olympic* soldiered on. Obviously, the port main engine had to be stopped or the vessel would have, literally, shaken herself to pieces, but she maintained speed on just the starboard main and central turbine engines — after all the 'Olympics' had originally been designed to steam at 20kts on just two engines producing a total of 30,000hp. The starboard main and central turbine engines between them produced 31,000hp. After dropping off passengers at Cherbourg and Plymouth, *Olympic* arrived at Southampton on 28 February, more or less on time.[36]

This tells us something of vital importance: that one main engine out of commission did not make the turbine unusable. The turbine was driven by exhaust steam from these main engines and produced its power from what otherwise would be wasted steam pressure. White Star, in common with any other competitive business, strove for efficiency and did all in its power to avoid wastage in all departments, coal being no exception. Why then did *Olympic*, when returning to Belfast from Southampton after the *Hawke* collision, use only the port main engine and allow the exhaust steam to go to waste unless the Parsons turbine was damaged and unusable? To go one step further, if the turbine or its propeller shaft sustained damage, situated as it was, on the centreline of the ship, then it is reasonable to surmise that the damage inflicted by HMS *Hawke's* steel and concrete ram extended at least that far; very much deeper than the claimed 8ft.

Hawke's point of impact, according to contemporary reports, had been 86ft from the stern, well aft of the turbine itself, indicating that any damage which rendered it useless must have been to the propeller shaft. This propeller shaft for the central engine ran through the stern frames of the ship, so these vital structural components must also have been damaged if the shaft was struck. Judging by the ship's performance immediately after the collision, the length of time it took to patch the hull (two weeks) and the fact that the vessel could only use one engine, it is logical to suppose that very serious structural damage had been occasioned by the collision.

We have seen that:

- The 'Olympic' class ships could use the central turbine engine even if one of the main engines was out of commission and could maintain cruising speed on just one main and the turbine engine;
- The turbine engine was not used during *Olympic's* voyage from Southampton to Belfast following the *Hawke* incident, telling us that the engine was damaged in some way and was inoperative;
- The damage inflicted on the liner by the *Hawke* extended far deeper into the hull than the eight feet usually accepted.

Planning the Switch

After disembarking her passengers at Southampton, *Olympic* made her way, still steaming on just her port main and central turbine engines, to Belfast for repairs to the damaged propeller, arriving on 1 March 1912.[1] At best, the remnants of the broken blade would have to be removed and a replacement bolted into place. At worst, the whole propeller would have to be changed. This work, which in any case should have been completed in one day, actually took a week. Why, one wonders? What else was happening?

What follows is mostly conjecture, but there is some photographic evidence to help us along the way. This photographic evidence, although available for many years, has not been recognised for what it truly is.

As was pointed out toward the end of *The Riddle of the Titanic*, a piece of equipment from the wreck of *Titanic*, a helm indicator, at the time on display at the National Maritime Museum at Greenwich, was deeply incised with the number 401, *Titanic's* build number.

This seemed, at first, to prove that a switch could not have been planned, or at least executed, during the week *Olympic* was back at the builder's yard to have a new port propeller fitted. What it actually means is that any switch had to be planned and at least partially executed during the five months between the *Hawke* incident and *Olympic's* return to the Belfast yard in early March of the following year.

I have no doubt that a switch indeed took place. Although the sequence of events following the collision between HMS *Hawke* and *Olympic*, including the circumstances of the *Titanic* disaster and the cover-up which followed, made the substitution of the vessel a distinct possibility, there seemed to be no hard evidence. As a result of the interest created by *The Riddle of the Titanic* (The *Titanic* Conspiracy), some new evidence has come to light and much of that which already existed has come under very much closer scrutiny than ever before. The original glass plate photographs of *Titanic* and *Olympic* stand up to massive enlargement far better than many more modern pictures. Under that sort of examination these photographs, more than 80 years old, reveal some intriguing surprises.

What follows is a possible scenario based partly on what the photographs suggest and partly on other evidence.

When *Olympic* was towed into Harland & Wolff's repair installation at Southampton after her collision with HMS *Hawke*, divers were sent down to inspect and evaluate the damage. Experienced men, they would have known straight away that the ship was in a bad way.

The divers may even have suspected that the ship's keel was damaged, something that they could have ascertained by diving inside the flooded compartments.[2]

Before the ship could go back to Belfast for more comprehensive repairs, it was necessary to ensure that the hull was at least watertight to the extent that the pumps could cope with any seepage. This is clearly what the repair yard at Southampton endeavoured to do. There must be a sound reason for the length of time it took the yard workers to fit patches to the hull. Two weeks is a very long time to spend bolting wooden or steel plates over a hole about 15ft wide by 40ft high at its extremities. It is not a long time to spend fitting emergency patches if the workforce were also engaged in reinforcing the vessel's frames and main structural steel girders.

On Wednesday, 4 October, able to operate on only the port main engine — something indicating that the damage was more extensive than has, even now, ever been admitted — the ship made the 570-mile trip back to her birthplace at something like 10kts. She had aboard only a minimal crew.[3]

Communications between Harland & Wolff's Southampton repair facility and the main construction yard at Queen's Island, Belfast, must have been a little tenuous. When *Olympic* limped into Belfast Lough, the dry dock she had struggled to reach and so desperately needed was occupied by her even more magnificent (and later much more famous) younger sister, *Titanic*.

In compliance with Ismay's suggested changes after *Olympic's* maiden voyage, *Titanic's* B Deck had been altered. (See Fig 5, showing *Titanic* with new B Deck window layout but missing tops of bridge wings and with unpainted funnels, with partially painted superstructure and with no gold band showing around the hull below the white areas of upperworks.)

At this time *Titanic* already sported the short aft promenade on B Deck which was a feature unique to this vessel at least until *Olympic's* late 1912 refit after the loss of the *Titanic*, or more probably 1914 when the ship was extensively refitted in preparation for service as a troopship.

Another useful recognition feature is also apparent on this photograph. The portholes clearly showing against the port side of the white painted forecastle (C Deck) are unevenly spaced and there are a total of 16 visible. Like the aft Promenade Deck, this porthole configuration was not supposedly incorporated into *Olympic* until late 1912 or 1914. The vessel in this photograph can be none other than *Titanic*, even though the specification changes ordered by J. Bruce Ismay are visibly incomplete, notably the forward end of A Deck.)

Titanic was removed from the Thompson Graving Dock and *Olympic* was manoeuvred in, but only after her stern had been lightened considerably. When she first arrived back at Belfast with her two aft compartments flooded she was drawing too much water to allow her to pass over the sill of the dry dock, which was only 8in beneath her keel under normal circumstances. *Olympic's* normal draught was 34ft 7in,[4] so there wasn't a great deal of room for error at the best of times and this was, for her, not the best of times.

The flooding of the rearmost two compartments indicates that the emergency patch to the hull had failed. There is no obvious reason for the failure of the patch unless the rigidity of the hull had been lost in the collision with HMS *Hawke*, with all that possibility's attendant ramifications.

The decision to switch the ships must have been taken shortly after draining the dry dock and inspecting the damage. It would have been obvious to the men examining the crippled vessel that the repairs required were extensive and would take months to complete. In that time work on the second ship, *Titanic*, would be held up as workers were diverted to repair her disabled sister. With £3 million[5] already tied up in the new ships and with no likelihood of them returning so much as a penny in the foreseeable future, the prospects for the owners looked bleak.

The courses of action open to the owners and builders were limited if anything was to be saved from the situation.

Obviously exchanging the identities of the two vessels could not be done overnight. The partially converted *Titanic* would have to be reconverted to *Olympic* specifications before she could hope to pass herself off as that ship. It appears that Harland & Wolff lost no time in getting the work under way.

Fig 4 shows a vessel identified by Harland & Wolff as *Olympic*. If these pictures were taken before *Olympic's* 1912 refit, which according to the Harland & Wolff chronology they were, then the identification has to be erroneous. The vessel shown has the short promenade on the aft end of B Deck, which was unique to *Titanic*, and 16 portholes in the forecastle, which show perfectly clearly against the white background. It will be remembered that the 16-porthole arrangement was also peculiar to *Titanic* until late 1912 or 1914. *Olympic* had only 14 until a later refit after *Titanic* had been lost. These photographs must have been taken later than Fig 5, as they reveal the funnels painted, the superstructure painted and the gold band in place. They also show B Deck windows in the original *Olympic* layout. The ship shown is neither fish nor fowl, but is somewhere between *Olympic* and *Titanic*. Because of the short Promenade Deck and the 16-porthole configuration to the forward end of C Deck, the ship shown has to be *Titanic*. But her B Deck windows were converted long before these pictures were taken, as we have seen. What these photographs appear to show is a vessel being reconverted from *Titanic* layout to that of *Olympic*. There can be no legitimate reason for such a conversion in 1912.

It has been suggested that these pictures are in fact of *Olympic*, taken at a much later date than is usually ascribed to them. However, immediately after the *Titanic* disaster and before any other structural alterations were made to the vessel, *Olympic* was outfitted with 40 more collapsible lifeboats. Then, later in 1912, she was fitted with extra davits and proper boats, enough to accommodate more than 3,500 people. These extra davits and the boats to be swung from them are nowhere apparent in either picture, indicating that the photographs were taken before the alterations were carried out, ie before 24 April 1912 — this seems far more believable than that Harland & Wolff could make such a monumental error in dating the photographs, not once but twice. Photographs taken in the shipyard are numbered for identification purposes,[6] which serves to bear out the deduction that the pictures are correctly dated.

The next photograph, Fig 6, shows *Titanic* and *Olympic* in echelon and can be positively dated as taken prior to 6 March 1912, the last time the two vessels were together at the builders. Close inspection of the number of portholes on the port side of C Deck, clearly visible against the white paintwork of the forecastle, shows *Olympic*, in the foreground, sporting the 16-hole arrangement. In 1912, when this photograph was taken, the layout of these portholes had yet to be changed (a telephone conversation with a representative of the Ulster Folk & Transport Museum revealed that this alteration was not carried out on *Olympic* until 1914). According to the evidence of this photograph in particular, both ships appear to have their forecastles transposed. In other respects, the layout of the ships is as it should be.

Fig 7, a photograph taken in New York harbour after completing the first half of her maiden voyage, shows the port side of *Olympic's* bow sporting the 14-porthole arrangement, which is as it should appear on all pre-1914 pictures of that ship. This is solid evidence of something very peculiar going on at Harland & Wolff. The same photograph also shows a large white cowling on the port side of the Forecastle Deck abaft the foremast. This cowling is not in evidence on early pictures of *Titanic* or on post-disaster photographs of *Olympic*. It is, however, clearly visible on a picture of *Titanic* setting out on her maiden voyage (Fig 8).

This same cowling also appears on a photograph taken on *Olympic's* Forecastle Deck, facing aft. This picture, taken during the 1912 refit according to Harland & Wolff, plainly shows the cabins on the extreme ends of the bridge to be incomplete and seems therefore to have been taken well before the ship entered service in May 1911.

The only theory to account for these pictures, other than that the photographs themselves might have been tampered with, is that the partly built *Titanic* was reinstated to her original layout or, less likely, that *Olympic* was being altered to resemble her younger sister. The only reasonable explanation for such a costly expenditure of time and effort has to be that they were preparing to switch *Titanic* for the heavily damaged *Olympic*.

The reason why diverting labour for a matter of six weeks from the fitting out of *Titanic* to the urgent repair of *Olympic* only put the completion date of the former back by three weeks, has been a puzzle for many years. A possible solution is that the workforce, instead of repairing *Olympic*, were engaged in removing alterations already carried out to *Titanic*, at least as far as B Deck was concerned. The ship would then have to be painted, but that would present no problem to the builders. What interior fitting out could be completed in the time available would be done. The rest would be carried out once the ship was back in service. At the end of the six weeks, *Titanic*, almost completely altered back to her original layout, with the exception of at least the forward end of C Deck, sailed from Belfast as *Olympic*.

It can clearly be seen that a conversion was well under way while both vessels were in the builders' yard following the *Hawke* incident. The photographs are claimed by Harland & Wolff to have been taken in March 1912. They show *Olympic* entering the graving dock, supposedly to allow the work on her port propeller. The sun is striking both ships from above the port bow. To enter the Thompson graving dock *Olympic* would have to be heading just west of due south (190°). From this it is possible to deduce that the photographs were taken at about noon.

Records show that the sun set shortly after 6pm in early March 1912 but high tide on the relevant day did not occur until almost an hour later. If the date on the photographs was correct and, given that *Olympic* could only enter the dock at fully high tide, then the sun should have already set. The only explanation for the combination of high tide and the sun still being well above the horizon is that the pictures were not taken on 3 March 1912. The only other time when both vessels were together at the builders was following the *Hawke/Olympic* collision, in October 1911.

Work is evidently progressing on the superstructure of the vessel to the right of the picture. Curiously, both vessels look to be all but complete and both show fully painted funnels and upper works. However, another picture dated by the builders to October 1911 allegedly shows *Titanic* with painted funnels, partly painted superstructure and with her bridge incomplete. The vessel in this photograph seems to be closer to completion than either ship portrayed in the wrongly dated ones or in Fig 6.

While all of this going on, *Olympic* was thoroughly examined and then superficially repaired, at least externally. The collision point, 87ft from the stern, is perilously close to one of the huge, 45ton, cast steel frames of the vessel which were to carry the bearings for the three propeller shafts (the forward propeller bracket).[7] There is no record of any damage to this frame, but if the casting had been fractured, which seems likely, then the results would be catastrophic. (We already know that the damage to *Olympic* was played down by the builders.) In all probability such a repair would have been beyond the pocket of James Pirrie. Without completely rebuilding the rear of the vessel, it was extremely unlikely that a certificate of seaworthiness would ever be granted again. Not, at least, if the inspectors knew where to look and what to look for.

That the immense cast frames at the stern of the 'Olympic' class ships were nothing like as strong as they looked is illustrated by the relatively minor collision between *Olympic* and the Furness Bermuda liner *Fort St George* on 22 March 1924. Leaving pier 59 at New York, *Olympic* backed into the Furness vessel breaking her mainmast, damaging lifeboats, decking and about 150ft of railings. Initially it was thought that *Olympic* had suffered nothing worse that a few scratches — after all the accident had happened within the confines of the harbour where both vessels would have been operating at reduced speeds. Nevertheless, it was soon apparent that the cast stern frame, which supported the huge rudder and the central turbine shaft, had been fractured. Attempts by Harland & Wolff to patch up the damaged frame proved abortive, and during the winter of 1925/26, *Olympic* returned to the builders to have the entire assembly replaced. This was the first time that such a repair had been carried out.[8] To have attempted a similar cure for *Olympic* following the *Hawke* collision would have entailed a great deal more work and, consequently, expense. The damage occasioned in the much less violent New York accident was to the extreme rearmost frame, while that resulting from the encounter with the Royal Navy's cruiser was some distance further forward.

Given the tremendous investment already tied up in the two ships, it is hardly surprising that White Star pushed as hard as they did to get the verdict of the Naval Inquiry on the *Hawke/Olympic* incident overturned. While the IMM vessel was held to blame for the accident, the company could expect to recover none of the cost of repair or reconstruction from their insurance company (Atlantic Mutual).

The management of White Star and Harland & Wolff must have known from quite early on in the court battles which followed the *Hawke/Olympic* fiasco that they were extremely unlikely to win. After all, they had taken on the Government — not an organisation noted for playing fair — and their only hope that the decision in the Royal Navy's favour would be upset was ultimately to rest in the hands of another branch of that same Government, the House of Lords.

Fully appreciating their position, it would be hardly surprising if the controllers of the White Star line began to devise some other way to recoup their considerable losses. Of course there was always the outside chance that the appeal court might take the facts of the matter into consideration. If that were to happen, then the owners might well come out of the affair rather well if they took the necessary steps immediately.

If the appeal were to go in their favour they could recover £1 million from the insurance companies and the cost of *Olympic's* repairs from the RN. Of course, these repairs had in fact cost nothing like as much as the estimates, simply because they had not been done.

An accident to the supposedly brand-new *Titanic*, actually her older sister, would answer their requirements nicely. An answer that would rid them of the white elephant *Olympic* had become and, at the same time, finance her replacement, must have seemed like manna from heaven. All they needed to do was sail the damaged ship out into the middle of the North Atlantic, somewhere nice and deep, and a staged collision with an iceberg would do the rest. The ship, masquerading as her younger sister, could be quietly allowed to sink after all those on board had been taken off.

It was a good plan and with even a modicum of luck it could be made to work. Luck, however, was not something that the White Star line had in abundance.

The next stage of the plan was to convert the damaged *Olympic* into a *Titanic* look-alike. There was no need to go to extremes. Ismay's suggested extra cabins on B Deck need not really be built in, as long as the windows along the outside of the deck were made to look as if the work had been completed. Some partitions would have to be put up, of course, to fool passengers into believing they were aboard the new *Titanic*.

While there was no need to have new bells made for the ship, she could hardly go to sea as *Titanic* with *Olympic* written all over them. The simple way around that little problem was to grind the names off the bells or to switch those bearing the ships' names. One of the ships' bells was recovered from the wreck but, although in excellent condition, there was no name on it. Small items of equipment bearing identifying marks could easily be moved from ship to ship, either during the six and a half weeks both ships were in the yard following the *Hawke* débâcle, or in the week following the propeller blade shedding in early March 1912. The timing is unimportant, as long as we appreciate that there was ample opportunity to move anything which Harland & Wolff might have considered advisable. Items which ordinary crew members might conceivably notice, such as bridge instruments, portable furniture (which had the ship's build number), lifeboats, lifebuoys, etc could all have been moved in the time allowed. Certainly there was nothing beyond the capabilities of the greatest shipyard in the world.

How could they keep the secret with a workforce of thousands privy?

Working conditions for manual workers in the early part of the 20th century were not dissimilar to those of today. There was no security of employment. If a man did not do as he was told, he was fired and somebody else was brought in to replace him. Moreover, in an age preceding social security, an unemployed person was thrown on the charity of the parish — and parishes were not remarkable for their charitability. The shipyard, the area's major employer, also had the option of dispensing with the services of all the male members of a clan if any one of them upset the company applecart, which would automatically reduce the entire family to starvation level. Then, of course, there was the simple expediency of bribery. The expenditure of a few pounds would normally be sufficient to satisfy the curiosity or pacify the misgivings of a worker. If all else failed, then there was always the threat of the Official Secrets Act. Keeping the secret, at least for the foreseeable future, would not have presented very much of a problem.

Early in June 1912, a mere seven weeks after the *Titanic* disaster, *Olympic* narrowly avoided running onto the rocky northern shore of Land's End, the southwest tip of England. This near calamity was brought about by abysmal navigation aboard the liner, which should have been miles away to the south. The vessel was saved only by a last-minute reversal of engines.[9] Although Captain Haddock was not officially censured for the negligent navigation of the ship, for the next few voyages the owners insisted that a monitor be aboard to keep an eye on things.

Despite passengers, crew, management and the master mariner put aboard to oversee Captain Haddock all being aware of the incident, this near catastrophe was kept hidden for 75 years[10] without recourse to the Official Secrets Act.

Luckily for everybody concerned, world events were to take a turn which would make any scandal from the shipyard seem like very small beer!

Even in 1912 the clouds of war were gathering over Europe. During the preceding three-quarters of a century Germany had become one of the world's most powerful countries with obvious ambitions toward territorial gain. Around its borders other countries, unable to stand alone, formed uneasy alliances. While still hoping for the best, the governments and heads of state in Europe prepared for the worst.

We know that:

- By the time *Olympic* had made the voyage from Southampton to Belfast, the after compartment had filled with water despite the two weeks of emergency repairs that had been intended to prevent just such an occurrence;
- The White Star line was quite capable of keeping a secret for long periods of time, even to the extent of stopping witnesses spreading word of what had happened.

6

Trials and Fiery Tribulations

On the morning of 29 May 1911, *Olympic* steamed slowly down Belfast Lough to begin her sea trials. Aboard were 3,000 tons of best Welsh coal and a special crew of 250 men, many sent over from Liverpool to navigate the ship. While still in the lough her compasses were adjusted to compensate for the magnetically attractive mass of the ship. This could not be done in the shipyard because of the huge quantities of iron and steel surrounding the vessel.

Of all the life-saving equipment aboard, the lifeboats themselves should have been beyond reproach. Mr W. Chandler, Board of Trade Ship Surveyor at Belfast, said that, 'On 19 May 1911, he received special instructions to look closely into the construction of all new boats [lifeboats]'.[1]

The sea trials lasted two days and during them the ship greatly exceeded the expectations of both builders and owners. Her design speed of 21kts was exceeded by at least three-quarters of a knot. At the end of these vigorous trials, the management of the White Star line expressed itself more than satisfied with the new vessel and took possession of the forerunner of the new fleet.[2] After waiting so that eminent visitors aboard could watch the launch of the second vessel of the new class shortly after midday, *Olympic* sailed from Belfast for Liverpool at about 4.30pm on 31 May.[3] Two years and five months after her keel was laid, and a mere seven months and 11 days after her launch, *Olympic* was in the hands of her new owners.[4]

Arriving off the Mersey on 1 June, *Olympic* was thrown open for public inspection for the day. In the evening of the same day she sailed for Southampton to begin preparations for her maiden voyage scheduled for 14 June.[5] Eleven full days had been allowed to prepare the vessel for her first fare-paying passenger-carrying voyage.

At 10am on 2 April 1912, a day late because of bad weather, *Titanic* began her acceptance trials. Aboard the vessel were 78 members of the 'black gang' — firemen, greasers and other engine room and stokehold personnel — as well as 41 officers and senior crewmen. With less than half the number of crew members to man the vessel, putting this ship through her paces would, of necessity, be a very different affair from that of her elder sister. *Titanic's* trials lasted for just one day, or rather one working day and four hours of this was utilised for what were known as running tests, 2hr outbound at a mere 18kts and 2hr back.[6] The American Inquiry into the loss of the *Titanic* noted the hasty inspection and trials of the ship by the Board of Trade[7] but did not follow it up. Aboard the vessel for the truncated trials were Harold Sanderson for White Star and Thomas Andrews, accompanied by Edward Wilding, for the builders. In the morning a few high speed (about 18kts) twists and turns were tried. After some of these the ship was allowed to drift to a halt and was then restarted. At about lunch time the ship accelerated up to just over 20kts and the helm was put hard over. The ship steamed a complete circle with a diameter of about 3,850ft (1,280yd; just over three-quarters of a mile). During the turn, the ship's forward movement was about 2,100ft (700yd).[8] This meant that a solid obstruction, completely blocking the vessel's course, such as a cliff face, could be avoided provided the helm was put over while the vessel was more than 1,000yd from the obstacle. If a course change of only 30° was required, then the distance needed to achieve this would be more in the region of 500yd. After lunch the main stopping trial was conducted at about 20kts. *Titanic* required about 850yd (just under half a mile) to come to a complete standstill. 'The entire vessel shuddered as the stress of full speed astern was imposed on her hull' at a forward speed of 20kts.[9]

This means that any obstacle, no matter how huge, should have been avoidable provided it was seen and reported at more than half a mile and at a considerably shorter distance if a turn of less than 90° was needed. Even if the obstacle was sighted at less than half a mile, the ship's speed could and should be reduced to the point where the inevitable collision and its effects were reduced to manageable proportions.

At about 7pm the Board of Trade inspector requested one last trial: port and starboard anchors were dropped. With the completion of her far-from-adequate trials, Mr Carruthers, the Board of Trade inspector, signed the certificate of seaworthiness, valid for one year from 2 April 1912.[10]

Because she was capable of carrying more than 50 steerage passengers, *Titanic* was classed as an immigrant ship[11] and should therefore have been subject to a more than ordinary inspection by the Board of Trade. *Titanic* was licensed to carry 2,603 passengers and 944 crew members; 3,547 in all[12] This certificate would become automatically invalid less than a fortnight from its date of issue.

Unknown to the Board of Trade inspector, even as he signed the certificate of seaworthiness, a fire raged unchecked deep in the bowels of the ship and it wasn't in any of the furnaces! Coal in Number 10 bunker at the aft end of the forward boiler room had been alight since before the ship's trials had begun.

Shortly after 8pm this floating nightmare, believed by many to be the safest vessel on the high seas, weighed anchor and set off toward Southampton. There was to be no layover in Liverpool, supposedly because of the one-day delay in beginning the trials.[13] This, however, is hardly a convincing reason when one allows that a full day, as compared to *Olympic*, was saved on the trials themselves.

In an era where moving pictures (cinema) were in their infancy and television was undreamt of, what better advertising could there be than to allow newspaper reporters and photographers to describe and record the wonders of the new vessel. She was, after all, presumably *Olympic* perfected, with carpets where her sister had tile or linoleum covered floors, more ornate suites and more lavish decoration.[14] Curiously, very few photographs of the interior of *Titanic* survive: pictures of *Olympic* usually substitute. The hard-headed businessmen who formed the management of White Star and IMM were well aware of the value of newspaper advertising, as is illustrated by the carefully stage-managed launching of *Titanic* on the same day as *Olympic* was to leave the builders — a nice piece of media manipulation. One is forced to the conclusion that these same businessmen must have had a very compelling reason for denying the press, and an interested public, access to the newly completed *Titanic*. Could it be that they were afraid that people might notice that the ship was visibly incomplete?

Titanic made her way out into the Irish Sea and turned southward. She was expected to arrive at Southampton in time to catch the midnight tide the following night, 3/4 April.[15] Again, there would be no time for civilians to inspect the ship, she was due to leave on her maiden voyage only six days later at noon on the 10th. Only just over half the time *Olympic* had needed to prepare for her inaugural voyage was allowed to *Titanic* and of these six days, Easter would account for some. It was almost as if she was already at least partially prepared!

The conditions aboard the liner, as she steamed toward St George's Channel, were hectic as measurements were taken and equipment tested under actual seagoing conditions.[16] To arrive on time a sustained speed of 18kts had to be maintained, but short bursts well in excess of this were achieved. Although the ship was surrounded by fog from 2am until 6am,[17] the unfavourable conditions did not stop Captain Smith from seeing just what the vessel could do. In one high speed burst, *Titanic* reached 23.5kts[18] (another example of Smith's contempt for adverse or dangerous conditions).

Titanic was equipped with the latest Marconi wireless apparatus (as was *Olympic*) and throughout this first night it was in almost constant use. Signals were sent to the White Star home office in Liverpool, describing the trials, the vessel's exceptional speed and ease of handling.[19] The wireless operators, Jack Phillips (aged 24) and Harold Sidney Bride (aged 22), adjusted and tuned their equipment, establishing contact with other wireless equipped ships. The *Titanic's* wireless was amongst the most powerful afloat and although only specified as having a 350-mile daytime range[20], at night this could be significantly improved. As *Titanic* rounded Land's End and turned eastward into the English Channel, the wireless operators were in touch with Tenerife 2,000 miles away and with Port Said, more than 3,000 miles distant.[21]

The officers had joined the ship at Belfast and had been aboard for the trials,[22] although there was to be one late change at the very last moment before the ship began her maiden voyage. However, for the trip from Belfast to Southampton, the officers aboard believed themselves to be those who would take the ship on her first Atlantic crossing. In command was Captain Edward John Smith, who had been with White Star for 32 years,[23] their most senior captain, having commanded no less than 17 White Star ships[24] and who had sailed more than two million miles. He was the highest paid seaman afloat at almost £150 a month.[25] He was also a bit of a show-off[26] who, according to his first officer, used to take his ship into New York harbour at full speed.[27] Even in the golden age of steam Captain Smith was special in the way that he handled ever-larger liners like enormous speed boats.

Under Chief Officer William McMaster Murdoch, who had been 12 years with the company, there were six officers on board *Titanic*. The first officer was Charles Herbert Lightoller, also with 12 years' service.[28] He had been shipwrecked four times, cast away on a desert island and had also survived a fire at sea[29] amongst his other exploits. Lightoller was 26 when he joined White Star,[30] having gained his master's certificate three years earlier and he was what the sailors called a 'hard case' (an adventurer). There were now a number of ports where he dared not go ashore for fear of the local authorities. In his time Lightoller had served with Bully Waters running guns for West Africa. When the excitement of this dubious pastime wore off, he tried his luck in the Yukon gold rush, without any conspicuous success.

Even his 12 years with White Star had not passed without incident. While serving on the *Medic*, 12,000 tons and launched in 1899, Lightoller had made a number of visits to Sydney, Australia. On one of these visits the spirit of the *Holt Hill* must have overtaken him as he raised the Boer flag and fired a cannon sited on Fort Dennison, in Sydney Harbour.[31] This was the man that White Star had appointed to be first officer of the *Titanic* for her maiden voyage (although they were, understandably, later to change their minds) and on whose evidence so much of what is generally accepted about the events surrounding her loss is based.

The second officer was David Blair, who was ultimately to miss the fateful voyage but who does have a claim to fame as the navigating officer of the *Oceanic* when she ran aground on a Scottish island and was totally wrecked during World War 1.

Third Officer Herbert Pitman with five years' service[32] had checked that life-jackets were stowed aboard. He had found about 3,600[33] of them, although in the event they were to prove useless. Pitman had also checked the lifeboats while the ship was still at Belfast and found that they were fully equipped. Lamps were not stored in the lifeboats but in a lamp-room on the ship and the compasses were kept in a locker,[34] handy for the boats he had noted.

Fourth Officer Joseph Groves Boxhall, four years with White Star,[35] had been at sea for 13 years. Boxhall was a specialist in navigation and had spent 12 months training at a navigation school in Hull.[36]

Fifth Officer Harold Godfrey Lowe, one year with White Star, was about to make his first Atlantic crossing.[37] Lowe, like Lightoller, had spent some time trading on the West African coast.[38]

Sixth Officer James Moody had been with the company for only eight months[39] and after a week aboard was still trying to find his way about the ship.[40]

The crew, such as they were, had been mainly recruited in Ireland for the voyage as far as Southampton, where they would, if they so chose, be paid off. There was nothing to stop them signing back on for the maiden voyage when the time came, but, significantly, only one man seems to have left the ship only to rejoin it a few days later. However, at least 11 crew members, whose names do not appear on the Southampton signing-on list, survived the disaster. Presumably these men did not sign on at the Hampshire seaport but had joined the vessel in Ireland and remained aboard for the maiden voyage. As only slightly less than a quarter of the crew members known to be aboard survived, it is reasonable to assume that only a similar proportion of those not known to be on the ship did the same. This leads to the conclusion that there could have been as many as 50 more crew members aboard *Titanic* than has hitherto been believed.

Then, as now, merchant naval seamen signed aboard a vessel for one voyage at a time. There was no obligation upon them to sign aboard the same vessel for the next voyage (although many did), nor was there any guarantee that a ship's master would accept them even if they did wish to rejoin.

Because of White Star's policy of only taking on lookouts that had undergone a sight test, at their own expense, this section of the crew was fairly consistently employed by the company. At that period in history the White Star line was the only major shipping company to adopt this policy, so those few who had made the investment in an eye examination were reasonably certain of finding a position with them.

The trip down from Belfast to Southampton was no exception to this general rule. Up in the crow's-nest the ever-watchful lookouts strained their recently tested eyes into the darkness. As the fancy struck them they would periodically peer through the binoculars, which the company provided. Although these binoculars were officially issued to the care of the second officer, in this instance David Blair, they were intended for use by the lookouts and were normally kept in a special cupboard built into the crow's-nest.

Deep within the hull of the vessel the stokers, firemen and trimmers sweated in the stokeholds, at the ends of the boiler rooms. Number 6 boiler room must have been even warmer than the other five. Not only were the furnaces blazing merrily: so was Number 10 coal bunker.[41] Situated at the rear end of the boiler room, against the bulkhead which separated it from the next boiler room aft,[42] the fire here was generating a considerable amount of heat[43] — heat which would inevitably weaken the bulkhead to the point where it would prove to be of no practical value at all. Murphy's Law, as we all know, states that if anything can go wrong, it will go wrong. The boiler room immediately aft of Number 6, with its fire-weakened forward bulkhead, was in turn separated from Number 4 by another bulkhead.

This bulkhead, primarily designed to contain flooding to either Number 4 or 5 boiler rooms (whichever was breached), reached only as high as F Deck, about 2½ft above the waterline, unlike all the others which reached at least one full deck higher.[44]

One wonders why on earth White Star ever accepted a burning ship from the builders. If the fire was unknown when the new owners first took delivery but was discovered soon afterwards, why didn't they simply return to Belfast to have it dealt with? Coal bunker fires were not unknown in the heyday of steam but they were not at all common. There is no danger more feared by sailors than fire at sea and a coal bunker fire was at least to be feared as much as any other.

Coming down from Belfast Second Officer Lightoller, then acting as first officer, said that he was unaware of the coal bunker fire. He went on to say that such a fire would not be reported unless it was serious and that then 'it might be' reported to the captain.[45] This example of buck passing is a foretaste of this officer's reliability as a witness throughout. 'It would be the engineer's responsibility to see that a bunker fire was put out,' he added,[46] again shifting responsibility from himself. In reality, each potentially life-threatening situation that arose aboard the ship was the responsibility of any and every senior officer. There can be no doubt that a coal bunker fire was an inherently life-threatening problem. More than one vessel had gone to the bottom, torn apart by explosions originating in their coal supplies. Such explosions would happen in the future. A particularly notable example was aboard the third of the 'Olympic' class vessels, *Britannic*, which had a huge hole blasted in her side when a bunker exploded soon after the ship struck a mine during World War 1. As a result of the bunker explosion, the ship sank in slightly more than three-quarters of an hour. Had the bunker not exploded, then a single mine, which could only have opened two compartments to the sea if it had exploded close to a bulkhead, should not have caused the vessel to founder.

At shortly before midnight on 3 April, *Titanic* steamed up Southampton Water where she was met by five Red Funnel Line tugs (the Southampton-based Red Funnel Line is still in existence and operates the Southampton-Isle of Wight ferries from that port). The attendant tugs – *Ajax*, *Hector*, *Hercules*, *Neptune* and *Vulcan* – assisted as the *Titanic* was turned around in the specially deepened turning area in the River Test. Slowly the tiny tugs eased the huge liner into her berth, stern first, with her bows pointing south, ready for an easy departure on the 10th. The reason for these rather elaborate preparations was simply that noon on the planned day of departure would be low tide and there would be very little room for the leviathan to manoeuvre.[47]

Meanwhile, a coal strike that had begun on 22 February had closed practically all the country's mines. Shipping was severely affected. One by one, vessels were returning to port with no coal to fire their boilers. Owners took advantage of the lay-ups to carry out maintenance, repainting and even dry docking their ships. *Lusitania* went to Liverpool for maintenance and repairs. At Southampton the port became so crowded with idle liners that they were tied up side by side because there was no more room at the quaysides.[48]

To help offset the coal shortage, and possibly to keep nosy passengers out of certain parts of the ship, *Olympic* filled her bunkers to capacity in New York and even supposedly carried coal, in bags, in empty first class cabins and any other available space. In this way she had been able to add to the White Star stockpile at Southampton. *Olympic* had only vacated the dock now occupied by *Titanic* hours before the latter arrived, taking with her most of the stockpiled coal. What remained on the quayside was wholly inadequate to fuel the new liner for her maiden voyage. Desperate situations require desperate remedies, and to make good the shortfall in coal White Star would have to resort to one of these.

We know now that:

- While *Olympic* underwent two full days of trials before being handed over by the builders to her new owners, *Titanic's* trials only lasted for little more than half a day;
- Even as White Star line accepted the ship from Harland & Wolff, there was a fire in forward coal bunker No 10 which had started before the ship's trials had begun.

7

Southampton and Supplies

Events ran no more smoothly for *Titanic* at Southampton than they had in Belfast. The ship was nowhere near ready to receive passengers. There were still carpets to lay, panelling to fix and cabins to paint.

Mrs Maude Slocombe, the masseuse, worked desperately to clear half-eaten sandwiches and empty beer bottles from the Turkish baths before sailing day.[1] Owing to the amount of work that was still going on aboard, public rooms and alleyways were a jumble of stores, tools, boxes, rolls of wire, rolls of carpet and all the rest that was required to make this the finest vessel in the world. Such was the quantity of litter, there was nowhere sightseers could safely visit.[2] All of this detritus had to be cleared away before the stores could be brought on board.

It was so unusual for a vessel this close to her maiden voyage to be so ill-prepared that a local newspaper ran an article on the extraordinary state of the ship. 'Sightseers Need Not Apply' one of the paragraphs was headed; 'The officials have had so much worry lately that we gladly accede to their request for our help in making it known that the *Titanic* will not be open for inspection.'[3] That the *Titanic* was still incomplete so close to her maiden voyage hints that Harland & Wolff had run into unexpected snags. Given their experience in ship construction, this seems unlikely in the ordinary course of events. However, the extra labour involved in removing fittings and altering the vessel's appearance from that of her sister could perhaps account for a serious miscalculation of the time the work might take.

There were only six days remaining before *Titanic* was due to depart, one of these being Easter Sunday, a public holiday even in 1912. The ship had no crew except the transit crew that had brought her down from Belfast. Many of these had elected to be paid off and returned home soon after the vessel docked. There was not enough coal stockpiled to fill her bunkers. She was incomplete and still had 'civilian' workers aboard. To cap it all, she was on fire. Not, you could be forgiven for thinking, a very auspicious start to the career of the largest and most sumptuous liner the world had ever seen.

The coal strike, which had begun on 1 March[4] was both good and bad news for *Titanic*. The bad news was that not enough coal was readily available to fuel her furnaces for the maiden voyage even though *Olympic* had brought extra with her from New York. The good news was that the strike had left so many ships stranded that enormous numbers of sailors were available to sign on as crew. Captain Smith and his officers had the pick of these and should have been able to assemble a crack crew. That the good Captain and his band of piratical (as we shall see) officers failed hopelessly to pick such a crew is amply illustrated by later events.

On Saturday, 6 April 1912, in halls throughout Southampton, the crew was signed on, each man having to produce his licence to work, his Certificate of Continuous Discharge. This was a record of his service aboard other ships and usually had a one word comment from the masters of those vessels, provided the holder of the certificate had signed on and off. No comment shown meant that either a master had refused to give the man a reference or that he had not completed that particular voyage, ie he had jumped ship or deserted. Such a lack of entry would normally disbar a seaman from finding employment aboard another vessel belonging to a reputable company. However, this was not always the case. It is a fact that a sailor who deserted *Titanic* was, within weeks, given a berth aboard Cunard's flagship *Mauretania*; but more of John Coffy later.

Many of the crewmen who signed on that Saturday in Southampton had previously served on *Olympic*, which would have helped them find their way about the new ship,[5] but others were from *Oceanic* and *New York*[6] and consequently would have had no more idea of the vessel's layout than the passengers who were to join her four days later.

Incredibly, even with the glut of unemployed lookouts available, at least one of *Titanic's* had not served with White Star before and had not been eye-tested.[7] Lookout was regarded as a 'cushy' job in 1912, even though it entailed working two-hour shifts with only a four-hour break between.[8] Undoubtedly it was preferable to working in the abysmal conditions of the stokeholds.

There was inevitably a certain amount of confusion over orientation; Second Officer Lightoller said that it took him a fortnight before he could find his way about the ship with any confidence. Lightoller's statement is of interest in as much as the ship sank only 13 days after leaving the builders.[9]

Over and above the crewmen needed efficiently to run the ship, a number of extra men were provisionally signed to make up for any crew members who failed to appear in time for the departure, of whom there were a few. Despite this, 12 more firemen were transferred from *Oceanic*[10] specifically to deal with the fire which still blazed down in Number 10 bunker.[11] Why these 12 firemen were not selected from among the provisional party, who were obviously keen to make the journey because of the difficulty in finding employment, is unknown. Here though, at last, we have our first indication that the ship's officers were beginning to take the bunker fire seriously.

As previously mentioned, there was not enough coal stockpiled to fill *Titanic's* cavernous bunkers. She had arrived in Southampton with 1,880 tons on board, of which she would consume 415 tons producing steam to operate cargo winches and to provide heat and light throughout the ship during her time in port. Another 4,427 tons was scraped together from that left by *Olympic* and from the bunkers of five other IMM ships stranded in Southampton: *Oceanic, Majestic, New York, Philadelphia* and *St Louis*.[12] *Olympic* had consumed about 620 tons of coal a day, on her maiden voyage although she had been expected to use 720 tons.[13] *Titanic* must have been expected to burn something between these amounts in the same time.

The coaling of a steamer was a hellish task at the best of times, leaving a ship covered in coal dust and needing cleaning from stem to stern, but hauling coal in bags and baskets from deep within the five donor vessels must have been a nightmare. The very nature of coaling a ship meant that it was universally hated by officers and crew alike. Everybody aboard was obliged to help, the only exception being the skipper. Coal was supplied to White Star ships by R. & J. H. Rea and was brought alongside in barges. This same company would have inherited the unenviable task of manhandling the coal up from the bunkers of the five IMM ships and transferring it to *Titanic*.[19]

Eventually all the coal thundered its way down the chutes into *Titanic's* waiting bunkers, including Number 10, which as we know was already on fire. Coal dust must have hung in the air or drifted into every tiny opening. As coal miners are very well aware, coal dust, when suspended in the atmosphere, can be extremely explosive, requiring only the tiniest spark to ignite it. To alleviate this potentially lethal situation, the coal was generally wetted down to lay the dust, before it was tipped into the bunkers, but this by no means eliminated the problem. Fireman J. Dilley described the bunker fire thus:

> 'The coal on the top of the bunker was wet, as all the coal should have been, but down at the bottom of the bunker the coal had been permitted to get dry. The dry coal at the bottom of the pile

took fire and smouldered for days. The wet coal on top kept the flames from coming through, but down at the bottom of the bunker the flames were raging.'[14]

Coal, wet or dry, gives off coal gas, predominantly hydrogen, when heated. This gas is extremely susceptible to exploding or, at least, rapid burning as is evinced by the *Hindenburg* disaster. That coal gas is readily ignited by the source of heat that initially released it from the coal can be seen by the jets of burning gas apparent in any household coal fire.

Instead of dealing with this potentially lethal fire at Belfast, as they undoubtedly should have, or even at Southampton, where all the firefighting capabilities of a great port were available to them, *Titanic's* senior officers actually allowed about 400 tons of coal to be poured into the bunker on top of it. They stoked up the fire rather than put it out. Captain Smith must have known how dangerous a bunker fire could be and yet instead of attempting to avert the possibility of a major explosion by filling the burning bunker with water, he increased the probability that one would take place. Left unchecked, the fire must inevitably have meant disaster for the ship.

We see in the cavalier attitude to the inherently dangerous bunker fire, clear evidence that the commander and senior engineering officers of *Titanic* were not greatly worried whether their ship was fit for sea or not. Only a fool would expect a burning ship to be able to steam all the way from Southampton to New York without serious problems. Captain Smith might have been many things, but he was not a fool, and must therefore have had a very compelling reason for setting out from Southampton knowing there was every chance that an explosion could prevent the vessel completing the crossing.

The captain would also have been aware that a bunker blast posed not only the threat of immediate injury to his passengers and crew, but might easily cause fire to spread throughout the rest of the ship.

Fireman Dilley described the steps taken to control the fire:

'Two men from each watch were told off to fight that fire, working four hours at a time. No, we didn't get that fire out and among the stokers there was talk that we'd have to empty the big coal bunker after we'd put our passengers off in New York and then call on the fireboats there to help us put out the fire. The stokers were alarmed about it but the officers told us to keep our mouths shut. They didn't want to alarm the passengers.'[15]

From what Dilley, one of those aboard *Titanic* specifically to fight the fire, had to say, apparently this was no minor, insignificant conflagration but a profound threat to the safety of the vessel.

Titanic's maiden voyage had already been postponed once due to delays caused by urgent repairs to *Olympic*. There can be no doubt that passengers and crew would have preferred another relatively short delay rather than sail on time aboard a vessel in such an unpredictable state. A day or two more spent at Southampton would also have eased the panic to prepare the ship for sea in other ways. Why was Captain Smith in such a hurry to get his vessel onto the North Atlantic?

No sooner was the builders' rubbish squared away, than supplies and other necessities of life began to be brought aboard. There were 57,600 pieces of crockery and 29,000 pieces of glass from Stoniers, a Liverpool-based company that kept a store in Southampton specially for replenishing ships — particularly after stormy crossings when large quantities of crockery and glass could be broken. Some of *Titanic's* stock of china had been put aboard in Belfast for the use of guests during the trials and the trip down to Southampton.[16] Some 44,000 pieces of cutlery were also carried aboard.

Bottled beer came from Charles George Hibbert & Co of Southampton and London, in the shape of 15,000 bottles. Hibbert's was particularly proud to be supplying *Titanic* and had special postcards printed to commemorate the event.[17] Cut flowers, potted plants and palms were brought aboard by F. G. Bealing & Son of Highfield. In the early days of transatlantic steamer travel a first class male passenger might well have found a 'buttonhole' waiting at his place in the dining saloon, a nice touch by the horticulturists.[18]

Fruit and vegetables came from Oakley & Watling of 118 High Street, Southampton. Grey and Co, another Liverpool firm with a branch in Southampton's Queens Terrace, put meat, poultry and tinned food aboard the liner.[20] Southampton traders supplied a large proportion of comestibles but by no means all of what was required.

The provision list for the ship is almost as impressive as the vessel herself:

Fresh meat	75,000lb
Fresh fish	11,000lb
Salt and dried fish	4,000lb
Bacon and ham	7,500lb
Poultry and game	25,000lb

Fresh eggs 40,000
Sausages............................... 2,500lb
Potatoes.............................. 40 tons
Onions 3,500lb
Tomatoes............................. 3,500lb
Fresh asparagus .... 800 bundles
Fresh green peas................... 2,500lb
Lettuce .... 7,000 heads
Sweetbreads 1,000
Ice cream 1,750qt
Coffee 2,200lb
Tea 800lb
Rice, dried beans, etc.......... 10,000lb
Sugar................................. 10,000lb
Flour .... 250 barrels
Cereals............................... 10,000lb
Apples 36,000
Oranges.............................. 36,000
Lemons 16,000
Grapes................................ 1,000lb
Grapefruit 13,000
Jams and marmalade 1,120lb
Fresh milk 1,500gal
Fresh cream 1,200qt
Condensed milk 600gal
Fresh butter 6,000lb
Ales and stout .... 15,000 bottles
Wines .... 1,000 bottles
Spirits .... 850 bottles
Minerals .... 1,200 bottles
Cigars 8,000

White Star's linen was interchangeable throughout the fleet and unremarkable except in the quantity which *Titanic* took aboard at Southampton — 196,100 separate items, all to be entered in the inventory along with the other equipment and sundry supplies boarding.[21]

Cargo was loaded even while household items were being distributed throughout the ship. One of the more spectacular items listed as cargo was a Renault motor car belonging to first class passenger W. E. Carter. It was carefully stowed in Number 2 hold along with rolls of linoleum, furniture, books and periodicals. One deck directly below this assortment of cargo a large percentage of the 40 tons of potatoes needed to feed the passengers and crew were stored.

In the specie room, under lock and key, were cases of opium and some parcels. The total cargo weighed 559 tons and was made up of 11,524 separate pieces.[22] Noticeable amongst the items destined for the ship's hold is Mrs Charlotte Drake Cardeza's remarkable quantity of luggage, which comprised 14 trunks, four cases and three crates.[23]

Passengers' trunks and other heavy items of luggage often arrived well before the passengers themselves and had to be carefully stowed in their cabins or the holds under the watchful eye of *Titanic's* officers and crew.

Distributed throughout the double bottom of the ship, and in the fore and aft peak tanks, was storage space for over 3,500 tons of water ballast, used for trimming the ship (keeping the vessel on an even keel). This elaborate system for keeping her level was unable to cope with a persistent tendency for *Titanic* to list to port. Two midship sections of double bottom space were given over to the storage of fresh water for services such as flush toilets, showers, etc. These tanks contained 664 tons of non-drinkable water. The fresh (drinking) water, 792 tons of it, was stored in six tanks situated on either side of the electric engine (generator) room.

While *Titanic* was at Southampton, changes were made amongst the officers. Henry T. Wilde, chief officer of *Olympic*, was, against his will, drafted aboard *Titanic*, joining the ship only on the morning of departure, 10 April. As *Olympic* had sailed from Southampton just a week before, the orders detailing Wilde to leave that ship must have been received before the third, considerably before. It appears that Captain Smith may have personally asked for Wilde to be aboard,[24] but this seems unlikely judging by what we know of Smith's overconfident attitude. To have asked his employers for assistance over and above that which they thought adequate was completely out of character for the captain. That Smith should have as his two most senior officers men who did not hold an extra master's certificate, when it was company policy to employ only bridge officers who held that qualification, is of itself worthy of comment.

A new chief officer was assigned to assist an equally new and inexperienced Captain Haddock in running *Olympic*. One cannot help wondering if the experienced Wilde might not have been more use to Haddock than to the more experienced Captain Smith. As it was, *Olympic* was at sea with its two senior officers completely new to, and ignorant of, the idiosyncrasies of the 'Olympic' class, an accident looking for somewhere to happen. It was a general regulation of White Star that the safety of the ship should be paramount[25] although the company seems to have overlooked that in this instance. Some years earlier T. H. Ismay had written, in a letter to the Inman Line, 'We have enjoined the masters and officers under our charge to act on all occasions even in excess of mere prudence to avoid the possibility of danger.'[26] Obviously these rules only applied to the masters and officers of the line and not to the management.

Wilde was not pleased about the transfer, which had happened without his consent, but as it was for the one voyage only, he reported aboard as ordered. Consequently *Titanic's* existing chief, first and second officers were considerably inconvenienced. Murdoch was demoted from chief to first officer and First Officer Lightoller was downgraded to second with a corresponding cut in pay. Second Officer Davie Blair was obliged to quit the ship altogether. When he left, he took with him the keys to the crow's-nest binoculars cupboard, but not his own binoculars, which were locked in his cabin.[27]

Titanic's senior officers were issued with binoculars, which were marked 1st, 2nd officer, *Titanic*, etc.[28] Those marked '2nd officer, *Titanic*', which should have been in the crow's-nest for the benefit of the lookouts, were recently discovered on the sea-bed close to the wreck. This is where they would have been more likely to come to rest had they fallen from the crow's-nest when the foremast collapsed than if they had been locked away in the second officer's cabin.

On sailing day, 10 April 1912, the wind was from the west to northwest and gusty. The crew began to arrive soon after sunrise, which was at 5.18am on that fateful Wednesday. They entered the dock yard by Number 4 gate and had to cross the railway tracks to reach Berths 43 and 44 where *Titanic* lay moored.

At about 7.30am, Captain Smith came aboard and went straight to his cabin to receive the sailing report from Chief Officer Wilde, who had set foot on the vessel for the first time that morning.

Boarding at about the same time as Captain Smith was the assistant Board of Trade immigration officer, Captain Maurice Harvey Clarke.[29] His function was to clear *Titanic* under the Merchant Shipping Acts, as an emigrant ship. He had already visited *Titanic* a number of times during the preceding three days to check on such mundane items as food storage, sanitary arrangements and the fresh water supply.[30] Today he would inspect everything he could think of.[31] Clarke was well known to White Star officers and was regarded as something of a pain in the neck.[32] Conscientious to the point of nit-picking, the Board of Trade inspector would allow nothing to pass untested.

On this morning he insisted that two starboard lifeboats were lowered to satisfy himself that the tackle worked and the crew knew how to operate it effectively.[33] Somehow the fire below was kept from Captain Clarke, who would undoubtedly have insisted that it was extinguished before the ship sailed. This oversight on the part of the inspector can be attributed to lack of time. Amongst his other duties Clarke saw every one of the crew members aboard and checked that their details were correct[34] — including one Thomas Hart, we have to assume.

After completing the inspection, Captain Clarke reported his findings to Captain Smith and Captain Benjamin Steele, White Star's own marine superintendent, who were awaiting him on the bridge.[35]

By this time the passengers had begun to arrive. Third class embarked between 9.30am and 11am through the aft entrances near the stern on C Deck and by way of the forward gangway which led them into the maze of corridors close to the bow on D Deck. As they came aboard, these third class passengers were medically inspected and sorted into 'steerage' and 'immigrants' — steerage being a part of the ship allotted to passengers travelling at the cheapest rate. British passengers were quickly passed in the medical inspection but foreigners, particularly Scandinavians, were subjected to closer scrutiny.[36] White Star had no desire to carry a passenger all the way to America just for the authorities to turn them away, forcing the company to bring them all the way back again. Steerage was, at this time, by no means a one-way traffic and at one time 100,000 disillusioned Europeans were returning across the Atlantic annually.[37] The stewards helped incoming third class passengers to find their berths, but owing to the numbers boarding and the lack of stewards, there was no time to do more. These passengers were not shown their way about or even the whereabouts of the stairs and passages that would lead them to the open decks or their public rooms. Passengers wandered about with absolutely no idea of where they were in the vessel or how to reach anywhere else. Language differences only aggravated the problems faced by third class.[38]

Very shortly before 11.30am the boat train from Waterloo drew up alongside the ship and disgorged its load of first and second class passengers. First class entered the ship by way of the midships gangway leading to B Deck. The company supplied guide books for these passengers to use as an aid to finding their way about the enormous vessel.[39] (As we shall see, the company might well have done better to have supplied these guide books to the crew, some of whom had to ask directions from passengers.) The chief steward, A. Latimer, and his staff waited to lead them to their cabins through the blue carpeted corridors.[40]

Second class passengers were also escorted to their cabins by their stewards. Although there were fewer second class stewards than there were first, this overworked band managed to settle everyone.

By the time the quayside was devoid of persons waiting to board, the ship had taken something more than 900 passengers.[41] Amongst these were some of the richest and most famous people of the age, and some of the poorest and most anonymous.

So now we know that:

- Not only was the *Titanic* on fire when she reached Southampton but that instead of putting that fire out her officers allowed more coal to be put into the bunker, stoking it up;
- There were still civilian workmen aboard and there was so much work to do to complete the ship that she could not be opened to the public;
- Twelve extra crewmen were taken aboard to help control the bunker fire but a Board of Trade inspector, who was notorious for checking every detail, failed to notice the blaze.

8

The Passengers, and a Brush with New York

The wealthiest man aboard *Titanic* by a wide margin, was Col John Jacob Astor, with an estimated fortune of around £30 million, which had been amassed from property speculation. Col Astor had put up more hotels and skyscrapers than any other New Yorker. At one time he was a director of more than 20 large corporations, including railways. In 1891 Astor had married Miss Ava L. Willing of Philadelphia and produced a son, William Vincent, and a daughter, Alice. Late in the first decade of the 20th century it became known to the majority of New York society that relations between the colonel and his wife were not harmonious. In fact the couple saw very little of each other. As one entered a country the other, as a rule, left. In May 1909 Col Astor returned home just in time to see his wife off on a trip to Europe. She returned in October, just three days after he and 17-year old William Vincent had sailed for southern waters aboard Astor's yacht *Normahal*. This was obviously the last straw. Mrs Astor filed for a divorce, which was awarded on 8 November 1909. Grounds for the divorce were not made public at the time. There was no mention of alimony in the decree but Mrs Astor was awarded $50,000 a year.

At about this time a worldwide search was started for the colonel and his son who were believed shipwrecked in the Caribbean. It was a false alarm: the yacht and its passengers turned up at San Juan, Puerto Rico, none the worse for wear.

In July 1911, Astor announced his engagement to Miss Madeleine Talmage Force, the 18-year old daughter of William H. Force of New York, after an acquaintanceship of less than a year. Astor and Madeleine were married on 9 September 1911 by the Reverend Joseph Lambert, pastor of the Elmwood Congregational Church at Providence, but only after several other ministers had refused to conduct the ceremony, in view of Col Astor's divorce. Astor's new wife was a year younger than his son, which must have complicated their domestic relationship.

Soon after the marriage, Col Astor and his new wife set off on their honeymoon; Astor's divorce and subsequent re-marriage had not gone down well with New York society, to the extent that he (and she) were ostracised. To allow time for feelings to cool before facing his peers,

Astor planned a long honeymoon and only in April of the year following his marriage were he and his wife prepared to return to New York to face the music. As events were to turn out, he was spared the disdain of New York society hostesses.[1]

Another of the very wealthy aboard the ship was Isador Straus. Straus had moved to America in 1852 at the age of seven years. Nine years later, on the eve of the American Civil War, he volunteered for the Confederate Army. Desperately short of funds for the procurement of weapons, the Confederacy supposedly turned him down so he went to work as a clerk in his father's store. In fact the Confederate authorities had enlisted the young Straus to secure weapons and financial aid from Europe.[2] As soon as the opportunity presented itself, he moved to England where he remained for two years, until the war was over. After his return to America he moved with his father, Lazarus, to New York where they set up in business dealing in earthenware. So successful was this venture that the Straus family branched out into porcelain and chinaware.[3] As his younger brothers came of an age to join the company, the name was changed. The name of L. Straus & Sons was known worldwide.

In 1874 the Straus family joined forces with R. H. Macy & Company, becoming partners in 1888 and setting up the very first department store, which exists to this day: Macy's.

Isador Straus began to take an active interest in politics when Grover Cleveland became a presidential possibility. He supported Cleveland who was elected and became president in 1885 and again in 1893 at which time Straus became a presidential counsellor.[4] As a reward for his services, Isador Straus was elected to the 53rd Congress.

In common with many extremely wealthy men of his age, Straus was something of a philanthropist and supported almost every charitable institution in New York, regardless of creed. He was a director of the Hanover National Bank, vice-president of the Chamber of Commerce and Board of Trade. On top of all this, as if he still had time to spare, he was vice-president of the J. Hood Wright Memorial Hospital. Straus was travelling with his wife, Ada, in a style befitting a man of considerable means. What could be more natural than that they should travel aboard the very last word in style and luxury?

Clarence Moore, a Washington banker and one of the best known sportsmen in America, was also making the trip. He had been in Europe purchasing 50 foxhounds for the Chevy Chase Hunt, of which he was master, from the best packs in the north of England. He was travelling alone; his wife later confirmed this saying that her husband's trip abroad had been for pleasure! A member of the New York Yacht Club, the Travellers' Club of Paris, the Metropolitan, the Chevy Chase and the Alibi Club of Washington, Mr Moore was instantly recognised by his peers.

The noted war correspondent and artist, Frank D. Millett, 66 years old, was yet another eminent traveller. Never one to remain too long in one place, Millett had visited just about every country on earth by the time he booked passage on *Titanic*. Although resident in Great Britain, he still had strong ties to his mother country and was engaged in producing murals for a number of American public buildings, including the State Capitol at St Paul, Minnesota; the Court House at Newark, New Jersey; the Customs House at Baltimore; and the Federal Building at Cleveland, Ohio.[5] Naturally, living in England and working in America meant that Mr Millett was something of a commuter as well as an inveterate visitor to countries new. I don't suppose he was very worried which ship he made the crossing on, but *Titanic* was available.

One of the more influential persons aboard was Major Archibald Willingham Butt, President Taft's military aide and friend, who was returning to Washington after a visit to Rome where he had an audience with the Pontiff and King Victor Emmanuel. Archie Butt had gone to Rome as a personal messenger from the President and was bearing home to Taft an important message from the Pope.[6] It appears that Archie Butt had been in need of a holiday and Frank Millett had persuaded President Taft to send him to see the Pope on official business. Rome was especially appealing in the spring and such a trip would serve as a holiday for the major.[7]

Charles Melville Hays, President of the Grand Trunk Railway and the Grand Trunk Pacific Railway companies, also boarded. At a 1912 dinner at the Canadian Club of New York, held at the Hotel Astor, Sir Wilfred Laurier said of Charles M. Hays, 'Mr Hays is beyond question the greatest railroad genius in Canada. As an executive genius he ranks second only to the late Edward H. Harriman.'[8]

Hays did not wholly believe that the tendency among major ship owners to build ever larger and more opulent vessels was the most sensible course that they could take. On the subject he wrote, 'The White Star, the Cunard, and the Hamburg-American lines are now devoting their attention to a struggle for supremacy in obtaining the most luxurious appointments for their ships, but the time will soon come when the greatest and most appalling of all disasters at sea will be the result.'[9] He was soon to learn that his foresight was all too accurate.

The well-known writer and author of *The Thinking Machine* and many short stories, Jacques Futrelle was yet another of the famous people making the voyage to New York. Mr Futrelle (37) was another ex-newspaperman — a type that seemed to be in abundance on the ill-starred liner.

Another noted author aboard was an Englishman, 63-year old William T. Stead, editor of the *English, Australasian* and *American Review of Reviews*, which journals he used to air his advocacy of international peace. As well as his pacifist tendencies, William T. Stead was also interested in psychical phenomena, which expressed itself in many of his articles such as 'If Christ came to Chicago' and 'Maiden Tribute'. In 1900 he proposed the formation of the International Union to combat militarism and to secure the adoption of the recommendations of the Hague Conference.

There are many claimants to prophecy where the loss of RMS *Titanic* is concerned, but in truth only two of these can really be accepted as foreshadowing the events of 14/15 April 1912. One of these prophets is none other than William T. Stead who wrote in the *Pall Mall Gazette* of 22 March 1886 an article 'How the Mail Steamer went down in Mid-Atlantic, by a Survivor', in which an unnamed steamer collides with another vessel and consequently sinks. Many lives are unnecessarily lost because the ship is equipped with too few lifeboats. Stead concluded the article with a prophecy: 'This is exactly what might take place and will take place if the liners are sent to sea short of boats. — Ed.'

Six years later, Stead wrote another article, this time for the *Review of Reviews*. In the 1892 special Christmas edition appeared the 123-page mini-novel *From the Old World to the New*. In it, during a fictional Atlantic crossing aboard *Majestic* in early May, a clairvoyant passenger has a vision of survivors from a vessel which sank after striking an iceberg. In response to the clairvoyant's vision *Majestic* steers for the wreck site, rescues the survivors and then moves southward to avoid meeting the same fate as the unfortunate ship.[10]

In April 1912 William T. Stead was on his way to the New World (New York) at the personal invitation of President Taft[11] to address a great peace rally to be held on 21 April at Carnegie Hall. There was no possible way that Stead could have known that his prophecies of doom were to be fulfilled on this trip, or he might have been excused for postponing or bringing forward his visit to New York, or even refusing to accept the president's invitation at all.

The Chairman and Managing Director of IMM and White Star was booked aboard for the trip in suite B52.[12] Not surprisingly, the line's supremo had taken the port side millionaire suite with its own private promenade deck, one of only two on the vessel. It should, perhaps, be mentioned here that Ismay believed that a ship was the responsibility of her captain. He even carried this belief over to his motorcar, believing it to be the responsibility of his chauffeur. Even though the chauffeur drove much too fast to suit his employer, he was never reprimanded. When asked about this Ismay replied, 'He is in charge, and if he thinks we should go so fast it is not up to me to interfere.'[13] After the disaster Ismay was accused of influencing Captain Smith as to the speed of the *Titanic*, which, in the light of this statement, seems unlikely.

During the disaster he was, undeservedly, to win everlasting infamy as the man who should have gone down with the ship but didn't. The fact that J. Bruce Ismay survived the wreck of *Titanic* blighted the remainder of his life, although not quite as much as if he had not managed to board a lifeboat at all!

The other promenade suite should have been occupied by the shipping combine's owner, J. P. Morgan, but, ostensibly for reasons of health, Mr Morgan had cancelled his passage. (In fact, he was enjoying the company of his French mistress in Aix-les-Bains.) Luckily for Mr Morgan a shipment of bronzes that should have been on *Titanic* with him had 'by pure chance' not been included in the cargo manifest and were consequently not aboard. His booking had been taken over by Horace Harding but he, too, had cancelled and then sailed on the *Mauretania*.[14] For the maiden voyage the suite would be occupied by the Cardezas.

Of the lesser mortals aboard, Sir Cosmo and Lady Duff-Gordon (of London Dry Gin fame) were destined to make a name for themselves by escaping the disaster with three friends in a lifeboat designed to carry 40.

George Wright, a very prominent, if somewhat eccentric, Halifax property developer also appears on the first class passenger list. He was a big man who wore a waxed moustache. The owner of a 57ft boat, he was a leading yachtsman and something of an extrovert — all in all the sort of person who did not go through life unnoticed. Curiously, not a single survivor from the *Titanic* mentioned ever seeing him, nor is his name on any survivor list.[15] Nothing seems to be known of him after the liner set sail.

First class passenger George Quincy Clifford may have had misgivings about the voyage. Shortly before sailing day he took out a $50,000 life insurance policy, which as things were to turn out, was quite a shrewd investment.[16]

The safety record of the White Star line for the 10 years up to the *Titanic* disaster was exceptionally good, at least as far as first class passengers were concerned. Of the 2,179,549 persons carried, only two first class passengers had been lost, both of them when the *Florida* collided with the *Republic*.[17] (Obviously a criminal lunatic lost overboard on the return leg of *Olympic's* maiden voyage did not qualify!)

In the few weeks following 10 April 1912, many people who would otherwise have never attained public recognition were to become household names as the roles they played became sometimes apparent.

Col Archibald Gracie, in stateroom C51, upon boarding the ship sought out every unattached first class female he could find and offered his services and protection. Amongst this throng were three sisters — Mrs E. D. Appleton, Mrs R. C. Cornell and Mrs J. Murray Brown — all friends of his wife. The sisters were returning from burying a fourth, Lady Victor Drummond. Although the colonel had known of the funeral he had not attended, for reasons of his own. Travelling with his wife's friends was Miss Edith Evans.[18] It was common practice in those far-off days for a gentleman to offer his protection to a lady travelling alone, but not to a ship-load of them. In fact, one of the few first class female passengers lost in the disaster just happened to be under the dubious protection of the colonel. At the time *Titanic* was sinking, instead of actually assisting the ladies to whom he had offered his protection, Col Gracie was searching the ship for Mrs Churchill Candee, as it seems were a good percentage of the unattached first class male passengers. Gracie's account of the disaster, long viewed as accurate, in the light of subsequent events must be treated with suspicion.

Among the second class passengers was a young schoolteacher, Lawrence Beesley, who was watching everything and taking notes of what he saw. This was to be his first voyage and he wanted to miss nothing. In fact Beesley's notes, taken before, during and after the sinking, formed the basis for his book, *The Loss of the Titanic*, which is, without doubt, the clearest survivor account of all, with no attempt at self-aggrandisement.

Mr Hoffman and his two young children did their best to keep out of the way. This was unsurprising as the family name was not Hoffman but Navratil and the father was in the process of kidnapping his own two children in a desperate attempt to save his failing marriage.[19]

John Pierpont Morgan was not the only person to cancel his booking on the *Titanic* at the last moment. Jack Binns, who had won fame as the wireless operator of the *Republic* when that vessel sank, was another. After that collision Binns had stayed with his apparatus, under appalling conditions, until his distress signals were answered and help arrived. He could not wait for *Titanic* and so sailed earlier on the *Minnesota*.[20] In all, over 50 people decided not to sail on the maiden voyage.

As the passengers boarded, some crewmen, mostly members of the 'black gang', who were not on duty, were allowed to go ashore again on the understanding that they would rejoin the ship in time for departure. At least some of those liberated took advantage of this extra time ashore to visit local hostelries. Most were back in good time but a few remained in the pubs for just too long. John Podesta, William Knutbean, the Slade brothers (Bertram, Tom and Alfred) all entered the docks at the same time, but the Slades waited for a train to pass while Knutbean and Podesta managed to scurry ahead of it and reach the ship. The Slades ran alongside the vessel shouting to be allowed to board, but the sixth officer, Moody, would not allow it. The Slades, along with stokers Shaw and Holden and trimmer Brewer, were left behind, luckily for them. Replacements had been signed on from the extra men waiting aboard for a situation just like this.[21]

Round about midday, the huge vessel moved clear of the harbour wall and began, with the aid of tugs, to creep out of the White Star (Ocean) Dock. On a previous voyage, aboard *Olympic*, Smith had told the pilot, George Bowyer, that he was getting used to this class of vessel's huge proportions.[22] He was mistaken.

Even as gently as the ship was moving, it was still too fast for the confined area of the dock, cluttered as it was with moored ships. As *Titanic* moved forward, the movement of water caused by the passage of her great hull, pulled the SS *New York*, which was tied up alongside *Oceanic*, away from the vessel she was moored to. With a sound like shots being fired the thick ropes holding her in place parted like cotton and *New York's* stern swung toward *Titanic. Oceanic* was also caught up in the suction created by the movement of the enormous hull in such a limited space and keeled over several degrees; luckily her mooring lines held.[23]

Only the quick action of Captain Gale of the tug *Vulcan* averted a disaster. Leaving *Titanic* he took his tiny vessel around the *New York* and, at the second attempt, got a line on her. The tug's powerful engines strained and eventually arrested the swing of *New York's* stern. A mere 4ft was all that separated the two ships.[24] Reacting far more quickly and decisively than during the *Hawke* incident, the pilot Bowyer had *Titanic's* engines put astern, which helped push the *New York* clear, and Smith prepared to drop the bow anchors to stop the ship's forward momentum before a collision occurred. It seemed as if disaster had been averted, if only for this trip. Nobody knew that *Titanic* had just come as close to New York as she ever would!

Why Smith and the pilot underestimated the suction problems of moving this type of ship out of Southampton is another mystery. Both men had taken *Olympic* through those same restricted waters on a number of previous occasions,[25] although because of the coal strike, it is true that there was an unusually large number of idle vessels crowding the harbour this time and this may have contributed to the problem.

After an hour's delay, *Titanic* slipped quietly down Southampton Water and turned left into the Solent. Perhaps during the delay Captain Smith noticed Sailing Order Number 4, posted in the chart room:

> 'No thought of making competitive passages must be entertained, and time must be sacrificed or any other temporary inconvenience suffered, rather than the slightest risk should be incurred.'[26]

One reason for this insistence by the owners that no risks should be taken with their property might have been that White Star vessels were under-insured by about a third of their value.[27] While insurance premiums at the time could hardly be described as excessive — *Titanic's* was 3% and her cargo's 15%[28] — the owners were not about to lay out any more money than was absolutely necessary.

The weather was cold and the wind gusty when the liner moved majestically out of Southampton.[29] As the ship steamed past Cowes on the Isle of Wight, a local pharmacist waited in a small boat to photograph the new liner. This man had similarly photographed *Olympic*. He had also been a witness to the *Hawke* incident and had given evidence at that inquiry. Captain Smith recognised the photographer and gave four blasts on the whistle in salute.[30] The ship stopped briefly to allow surplus crewmen and civilian workers to leave the ship by tender (tug) before moving on, swinging right around the eastern end of the Isle of Wight and shaping course for Cherbourg. The most famous maiden voyage in history had begun.

We know that:

- A number of people cancelled their passage aboard the *Titanic* at the last moment, including the vessel's owner J. P. Morgan;
- Mr Morgan's bronze statuary, which should have gone aboard the ship, was overlooked and left on the quayside;
- George Wright, a well-known Halifax businessman who supposedly joined at Southampton, was never seen again, either aboard the vessel or afterwards.

From Southampton to Queenstown and Onward

The voyage as far as Cherbourg was uneventful,[1] except that for the first time the lookouts found they no longer had binoculars.[2] The glasses had been locked in Second Officer Lightoller's cabin on the instructions of the man he had replaced, former Second Officer David Blair.[3]

Why the outgoing officer would order the confiscation of the lookouts' binoculars is something of a mystery in its own right. The glasses were not the personal property of Davie Blair but were ordinary company issue. To avoid confusion and identify which officer was responsible for which pair of glasses they were stamped with his rank.

While not obligatory, it was normal practice aboard White Star vessels for the second officer to lend his glasses for use in the crow's-nest. This was a practice that both Captain Smith and Second Officer Lightoller, who had held that rank aboard other vessels belonging to the line before being promoted, for however short a time to first officer, must have been well aware of.

The lookouts could not understand why they were denied binoculars. Glasses had been provided for them on the way down from Belfast and on other vessels belonging to the line.

Not long after setting out from Southampton, lookout George Symons went to the second officer and reported the disappearance of the glasses from the crow's-nest. Lightoller took the query to First Officer Murdoch, who told him that he knew all about it and would deal with the matter.[4] The lookout went so far as to ask Chief Officer Wilde about the missing binoculars, 'There is none,' he replied.[5] 'I asked for the glasses several times,' said Symons. 'It is always customary to have glasses in the crow's-nest. I served for three years and five months on the *Oceanic* and they had glasses all the time.'[6] Lookout George Hogg said, 'I have always had night glasses in the White Star boats. I asked for glasses and I did not see why I should not have them. I had them from Belfast to Southampton but from Southampton to where the accident occurred we never had them.'[7] Hogg also said that 'he had only ever had glasses supplied on White Star ships'.[8]

Ismay explained at the British Inquiry that while it had once been White Star practice to supply binoculars for the lookouts, this had stopped in 1895. After that date it was left to the discretion of individual captains as to whether or not binoculars were provided to lookouts.[9]

During the evening, passengers and crew alike found time to explore the huge ship or at least a small part of it. One first class passenger's impression of the vessel and its performance was published in the *Belfast Telegraph* on 15 April 1912:

' "Look how that ship is rolling. I never thought it was so rough." The voice was a lady's and the place was the sun deck (sic) of the Titanic. We had just got well clear of the eastern half of the Isle of Wight and were shaping our course down the English Channel toward Cherbourg.

'The ship that had elicited the remark was a large three-masted sailing vessel which rolled and pitched so heavily that over her bow the seas were constantly breaking. But up where we were — some 60ft above the waterline — there was no indication of the strength of the tossing swell below. This indeed is the one great impression I received from my first trip on the *Titanic* — and everyone with whom I spoke shared it — her wonderful steadiness. Were it not for the brisk breeze blowing along the decks one would scarcely have imagined that every hour found us 20 knots further upon our course.

'But other things beside her steadiness filled us with wonder. Deck over deck and apartment after apartment lent their deceitful aid to persuade us that instead of being on the sea we were still on terra firma. It is useless for me to attempt a description of the wonders of the saloon – the smoking room with its inlaid mother of pearl — the lounge with its green velvet and dull polished oak — the reading room with its marble fireplace and deep soft chairs and rich carpet of old rose hue — all of these things have been told over and over again, and only lose in the telling.

'So vast was it all that after several hours on board some of us were still uncertain of our way about — though we must state that with commendable alacrity and accuracy some 325 found their way to the great dining saloon at 7.30 when the bugle sounded the call to dinner. After dinner, we sat in the beautiful lounge listening to the White Star orchestra playing The Tales of Hoffman and Cavalleria Rusticana selections, and more than once we heard the remark "You would never imagine you were on board a ship." Still harder was it to believe that up on the top deck it was blowing a gale.

'But we had to go to bed, and this reminds me that on the *Titanic* the expression is literally accurate. Nowhere were the berths of other days seen and everywhere comfortable oaken bedsteads gave ease to the weary traveller.

'Then the morning plunge in the great swimming bath, where the ceaseless ripple of tepid sea water was almost the only indication that somewhere in the distance 72,000 horses in the guise of steam engines fretted and strained under the skilled guidance of the engineers. After the plunge a half hour in the gymnasium helped to send one's blood coursing freely and created a big appetite for the morning meal.

'But if the saloon of the *Titanic* is wonderful, no less so is the second class and, in its degree, the third class. A word from the genial purser opened a free passage through all this floating wonder. Lifts and lounges and libraries are not generally associated in the public mind with second class, yet in the *Titanic* all are found. It needed the assurance of our steward guide that we had left the saloon and were really in the second class.

'On the crowded third class deck were hundreds of English, Dutch, Italians and French mingling in a happy fellowship and when we wandered down among them we found that to them, too, the *Titanic* was a wonder. No more general cabins, but hundreds of comfortable rooms with two, four or six berths each, beautifully covered in red-and-white coverlets. Here, too, are lounges and smoking rooms, less magnificent than those amidships, to be sure, but nonetheless comfortable, and which, with the swivel chairs and separate tables in the dining rooms, struck me as not quite fitting with my previous notion of steerage accommodation.

'Dusk fell as *Titanic* rode at anchor while 274 passengers joined the ship and 22 left her. At 8pm, ninety minutes after arriving, orders were given to weigh anchor and ten minutes later the liner was under way, setting a course for her next and last port of call, Queenstown, Ireland. The lights of Cherbourg slowly disappeared astern as the vessel picked up speed. Through the silent night she steamed westward along the English Channel before swinging port

around Land's End, the extreme south western tip of England, into
St George's Channel and onward toward Ireland.'

Although much of the description in the above newspaper article is
erroneous, it is painfully obvious that whoever wrote it was more than
a little impressed by the *Titanic*.

Titanic arrived off Cherbourg, still an hour behind schedule, and
dropped anchor in the roadstead at 6.30pm.[10] Cherbourg, like
Southampton only 77 nautical miles away, was a deep water port. It
had a good harbour, protected from the elements by a long sea wall.
It also boasted a naval station and a small inner harbour, but while
these facilities were adequate for most commercial and coastal
shipping, they could not cope with anything like the new giants,
Olympic and *Titanic*.[11] These had to drop anchor outside the harbour.
Passengers had to be ferried to and from these ships in smaller vessels
specially built for that purpose.

While the new super-liners were under construction in the Belfast
yard, Harland & Wolff were also busy building two new tenders to
ferry passengers and mail to and from the ships as they lay offshore at
Cherbourg. First and second class passengers went aboard the *Nomadic*
and third class travelled on *Traffic*.[12] *Traffic* was scuttled at Cherbourg
in 1940, but was raised and refurbished by the Germans. She was sunk
in the English Channel by a British torpedo boat on 17 January 1941.
Nomadic, however, survives to this day as a floating restaurant,
anchored on the River Seine near the Eiffel Tower in Paris — the last
of the White Star fleet.[13]

Waiting to board the overdue liner were 102 third class passengers,
30 second and 142 first class passengers. Prominent among the first
class were the Cardezas — Thomas D. M., his wife Charlotte Drake,
his valet Gustave Lesneur and Mrs Cardeza's maid, Anna Ward.[14]
Obviously a seasoned traveller, Mrs Cardeza had sent the bulk of her
luggage to be put aboard ship at Southampton. As we saw earlier, her
goods were packed into 14 trunks, four suitcases and three crates[15] all
of which she later valued at £36,567 2s.[16]

Among other first class passengers joining the vessel at Cherbourg
were Benjamin Guggenheim and his valet Victor Giglio. Forty-six-
year old Guggenheim was also taking passage with his wife. When he
was only 20 years old his father sent him to Leadville, Colorado, to
take charge of the family mining interests, which were becoming
tremendously productive at about that time. While the young

Guggenheim was in the mining town he recognised the huge potential for a smelting plant in the area. This plant was but the first of many and it was smelting that formed the basis of the Guggenheim fortune,[17] estimated at £20 million.[18] The Guggenheim interests were closely associated with those of J. P. Morgan.[19] Guggenheim's chauffeur, Rene Perot, was travelling second class.

Also boarding at the French port were Mrs James J. (Margaret) Brown, better known as Molly; Miss Rosenbaum, also known as Edith Russell; Mr and Mrs Morgan, who were to figure prominently in later events under their own names; Sir Cosmo and Lady Duff-Gordon; and Mr and Mrs Ryerson and their three children.[20]

Life aboard the vessel as she ploughed steadily onwards toward Queenstown was not all 'beer and skittles'. Somebody had to feed the hungry furnaces, tend the engines, prepare and serve the food, wash up afterwards, and steer the ship.

Not all the workers aboard were employees of the White Star line. There were two wireless operators, who were employed by both White Star and the Marconi Company. John (Jack) Phillips, the senior man at 24 years old, was to celebrate his 25th birthday the following day, the 11th.[21] With him was Harold Sidney Bride, aged 22. Bride said later that he was paid £2 5s a month by White Star and a further £4 a month by Marconi.[22] Phillips, as the senior man, was slightly better paid at £4 5s a month by the shipping line[23] and, presumably, received a similarly increased sum by his nominal employer.

A large proportion of the waiters and kitchen staff operating the new á la carte restaurant worked for Gatti's of London and were effectively subcontracted labour. They do not appear to have been paid anything at all by White Star directly.

The ship's Post Office was located deep within the ship, forward, on G Deck. Americans John S. Marsh, William C. Gwynn and Oscar S. Woody worked in this office along with two English Post Office employees, Jago Smith and E. D. Williamson.[24] All five postal workers were employed by their respective national postal services. Nine men from the builders were also aboard to sort out any minor defects which might show themselves during the maiden voyage. Heading this group was Thomas Andrews[25] who was William James Pirrie's nephew and the Managing Director of Harland & Wolff. Judging by the respect and affection in which Mr Andrews was held by management and workers alike, one suspects that he was not above getting his hands dirty if the occasion demanded. On a cruise like *Titanic's* there would certainly be plenty of opportunity for an engineer of Mr Andrews' undoubted capabilities to roll up his shirt sleeves and practise what he preached.

It seems strange that such a senior man should accompany the Belfast workforce, unless of course something was expected to go seriously wrong with the ship, as it might be if she was in fact the mortally wounded *Olympic* in disguise. In that event one would have expected at least some of the guarantee party to be equally experienced and highly qualified so as to be able to cope with practically any emergency that might foreseeably arise as a result of the vessel's earlier contretemps with the armoured cruiser. There would also, of course, have to be somebody to do the dirty work. Just as in industry today, labourers and apprentices do the jobs which nobody else wants to tackle. The guarantee party fits these requisites perfectly and consisted of William Henry March Parr, assistant manager, electrical department and Roderick Chisholm, chief ship's draughtsman. These two men, with Andrews (also a draughtsman and assistant designer of these vessels) travelled first class. Six more men (the workers) had to make do with second class accommodation. These were Anthony (Archie) W. Frost, outside foreman engineer; Robert Knight, leading hand fitter engineer; William Campbell, joiner apprentice; Alfred Fleming Cunningham, fitter apprentice; Francis (Frank) Parkes, plumber apprentice and Ennis Hastings Watson, electrician apprentice.[26] The whole party were on 24-hour standby, but it doesn't take a genius to work out which of the nine would be most likely to have their night's sleep disturbed in the normal course of events. Officially the Belfast men were at the beck and call of the ship's various engineers, which seems an upside down arrangement because, at that point, Harland & Wolff's people would have known more about the ship than her own crew.

The reporter from the *Belfast Telegraph* was still more than a little impressed by the gentle motion of the ship: 'And this morning, approaching Queenstown through the clear dawn, when the full Atlantic swell came upon our port side, so stately and measured was the roll of the mighty ship that one needed to compare the moving of the side with the steady line of the clear horizon.'

On the morning of the 11th, before reaching Queenstown, Captain Smith ordered an emergency drill. The alarm bells all rang for 10sec before all of the automatic watertight doors throughout the vessel were closed, wrote Assistant Electrician George Irvine in his last letter to his mother.[27] (Curiously, there was no general alarm, nor were bells sounded after the vessel apparently struck an iceberg.) There is no record of the boats having been swung out, nor did the passengers assemble on the Boat Deck, so this trial (if it were a trial) was purely to test the efficiency of the watertight doors. Presumably these same watertight doors would already have been thoroughly tested by the builders, by the new owners during the vessel's trials and again by Captain Clarke when he examined the ship in Southampton harbour. Unless Captain Smith suspected that there was something amiss with the doors there was absolutely no reason to test them again. It might have been done to impress the passengers, whom it was more likely to alarm than reassure.

The most likely explanation for the watertight doors being closed is that either the officer of the watch thought that a real emergency had arisen or that the vessel was taking in water. The latter reason is the more plausible as we shall presently see and is only explainable if the watertight integrity of the hull had been previously compromised. Dismissing the idea that the door closing was a test leads us to the conclusion that the ship was taking in water faster than the pumps could clear it, or that eventuality was expected to arise at any moment. Even at this early stage in the maiden voyage the ship had a persistent and, apparently, incurable list to port.

As *Titanic* approached Queenstown at about 11am, she came up on the Daunt light vessel which marked the entrance to the harbour. A long slow turn to port brought her close to the lightship where she stopped to pick up the pilot before proceeding toward the harbour mouth. Sounding lines were in constant use as the great ship eased gently toward the harbour before coming to a halt and dropping anchor about two miles offshore. The time was 11.30am.[28]

There was a delay of about half an hour as the tenders *America* and *Ireland* ferried passengers and mail from the pierhead, situated at Queenstown railway station. A total of 120 passengers were joining the vessel here, seven for second class and 113 third. Mail bags were taken aboard: 1,385 sacks.

Eight people left the ship at Queenstown, seven of them legitimately as passengers and one presumed deserter, fireman John Coffy of 12 Sherbourne Terrace, Southampton. Coffy had signed aboard *Titanic* for the round trip, Southampton to New York and back. Seemingly, on reaching Queenstown he secreted himself amongst the mail leaving the ship and thereby managed to get ashore.

Unless he actually hid inside a mail bag, this explanation is patently absurd. With so few passengers leaving the vessel the fireman could hardly have lost himself in the crowd.

Why would a man go to such lengths to leave a ship when employment was at a premium and had been for some weeks, owing to the coal strike?

An alternative explanation might be that he was allowed to leave the ship by Captain Smith for whatever reason. In this way his continuous discharge certificate would have been filled in enabling him to get work on another ship, which is exactly what he did. But the question remains. Why was Coffy so desperate to leave *Titanic*?

Among the letters brought ashore at Queenstown was a missive from Chief Officer Wilde to his sister. It must be remembered that Wilde had joined the ship only on the morning of her departure from Southampton and as this was her maiden voyage he could not have served on her previously. In his letter Wilde wrote, '... I still don't like this ship ...' STILL? How could he still dislike a ship he had never been aboard before. He didn't say, 'I still don't like this type of ship.' He wrote very specifically 'this ship', surely evidence that Wilde had indeed served on the vessel before and had not enjoyed the experience. Interestingly, Wilde had served aboard *Olympic* and had witnessed her accidents, most notably the encounter with HMS *Hawke*.

Although it was Ismay's stated policy never to interfere with the captain's general running of the ship, while the vessel lay stopped at Queenstown the line's chairman called for a meeting with Chief Engineer Bell. At this meeting Ismay informed the engineer of exactly what speed he expected the liner to attain, day by day. Supposedly the White Star executive informed Bell that he wanted the ship to arrive in New York not before Wednesday morning, certainly not on the Tuesday afternoon[29] (although this is contradicted by other evidence which shows that passengers expected the ship to arrive on Tuesday). A completely unnecessary high speed trial was also seemingly arranged for the following Monday, even though the ship was short of coal. The *Titanic* had already exceeded her sister's previous best speed on the short run down from Belfast to Southampton when she had reached 23½kts. Unlikely as it seems, Ismay and the chief engineer didn't consult the captain about any of these arrangements.[30] After all, what business was it of the captain's what speed his ship was travelling at? He was only responsible for its safe navigation!

Soon after 1.30pm *Titanic* again weighed anchor and the world's largest reciprocating steam engines began to turn. The ship's whistles sounded three deep melancholy blasts to announce her imminent departure.[31]

On the aft third class Promenade Deck, Irish emigrant Eugene Daly played the dirge *Erin's Lament* on his Irish bagpipes[32] Even before the ship began to move, the smoke-blackened face of a stoker appeared at the top of the aft funnel, either as a joke or simply for a breath of fresh air. The man had climbed up the inside of the giant funnel, which was a dummy used purely for ventilation.[33]

Slowly the ship gathered way until stopping again by the Daunt light vessel to drop off the pilot. Then there was a long sweeping turn to starboard, reversing her inbound course precisely and *Titanic* pointed her bows westwards toward America.[34] It was growing dusk as the liner took the first Atlantic swells when a French fishing trawler was sighted. Dangerously close, the liner swept past the small vessel, the spray from her bow soaking the fishing boat. The French fishermen waved and cheered *Titanic* on her way. (One wonders if the waving and cheering was, in fact, fist shaking and swearing.) In return the officer of the watch on the liner's lofty bridge ordered a salute of one blast from the whistles: a raspberry?

Titanic settled on her course into the setting sun.[35]

We now know that:

- *Titanic* had hardly cleared Southampton before the lookouts were complaining about the lack of binoculars for the crow's-nest;
- The ship had a persistent list to port;
- At Queenstown a fireman deserted the ship and the Chief Officer, Wilde, posted a letter to his sister saying that he STILL didn't like the ship. Wilde had supposedly first set foot aboard the *Titanic* the previous day.

West, Toward Disaster

It is a commonly held belief that the course steered by RMS *Titanic* on her fateful maiden voyage was the usual route for outbound liners at that time of year. This is not the case. Instead of taking the 'Outward Southern Track' as she should have, *Titanic's* captain elected to follow the 'Autumn Southern Track'.[1] This was the more direct route to New York, but it took the liner 60 miles north of the safer alternative path. It was not unusual in 1912 for vessels to steer well to the north of the agreed safe routes across the North Atlantic to save time. White Star was not alone in this practice: all the major lines were equally culpable.[2] Smith's choice of routes is questionable, however, as shipping papers had been publishing reports of ice in the North Atlantic shipping lanes throughout the early spring of 1912.[3]

White Star standing orders clearly forbade the use of the 'Autumn' route. It was White Star policy only to use this track from the middle of December to the middle of March, as field ice is then building up on the edge of the Grand Banks.[4] *Titanic* should have taken an alternative route many miles further south than the one chosen by Captain Smith to avoid this known danger area.[5]

As mentioned in the previous chapter, while the vessel was stopped at Queenstown, Ismay supposedly had talked to Bell, the chief engineer. Between them they had agreed to a speed trial the following Monday. *Titanic's* top speed was thought to be about 24 or 25kts.[6] Ismay and Bell had also agreed that the ship would increase speed, day by day, in the build-up to this trial in an effort not to use too much coal.[7] Captain Smith was in command of the ship, but this agreement, apparently made without his knowledge, would seem to make a sham of that. However, it is more than likely that the chief engineer would have informed the skipper of what was going on.

Under normal circumstances the captain is the absolute ruler of a ship at sea, but not if the owner is aboard. As his employer, the owner could dismiss a captain in mid-ocean if it so pleased him.[8] The mere presence of Ismay on board his ship could have put Captain Smith under pressure to put up an impressive performance,[9] but this seems unlikely. In fact, the company chairman appeared to be so disinterested in the day-to-day running of the ship that he did not visit the bridge once during his first four days on board.[10]

On paper it seems that there was no possibility of *Titanic* capturing the Blue Riband from *Mauretania*, which held the record for crossing the Atlantic at better than 26kts. If *Titanic*, capable of considerably more than 23kts, crossed the Atlantic by the shorter northern route then it became just possible for her to complete the journey from Queenstown to Sandy Hook (New York) in the same or slightly less time than the Cunarder. This, I suspect, has given rise to innumerable theories that *Titanic* was trying for the record.[11] In truth, to have attempted any such thing on a maiden voyage and with a crew unused to the workings of the ship would have been questionable in the extreme. There is almost no evidence to support the idea of a record attempt except a statement from a member of the 'black gang' who swore that the engines were running flat out right from the time that the vessel left Ireland.

Ismay had supposedly instructed Captain Smith, 'Under no circumstances whatsoever is the *Titanic* to arrive before 5am on Wednesday morning at the Ambrose light vessel.'[12] The last thing that the White Star line would have wanted was for the ship to arrive before the reception committee, press and crowds had assembled to greet her on the completion of a triumphal maiden voyage. Nevertheless, many survivors made persistent references to their belief that the *Titanic* would have arrived in New York late on Tuesday night instead of when scheduled.[13] If the *Titanic* had only maintained the speed she was making on the 14th she would indeed have arrived on the Tuesday evening.[14]

Later on the 14th it was planned that the vessel would put on more speed and yet more again on the following day. So we know that the ship was going faster than she needed to arrive on time. Clearly there was an intention to get somewhere in a hurry, but not to New York. The question that arises is why?

The first full day out, from 12 noon Thursday to 12 noon Friday, was relatively uneventful. The engines were running at 70rpm[15] and during that time the ship covered some 386 nautical miles.

In the radio room the two radio operators, Phillips and Bride, were occupied in sending passengers' personal messages. Describing his duties Bride said, 'I didn't have much to do aboard *Titanic* except to relieve Phillips from midnight until sometime in the morning.'[16] To send a Marconigram, as the radio telegrams transmitted by operatives of the Marconi Company were known, was almost the ultimate status symbol at sea.

In order of priority, passengers' personal messages did not come at the top of the list. 'There was an arrangement whereby Atlantic Steamer companies supplied one another with information regarding ice.'[17] Navigational messages, important to the safety of the ship, were supposed to take precedence over all others. The wireless men were obliged to take down any such message and immediately convey the information to the bridge.[18]

During that first 24-hr period, the 11th and 12th, five such messages were received by *Titanic* reporting heavy ice on or near the vessel's course, ahead of the speeding ship.

The following day, 12 April, the *Avala, East Point, Californian* and *Manitou* all encountered ice, again ahead of *Titanic*, and wirelessed warnings. In response to these early indications of the danger which lay ahead, the liner increased speed, engine revolutions rose to 72,[19] and the vessel covered 519 miles in the 24 hours up to midday on the 13th. The ice was still over 800 miles away, so *Titanic* increased speed yet again. In the 24 hours ending at noon on the 14th, another 546 nautical miles passed beneath her keel.

In that same period, the 12th to the morning of the 14th, another 10 reports of ice lurking ahead of the ship were transmitted by various vessels in the area. Each day the ship travelled faster than on the previous one.[20] On the morning of Sunday the 14th more boilers were lit ready to push the ship ever faster.[21]

Meanwhile, the days passed calmly for the passengers and crew alike. White Star treated their travellers like adults and did not provide organised entertainment. Passengers were left to find their own amusements, which no doubt suited the majority. The gymnasium, swimming pool, sauna and electric baths would provide plenty of opportunity for the more athletic in first and second class, while the library and numerous bars would cater for the needs of the less active travellers. In third class, a piano was provided for singsongs in the public rooms. Deck games were available to all and third class passengers had their own bars and smoking room.

Meal times were about the only organised events aboard, something that was unavoidable with the numbers involved if hot food was to be available to all. Breakfast was served from 8.30 to 10.30am; luncheon, in first and second class, from 1 to 2.30pm; dinner being served in steerage (third class) during the same time.

Dinner for first and second class, tea for third, was available from 6 to 7.30pm.

Hot meals for first class were available from 8am to 11pm daily in the á la carte restaurant on B Deck. This was staffed by employees drawn from Luigi Gatti's two famous London restaurants and catered for those whose tastes exceeded even the variety of foods on offer in the dining room. Gatti held a concession from White Star and the predominantly Italian staff of the á la carte restaurant, although not officially a part of the ship's crew, were subject to ship's discipline. Being neither fish nor fowl so to speak, neither crew nor passenger, the restaurant staff were in an unenviable position when the worst happened. The fate of the Italian restaurant staff is, without doubt, one of the more shameful aspects of the whole disaster.

One entertainment available to first and second class passengers alike was the ship's orchestra, which was made up of eight musicians recruited mostly from other ships and other lines. The band leader, 33-year old Wallace Hartley, a violinist, had joined the White Star ship from the Cunarder *Mauretania*. The cellist, in whom I have a particular interest as he was a local man, was John Wesley Woodward of The Firs, Windmill Road, Headington, Oxford. Woodward was to make a lasting impression on at least one passenger during the night of 14/15 April 1912 as he dragged his instrument towards where the rest of the band were assembling.

Normally the band was divided into two groups: one of three musicians, piano, violin and cello, played in the second class dining saloon and lounge, while the others played in first class. This division was not unalterable; members moved from group to group or formed duos or trios who acted as strolling players. When playing in second class, members wore blue jackets; in first class, white jackets and blue trousers were the order of the day. Each member of the orchestra was expected to know each and every song in the White Star song book and to recognise any of the 352 tunes from its number when called upon to do so by Hartley.

The morning of 14 April 1912 dawned cold and clear, but with a slight haze. Mrs White commented to fellow first class passenger Miss Young that it was so cold that they must be near icebergs.[22]

Until now only 20 of the 29 boilers were lit, but early on this Sunday morning, at about 8am, two or three more were fired[23] in preparation for the special trials the following day. These preparations were a little premature: it would not have required a full day and night for the six furnaces per boiler to raise the necessary 215lb/sq in steam pressure required by the engines.[24]

Sometime during the day the ship's purser told Lawrence Beesley, 'They are not pushing her this trip and don't intend to make any fast running.'[25] The engines were now turning at 75rpm,[26] the equivalent of more than 22kts. The notion that no attempt was to be made to make a fast passage is supported by a statement made by Lightoller at the British Inquiry. When he was asked by Thomas Scanlan MP, 'Were you not making all the speed that you could?' Lightoller replied, 'No, there was a shortage of coal and a number of the boilers were off, so that there could not have been the desire to make the most speed we could.'[27] But we already know that the vessel was ahead of schedule and preparing to accelerate.

At 9 o'clock on the morning of Sunday, 14 April, the first of a series of ice warnings was received in the wireless room. This first message, from the SS *Caronia*, was possibly the only one ever to reach the bridge or the eyes of the senior officers of *Titanic*. It read as follows:

'Captain, Titanic — Westbound steamers report bergs growlers and field ice in 42°N from 49° to 51°W, 12th April. Compliments — Barr.'

The reader will notice that this message referred to bergs, growlers and field ice sighted on 12 April, more than 48hr before the time of the coming collision. At the time this message was received aboard *Titanic* she was about 100 miles north and 300 miles east of the ice reported. It was known that, due to the exceptionally mild winter, more bergs than usual had found their way into the Atlantic and were getting down as far as Bermuda.[28]

Captain Smith acknowledged receipt of this message and the position of the ice was marked up in the chart room. From this point forward, communications between the wireless cabin and the bridge of *Titanic* appear to have suffered some slight disruptions.

Later that same morning, time had been set aside for a boat drill. These drills were not popular with the crew, particularly the firemen who refused to take part in the proceedings[29] — although it will be noticed that when use of the lifeboats became necessary, the firemen were not quite so backward. A surprising number of this contingent, which appeared to have an aversion to small boats in the ordinary way, found their way into them with amazing alacrity; 'like rats up a drainpipe' is the expression which springs to mind.

Probably in the interests of harmony between the upper decks and the hellish stokeholds, the lifeboat drill was cancelled and a Sunday morning church service held in its stead. This service may not have had the same life-preserving potential as a boat drill but it perhaps served to prepare at least some aboard for the coming ordeal.

Another possible reason for the lack of boat drill could be that the officers were in no hurry to let the passengers know that in the event of a real emergency there were not enough lifeboat places for all concerned to vacate the ship!

The vessel's course was set or checked daily, at noon, by the captain.[30] On the fateful Sunday, Second Officer Lightoller relieved Murdoch from 12.30 to 1pm so that the first officer could get something to eat. During his 30min stint on the bridge he failed to notice the ship's course[31] or speed.

Throughout the day Col Archibald Gracie was engrossed in a copy of Mary Johnston's *Old Dominion*, a book of adventures and extraordinary escapes.[32] This publication can have contained no more extraordinary escape story than the one the colonel told of his own getaway early the following morning.

Halfway through luncheon (dinner in third class) at 1.42pm, a wireless message from the SS *Baltic* was received by *Titanic*. The message read:

> 'Captain Smith, Titanic — Have had moderate variable winds and clear, fine weather since leaving. Greek steamer *Athenia* reports passing icebergs and large quantities of field ice today in lat 41°51'N, long 49°52'W. Last night we spoke German oiltank steamer Deutschland, Stettin to Philadelphia, not under control, short of coal lat 40°42'N, long 55°11'W. Wishes to be reported to New York and other steamers. Wish you and *Titanic* all success — Commander.'

At the time this message was received, *Titanic* was approximately 45 miles north and 180 miles east of the reported ice field and closing at about 22kts. Maintaining her present speed she should reach the ice in something less than eight hours.

Captain Smith acknowledged the message, which means that a wireless operator took the message at least as far as the captain, if not actually placing it in the hands of a watch officer where it might conceivably have done some good. There is clear evidence from three of *Titanic's* four surviving bridge officers, one of whom was the navigating officer, that the *Baltic/Athenia* ice warning never reached the bridge, nor was it plotted on the chart.

The simple explanation for this warning not being passed on to the navigating officers is that, almost immediately after receiving the Marconi form, Captain Smith handed it to J. Bruce Ismay. He supposedly did this to let Ismay know that an encounter with ice was to be expected. Ismay understood the message to mean that they would be up to the ice 'that night'.

Instead of taking the Marconigram back from the company chairman, Captain Smith allowed him to retain it until about 7.15pm, five and a half hours after its receipt. Smith should not have allowed Ismay to take custody of such an important navigational aid, but even without the paper itself the captain was in a position to take action. White Star standing orders clearly allowed the captain to reduce speed or take any other action he deemed advisable to safeguard the ship. On taking command of a White Star ship, her captain received a letter clearly saying that no risks to the ship or persons were to be taken under any conditions. This letter also instructed the master to be on deck in anything less than perfect conditions and further than 60 miles from land.[33]

As early as December 1871, T. H. Ismay had written a letter to the owners of the Inman Line. In it he said, 'We have enjoined the masters and officers under our charge to act on all occasions even in excess of mere prudence to avoid the possibility of danger.'[34] With such a definite indication of danger, Captain Smith should, if company policy was really to avoid danger, have slowed the ship down.

In practice things were not quite as White Star policy would appear to indicate. Captains did not slow down because of little problems such as ice or fog, or both, but relied on the lookouts and reactions of the officers on the bridge. Robust captaincy is the usual description for this madness and Smith was more robust than most. He was relentless in the way he pressed on despite fog and heavy seas in his desire to maintain schedules.[35] The White Star line had a reputation for following a particularly daring policy as to captains keeping to, or beating, advertised arrival times. This absurdly competitive tendency was the result of rivalry between the major shipping lines.[36] On more than one occasion, Smith's luck had turned on him and he had run ships hard aground off the entrances to New York harbour and other places.

So when he received the ice warnings, true to form, Smith did nothing and *Titanic* sped onwards. Curiously, Ismay also did nothing to ensure the safety of the ship. He, too, was aware that large quantities of ice lay ahead and, although he was in a position to suggest to the captain that he reduce speed, the chairman of the line merely spread the word that ice was to be expected.

At 1.45pm, only three minutes after the *Baltic* warning, *Titanic's* wireless operators received a message from the German steamer *Amerika* for relay via Cape Race to the Hydrographic Office in Washington, saying: 'Amerika passed two large icebergs in 41°27'N, 50°8'W on 14th April.'

This message, although it bore directly on the navigation of *Titanic*, showing as it did large icebergs well to the south of any mentioned in previous warnings, was never handed to any officer aboard the ship. Why it wasn't taken, along with the *Baltic* message, to Captain Smith, is yet another mystery. As it showed ice in latitude 41°27'N, the captain might not have chosen to steer to the south of his intended course. This message could not have been passed on to Cape Race until *Titanic* came within range of the powerful shore station between 8 and 8.30pm.

Sometime between 5.45 and 5.50pm, half an hour after she would normally have made the manoeuvre, *Titanic* changed course from S62°W[37] on to S86°W. Quartermaster Rowe was at the wheel as the liner turned[38] onto the more northerly heading.[39] In his evidence to the British Inquiry, Rowe who was on the 4–6pm watch, stated that the course change was from S85°W to S71°W, or that *Titanic's* bows swung 14° toward the south.[40] Two days earlier Pitman had made a similar statement to Lord Mersey's Board of Assessors, '… the course marked out at noon that day was 10 miles further south than necessary. At 5.50 the commander altered the course yet more southerly.'[41] If the third officer and the helmsman are correct then the ship was on a route well to the north of the 'Outward Southern Track' and had to head to the south-west to reach New York. This confirms that *Titanic* was on the 'Autumn' route. While keeping in mind this indication that the ship was far to the north of the 'Outward Southern Track' at 5.45pm we will, for the present, continue as if she were on her allotted course.

On Smith's instructions the course change had been made late and the extra three-quarters of an hour would have put the vessel about 18 miles further on her course (S62°W) and about six miles south of where that change would normally have been made. Lowe and

Boxhall, when looking at the chart later, noticed that the ship had not altered course when she should have done but had delayed the turn by about 45min.[42] Boxhall had remarked to the chief officer sometime between 4 and 6pm that the course change should have been made earlier. The navigating officer believed that the ship's course had been changed by only one degree in the 5.50pm turn, from S85°W to S86°W and that this was merely an attempt to regain their intended route.[43] It seems as if the senior officers had no clear idea of what heading the ship really was on.

A detour of four to six miles to the southward of the intended course of the ship could hardly be construed as a measure calculated to take the vessel clear of the ice. The turn would normally have been made in latitude 42°N; Smith's delay merely meant that the change now occurred close to 41°55'N.

The new course of S86°W meant that for every 100 miles along that route the vessel steamed, she would move just over five miles to the south (one mile to north or south equals one second of arc or 1/60th of a degree). Allowing for the Labrador current which flows from north to south in that part of the North Atlantic and which would be pushing the ice slowly that way, Captain Smith, by choosing the course which he did, appears to have been aiming directly for the ice indicated in *Baltic's* warning. *Titanic* must have come within a couple of miles of that ice, which under the prevailing conditions was much too close for comfort.

It is possible that sometime during the evening the 10-day old bunker fire in Number 6 boiler room was finally reported to be out.[44] According to Fred Barrett the coal had been removed from the bunker[45] by himself and the specially enlisted crew from *Oceanic*. Leading Fireman Charles Hendricksen inspected the damaged bunker and found that the bulkhead was scorched and warped. Fred Barrett described it as 'dinged'.[46] By way of rectification of the damage, Hendricksen said, 'I just brushed it off and got some black oil and rubbed over it, to give it its ordinary appearance.'[47]

However, there is a body of evidence to suggest that the bunker fire was not extinguished by the Sunday evening and in fact continued to blaze until the sea reached it, which we will look at later.

At 6pm Lightoller returned to the bridge to begin his four-hour watch. The engine room telegraph, he noticed, was at 'full ahead', which was quite normal and the vessel's course was S86°W true.[48] The engines were making 75 revolutions, which would be about 21.5kts, or 700yd/min he estimated. He had noticed at one point in the voyage that the engines had been turning slightly faster than they were now, on the evening of the 14th.[49] As far as Lightoller was aware there were no alterations in course or speed during his spell of duty.

Throughout the day the ship maintained 75rpm or about 22kts. The three extra boilers, lit that morning, were connected to the engines at 7pm, giving the ship another knot or so. Many passengers noticed the increased vibration caused by the extra rpm.[50] The five auxiliary single-ended boilers were never lit[51] thought Ismay, who on his own admission had nothing to do with the running of the ship. In reality the five single-ended boilers were lit on the Sunday afternoon but were not connected up to the engines and therefore did not affect the speed of the ship.[52]

At 7.30pm a fourth wireless ice warning was intercepted in the radio room of the *Titanic*. This message was from the SS *Californian* and was intended for the SS *Antillian*; it read:

> 'To Captain, *Antillian*: 6.30pm apparent ship's time; lat 42°3'N, long 49°9'W. Three large bergs five miles to southward of us. Regards — Lord.'

The second wireless operator, Harold Sidney Bride, who initially believed that the message came from the *Baltic*,[53] said that he delivered this message to the bridge where he placed it in the hands of an officer, but he could not remember just who. None of the surviving bridge officers from the ship had any recollection of this message ever reaching the bridge, which judging by Bride's subsequent evidence is almost certainly true.

Third Officer Pitman certainly never saw this warning and was convinced that the ship was not even heading toward ice.[54] Whether the warning reached the bridge or not has no bearing on the disaster as the ice, at the time the message was received, was slightly astern on *Titanic's* starboard quarter. However, it does serve to throw considerable doubt on the reliability of Bride as a witness to subsequent events.

Titanic sped onwards. Captain Smith, disregarding standing orders, was not on deck but attending a private dinner party given for him by the Wideners in the á la carte restaurant;[55] at table with him were the Thayers, Carters, Butt and Harry Widener. The captain made his excuses and left the party at about 8.55pm and made his way to the bridge where Second Officer Lightoller was on watch. He had relieved

Chief Officer Wilde as watch officer at 6pm and would relinquish the position at 10pm to First Officer Murdoch.

Much had happened during the watch. The weather had been fine and clear since the second officer had taken over, but the temperature was falling steadily. Between 5.30 and 7.30pm the temperature had fallen from 43° to 39°F (6° to 4°C) and was still dropping. At 7.35pm Murdoch, who had relieved Lightoller for dinner, told his subordinate that the temperature had fallen another 4°. By 9 o'clock the air temperature had fallen to 33°F (1°C).[56] The rapidly falling temperature was an indication that there were icebergs close by. Lightoller, on taking over the watch, had noted a footnote in the night order book about keeping a sharp lookout for ice. He initialled the note, as had the other watch officers.

Having seen the *Caronia* warning, Lightoller had asked Sixth Officer Moody, who was also on duty, to let him know 'at what time we should reach the vicinity of ice'. Moody told him 'about 11 o'clock'. This did not agree with Lightoller's calculations which showed 9.30pm to be the time they would meet the ice, working from the *Caronia's* message.[57] Lightoller thought that Moody might have based his calculations on a different message.[58] The second officer didn't comment on the discrepancy between his own and Moody's calculations because the sixth officer was very busy at the time.[59]

We now know that:

- Contrary to company standing orders, *Titanic* was on the Autumn Southern Track, to the north of the usual route;
- Despite an almost continuous stream of wireless messages warning of ice ahead of the ship, the vessel increased speed daily.

Into the Ice

At 7.15pm Lamp Trimmer Samuel Hemmings made his way to the bridge to report that all the ship's navigation lights were in place. First Officer Murdoch ordered him to go forward and see the forescuttle hatch closed,[1] 'as we are in the vicinity of ice and there is a glow coming from that, and I want everything dark before the bridge.' This was obviously to help the lookouts' view forward. We can gather from this that Murdoch knew of ice but not its exact position and that he was aware the ship was entering the general area mentioned in the *Caronia* warning, even though the ice in that message was to the north.

Lightoller, the officer of the watch, took a star sight at 7.30pm, as would all the officers on the bridge. The officers took solar observations in the mornings and stellar ones in the evenings.[2] It was normal practice for every officer to take two or three star sights before working out the ship's latitude from each one, independently.[3] This made the system self checking as all calculations had to agree before a position was accepted. As the second officer called out his sights, Third Officer Pitman noted the time by the ship's chronometer.[4] In this instance Lightoller did not bother to work his sightings out for himself, but passed his sextant readings to Joseph Groves Boxhall, the fourth and navigating officer,[5] 'and they were beautiful observations,' the navigator thought.[6] Boxhall worked out the vessel's position and wrote it on a memo which he left on the chart for the captain to enter later. He noticed that the ice marked on the chart was to the north of their present course.[7]

Pitman also checked the chart. 'The course of the ship was several miles north from the spot where the ice was indicated,' he thought.[8]

Fifth Officer Lowe also worked out the ship's position at 8pm, using dead reckoning and a set of tables for calculating how far the ship would travel for a given number of propeller revolutions.[9] It is popularly believed that Captain Smith entered the ship's 7.30 position on the chart at 10pm, but he had apparently retired at about 9.20pm so in all probability he did this immediately after leaving the bridge.

At 8 o'clock Archie Jewell and George Symons had taken over as lookouts from Hogg and Evans.[10] Symons was well aware that on such a dark night his nose could prove as useful as his eyes. 'As a rule you can smell ice before you get to it,' he said.[11]

As the evening wore on, Miss Elizabeth Shutes, a first class passenger, detected a strange odour on the cold night air.[12] High above in the crow's-nest, George Symons had also detected the smell of ice.[13]

From 8.30pm until well after 10pm more than 100 passengers gathered in the second class dining saloon for a hymn singing session. This vociferous religious extravaganza had been organised by the Reverend E. C. Carter and was accompanied by a pianist. One hymn which enjoyed some popularity that evening was Eternal Father, Strong to Save. Particularly relevant was the passage 'O hear us when we cry to Thee for those in peril on the sea.'[14] How little those passengers imagined that shortly they were to be 'those in peril', or how little help some of them were to receive from on high.

Boxhall and Moody had also come on duty at about 8pm.[15] They were to keep a careful eye on air and water temperature, checking these regularly.[16] Just 10min later Lightoller ordered Quartermaster Hitchens to tell the ship's carpenter, J. Maxwell, to look after the ship's fresh water tanks as the temperature had fallen below freezing point. Lightoller ordered Maxwell to pass the message on to Chief Engineer Bell regarding the fresh, but not drinkable, water stored in the double bottom of the ship, for use in the boilers. Even with *Titanic's* condensing apparatus, some steam would inevitably escape into the atmosphere, resulting in a lessening of the amount of water circulating in the boilers. This water was replaced from the supply kept in the double bottom tanks. The instructions to Bell show that the second officer was expecting the sea temperature to fall below freezing point as well as that of the air. Bell's water tanks were well below the waterline and unaffected by the air temperature. The second officer then sent word to the engine room instructing them to take all necessary precautions to stop winches from freezing. When Hitchens returned to the bridge, he was sent to find the deck engineer and to obtain from him the key to turn on the heaters in the chart room, wheelhouse and the corridor of the officers' quarters, it was so cold.[17]

The actions of all of the officers show that they were well aware that the ship was entering an area where ice abounded.

As mentioned earlier, Captain Smith made his excuses and left the Wideners and their other guests to continue the party. Going straight to the bridge he found Lightoller in occupation.[18] In all his years of experience, it was the first time Lightoller had seen a perfectly flat calm sea,[19] there was no swell.[20] Although there was no moon, visibility was very good and they could see the stars 'heading down toward the horizon'.[21] The air was so clear that as the stars set they appeared to be cut in half by the horizon.

The master and his second officer struck up a conversation which lasted about 25min. This conversation, so far as it is material, is described by Lightoller in the following words:

> 'We commenced to speak about the weather. He said "There is not much wind." I said, "No, it is a flat calm." As a matter of fact he repeated it he said, "A flat calm." I said, "Quite flat; there is no wind." I said something about it was rather a pity the breeze had not kept up whilst we were going through the ice region. Of course my reason was obvious; he knew I meant the water ripples breaking on the base of the berg ... We then discussed the indications of ice. I remember saying, "In any case, there will be a certain amount of reflected light from the bergs." He said, "Oh yes, there will be a certain amount of reflected light." I said or he said — it was said between us — that even though the blue side of the berg was towards us, probably the outline, the white outline, would give us sufficient warning, that we should be able to see it at a good distance and as far as we could see, we should be able to see it. Of course, it was just with regard to that possibility of the blue side being toward us, and that if it did happen to be turned with the purely blue side towards us, there would still be the white outline.'[22]

Lightoller was sure that in the clear atmosphere an iceberg would be as easily seen from the bridge as from the crow's-nest.[23]

Lightoller didn't mention his calculation as to when he expected the ship to reach the ice, less than half an hour away. Nor did he mention when Moody expected to meet the ice.

The captain had first shown Lightoller the *Caronia* warning at about 12.45pm when the second officer was just about to go off duty. He, Lightoller, had performed a quick mental calculation at that time and concluded the ship would not come up to the ice before he came back on duty at 6pm.

Lightoller was perfectly sanguine about meeting icebergs even on a calm, moonless night. The problems of traversing an ice field littered with bergs and growlers (low-lying bergs) held no terrors for the overconfident officer. Asked at the British Inquiry if he suffered any fears on this score he replied, 'No, I judged I should see it with sufficient distinctness' and at a distance of a 'mile and a half, more probably two miles'.[24] He then added, 'In the event of meeting ice there are many things we look for. In the first place, a slight breeze. Of course, the stronger the breeze the more visible will the ice be, or, rather, the breakers on the ice.' He was then asked whether there was any breeze on this night. He answered, 'When I left the deck at 10 o'clock there was a slight breeze. Oh, pardon me, no; I take that back. No, it was calm, perfectly calm.' And almost immediately afterwards he described the sea as 'absolutely flat'. What are we to believe?

Captain Smith had said that there was not much wind, indicating that there was some. Lightoller's first statement that there was a slight breeze agrees with what he stated the captain had said shortly before 9.30pm. The slight breeze, which would have made a berg visible at a considerable distance, is very much more believable in the light of subsequent events, which show that ice was indeed spotted miles ahead of the ship.

The North Atlantic is not noted for its stillness but for the tremendous gales and huge waves which it produces without warning. The area around the Grand Banks, where the cold water of the Labrador current meets the warmer waters of the Gulf Stream, is particularly famous for the dense fogs which can spring up almost instantaneously, as if by magic. There is no more favourable hunting ground on earth for that most prodigious of ship killers, an iceberg. However, according to *Titanic's* second officer, apart from a lack of moonlight and no breeze, conditions were about as favourable as could be expected in this inhospitable area. Again, according to Lightoller there was none of the mist or fog for which these seas were justifiably feared. But, both of the lookouts on duty for the 10pm to midnight watch reported seeing patchy fog and mist.

When, shortly before 9.30pm, Captain Smith decided to call it a day, his last words to Lightoller before leaving the bridge were, 'If it becomes at all doubtful let me know at once; I will be just inside.'[25] This remark undoubtedly referred to ice.

Titanic crossed the 49th meridian at about the same time as Captain Smith left the bridge.[26] The captain must have gone to the chart room after leaving the bridge and to have brought the chart up to date. At least as up to date as entering the ship's position worked out by Boxhall two hours before.

It has always seemed a little odd that Captain Smith didn't actually go to bed on retiring but remained fully dressed. He cannot have believed that the ship was in any way threatened by the weather conditions or anything else beyond his control or he would have stayed on the bridge, as the White Star company instructed. He was behaving very similarly to Captain Lord of the *Californian*, perhaps for similar reasons.

Showing, for the first time, a sense of responsibility toward the safety of the ship and its passengers, Lightoller ordered Sixth Officer Moody to convey a message to the crow's-nest, 'to keep a sharp look out for ice, particularly small ice and growlers' until daylight. Moody didn't make a proper job of passing on the message, Lightoller thought, so the junior officer was made to do it again.[27] The men in the crow's nest, Archie Jewell and George Symons, were also instructed to pass this message on to their reliefs when they went off duty at 10 o'clock.

Meanwhile, Col Gracie had booked the squash racquets court for an early workout the following morning and so decided to get an early night. He was sure that this forearmed him for what the night held in store better than if he had been forewarned.[28]

Sometime between 9 and 10 o'clock, third class passengers were ordered below decks.[29] Unlike first and second class, who could come and go as they pleased at all times of the day and night, third class was strictly controlled.

Throughout the voyage passengers had continued to notice that the ship had a permanent and unexplained list to port.[30] For some reason the trimming tanks in the double bottom of the vessel could not cope with this persistent tendency to lean to the left. Nor could the coal trimmers, part of whose job was to keep the coal in the bunkers so distributed as not to upset the trim of the ship.

Another message was received in the wireless room a mere 10min after the captain had left the bridge. At 9.40pm the penultimate wireless warning of the perils confronting *Titanic*, the last complete warning by wireless, arrived. 'From *Mesaba* to *Titanic*. In Latitude 42ºN to 41º25'N, Longitude 49º to Long 50º30'W. Saw much heavy pack ice and great numbers large icebergs, also field ice. Weather good, clear.' Stanley Howard Adams, the *Mesaba's* wireless operator received an acknowledgement, 'Received, thanks', which he thought came from Phillips rather than Captain Smith. At the time this message reached her, *Titanic* was close to 49ºW and a few miles south of 42ºN, heading right into the field of ice described in *Mesaba's* message. Surely no sane officer could possibly disregard such a warning. Unfortunately,

Lightoller was never given the opportunity to ignore the warning, or otherwise, because it never got any further than the wireless room. Contrary to the rules governing the treatment of navigational messages vital to the safety of the ship, which called for such messages to be carried to the bridge immediately, this one was spiked and forgotten. The Marconi operators were far too busy to worry about trivialities such as ice warnings. They were fully occupied in sending and receiving more lucrative personal messages for passengers.

At 10 o'clock the watch changed. On the bridge Charles Lightoller handed over to First Officer Murdoch. Sixth Officer Moody remained. According to Boxhall, only the fourth and fifth officers should have been on duty; Murdoch was keeping a look out but he only came on the bridge at gone 11pm.[31] The air temperature was down to 32ºF (0ºC), freezing point.[32] True to form, Lightoller omitted to tell Murdoch that the captain had left instructions that he was to be called immediately 'if things became at all doubtful'. This omission may well be interpreted, if the received version could be believed, as one of the more important contributions to the disaster; almost as big a contributor as the mountain of ice which now lurked just over the horizon, about 40 miles away.

At the ship's wheel Quartermaster Robert Hitchens took over from fellow Quartermaster Alfred Olliver. He noted the ship's speed of 22.5kts and her heading N71ºW, which confirms Rowe's earlier statement.[33] *Olympic's* best speed for a westbound crossing had been something less than 22kts,[34] which again casts doubt on the value of the speed trials planned for the following day. Quartermaster Olliver remained on the bridge as standby helmsman, ready to take over from Hitchens if it should become necessary.

Up in the crow's-nest the lookouts were also changing. Jewell and Symons handed over to Fred Fleet and Reginald Lee, passing on the message that a special watch should be kept for ice. Lee sniffed the air, picking up the subtle yet unmistakable scent of icebergs.[35]

Murdoch, knowing of the ice threat, kept wandering out onto the open bridge wing, where his view forward was unobstructed by glass. Hitchens kept the bows pointing just south of due west. Lightoller went to his cabin and turned in.

At about 10.30pm a steamer was sighted to starboard, eastbound from Halifax. She turned out to be the SS *Rappahannock* (Albert Smith acting Master, no relation to *Titanic's* Captain Smith, regular captain sick). Morse signals were exchanged in which the cargo ship reported that her steering gear had been damaged by ice. Albert Smith also displayed a slightly eccentric sense of humour when he signalled, 'Have just passed through heavy field ice and several icebergs.' This signal was acknowledged from *Titanic's* bridge, proving that either Murdoch or Moody (or indeed both) were aware of it as one or other of the officers would have had to order the reply, 'Message received. Thank you. Good night.'

The message had certainly been received: what a pity it had not been understood. No alteration in course or speed was ordered. Nor was the captain called, as he had requested.

Had Lightoller passed on the captain's instructions to Murdoch it is very probable that the first officer would have roused Smith. Without those specific instructions, however, the situation would need to be very hazardous indeed before anybody would dare disturb the slumbering master. Anyway, in all probability Captain Smith would have taken no more notice of this warning than he had of the others. It is much more likely that he would have stuck to his normal principle and bashed on regardless!

Murdoch would have known that a change in speed or course, without the captain's authorisation, would take some explaining. It was an unwritten law that even senior officers touched the engine room telegraphs or gave helm orders only in dire emergencies without the authority of the captain.[36] Murdoch obviously didn't think conditions were as yet dire enough. One by one, *Titanic's* chances were slipping or being thrown away.

Still the liner accelerated. Passengers noticed that late on Sunday night the ship's engines were running faster than at any other time in the voyage.[37]

Another 25min slipped by before the next wireless alert came through to the radio room. At the time, 10.55pm, Jack Phillips was extremely busy sending passengers' personal messages to Cape Race. Earlier the wireless equipment had gone on the blink and a large backlog had built up, which the operator was now working frantically to reduce. Suddenly, an incoming signal cut across everything else. It was so loud that Phillips jerked the earphones from his head.

Californian, 19½ miles to the north, lay stopped, drifting with the field ice. There were no bergs in sight from the Leyland Line passenger cargo ship. If icebergs as tall as *Titanic* were invisible from the crow's-nest of *Californian*, then it follows that the White Star liner would also be invisible when it reached the icebergs.

Captain Lord had stopped his vessel at 10.15pm, as soon as he met the floating ice. Shortly afterwards he had worked out *Californian's* position and then given Cyril Evans, his wireless operator, instructions to alert other ships in the area to the fact that *Californian* was drifting. At 10.55pm, Evans tried to pass the message on to *Titanic*, only to provoke an angry 'Keep out! Shut up! You're jamming my signal. I'm working Cape Race.' Thus reprimanded, Evans stopped trying to warn the liner and instead listened to *Titanic's* traffic with the shore station until finally switching off his set and preparing for bed at 11.30pm. Shipboard times between *Titanic* and *Californian* were very close if not identical.[38] More about *Californian* later, and other vessels which were much closer than they ever admitted.

All warnings of the proximity of ice from external sources had now reached *Titanic* and all had been either stopped at the wireless room or studiously ignored by the bridge officers. *Titanic* ploughed onward into the centre of the area containing many icebergs, growlers and floating ice, defined in the wireless messages.

So far, on the 14th, the vessel had increased speed (despite warnings on previous days), received six and part of a seventh wirelessed ice warnings, and been in contact by Morse lamp with a vessel which had just emerged from the ice field after suffering significant damage. The air temperature had been falling steadily and was now below freezing point, as was the sea temperature.

At least two watch officers had taken the trouble to calculate roughly when ice was likely to be encountered. The captain had discussed the problems of spotting an iceberg under the prevailing conditions. There had been more than enough reasons to have slowed the vessel to a speed where she could, if necessary, be brought to a stand-still within the range of the lookouts' vision.

Once the last warning had been ignored, the fate of all aboard rested with the alertness and efficiency of the two men huddled in the crow's-nest, shivering from the intense cold, made all the more chilling by the biting wind caused by the ship's 22½kt speed. Even so, all might still have been well if only those same shivering lookouts had direct control of the ship. The delay between the first alarm from the crow's nest and the reaction from the officers on the bridge was to prove fatal to more than 1,500 people. A delay that, like so many other incidents or omissions aboard *Titanic* that day, should never have occurred in the normal course of events. But why were events not following their normal course?

Something very strange was happening, so strange that it cannot be satisfactorily explained by the usual oversight or misunderstanding theories which are put forward, or by the presence of the company chairman. The captain had not ignored the ice warnings he had seen: on the contrary, he had aimed the ship directly at that ice. The company chairman on seeing one of the ice warnings had not advised the captain to take extra care; instead he had allowed the continued acceleration of the vessel up to her maximum speed.

The captain, knowing full well when the ice was likely to be encountered, instead of following company orders and remaining on deck throughout the period of danger, had gone to bed, or at least to have a lie-down, at the very time the ship entered the ice region, even though his employer was aboard. The officers of the watch had neither increased the number of lookouts, nor placed a man in the very bows of the ship where his forward view would be unobstructed, a precaution taken by Captain Lord of the *Californian* and Captain Rostron of the *Carpathia*. Even though aware of the likelihood of meeting a berg and of how difficult it would be to see such a berg under the weather conditions prevailing, no officer, Second Officer Lightoller in particular, deemed it necessary to supply the crow's-nest with a pair of binoculars.

More outstandingly, the wireless operators contravened Marconi Company rules by not passing important navigational messages directly to the bridge. Six of the seven messages received in the wireless room possibly never reached the bridge. Four of them almost certainly never left the wireless cabin. Lightoller, Boxhall and Lowe were positive that the only ice warning to reach the bridge was the one from *Caronia*.[39] Third Officer Pitman had seen some Marconigrams in the chart room, but none of them indicated ice on *Titanic's* track.[40]

How on earth could Second Officer Lightoller forget to pass on the captain's instructions that he was to be called if conditions became 'at all doubtful', when these instructions had been given to him by the master only half an hour before? One wonders if such instructions were given at all, as they should have been entered in the night order book and initialled by each officer as they came on duty. The response of both First Officer Murdoch and Sixth Officer Moody to the morsed information from the *Rappahannock*, beggars belief. Acting Captain Smith, of the *Rappahannock* had done his level best to alert the bridge officers of *Titanic* to the immediate danger, only to be met with the response, 'Thank you and good night.' Just what one might have expected from a Victorian music-hall turn.

Events up to this time point toward the senior officers of *Titanic* cold-bloodedly driving the ship into an area where they knew that the chances of striking ice were considerably better than good. By doing little or nothing to keep the vessel out of danger, the ship's officers were breaking the primary rule of the line.

By far the most startling piece of apparent ineptitude by the watch officers of *Titanic* was about to unfold — so startling, in fact, that the events about to be related would be unbelievable were they not so strongly supported. And these events on their own would have been enough to prove a case of criminal negligence against the officers of the *Titanic*.

In the crow's-nest, 50ft above the Forecastle Deck, Fred Fleet on the port side and Reginald Lee on the starboard strained their eyes into the blackness ahead and to the sides of the ship. Describing the conditions, Fleet said, 'It was the beautifullest night I ever seen. The stars were like lamps.'[41] Later in the watch, sometime after 11pm, a slight haze had developed ahead of the ship, about three points on either side.[42] It was terribly cold.[43] Reginald Lee described a, 'Clear, starry night with haze extending more or less round the horizon, very cold.'[44]

Charles Lightoller was adamant that there was no haze on the night of the 14/15 April.[45] As usual, the second officer's statements need to be treated with caution because at the time the lookouts thought that they detected haze, Lightoller was in bed.

Suddenly Fleet leaned across, grabbed the rope hanging from the crow's-nest bell and rang it three times to alert the bridge of an obstruction ahead: the time was 11.15pm. The lookout had seen, 'A black object, high above the water, right ahead.'[46] He then picked up the phone and tried to make contact with the officers on watch. There was no response. Fleet's impression at the time, incredible as it seems, was that there was nobody on the bridge.[47] *Titanic* sped onward, directly toward the bluish coloured berg, with its attendant mist patch, which the lookouts could plainly see silhouetted against the black sky. At this point the berg would have been about 10 or 11 miles away from the ship, on the horizon.[48]

Fireman John Podesta, who came off duty at 8pm, had gone to the mess room for supper after getting changed. When he had finished his meal and was returning to his quarters he heard a lookout shout, 'Ice ahead sir.' After about 1hr, or slightly more, as Podesta and his mate were lying in their bunks talking, they heard the cry again, several times. 'Ice ahead sir'. Podesta described how, 'Nothing was done from the bridge to slow down or alter course, so the crash came.'[49]

Mrs Herbert Chaffee, recounting a conversation with Fred Fleet in the lifeboat, said that he told her, 'There was only one lookout in the crow's-nest just before the ship struck the iceberg.'[50] Initially this seems unlikely, but it was confirmed in 1964 when Leslie Reade interviewed the lookout.

Two or three times Fleet tried to raise the bridge by ringing the bell and trying the phone, finally getting a response and reporting the presence of a berg directly ahead of the ship. The officer on the bridge took no action at all, no reduction in speed or change of course. This caused the lookouts much indignation and astonishment. Again Fleet telephoned the bridge and reported that he thought there was an iceberg ahead of the ship. Again there was no response from the bridge. Yet again Fleet, by now fairly certain that they must strike the berg, attempted to sting the watch officer into action by telephone, yet again without result. Fred Fleet and Reggie Lee stood helplessly in the crow's-nest and watched the mountain of ice as *Titanic* relentlessly advanced upon it. Fleet realised that the ship might smash head on into the berg and that if it did, then the foremast, with the crow's-nest, could well fall either to the deck or over the side of the ship into the freezing sea. Showing a generosity of spirit not normally attributed to him, Fleet ordered Lee to abandon the crow's-nest while there was still time. Lee didn't want to leave his mate alone to his fate, but in obedience to orders he started down the ladder when Fleet insisted. However, Lee's conscience and his sense of responsibility toward his fellow lookout got the better of him. Disregarding his orders he climbed back into the crow's-nest and stood beside Fleet; both men were at their stations when the ship struck.[51]

Even as Fred Fleet watched the approaching berg, he strove once more to provoke some response from the bridge. He rang the bell again three times and tried the phone. Moody answered. 'Yes. What did you see?'

'Iceberg right ahead,' said Fleet.

'Thank you,' said the sixth officer.

Before the exchange was completed Fleet noticed the bows of the ship beginning to swing to port.[52]

After rescue, aboard *Carpathia*, Fleet described his conviction that he would not avoid condemnation for the disaster. He said to Mrs

Catherine Crosby, 'I know they will blame me for it, because I was on duty, but it was not my fault; I had warned the officers three or four times before striking the iceberg that we were in the vicinity of icebergs, but the officers on the bridge paid no attention to my signals.'[53]

Helmsman Robert Hitchens didn't hear the telephone message from the crow's-nest but he did hear Moody report to Murdoch.[54] One can only assume that Hitchens was too busy spinning the ship's wheel to take much notice of what Moody had to say to the lookout.

Murdoch had been out on the starboard, open wing of the bridge when he finally saw the berg for himself, about 800yd ahead. Rushing back inside he immediately called for 'hard a-starboard', scurried to the engine room telegraph and rang, 'Stop: Full Speed Astern'. Quartermaster Robert Hitchens spun the wheel even as Moody, now standing beside him, repeated Murdoch's order. In a classic example of too little too late, First Officer Murdoch had succeeded in not quite avoiding contact with the iceberg, or whatever obstruction lay ahead of the ship.

It is evident that Lightoller's thought that a man on the bridge would see an iceberg as soon as one in the crow's-nest was over-optimistic. It seems that the crow's-nest lookouts had seen the iceberg 25min before the officer on the bridge.

Had Murdoch not attempted to avoid the iceberg but had rammed it head on, then the ship would probably not have sunk. It was designed to withstand just such collisions. Instead the first officer seemingly took the more natural and understandable course of trying to swerve the vessel around the obstruction. Of course, Murdoch might have been attempting to come alongside and bring the ship to a halt next to an iceberg, giving the impression that the ship had struck it a glancing blow. The vibration brought about by reversing the ship's engines from 'full ahead' to 'full astern' would have reinforced this impression. Just the sort of vibration that many of the witnesses reported.

Only a couple of witnesses mentioned any sort of impact at all. Most merely noticed a slight shuddering such as might be produced by the ship dropping a propeller blade, or they didn't notice anything except the engines stopping.

No witnesses reported hearing or feeling anything of the magnitude needed for an iceberg to have inflicted the sort of damage which *Titanic* supposedly sustained.

The received information about the accident itself can be summarised as follows:

- An iceberg was sighted a mere 500yd ahead of the speeding ship.
- The lookouts frantically signalled the danger and sent a message to the bridge.
- The watch officers coolly received the message and took the appropriate action, first by swerving to the left and then putting the ship's engines full astern. That these reactions to the situation were too late is hardly the fault of the officers who received the warning only when the accident was unavoidable.
- Then we have the grinding crash as the vessel scrapes along a submerged ledge of ice tearing a huge gash in her side.

We now know that most of this scenario is false, but it has served to distract attention from a more relevant detail. A point normally overlooked is that steel, even of the quality in use in 1912, is very much harder than ice. Only sustained heavy pressure could account for the sort of damage suffered by *Titanic* in her brush with an iceberg, and that is not what witnesses described.

We know that:

- At 11.15pm Fleet and Lee first saw ice ahead of the ship;
- Try as they might to report this ice to the officers on the bridge, the lookouts could get no answer to their telephone calls for about 25min;
- Even as Fleet finally got through to the bridge, he noticed that the ship was beginning to turn to port, indicating that ice had been seen from the bridge before his report reached there.

Impact — Softly Softly

Even as *Titanic's* bow swung to port the starboard side of the hull, just forward of the foremast,[1] brushed against the iceberg. In the crow's-nest Fleet and Lee watched spellbound as the dark shape, almost indistinguishable from the blackness surrounding it (Gracie describes the iceberg as black[2]) slid alongside. Fleet noticed no jar or impact, only a slight grinding noise lasting 'a matter of a few seconds'. So slight was the impact, in fact, that he believed the ship had just missed the berg. 'I thought it was a narrow shave.' Relieved, Fleet and Lee settled down to finish their watch, or so the official version goes.

Until they went off duty at midnight, the lookouts saw no sign of another ship in the area.[3] Had there been one, their vision no longer impaired by the wind caused by the speed of the ship's passage, they must surely have seen it. Even if it had not stopped, the ship had slowed considerably.

Approximately 37sec had elapsed between Fleet speaking to Moody and the moment of impact.[4] Evidently Murdoch had issued the wrong series of orders if a collision with an effectively stationary object was to be avoided. The first officer must have known that, 'by reversing one prop and going ahead with the other and putting the helm over, *Titanic* could turn a circle in three times her own length, as demonstrated in her sea trials'.

Titanic was in contact with the obstruction for about 10sec.

With the rudder still hard over to port, instead of the bow being pushed clear as one would expect, the ship then scraped along the berg until over 300ft of her hull was open to the sea. Analysing the progressive flooding of the ship and the time that it took to sink as described by survivors, Edward Wilding, a marine architect and member of the design team of the 'Olympic' class vessels, described the likely extent of the damage. He concluded that the collision must have resulted in an intermittent gash extending over 500ft of the hull (*Titanic*, remember, was 882ft 6in long). This series of punctures was equivalent to a hole three-quarters of an inch wide and 200ft long. The area through which water was entering the ship was about 12sq ft[5] (about three-quarters of the size of a normal internal door).

Wilding's report goes on to tell us that the ship was still able to move under her own power and could have steamed toward any potential rescuer. Why, then, didn't Captain Smith make for any of the ships which he knew were coming toward the stricken liner instead of launching his lifeboats and thus effectively immobilising his command?[6]

In the process of scraping the berg, *Titanic* brought tons of ice, in small fragments, down onto her forward Well Deck. Quite how she managed this is another of those *Titanic* mysteries. For the ice to have fallen on to the deck the berg must have overhung it, that much is plain.

According to Gracie, the iceberg towered 50ft above A Deck, which — if true — would indicate a berg of over 100ft high.[7] Gracie's estimate is supported by Quartermaster Rowe, who from his vantage point on the Poop Deck also saw a 100ft iceberg close alongside.[8]

The Ice Patrol says that striking such a massive, though partially hidden, object as an iceberg would have the same effect as hitting an island. Icebergs are not only extremely unyielding but virtually indestructible.[9] It is certain that an iceberg of this magnitude would not have moved aside to allow the ship to slide past, quite the reverse in fact; the ship would be shouldered aside. This obviously didn't happen either because the ship was still in contact with the ice until it was well aft of the forward funnel, showing that *Titanic* was as close to the berg at that point as when the overhanging side deposited ice onto the Well Deck. How the starboard wing of the bridge and Number 1 emergency boat, which was kept swung out,[10] escaped damage from this icy overhang is a mystery. How the superstructure on that side of the ship as a whole survived undamaged in the collision is not just a mystery, but more of an impossibility. Either there was no ice on the Well Deck or the bridge wing and Number 1 boat, along with a substantial quantity of starboard side superstructure, must have come into contact with the ice. If that ice was tough enough to open the 1in-thick hull plating, pushing 10in steel girders aside in the process, it would certainly have had no trouble removing the much more lightly constructed bridge wing and wooden lifeboat.

One other possibility presents itself: that the ice on the Well Deck, which is testified to by too many people to be discounted, did not come from an iceberg at all but from the rigging of a ship, probably *Titanic* herself.

In the wireless cabin, Second Wireless Operator Bride didn't notice the accident and was barely aware that anything out of the ordinary had occurred until the captain told him.[11] This was hardly surprising as Bride was supposedly in his bunk and fast asleep until shortly after midnight.

As Bride dressed and put on the headphones in preparation for taking over from Phillips, the senior operator was getting ready to turn in. Phillips casually observed that they must have hit something as the engines had stopped.[12] 'It was 10min, Phillips told me, after he had noticed the iceberg, that the slight jolt that was the collision's only signal to us occurred. We thought we were a good distance away,' said Bride. This, of course, supports the lookouts' story that the berg was first seen some considerable time before the collision.

At the rear of the ship Quartermaster Rowe noted that the Cherub Patent Log indicated that the vessel had covered 260 nautical miles since it had been reset at midday[13] confirming that she was averaging something in the region of 22kts.

First class passengers Mrs Marian Thayer and her son Jack both noticed the time and said '*Titanic* struck at 14 minutes to 12.'[14] The 6min time discrepancy is easily explained by the Thayers forgetting to put their watches back in accordance with the ship's clocks as the vessel moved westward. *Titanic's* clocks should have been put back 25min during the 8pm to 12 midnight watch, but as Sixth Officer Pitman said of the latter part, 'We had something else to think of.'[15]

Jack Thayer describing the collision, said, 'If I had a brimful glass of water in my hand not a drop would have been spilled.'[16]

Profoundly unimpressed by the bump was Mrs Astor, who thought it was merely some mishap in the kitchen.[17] Nevertheless, she later wakened two other female passengers who had been overlooked by the stewards detailed to raise the alarm throughout first class.[18]

J. Bruce Ismay's first thought was that the ship had lost a propeller when he was awakened by the collision[19] or the vibration caused by the engines being put full astern. John Poigndestre described the sensation: 'There was vibration indicating that the engines were going full astern at the time of the collision.'[20]

Deep within the ship, Fireman Fred Barrett had been slaving away in boiler room Number 6. He had just paused to chat to Second Engineer James Hesketh[21] when all at once the alarm bell rang and the red warning light came on. Barrett and the second engineer both shouted 'Shut the doors', meaning the furnace ash doors, and then came a crash. A jet of water suddenly burst in through the side of the ship, about two feet above the stokehold floor.[22] Another fireman,

George Beauchamp, on duty in Number 10 stokehold did not agree with Barrett as to where the water entered the boiler room. He said, 'Water entered Number 10 stokehold through the bunker door.'[23]

Leaving the heroics to somebody — anybody — else, Barrett and the engineer fled aft into boiler room Number 5 moments before the watertight door between the two boiler rooms closed, about 3min after the collision.[24] According to Barrett the whole length of Number 6 boiler room was open to the sea and the damage extended about 2ft into the bunker at the forward end of Number 5.[25]

Marine Architect Edward Wilding initially thought that the damage extended only as far aft as Number 5 boiler room, 'but for some reason, unexplained, the water was rising in Number 4.' He pointed out, at the British Inquiry, 'that they were doing their best to pump out number 4.'[26] This led Wilding to consider the possibility that the damage extended as far as Number 4 boiler room.[27]

A few moments after the watertight doors closed, Barrett climbed the escape ladder from Number 5 boiler room (this was to become something of a habit with him) and peered down into Number 6:

'There was eight feet of water in there. I went to Number 5 fireroom when the lights went out. I was sent to find lamps, as the lights were out and when we got the lamps we looked at the boilers and there was no water in them. I ran to the engineer and he told me to get some firemen down to draw the fires. I got 15 men down below.'[28]

According to Trimmer George Cavell, working in the starboard bunker of Number 4 section, the lights went out almost immediately after the collision.[29]

For a while the forward bunker in Number 5 boiler room contained the water entering through the ship's side,[30] a function it had never been intended to perform and to which, ultimately, it was unequal, there being no watertight doors to any of the ship's bunkers.[31] Finally, the bunker collapsed under the weight of water within. Barrett described it thus: '(I) saw a wave of green foam come tearing through the boilers.' True to form, Fred Barrett 'jumped for the escape ladder', a practice with which he was, by now, quite familiar.

For the benefit of the Senate Inquiry, the US Hydrographic Office determined the force of the blow with which the *Titanic* had struck the berg as approximately 1,173,200ft tons.[32] This should have provided enough energy to throw *Titanic* 20ft sideways in an instant.

One wonders why it didn't do just that — but then there would not have been a 300ft gash, merely a huge hole at the point of contact, perhaps flooding two compartments. As we shall see, this tremendous impact, not dissimilar to the ship being struck by a broadside from a battleship, passed largely unnoticed by most of the passengers and crew. Second by second the whole story becomes increasingly incredible.

In the first class smoking room on A Deck, passengers Archie Butt, Hokan Bjornstron Steffanson, Spencer V. Silverthorne, Lucien P. Smith, Hugh Woolner and Clarence Moore, to name but a few,[33] dressed in evening clothes, were drinking, talking or playing cards, or any combination of the three. Normally White Star did not allow the playing of cards on a Sunday but on this evening the rule had been waived by the chief steward[34] who must have had authority from a senior officer. Woolner felt:

> '... a sort of stopping, a sort of — not exactly shock, but a sort of slowing down. And then we sort of felt a rip that gave a sort of slight twist to the whole room. Everybody, so far as I could see, stood up and a number of men walked out rapidly through the swinging doors on the port side and ran along to the rail that was behind the mast ... I stood hearing what the conjectures were. People were guessing what it might be and one man called out, "An iceberg has passed astern," but who it was I do not know. I never have seen the man since.'

Woolner himself caught a glimpse of an iceberg about 150yd astern.[35]

Among those who rushed out of the smoking room were Silverthorne and a steward who were just in time to see an iceberg close alongside.[36] First class passenger Washington Dodge could see nothing of interest and concluded that there was 'no iceberg in sight'.[37] He did notice that there were two stokers on the promenade deck, which was unusual, and that there was several cartloads of small ice fragments on the Well Deck just inside the starboard rail.[38] Archibald Gracie, who had been asleep at the time of the collision,[39] got fully dressed before making his way up to the Boat Deck from his cabin, C5141, where he was offered a pocketwatch-shaped fragment of ice by his friend Clinch-Smith.[40]

William T. Stead and Father Byles were strolling on deck, but neither of them thought that anything serious had occurred.[41] A middle aged couple were on the second class promenade deck, arm in arm, but they, too, took little notice of the collision.[42] Col Gracie made a complete tour of the Boat Deck, scanning all points of the compass, searching for whatever the *Titanic* had struck. 'There were no icebergs, ice or other ships in sight.'[43] In Col Gracie's own words, 'we strained our eyes to discover what had struck us. From vantage points where the view was not obstructed … I sought the object, but in vain, though I swept the horizon near and far and discovered nothing.'[44] Gracie expected to see at least some of the ship's officers on the Boat Deck and was a little surprised to find that there were none.[45]

First class passenger Mrs White said that, after the collision, Captain Smith ordered the passengers on the Boat Deck to put on their life-jackets and to go down to B Deck. He later ordered them to go to A Deck to board boats.[46] It seems that Mrs White, in recounting her version of events, confused Captain Smith's orders immediately after the accident with those of Second Officer Lightoller when he began loading boats more than half an hour later.

On duty at the forward end of B Deck was Alfred Crawford, a steward. Hearing a slight 'crunch' on the starboard side, Crawford scuttled over to the rail just in time to see 'a large black object' passing rapidly alongside. The object, he estimated, was much higher than B Deck.[47] He went back inside where 'there were a lot of passengers coming out' of their cabins.

Mr Dickinson Bishop was amongst these. He had been reading while his wife slept and, feeling the impact, had gone on deck but 'couldn't see a thing'. Bishop returned to his cabin and woke his wife (significantly, the collision had not roused her). Together they now went out onto the open deck where they noticed the 'intense cold'. The couple looked 'all over the deck', walking up and down a couple of times, before running into Steward Crawford, who found their apprehension amusing. Crawford said, 'You go back downstairs. There is nothing to be afraid of. We have only struck a little piece of ice and passed it.'

Mrs Molly Brown, seemingly, was thrown to the floor by the violence of the collision,[48] which almost everybody else barely noticed, but she didn't think it was anything to worry about.

In the second class smoking room, also on B Deck but further aft, the men were trying to estimate the size of the berg. One passenger, a motor engineer, was quite sure of what he had seen. 'Well I am accustomed to estimating distances and I put it at between 80 and 90 feet.'[49]

Obviously the impact had not been very impressive as far as these passengers were concerned. The atmosphere in the smoking room was still very convivial. Raising his glass one passenger said to his companion, 'Just run along the deck and see if any ice has come aboard, I would like some for this.'[50] With Steward Crawford wandering about B Deck and this passenger instructing his friend to run along it, we can fairly safely assume that there was nothing to stop people moving freely from end to end of that deck. This argues that B Deck was a promenade with easy access to the ship's rail, both fore and aft. However, this does not tie up with existing plans of *Titanic*, but does agree with the layout of her sister, *Olympic*.

Quartermaster George Rowe, on duty at the aft docking bridge, is a major player in the drama unfolding. He described his experience: 'I felt a slight jar and I looked at my watch. It was a fine night and it was then 20 minutes to 12. I looked toward the starboard side of the ship and saw a mass of ice … It was very close to the ship, almost touching it.' From Rowe's evidence it seems clear that the ship was most likely still in contact with the iceberg.

Seamen Brice, Buley and Osman were in the mess on the port side, forward on C Deck, 'smokin' and yarnin' '. Others sat reading. Suddenly they heard the three clangs of the crow's-nest bell. A moment later Edward Buley felt 'a slight jar. It seemed as though something was rubbing alongside of her at the time.' Brice thought it 'was like a heavy vibration'. This close to the point of impact some slightly more dramatic indication of a collision might have been apparent had the vessel struck as violently as the US Hydrographic Office calculated. Buley looked out onto the Well Deck and saw what he estimated to be a couple of tons of ice there.[51] Able Seaman John Poigndestre went out onto the Well Deck and collected a piece of ice, which he took back to the mess to show to his mates.[52]

Fireman Jack Podesta describing the noise of the collision said that it was 'like tearing a strip of calico, nothing more'.[53] Another fireman, Alfred Shiers, saw an iceberg off *Titanic's* starboard quarter about five minutes after the collision. The ship was still moving slowly forwards he noted.[54]

Mrs E. D. Appleton, a first class passenger, described the sound of the collision in an identical fashion to Podesta — like 'tearing calico'.[55]

Able Seaman Joseph Scarrott, about 8min after hearing the three bells, merely felt a kind of tremor as if the ship's engines had been put full astern. He didn't think that the vessel had struck anything.[56]

Frank Osman rushed out onto 'the forewell deck, just against the seamen's mess room. Looking in the forewell square, I saw ice was there.' Osman is not quite correct when he describes the seamen's mess as being adjacent to the forward Well Deck. To reach the seamen's mess it was preferable to enter the forecastle by the port side door from the Well Deck, then proceed straight along the corridor, past the third class stairway on the left, the hospital and galley stores, fan room and carpenters' shops on the right and the crew's galley and stairway to the left, before entering the mess, also on the left. Sailors who had accompanied Osman out onto the forward Well Deck were soon back in the warmth of the mess. One of them brought a chunk of ice back with him and saying to Frank Evans, 'Look what I found,' he threw it onto the deck. An iceberg had been seen by the seamen who had rushed out onto the deck. They thought that it looked like Gibraltar and was as high as the ship's deck.[57] Scarrott noticed that when he came on deck the ship was still moving forward and turning to starboard. Whether Scarrott meant that the ship was under a starboard helm and consequently turning to the left or that the vessel was actually turning to the right is unclear. The consensus is that *Titanic* did not turn to starboard either immediately before or after the accident.

In cabin C19 Margaret Graham was eating a chicken sandwich. With her in the cabin was her governess Elizabeth Shutes. Miss Graham's hands were shaking so badly that the chicken kept falling out of her sandwich. Elizabeth Shutes went to ask an officer if there was any danger: he told her that there was none. As the officer moved away Miss Shutes heard the officer say, 'We can keep the water out for a while.'[58]

Further aft on C Deck Mr and Mrs Walter Douglas had, shortly before the collision, been strolling past the aft first class grand stairway when they noticed 'that the boat was going faster than she ever had. The vibration as one passed the stairway in the centre was very noticeable.' Once in their stateroom, C86, the vessel struck, 'the shock of the collision was not great,' they said. Mrs J. Stuart White did not pay much attention to it either. She described it as '… just as though we went over a thousand marbles. There was nothing terrifying about it at all.'

Other passengers were equally unimpressed by the violence of the crash. Maj Arthur Peuchen likened it to a large wave striking the ship. Mrs Walter B. Stephenson thought it felt like the first shock of the

San Francisco earthquake. 'Like the Zurich lake ferry making a sloppy landing,' was Marguerite Frolicher's impression.[59] In the second class library (there was no first class library) aft on C Deck the librarian didn't take any notice of the crash and carried on counting loan slips.[60]

This still doesn't sound like an impact involving over one million foot tons of energy. However, a stoker later told Lawrence Beesley that the whole side of his stokehold had caved in when the ship struck.[61] This is very much more what one would expect from a collision with an iceberg and is in line with the Hydrographic Office calculation. Nevertheless, it is entirely inconsistent with the vast majority of damage reports and with the progressive flooding of the ship, leading up to its foundering.

C. E. Stengel had just been dreaming, which was why his wife had wakened him. Stengel described his experience '… as I woke up I heard a slight crash. I paid no attention to it until I heard the engines stop. When the engines stopped I said, "There is something serious; there is something wrong. We had better go up on deck." ' Stengel later said that he saw a large iceberg which looked similar to the Rock of Gibraltar.[62]

Yet deeper inside the vessel, down on D Deck, firemen in their quarters were in the main awake when the crash came. Many of them had been roused to prepare to go on duty at midnight. Here, for some strange reason, the impact was felt much more powerfully than it had been on the deck above, where it will be remembered, the seamen were relaxing in their mess, or on the deck below, as we shall shortly see. Fireman John Thompson:

> '… felt the crash with all its force up there in the eyes of the ship, and my mates and I were all thrown sprawling from our bunks. It was a harsh, grinding sound … I ran on the deck [up to C Deck] and found the forward Well Deck covered with masses of ice torn from the berg. We went below to grab some clothes. Our leading fireman, William Small, rushed in and shouts, "All hands below!" But we had no chance to go down the tunnels to the fireroom, for the water was rising and plainly to be seen. So we had to go up on the main deck. Next, the leading fireman rushed up there and orders us back to get lifebelts and go on the Boat Deck. We put out again for the forecastle, got our lifebelts on and then up to the Boat Deck. The chief officer wanted to know "what in the hell" we were doing up there and sent us down.'

Here we see the first indication that the watertight firemen's tunnel was no longer watertight. This is something which will come up again when we assess the damage to the vessel and how it might have been caused. We also see two entirely different descriptions of the collision: one a slight vibration and the other a violent crash.

Stewards in the dining saloon, further aft on D Deck felt a slight grinding jar.[63] James Johnson believed it was nothing more than *Titanic* dropping a propeller blade,[64] a belief shared by Joseph Thomas Wheat[65] and millionaire passenger Howard Case.[66] Fancy pastries were made by the day-shift bakers so Chief Night Baker Walter Belford, in the kitchen, was making bread rolls. He found the collision more noticeable than the stewards slightly forward in the dining saloon.[67]

At about 5min to midnight, Lookout George Symons noted that the water in the forward hold had risen as high as the D Deck hatch coaming and needed to rise only another 16ft to overflow the bulkhead into the next compartment aft.[68] Clearly Symons was unaware that the next compartment was already open to the sea and filling rapidly: in the first 10min following the accident, water had risen 14ft above the keel.[69] Water finding its way over the top of the bulkhead was irrelevant.

Mrs Henry Sleeper Harper, in D60, spoke to the ship's surgeon, Dr O'Loughlin, who told her that trunks were floating in the flooded hold and that they should make their way to the Boat Deck.[70]

Down on E Deck, forward, there was a certain amount of activity. Trimmers and firemen were berthed in this part of the ship and many would have been preparing to go on duty when the watch changed at midnight. Close to the bow, immediately aft of the forepeak store, 24 coal trimmers had their living quarters. The collision was felt here, but nothing like as violently as on the deck above. Lamp Trimmer Samuel Hemmings, who was lying in his bunk at the instant of impact, noticed a peculiar hissing sound immediately afterwards. As he got out of bed he noticed the time, it was 10min to midnight.[71] He described what he next did or saw:

'(I) went out and put my head through the porthole to see what we hit. I made the remark to the storekeeper, "It must have been ice." ... I went up under the forecastle head to see where the hissing noise came from ... I opened the forepeak storeroom. Me and the storekeeper went down as far as the top of the tank and found everything dry. I came up to ascertain where the hissing noise was still coming from. I found it was the air escaping out of the exhaust of the tank. At that time, the chief officer Mr Wilde puts his head around the hawse pipe and says, "What is it Hemmings?" I said, "The air is escaping from the forepeak tank, but the storeroom is quite dry." … We went back in our bunks a few minutes. Then the joiner came in and he said, "If I were you, I would turn out, you fellows. She is making water one-two-three, and the racket court is getting filled up." Just as he went, the boatswain came and he says, "Turn out you fellows … you haven't half an hour to live. That is from Mr Andrews. Keep it to yourselves and let no one know." ' (See deck plans.)[72]

This tells us that the damage extended very much further forward than is generally believed. The forepeak tank, right in the extreme forward part of the ship, was filling with water, from the bottom up. As this tank was watertight then something must have punctured it. Whatever *Titanic* had hit, the point of first contact was a long way forward of the foremast. For the forepeak tank to have sustained damage then the hull was breached as far forward as it possibly could be.

The damage further aft initially suggests a spur or shelf of ice some 25ft below the waterline. At this part of the ship's hull the 10in-thick channel section steel ribs were reinforced by triangular steel knees (webs) reaching up to about 5ft above the lowest deck.[73] Is it credible that a spur of ice could have been strong enough to penetrate far enough into the ship's hull to puncture the watertight firemen's tunnel despite the 1 in thick hull plating and the heavily reinforced 10in steel frames spaced at 2ft centres? The short answer must be no. With such damage sustained everybody aboard must have been instantly aware that a major collision had occurred.

We know now that:

- Incredible as it seems, although the forces involved are similar to the vessel being struck by a broadside from a battleship, the collision passes almost unnoticed by most aboard;
- During the collision, the watertight integrity of the firemen's passage, deep within the ship, is breached, arguing that something harder than ice had penetrated the hull.

Stopped

On the port side of the ship, aft of the trimmers' quarters and the firemen's and seamen's wash places and WCs lay the seamen's quarters. Lookout Archie Jewell was wakened by the crash and immediately went up on deck to investigate. Once there he saw a considerable amount of ice.[1] Seaman Fred Clench was awakened:

'... by the crunching and jarring, as if it was hitting up against something ... Of course I put on my trousers and I went on deck on the starboard side of the Well Deck and I saw a lot of ice [on] the Well Deck ... With that, I went in the alleyway again under the forecastle head to come down and put on my shoes. Someone said to me, "Did you hear the rush of water?" I said, "No."

'They said, "Look down under the hatchway [Number 1]." I looked down under the hatchway and I saw the tarpaulin belly out as if there was a lot of wind under it, and I heard the rush of water coming through.'

Over on the starboard side, in cabin E50, Mr and Mrs George A. Harder heard a scraping noise and felt the ship vibrate. On looking out of the porthole Mr Harder saw an iceberg passing alongside.[2] James R. McGough had a very similar experience to that of Mr and Mrs Harder, but in his case the porthole was already open and splinters of ice came in.[3] One cannot help marvelling at the wonderful variety of shapes the iceberg must have assumed as it passed close alongside *Titanic*. Initially, it was an overhanging mountain more than 100ft high when it first came into contact with the ship and deposited tons of ice on the Well Deck. Then it must have become more like the Rock of Gibraltar, as described by witnesses, in order to avoid crushing the outboard emergency boat and starboard bridge wing. Next it must have resumed something like its original shape to scrape along the ship's side sending showers of icy splinters into open portholes before changing to again resemble the Rock of Gibraltar. That icebergs change their appearance is a fact of life, but these changes normally take place over a much longer period than the 10sec or so that this one was alongside *Titanic*.

Luigi Gatti's secretary, Paul Mauge, was asleep in his berth when the crash came: it didn't waken him. He was wakened by a steward who told him that the ship had struck something but that there was nothing to worry about. This information so impressed Mauge that he almost immediately went back to sleep, only to be further disturbed by what he believed was an alarm bell. Convinced now that something was amiss he got up, dressed and went on deck.[4]

According to first class passenger Karl H. Behr, 'it was not until 40 or 50min after the collision that passengers were given any warning of danger.'[5] This delay was confirmed by Mrs Jacques Futrelle who said that her husband had been assured by an officer that there was no danger at all.[6]

Further aft on the port side, in the stewards' quarters, Frederick Dent Ray was wakened by '... a kind of movement that went backward and forward. I thought something had gone wrong in the engine room.' While things may not have 'gone wrong in the engine room' there certainly was a lot going on with the engines being put forward and backward in response to what now seems a random series of orders. A little later a man came into the stewards' quarters with a teacup-sized fragment of ice and told Frederick Dent Ray, 'There are tons of ice forward.'[7]

Steward J. Witter was already dressed, but sensing the gravity of the situation picked up the caul from his first child, which he habitually took with him, and then filled his pockets with cigarettes.[8]

Albert Pearcey, third class pantryman, was standing outside the pantry on F Deck when the ship struck. The motion caused by the collision was nothing to speak of, he thought.[9]

Samuel J. Rule, a bathroom steward was wakened by the engines stopping and then reversing.[10] He didn't notice the impact at all. Neither did John Edward Hart who also slept through the collision.[11]

William Ward, another steward, clambered out of bed, '... went to the port and opened it. It was very bitterly cold. I looked out and saw nothing. [Whatever the ship had struck was on the starboard side.] It was very dark. I got back into my bunk again. Presently two or three people came along there where we were all situated and said she had struck an iceberg, and some of them went and brought pieces of ice along in their hands.' Frederick Dent Ray also passed comment on the biting cold. When he first went on deck after the collision the chill struck him so forcibly that he returned to his cabin to put on warmer clothes and an overcoat.[12] At midnight the water temperature was down to 28°F and the air temperature was 27°F (-2°C).[13]

Steward Ray continued, 'I thought at first it was the propeller gone, the way she went. I lay there for about 20min and in the meantime the steerage passengers were coming from forward, aft, carrying lifebelts with them.'

As Ray lay in bed, about a quarter of an hour after the impact, the order reached E Deck to close the watertight doors.[14] The corridors known as 'Park Lane' and 'Scotland Road' were crowded with crew members and steerage passengers making their way aft to escape the incoming water.[15] When Hendricksen saw the third class passengers in the alleyway he noted that there was nobody directing them toward the Boat Deck.[16] Despite the exodus from the forward part of the vessel, which was gathering momentum, the crew closed the watertight doors shortly before midnight, cutting off that avenue of apparent escape.[17]

Ray described the steerage passengers he saw struggling to make their way aft. 'Some of them got their grips and packages and had them with them, and some were wet.' Even confronted by this clear evidence that the ship had sustained critical damage forward, Ray still 'did not think it was anything serious'.

This evidence shows that, in the third compartment counting aft from the bow, the water must have risen to above G Deck, the lowest forward third class accommodation, within the first 20min. The bows of the vessel had settled almost 8ft in about a quarter of an hour, which argues something much more severe than a half-inch slit in the plating in that area, or forward.

Working his way forward on the port side of D Deck, Second Steward George Dodds raised the alarm first in the bakers' quarters, banging on the door and shouting, 'Get up lads, we're sinking.' Then moving on to the waiters' quarters he found Saloon Steward William Moss already trying to rouse the sleeping crewmen. Dodds burst in shouting, 'Get every man up! Don't let a man stay here.' He then moved on to the stewards' quarters. While still trying to rouse his shipmates, Dodds overheard a conversation between Carpenter J. Hutchinson and Steward J. Witter, 'The bloody Mail room is full.' Just then William Moss arrived and said, 'It's really serious Jim.'

Mr Norman Campbell Chambers thought he heard:

'... jangling chains whipping along the sides of the ship. This passed so quickly that I assumed something had gone wrong with the engines on the starboard side ... At the request of my wife I prepared to investigate what had happened ... I looked at the starboard end of our passageway, where there was the companion way leading to the quarters of the mail clerks and farther on to the baggage room and, I believe, the mail sorting room. And at the top of these stairs I found a couple of mail clerks, wet to their knees, who had just come up from below, bringing their registered mailbags. As the door in the bulkhead in the next deck was open, I was able to look directly into the trunk room, which was then filled with water and within eighteen inches or two feet of the deck above. We were standing there joking about our baggage being completely soaked and about the correspondence which was seen floating about on top of the water.'

Even while the Chambers were passing the time of day, or night, with the postal workers they were visited on three separate occasions by Fourth Officer Boxhall, Assistant Second Steward Wheat and the captain, accompanied by Thomas Andrews. Still they didn't realise there was anything to worry about.[18] Mr Chambers' statement is a little ambiguous but I think he was saying that when he talked to the postal clerks, shortly after the collision, the water in that compartment had almost reached F Deck, but he might have meant E.

Thomas Wheat saw water rising up the stairway from the Orlop Deck but it had yet to reach the Post Office, 10min after the collision.[19] The mail room, on the Orlop Deck, had begun to flood at the time of the crash and within 5min the icy water was swirling around the knees of the postal clerks as they struggled to move 200 sacks of registered mail to the deck above.[20] One of the clerks, John R. Jago Smith, spotted Smith and Andrews on their tour of inspection and reported to the captain that the mail room was filling.

Mrs Celiney Yasbeck and her husband heard the collision and went to look down into the boiler room to see if anything was wrong. They saw engineers struggling to repair the damage and to get the pumps going. The Yasbecks, fearing the worst, returned to their cabin to dress in preparation for taking to the boats.[21]

At the aft end of F Deck, Mrs Allen O. Becker, travelling with three children, was roused '... by a dead silence. The engines had stopped. We heard people running through the halls and pounding above our cabin.' Concerned by the unusual goings-on, Mrs Becker went to ask a steward if anything was amiss. 'Nothing is the matter,' he told her. 'We will be going on in a few minutes.' As we know, it was a cold night so Mrs Becker decided that she had better go '… back to bed, but the longer she lay there the more alarmed she became. She decided to get up and inquire again.' Again Mrs Becker ventured out of her cabin and into the corridor where she met their cabin steward and asked him what the trouble was. 'Put your lifebelts on immediately and go up to the Boat Deck.' he told her. 'Do we have time to dress?' she asked. 'No Madam, you have time for nothing.' he replied.

George Harder was told a very similar story by the first steward he spoke to after the collision. The steward said to him that they would be on their way again in a few hours.[22] He neglected to mention that the vessel was now bound for a different destination from that shown on Harder's ticket.

Mr and Mrs Henry B. Harris, on C Deck, and Lawrence Beesley, on B Deck, also noted that the engines had stopped[23] immediately after the collision.[24] Jack Thayer, while in his cabin on B Deck, noticed that the wind coming in the porthole diminished as the vessel slowed.[25] He decided that he had better go on deck to find out what was going on.[26]

Baker Burgess, alerted by the crash and the engines stopping, put on shirt and trousers, left his F Deck quarters and made for the Boat Deck. He left his life-jacket behind.[27] Even at this relatively early stage it appears that the stewards were aware of how badly damaged the ship was and believed there to be very little time left. *Titanic* took a 5° list to starboard and was noticeably down by the head within five to 10min of the accident.[28]

Shortly afterwards, Steward John Hardy and 12 other men came down to F Deck. Hardy described how he 'went among the people and told those people to go on deck with their lifebelts on, and we assisted the ladies with the belts — those that hadn't their husbands with them — and we assisted in getting the children out of bed. I also aroused the stewardess to assist them.'

Only when the children were out of bed and the women had their life-jackets on did Steward Hardy and his 12-man crew get on with closing 'the watertight doors on F Deck'. It is strange how priorities become mixed in moments of crisis. If the watertight doors were going to do any good then the ladies' wearing of life-jackets was superfluous and if the life-jackets were to be of service then what was the point in closing the watertight doors? With the sub-freezing sea temperature, life-jackets would prove to be about as much use as an ashtray on a motorbike.

G Deck was the lowest passenger deck, with single male third class (steerage) passengers accommodated forward in open berths (dormitories) and women aft, strict segregation of unmarried male and female third class passengers being the order of the day.

Even further forward than the steerage accommodation, on the port side, were the leading firemen's quarters. Here Charles Hendricksen, 'Dead to the world', slept through the collision only to be wakened shortly afterwards by one of his mates and by the sound of seawater swirling around the foot of the spiral staircase connecting the firemen's quarters to the passageway leading to the stokeholds.[29] This passageway was supposedly a watertight unit in its own right, allowing access to the stokeholds even though the forward holds might be flooded. Hendricksen then went up on deck where he saw a berg astern of the ship.[30]

Immediately on impact, in the forward open dormitory berths, Olaus Abelseth awoke, surprised by the noise. 'What is that?' another passenger asked. 'I don't know,' Abelseth replied, 'but we had better get up.'

In the same small room, fellow passengers Daniel Buckley and Carl Johnson, who had not been roused by the collision, woke a few minutes later. Seeing other passengers getting up Buckley decided to do likewise:

'[I] jumped out on the floor and the first thing I knew my feet were getting wet. The water was just coming in slightly.[31] I told the other fellows to get up, that there was something wrong and that the water was coming in. They only laughed at me. One of them says, "Get back into bed. You're not in Ireland now." I got my clothes on as quick as I could, and the three other fellows got out. The room was very small, so I got out to give them room to dress themselves. Two sailors came along and they were shouting, 'All up on deck, unless you want to get drowned!'' '

Buckley's statement again shows us that within a very few minutes of the impact the water level inside the forward part of the ship had reached G Deck, after filling the Tank Top and Orlop Deck. If Buckley was correct about being in a small room, the only one that even remotely fits that description should have been in the fourth watertight compartment back from the bow.[32]

Greaser Walter Hearst was still in bed when his father-in-law came into the room with a piece of ice, which he threw onto Hearst's bed.[33]

In the third class smoking room, August Wennerstrom, who had left his bed immediately he felt the shock of the collision, remembers:

'[I] tried to get something to drink, but the bar was closed. Nothing else to do, we got someone to play the piano and started to dance. During this, about 50 Italian emigrants came in, dressed in life preservers and carrying their baggage in bundles on their backs. They acted like they were crazy — jumping and calling on their "Madonna". We made a circle about them and started a ring dance all around them.'

These Italians must have taken some time to pack their belongings and find their way from the bows of the ship to the stern, which indicates that they were alerted to the danger very soon after it arose. Either their stewards were very efficient, which would be entirely out of character, or the danger was obvious, even to these landlubbers, right from the word go.

Even lower, on the Tank Top, the lowest deck in the ship where the engines, boilers and other heavy machinery were situated, Fireman Fred Barrett, in the forward boiler room, supposedly had the terrifying experience recounted above where water burst in through the ship's side.

All the descriptions so far recounted, point not toward a collision with an iceberg but toward a very different chain of events.

In 1912, not everyone was convinced by the accident/iceberg story. Alternative theories were circulating. One of these in particular is of interest. This theory, for it could be nothing else at the time, concerned the fire known to exist in bunker Number 10. Had a coal bunker explosion caused the loss of the ship? This was quite a reasonable idea: after all, coal was known to exude explosive gases and give off highly inflammable dust. A bunker explosion in Number 10 would certainly have flooded both forward boiler rooms exactly as Barrett described, but had there been such a violent explosion, the chances of anybody from Number 6 boiler room surviving to tell the tale are negligible. In the theory's favour, it must be said, is that nobody noticed any serious rapid deceleration, which is consistent with an explosion but not a collision with something as unyielding as an iceberg. Only in the firemen's quarters forward on D Deck was any serious shock felt, as described by John Thompson, '... my mates and I were all thrown sprawling from our bunks. It was a harsh grinding sound.' This description is not consistent with an explosion, even a coal gas and dust eruption that might well have been a roar rather than a bang but could hardly be described as a 'harsh grinding sound'.

So far we are faced with a mystery. None of the evidence from passengers or lower ranked crew members fits the iceberg explanation. There appears to have been a substantial breach in the forward part of the hull, evinced by wet passengers making their way aft minutes after the accident with lighter damage farther aft. This is irreconcilable with the estimates of the damage accepted by both British and American inquiries. Obviously there must be some other explanation which would at least cover most of the known facts. It is only too apparent that the established version of events does not.

We know that:

- Ten minutes after the collision *Titanic* had taken a five-degree list to starboard and was noticeably down by the head;
- Although it should have been obvious within a few minutes that the ship was seriously damaged, about 45min elapsed before the passengers were given any warning of the danger.

Blowing off Steam

Shortly after the final warning from the crow's-nest, Captain Smith had been roused, whether by the impact, the engines going astern, the ship stopping or some other cause such as somebody actually having the wit to wake the master: after all, 'things had become … doubtful'. The captain emerged from his room onto the bridge, asking, 'What is that?' Murdoch replied, 'An iceberg.' Captain Smith then ordered, 'Close the emergency doors.' but Murdoch said, 'The doors are already closed.' In fact the watertight doors were not closed until 3min after the collision[1] and even then only the lower, automatic doors were closed,[2] which gives us an approximate time for the skipper's appearance.

Smith sent for Maxwell, the ship's carpenter, to sound the ship (find out how much water had come aboard). He then went to the wheelhouse, sited in the rear centre part of the bridge and checked the commutator, a clock-like instrument which measured any list the ship might have taken. This commutator was situated just in front of the compass and was visible to both the helmsman, Quartermaster Robert Hitchens, and the standby helmsman, Quartermaster Olliver. The ship was listing 5° to starboard.

Quartermaster Alfred Olliver described what happened next on the bridge of the *Titanic*. 'The Captain telegraphed half speed ahead.' Olliver went on to say that when the captain gave this order the ship had almost stopped. He did not know how long the ship continued at half speed because, as standby helmsman, he was expected to act as messenger for the officers of the watch. He was sent to deliver messages to various parts of the ship not connected to the bridge telephone, leaving only the helmsman, Hitchens, to witness what else happened.

After Olliver had left the bridge, other orders were sent to the engine room via the telegraph, as we shall see in a moment. There is no difficulty in establishing that a series of orders were transmitted to the engine room. Why those orders were given, before the captain was aware of how badly damaged his vessel was, however, is a puzzle.[3]

When the carpenter had completed his soundings he returned to the bridge and reported to Mr Lightoller. He told the second officer that Number 6 stokehold was dry,[4] confirming that the damage to the outer hull of the vessel extended only as far aft as Number 5 boiler room.

Immediately after the collision, according to the familiar version of events aboard *Titanic*, the order was given to draw the boiler room fires, to prevent the boilers exploding when the cold sea water reached them. This is not really what happened. Trimmer Robart Patrick Dillon on duty in the engine room was ordered to go forward and to tell the firemen to 'keep steam up'.[5] Dillon was unaware which stokeholds had been ordered to draw their fires, but he did know that the order did not apply to the four he visited.[6] He didn't say which boiler rooms those were, but as the single-ended boilers in Number 1 were probably never lit we can safely assume he was not referring to them. As he was moving forward, the most likely stokeholds visited would be boiler rooms 2, 3 and, perhaps, 4. No matter which he visited, 5 and 6 were out of the question because they were filling with water according to Barrett and Beauchamp. This means that no fewer than 10 and possibly as many as 20 double-ended boilers were maintaining steam pressure.

George Cavell, another trimmer, said that the boilers were maintaining a pressure of 225lb/sq in. The *Titanic's* engines were designed to run at a pressure of 215lb/sq in, so the vessel must have been capable of exceeding her design speed at that time at least. Even 10 boilers working at 225lb/sq in were more than the pumps, lighting, wireless and other functions aboard could possibly make use of, so there was adequate steam pressure to power the engines at somewhat reduced revolutions for as long as needed or at full power for a short time.

After going ahead at half speed for an, at present, undetermined time, the engines were stopped. Then they went slow astern for 2min before stopping again.[7] This was when the watertight doors were closed according to Frederick Scott, a greaser on duty in the turbine engine room at the time of the collision.[8] Dillon, who had been on duty in the main engine room, said that the watertight doors were closed about 3min after the collision. After some delay (about 15min[9]) the ship went slow ahead again for a while. She stopped again before going slow astern for about 5min, then finally stopped.[10] Scott then went on deck to find that all the starboard boats had gone but that there were still boats on the port side. The last starboard boat left at 1.40am so we can assume that for the whole time starboard boats were being launched, the vessel was under way. This is borne out by events when the boats were being lowered, which again we will have to come back to later.

Why Captain Smith considered it necessary to move the ship in so erratic a manner after the accident is yet another of the mysteries upon which it may be possible to shed a little light. Perhaps he believed there was another vessel close by that he could signal with the Morse lamp or rockets. Or could he have been moving to a prearranged position to await rescue?

Quite early on, water was noticed flowing into the watertight firemen's passage, which ran beneath cargo holds 2 and 3 from the stairway leading down from the firemen's quarters on D and F decks. At the British Inquiry one of the more pertinent questions asked concerned this phenomenon: 'Was the firemen's passage at any point in contact with the skin of the ship?' Board of Trade counsel Rowlatt asked Wilding, the naval architect. 'No, there was 3ft 3in between them.' Rowlatt continued, 'If water from the sea was running into the spiral staircase space, something must have penetrated through the skin to the extent of 3ft 3in?' Wilding replied, 'Yes.'

Mersey joined in, 'In other words, the ice must have penetrated through the skin of the ship and through the watertight way, that is more than 3ft 6in?' Rowlatt answered, 'Yes, and in sufficient bulk to break a partition at the end of three feet.'[11] In fact, at its nearest point, the passage was 5ft 3in from the skin of the ship, so 2ft has to be added to all of the distances discussed by Wilding, Rowlatt and Mersey. At this point the iceberg story should have been laughed out of court.

Meanwhile, back on the bridge, Fourth Officer Joseph Groves Boxhall, who had been approaching the bridge when he heard the three bells and the order to go hard a-starboard just before the ship struck, arrived at his destination. He noticed that the engine room telegraph was at full astern and that Murdoch was just pulling the lever which operated the watertight doors. Captain Smith was already on the bridge when Boxhall reached it.[12] Boxhall heard Murdoch say to the captain, 'I was going to port around it, but she was too close.'[13] Here is evidence that Murdoch never did give the order to reverse the helm, to try to swing the ship's stern clear of the obstruction, because there simply was not time.

Quartermaster Olliver later said, 'I heard hard a-port.'[14] but he was the only person aboard who did. If the order was given, which is doubtful, it was not carried out.[15] The helmsman was certain that the ship was never under a port helm immediately before or after the collision.[16]

No sooner was the wheel hard over to starboard than the collision came.[17]

Immediately after the collision the order was given to close the manually operated watertight doors on the higher decks within the hull. Pantryman A. Pearcey assisted in the closure of those on F Deck.[18] These non-automatic doors were hinged and held closed by 12 clips[19] and could be operated from their own deck or from the deck above.[20] The automatic doors on the lower deck were vertically sliding and were closed by gravity once the electro-magnets which held them open were deactivated.

The captain ordered Boxhall to go below and check on the damage. Steam from the boilers was not being vented when he left the bridge, but it was by the time he returned 10min later.[21] By the time any numbers of people had reached the Boat Deck, high pressure steam was escaping[22] from the vents on the three real funnels. The noise was deafening. So loud was the roar that wireless operator Jack Phillips asked the captain if it might be reduced because he could hear nothing in his headphones.[23]

While he was away on his inspection the fourth officer had seen no damage above F Deck. However, he had been told by John Jago Smith, a postal clerk mentioned earlier, that water was entering the mail room on the Orlop Deck and the postal workers were moving the sacks of mail to the deck above.

While on his tour of inspection Boxhall was presented with a piece of ice about the size of a small basin by a third class passenger.[24] After this very cursory examination of the ship, Boxhall on his way back to report to the captain, decided to alert Second Officer Lightoller and Third Officer Pitman.

Both of these senior officers had felt the accident, both had got out of bed and gone on deck to see what was wrong. Lightoller had even seen Smith and Murdoch on the bridge wing looking for the iceberg but attached no importance to it.[25] Seeing nothing consequential, they thought, both officers returned to their respective bunks. No doubt they would be called if they were needed.

At about 12.05am Captain Smith ordered Wilde to uncover the boats, Moody to get out the list of boat assignments and Murdoch began to muster the passengers.[26] Murdoch next came across George Symons, a lookout, who he seconded to help uncover the boats,[27] possibly in an effort to take some of the workload from Wilde, who was engaged on the same task. Lightoller said at the British Inquiry that he was ordered to uncover the boats, which he did, beginning on the port side.[28] As we now know, when the orders for the uncovering of the boats were given, he was still ensconced in his cabin.

On being alerted by Boxhall, Lightoller and Pitman hurried to the bridge to offer their services. The second officer took the simple precaution of wrapping a white scarf around his neck as protection from the biting chill of the night air.[29] Lightoller noticed, as he came on deck, that the ship was venting steam and he thought that this meant the engines had stopped.[30] On arrival Moody told Pitman of the ice on the Well Deck. Disbelieving, the third officer peered down from the bridge, satisfying himself that Moody was not pulling his leg.[31]

Some time before midnight the White Star chairman paid his first visit to the bridge since the voyage had begun. The skipper told him then that the ship was badly damaged and that the forepeak and four compartments were open to the sea.[32]

Immediately below the bridge, at the forward end of A Deck, Major Peuchen and Charles M. Hays watched people from third class playing with the ice.[33] Peuchen noticed that the ship was slightly down by the head and commented on it to Hays. Hays was unperturbed and merely remarked, 'You cannot sink this boat.'[34] From her cabin on B Deck, Mrs Natalie Wick also watched the games being played with the ice.[35]

Boxhall was next ordered by Captain Smith to work out the ship's position. Going to the navigating room on the starboard side of the wheelhouse and on the opposite side of the bridge from the chart room, he set about finding the ship's latitude and longitude. Using the 7.30pm position he had himself worked out by star sights taken by Lightoller and which the captain, despite having turned in 40min earlier, had supposedly entered on the chart at 10pm, calculating the ship's speed, course and known drift from that time, Boxhall worked out a position[36] and scribbled the figures on a scrap of paper. He then rushed back to the bridge and handed the paper to the captain who glanced at the figures, which were 41°46'N, 50°14'W.

Twenty-eight-year old Boxhall held an extra master's certificate and had been at sea for 13 years. He had spent a year studying navigation and nautical astronomy at a specialist school in Hull. If any guesswork was involved in working out *Titanic's* position on that fateful night, then at least Boxhall was well qualified to do it.[37]

Earlier, soon after midnight, the captain had visited the wireless cabin, just aft of the bridge on the port side. He alerted the operators that a distress signal might be needed.[38] He told them then that the ship had been struck amidships, or just aft of amidships.[39] Ten minutes later he had put his head round the wireless room door and told Phillips (senior operator) to send the call for help.[40] The position given in the earliest distress calls sent between 12.15 and 12.25am, was incorrect and must have been based on approximate positions worked out by either the captain, senior officers or the operators themselves.

The first message, received at 12.15am by *La Provence* and *Mount Temple*, gives the stricken liner's position as 41K46'N, 50K23'W and the next call, received at 12.18am by *Ypiranga*, gave 41K44'N, 50K24'W as *Titanic's* position. The captain took Boxhall's scrap of paper to the Marconi room himself and at 12.25am the corrected position was received by Harold Cottam, the lone operator aboard the Cunard liner *Carpathia*.

Bride said that when they received *Carpathia's* reply to the SOS, he reported to the captain, who was superintending the lowering of the boats from the starboard side of the Boat Deck.[41] Before looking on the Boat Deck, Bride first tried the bridge and the captain's cabin. While trying to reach the skipper's cabin the wireless operator struggled through a great press of people on the port side of the Boat Deck. He didn't see any fighting, but he did hear people talking about it.[42]

Cottam, at the British Inquiry, confirmed that the first distress call from *Titanic* was received at 12.25am, but John Durrant, wireless operator of the *Mount Temple*, said that he heard *Carpathia* and *Titanic* working together at 11.35pm[43], or about the time of the accident. With the receipt of the 12.25am distress call began one of the most heroic and bizarre rescue attempts in maritime history.

Fred Fleet and Reginald Lee had been relieved in the crow's-nest at about midnight by Hogg and Evans. Between that time and 12.25am the lookouts tried, by telephone, to contact the bridge on a number of occasions without success. Without ever establishing communications with the ship's nerve centre, the lookouts deserted their post shortly before 12.30am.[44] The telephone link between the crow's-nest and the bridge seems to have been a little tenuous at best.

Nineteen and a half miles to the north the Leyland passenger/cargo ship *Californian* lay drifting with the ice. Her radio operator had switched off his equipment and turned in for the night at 11.30pm after receiving a brusque telling off from Jack Phillips for interfering with *Titanic's* commercial wireless messages. The only ship supposedly close enough to help those aboard *Titanic* would apparently know nothing of the disaster before morning came.

Down in *Titanic's* boiler room Number 5 Fred Barrett was helping Junior Assistant Second Engineers Jonathan Shepherd and Herbert Harvey operate the pumps. Shepherd had been with Barrett in Number 10 stokehold at the time of the collision and had escaped into the next compartment aft with the fireman. Senior Assistant Engineer B. Wilson was also working on the pumps along with a few other firemen.[45]

During the early panic Shepherd had stepped into an open manhole and broken his leg. He had been carried to a pump room at one end of the boiler room where he lay, unable to move, but nevertheless capable of giving instructions to Barrett and other unskilled firemen. Wilson and Harvey had managed to get a pump going and were keeping ahead of the incoming water in the boiler room.[46] The engineers seemed to have everything under control in the compartment when Harvey ordered Barrett to draw the fires as the pressure was lifting the safety valves and threatening to burst steam pipes.[47] Then the fire-damaged bulkhead collapsed. All of *Titanic's* engineers performed to the same impeccable standards as Wilson, Shepherd and Harvey, with no regard for their own safety. All perished.[48]

Thomas Andrews was sent for by Captain Smith to accompany him on an inspection of the forward part of the ship. Using the crew's companionways to avoid alarming the passengers, the two men made their way to the damaged areas of the ship. Within 10min they were back on the bridge. Andrews explained the problem to Smith. With the first five compartments flooding, the bows of the ship would be pulled down until water poured over the top of the bulkhead between the fifth and sixth compartment. Inevitably the bows would then sink even lower, allowing the water to overflow the next bulkhead and so on. About 16,000 tons of water had found its way into the ship in the first 40min.[49] Quite simply, the ship was doomed.[50]

In fact, there were a number of courses of action still open to them, if only the crew had been told what to do. Instead, the senior officers of *Titanic* allowed their ship to sink beneath their feet without making the slightest effort to prevent it.

On the Boat Deck, Second Officer Lightoller asked the chief officer if it was time to swing the boats out. Wilde told him to wait until the orders came, but Lightoller must have been getting a little apprehensive by this juncture because he next went directly to the captain for permission to swing out the boats. Captain Smith gave Lightoller the necessary authorisation to swing the boats out but not to load them. Lightoller then returned to the Boat Deck to carry out the instructions. No sooner had he done so than he asked for Wilde's consent to begin loading. Again Wilde told him to wait for instructions. Again Lightoller ignored his superior officer and went to see the captain and once again Smith allowed him to have his own way.[51]

Soon after the collision Quartermaster Wynne had been ordered by the captain to prepare the two emergency boats.[52] At 12.25am orders were passed to begin loading the lifeboats, women and children first. For the starboard side lifeboats this order was taken at face value and male passengers were allowed to enter the boats after the women and children. On the port side the order was interpreted to mean women and children only, resulting in families being needlessly split up and male passengers pointlessly sacrificed as boats left the sinking liner less than half filled.

We know that:

- Ten minutes after the collision the ship was venting steam, indicating that the boiler room fires had not been extinguished;
- The fires in the aft boiler rooms were not put out before the vessel foundered and that there was nothing to prevent Captain Smith moving *Titanic* closer to the mystery ship about five miles away.

Signals of Distress

Many of the passengers and crew were unaware that anything was amiss even as the boats were being uncovered. However, the very rich among them were all sought out and informed of the seriousness of the situation before the less affluent were made aware.[1] This preferential treatment was probably to ensure that they secured early places in the lifeboats. That they don't appear to have done so, at least not at first glance, was hardly the fault of *Titanic's* senior officers. Reinforcing the concept that the wealthier passengers were to be offered the chance of saving themselves before those from second and third class, there had been no general alarm and nor would there be.

Titanic, although in many respects fitted with the most up to date electrical equipment available had no public address system. Almost all of the information that passengers could obtain had to be gleaned from the stewards. Some of these stewards, whether through a desire to prevent a panic or through sheer inefficiency, were not as forthcoming as they might have been. There is some indication that this policy of keeping the passengers in the dark as to the true state of affairs was sanctioned aboard by the powers that be.

Nevertheless, a number of passengers, although only recently awakened, had their wits about them and would obviously feel happier having their valuables about them as well. They formed an orderly queue at the counter of the purser's office to claim possessions, which had been deposited in the ship's safes. There might have been an air of urgency about the proceedings but there was no panic or confusion as the staff, including purser's clerk Ernest W. King, handed out the valuables to their owners.

When, relatively recently, a safe was brought up from the wreck and opened amid great publicity it proved to be empty — silent testimony to the efficiency of the purser and his staff. It is faintly disturbing to think that every item left with the purser was claimed. It is a matter of recorded history that passengers left articles of very considerable value in their cabins as they prepared to leave the ship.

Perhaps the purser took whatever remained in the safes with him, intending to return them to the rightful owners at a later date, an occasion that never arose. This is what Mrs Sloan thought when she saw the purser carrying the contents from the ship's four safes. She understood that he intended to put them into a lifeboat, but the purser and the valuables were never seen again.[2]

Although many people were unaware that they were in any danger, yet more, despite repeated warnings from their stewards, refused to believe that the *Titanic* could and would sink. During the first hour following the accident most of the passengers made no preparations of any kind to leave the doomed liner. Many of these passengers, who were either not aware of the danger or chose to ignore it, did not react until it was too late and the boats had gone. There was no excitement whatever, nobody seemed frightened, nobody panicked.[3] They stayed away from the Boat Deck in droves. In others the instinct for self-preservation was stronger.

Maj Arthur Peuchen, realising the gravity of the situation, took the precaution of dressing warmly before venturing out into the night air. Behind him, on the cabin table, after serious consideration, he left a box containing over $300,000 in securities. There is no reason to suppose that the major's tin box is not locked in his cabin to this day.

Female passengers were, at first, slow to don their life-jackets, as was at least one stewardess. Mrs Robinson was spotted by Thomas Andrews without her Forberry's of London life preserver.[4] Andrews told her to put it on and to allow passengers to see her wearing it in the hope that it would encourage them to do the same.[5]

Stewards moved from cabin to cabin ostensibly checking that they were empty before locking the doors.[6] Inevitably, some doors were locked before the occupants had vacated their cabins, at least one having to be broken open to release the occupant, much to the annoyance of another steward who threatened to report the rescuer for damaging company property!

At about the same time, Chief Baker Charles Joughin, who had 13 staff to assist him, sent each of them to the Boat Deck with 40lb of bread.[7] He thought the time was then about 12.15am because the boats had been swung out but were not yet being loaded.

Col Archibald Gracie, searching for extra blankets for the lifeboats, he said, came across the squash racquets instructor Frederick Wright. 'Hadn't we better cancel that appointment for tomorrow morning?' the colonel joked. Fred Wright agreed but omitted to tell Gracie that the court was already completely submerged. The colonel went on his merry way, when perhaps he would have been better employed collecting together all of the unattached females to whom he had offered his protection when first they boarded the ship. These ladies were Mrs E. D. Appleton, Mrs R. C. Cornell, Mrs J. Murray Brown and Miss Edith Evans.[8] To be fair to the colonel, he did look in all of the cabins off the A Deck promenade, but he was looking for Mrs Churchill Candee and Mr Edward Kent. Although he found nobody in any of the cabins, he noticed four people in the smoking room playing cards: Clarence Moore, Frank Millett, Archie Butt and a stranger. In his account of the disaster he says that he never saw any of these people again.[9]

Colonel Gracie had, however, missed at least one first class lady passenger to whom his protection might have been useful. Throughout the voyage he had not so much as clapped eyes on his neighbour, Miss A. E. Icham.[10] Neither he nor any other gentleman aboard would prove of any assistance to Miss Icham on the night of the disaster.

Of those ladies fortunate enough to come under the colonel's protection, Edith Evans did not find a place in a lifeboat and Mrs J. M. Brown escaped only at the last moment in a collapsible boat.[11] As is the case with many of the acknowledged heroes of the *Titanic*, the colonel's fearless behaviour doesn't bear close examination.

Shortly before 12.30am Quartermaster Rowe, still at his post on the Poop Deck, telephoned the bridge to report that there were two lifeboats in the water on the ship's starboard side.[12] This was his first indication that there was anything wrong. Whoever he spoke to on the bridge was unaware that any boats had been launched, saying, 'No — is there?'[13]

Is it possible that these boats, in the water a full 20min before *Titanic* supposedly launched the first of her own, had come from another vessel?

At about the same time, 12.25am, Captain Smith finally gave the order to start the ship's pumps, 45min after the accident. Why the order was not given earlier has never been explained. Even if the captain had been too preoccupied to think of this basic means of extending the life of the ship, then any one of the senior officers should have done so. Failing this, Ismay and Andrews were both aboard and in a position to influence the skipper.

Other basic and usual precautions were not taken. Precautions such as counter flooding to keep the bows of the ship up for as long as possible and disposing of removable heavy items from the forward part of the ship, such as the anchors and chains. One particular measure, tried with ships which had far larger holes torn in their hulls than

Titanic, was the simple expedient of draping sails over the side of the ship. The inrushing water would carry the heavy canvas into the hole, or split, at least partially sealing the opening and slowing the influx of water. All liners of the period carried sails for use in emergencies and the practice was continued long afterwards. (*Teutonic* had been the first Atlantic liner not to need sails, but she had still carried them for use in an emergency, as did every other liner up to and including the *Queen Mary*.)

Captain Smith must have been aware of this simple emergency patch technique, which had been used by another White Star liner a little over three years earlier. On a foggy 23 January 1909 the *Republic* was rammed by the *Florida*. A huge hole was torn in *Republic's* side just aft of her funnel and 30ft of *Florida's* bow was crushed like a concertina.

Photographs taken shortly after the collision show both ships with tarpaulin patches over their wounds. Sadly the canvas patch was not enough to save *Republic* and she finally sank almost 40hr after the collision. Three people died as a direct result of the collision, two almost instantly and another after reaching New York. The death toll would undoubtedly have been much higher but for the heroic behaviour of Jack Binns, who operated the then novel wireless equipment. Binns, working under almost impossible conditions and holding his equipment together with his bare hands, managed to summon another White Star liner to their assistance. At about 7.30pm, more than 12hr after the collision, the *Baltic* arrived on the scene and four hours later had taken aboard all of *Republic's* passengers. Shortly before midnight she began to evacuate the passengers aboard *Florida*, taking no fewer than 1,650 from that vessel.

Binns remained at his post, repairing as best he could the wireless cabin which had been wrecked in the collision, and passing messages to other ships standing by. After almost 36 hours at his key, Binns abandoned the remains of his wireless cabin and the sinking liner at about 4pm. Shortly after 8.30pm *Republic* finally disappeared beneath the waves.

Binns was lionised for his part in what was then one of history's greatest and most dramatic maritime rescue operations. Before the applause had died away, Binns signed aboard another White Star ship, the *Adriatic*. His new captain was E. J. Smith and when the skipper transferred to the new *Olympic* when she entered service in 1911 Binns transferred with him.

By 1912 Binns had left the employ of the Marconi Company and joined the staff of the New York American as a reporter. Originally planning to cross the Atlantic aboard *Titanic* to join his new employers, he was unable to contain his enthusiasm and transferred to an earlier steamer, the *Minnewaska*. He arrived in New York and started work for the New York American a matter of hours before the *Titanic* disaster. How very different things might have been had the hero of the *Republic* occupied the senior wireless operator's position aboard *Titanic*. Binns knew the value of remaining in touch with any vessel in the immediate vicinity and might have been a little less dismissive to Evans of the *Californian*.

Between 12.30 and 12.45am Lawrence Beesley saw the ship's cellist running along the starboard side of the Boat Deck, the steel spike on the bottom of the instrument scoring a furrow in the planking. A few minutes later the band began to play on the promenade deck.[14] Not everybody heard the band and of those that did, not all heard the same types of music. Mrs J. B. Mennel, Mrs Roberts and Miss Madhill never saw or heard the band at all. Colonel Gracie didn't hear any hymns although he remained on the ship until the end.[15]

The Allison family waited on the Promenade Deck, smiling at all around them. Mrs Allison held the hand of her husband with one hand, and that of her daughter, Lorraine, with the other.[16] They were destined to remain together as the vessel sank beneath their feet.

Second Officer Lightoller, efficient as ever, elected to fill and lower boat Number 4 first. Accordingly, at about 12.45am he ordered all the women and children to make their way down to A Deck[17] while he had the boat lowered to there, forgetting all about the windows enclosing the forward part.[18] The windows were locked closed, making access to the boats impossible. Lightoller, rather than have the boat brought immediately back up to the Boat Deck and loading it from there sent a crewman to look for the key to open the windows. Meanwhile a group of first class passengers waited helplessly on A Deck for the anonymous crewman to reappear with the missing key. Among this presumably hand-picked group of passengers were Mrs Astor, Mrs Ryerson, Mrs Widener and Mrs Thayer. This group of women who had been present at the dinner party given for Captain Smith earlier in the evening seem to have been earmarked for what was to be, hopefully, the first boat away.

The missing key wasn't the only thing preventing the lowering of boat Number 4. Directly below it the ship's sounding spar projected from the side of the vessel, effectively barring Number 4's descent to the sea. More crewmen were detailed to remove the spar, using axes. The passengers were to wait for more than an hour before they could board the lifeboat and make their escape.

When the second officer had first swung out Number 4, it was his intention to load all of the lifeboats from A Deck.[19] Why he should have made such an elementary blunder with the forward boats has never been explained, but it was a mistake shared by Murdoch. Assistant Second Class Steward J. Wheat heard Murdoch order the boats lowered to A Deck. Wheat was then ordered, by the same officer, to get the stewards up to man the boats.[20] Why Murdoch wanted stewards, most of whom wouldn't have known one end of an oar from the other, to man the boats is yet another mystery. What was needed in the small boats were seamen, not waiters.

Samuel Rule worked his way along the starboard side lifeboats putting bread and biscuits into each.[21] Colonel Gracie noticed him, or another seaman, rolling a small barrel of bread toward the boats.[22]

Not long after the order to uncover the boats was given, Fourth Officer Boxhall received permission to start firing distress rockets, or so the story goes. In fact *Titanic's* pyrotechnic signals were what are known as 'socket signals' — an explosive shell fired from a socket, or mortar, mounted on the side of the bridge. The shell rose to a height of about 800ft before bursting with an ear-splitting report,[23] throwing out stars.[24] Manufactured by the Cotton Powder Company Ltd, they were the latest device, advertised as 'a substitute for both guns and rockets in passenger and other vessels'. The Cotton Powder Co did not specify over what distance their signals were visible, but claimed that they could be, 'seen and heard further than any other means'.[25] These mortar bombs were normally stored on the Poop Deck, where Quartermaster Rowe was still stationed. The assistant helmsman, Quartermaster Olliver, was dispatched to fetch Rowe and the signals. They each brought a box of 12 shells to the bridge and, at about 12.45am, the fireworks display began, just as boat Number 3 was being lowered.[26] Lawrence Beesley described the firing of a rocket: 'Up it went, higher and higher, with a sea of faces upturned to watch it, and then an explosion that seemed to split the silent night in two.'[27]

Contrary to popular belief, the signals sent up by *Titanic* were not all white ones. Quartermaster Robert Hitchens, helmsman, saw red, white and blue shells burst overhead over a period of about half an hour.[28] The signals were fired at short intervals, the exact number is unknown, but by the end of the session Rowe testified that there were a couple left in the box, which indicates that something in the region of 18 to 22 were sent up — a much more believable number than the eight generally believed to have been fired. Steward Crawford testified that he saw a dozen or more rockets fired.[29]

Lowe was working on boat Number 3 when the first rocket exploded overhead. After that, 'they were incessantly going off; they were nearly deafening me'.[30] Again this sounds as if rather more than six or eight rocket signals were fired. George Symons estimated the interval between rockets as about a minute[31] but this seems to be too short a time.

Rowe assisted Boxhall in the rocket firing until 1.25am.[32] Common sense dictated that, in an emergency of this type, every and all means should be used to summon assistance. I would have expected there to be no pyrotechnic signals left aboard the ship by the time the attempt to alert any vessel within sight was abandoned.

Joseph Boxhall had first seen the masthead lights of another ship ahead of *Titanic* about 30min after the collision, which was what prompted him to send for the rockets in the first place.[33] He said:

'I saw the masthead lights first, the two steaming lights: then, as she drew up closer, I saw her side lights through my glasses, and up closer, I saw the red light. I had seen the green but I saw the red most of the time. I saw the red light with my naked eye … I do not know when she turned … I do not think she was doing much steaming, but by the time I saw the red light with my naked eye she was not steaming very much, so she had probably gotten into the ice and turned around.'[34]

From the layout of her masthead lights Boxhall judged that the mystery ship was a four-masted steamer.[35] At the American Inquiry Boxhall was asked to estimate the size and type of the vessel showing the lights.

'That is hard to state, but the lights were on masts which were fairly close together — the masthead lights.'

'What would that indicate?'
'That the masts were pretty close together. She might have been a four-mast ship or she might have been a three-mast ship, but she certainly was not a two-mast ship.'
'Could you form any idea as to her size?'

'No; I could not.'

'You know it was a steamer and not a sailing vessel?'

'Oh, yes, she was a steamer, carrying steaming lights — white lights.'[36]

Quartermaster Wynne also saw the stranger's red and white lights, without the aid of binoculars, about seven or eight miles off. Wynne thought that the lights disappeared after a while only to be replaced 10 or 15min later by the lights of another vessel.[37]

Crawford saw both the red and green sidelights of the mystery ship,[38] the vessel didn't appear to be under way. The lights were still plainly visible when the fourth officer gave up firing 'rocket distress signals' after sending up between six and a dozen.

Rowe, too, had seen a stationary bright light about five miles away, about two points on the port bow.[39] MacKay saw what he believed was the stern light of a ship, to starboard, and travelling in the same direction as themselves.[40]

Boxhall didn't think that *Titanic* was swinging around[41] as the lights remained fairly steadily on *Titanic's* port bow.

The lights of this mystery ship were seen by quite a number of people aboard *Titanic*. Colonel Gracie saw a bright white light, ahead of *Titanic*, which he thought to be a ship about five miles away. He and J. J. Astor had to lean over the side of the ship and look toward the bows for this light. After a while the light grew less and less distinct and passed away altogether.[42]

Lightoller saw a 'perfectly stationary' single light about two points off *Titanic's* port bow and about five miles away. This light remained stationary and the second officer didn't notice it disappear.[43]

Third Officer Pitman saw a white stern light about five miles off;[44] it was not moving at all.[45] Fifth Officer Lowe saw two static masthead lights on the port bow.[46]

J. Bruce Ismay also saw a ship's light, but this vessel was on *Titanic's* starboard side.[47]

Able Seaman Edward John Buley, making his first voyage as a merchant seaman after 13 years in the Royal Navy, said this of the mystery ship most often sighted that night:

> 'There was a ship of some description there when she struck and she passed right by us ... You could see she was a steamer. She had her steamer lights burning. She was off our port bow when we struck ... We could not see anything of her in the morning

when it was daylight. She was stationary all night; I am very positive for about three hours she was stationary, and then she made tracks ... I should judge she was about 13 miles ... I saw two masthead lights ...'

Asked when he had first seen the lights, Buley replied, 'When we started turning the boats out. That was about ten minutes after she struck.'[48]

The attendant quartermasters, Rowe and Olliver, made of sterner stuff than Boxhall, continued to signal for assistance with the mortar. Boxhall now tried the Morse lamp and believed for a while that he could make out a flickering lamp aboard the mystery ship, indicating that she had seen his signals and was replying.[49] By this time Boxhall estimated that they were within four or five miles of the mysterious stranger. There was a certain amount of confusion aboard *Titanic*; some people thought that she had replied to their signals, while others were equally sure that she had not. There is some evidence to suggest that *Titanic's* signals were received by another steamer and that preparations were made aboard that vessel to receive survivors.[50]

It was a particularly clear night with an abundance of shooting stars so that it was difficult to be sure if rockets were being fired by the stranger, but at least one passenger was certain that she saw another ship firing rockets.

Mrs Marian Thayer described coming on deck shortly after the collision:

'While still on the Boat Deck I saw what appeared to be the hull of a ship, headed in the opposite direction to our ship, and quite near us, from which rockets were being sent up. The vessel (visible and about one mile off) was half the size of the Cedric and higher out of the water at her bow than the Carpathia.'[51]

The exact timing of Mrs Thayer's sighting is unknown, but taking her report with Boxhall's statement that he thought that the mystery ship replied to his signals establishes the possibility of another rocket-firing ship flashing a signal lamp in *Titanic's* vicinity. Mrs Thayer also said:

'Upon looking over the side of the vessel I saw what looked like a number of long black ribs, apparently floating nearly level with the surface of the water, parallel with each other but separated from each other by a few feet of water. These long black objects were parallel with the side of the ship.'[52]

On such a dark night Mrs Thayer would have been unable to distinguish anything more than a few feet from the ship unless it had its own illumination. The plank-like objects described obviously had no such built in radiance and were therefore within the circle illuminated by *Titanic's* own lights. What these objects may have been has never been satisfactorily explained but coupled with the description of a nearby ship, with its bows high out of the water, firing rockets, the possibility of a collision between *Titanic* and another vessel arises.

Might this be the explanation for the two boats that Quartermaster Rowe saw from the liner's Poop Deck 20min before *Titanic* launched the first of her own lifeboats? If such a collision actually occurred and the damaged vessel moved away to the northward, or *Titanic* to the south then events aboard *Californian*, laying stopped some distance to the north suddenly become more easily explainable. However, we will look at *California's* role in greater detail at a later time.

We now know that:

- QM Rowe reported seeing lifeboats in the water close to *Titanic* more than 15min before the first of her boats was lowered;
- *Titanic* sent up red, white and blue distress signals, not just the white ones usually ascribed to her.

Women and Children First

Lifeboat Number 7 was the first to be readied for lowering. Despite having a capacity of 65 people, the boat was lowered at 12.45am with a meagre 28 people huddled inside it. Not enough women and children could be found to fill the boat, a curious state of affairs which afflicted many of *Titanic's* lifeboats. I suspect that what was meant by 'not enough women and children' was 'not enough first class women and children,' at least as far as the forward boats were concerned. First class passenger Mrs Warren summed up the officers' lack of urgency when she said that there was no panic but more a sort of aimless confusion and an utter lack of organised effort.[1] When Mrs Warren had first gone up to the Boat Deck there were very few passengers there.[2] She also said that another passenger told her that they had seen Andrews rushing by the bottom of the grand staircase looking terrified,[3] which is somewhat different from the usual depiction of the shipbuilder.

With an hour and a half left to get as many people off the ship as was humanly possible the officer in charge of boat Number 7 had allowed it to leave less than half filled. From this it is evident that there was panic aboard, if not amongst the passengers and crew then amongst the officers on the Boat Deck. Seaman Brice had not seen any sign of passenger panic at this stage.[4] Steward James Johnson noticed, 'Lots of ladies going down from the Boat Deck to lower decks as the boats were being filled',[5] indicating that they were in no hurry to board the small boats. He also saw the red and white lights of a second mystery ship on *Titanic's* port bow and about eight or 10 miles away.[6]

Seated in the seemingly spacious environment of lifeboat Number 7 were passengers Miss Dorothy Gibson, a model and actress, French aviator M Pierre Marechal, Philadelphia banker Mr James R. McGough and Mr William T. Sloper (who had lived up to his name). Lookout Archie Jewell had managed to find himself a place in the boat as a member of the crew as well.

Meanwhile many third class passengers had gathered in their dining saloon where they held a prayer meeting. That they might have stood a slightly better chance of survival had they fought their way to the Boat Deck is undeniable. It appears, however, that they knew their place and were content to leave the lifeboats for the more deserving upper class passengers.

There was a lot going on aboard *Titanic* at about 12.45am. As mentioned earlier, Thomas Wheat returned to his own quarters where he noticed that water was running down the stairwell onto F Deck from the deck above.[7] This was the moment that the fire-damaged bulkhead between boiler rooms 5 and 6 chose to collapse, an event which apparently went unnoticed on the bridge. By this time it appears that the watertight doors between the undamaged boiler rooms had been reopened,[8] probably to allow more pumps to be brought into play. These doors were worked from the bridge and could not be operated by hand, either to open or close, once the switches had been thrown. This was in accordance with Board of Trade regulations.[9]

Up in first class Mrs Helen Candee described what she saw:

'A solid procession of all the ship's passengers, wordless, orderly, quiet and only the dress told of the tragedy. On every man and every woman's body was tied the sinister emblem of death at sea, and each one walked with his life clutching pack to await the coming horrors. It was like a fancy-dress ball in Dante's hell.'

Mrs Candee obviously believed that she could afford the time to watch what was going on around her, after all she was under the protection of Colonel Gracie.[10] It appears that the personable Mrs Candee was not short of male passengers who were prepared to offer her their protection.[11]

In the gymnasium, on the Boat Deck, first class passengers worked out on the exercise machines while they waited for the boats to be made ready. In this effort to keep fear and panic at bay they were assisted by the ever-willing instructor, McCawley.

Around about this time the fifth officer, Lowe, sleeping soundly in his cabin on the port side of the Boat Deck, was awakened by the unusual activity outside his door. Realising that something must be amiss he scrambled out of bed and looked outside. Incredible as it seems, E. J. Smith, Wilde and Murdoch had not thought to rouse the off duty junior officers. Seeing passengers wearing life-jackets, Lowe immediately dressed himself and went on deck to help, where he found the boats being made ready 'to go overboard'.

He noticed that there was very little commotion, no panic, and that nobody seemed to be particularly frightened. Most of the people seemed to be interested in the unusual goings on. Many of these passengers had crossed the Atlantic 50 or 60 times before and had never seen anything like this.

Observing the preparations for launching boat Number 7 Lowe noticed a group of elite passengers standing by. First Officer Murdoch had the boat lowered to the rail while J. Bruce Ismay called out, 'Gentlemen, please stand back.' The passengers looked at one another, 'more stunned than anything else'.

Helen Bishop heard somebody say, 'Put the brides and grooms in first' so she and her husband climbed in,[12] along with two other pairs of newlyweds. J. R. McGough was grabbed and propelled toward the lifeboat, 'Here, you're a big fellow, get in that boat.' McGough, along with some other gentlemen, obviously believing that the voice was referring to them, obliged!

Lookout Hogg was already in the boat,[13] scrambling about in the bottom, trying to put the plug in. At the falls Steward Etches struggled to untangle the ropes from around the passengers' legs; 'they kept catching in the passengers' feet'.

No sooner were the 25 passengers and three crewmen aboard than Murdoch ordered the boat lowered away.[14] It had taken about half an hour to prepare and load the boat.[15] Mrs Bishop peered down at the water far below. It was '… like glass. There wasn't even the ripple usually found on a small lake.'

Whatever Mrs Thayer had seen in the water, soon after the accident, was no longer in evidence and had probably been left astern by the slowly moving liner. Number 7 stayed close to the sinking *Titanic* until all the other starboard boats were in the water,[16] which appears to have been very handy for Thomas Whitely.

A newspaper article appeared on 21 April 1912 based on an interview with Whitely:

> 'After being thrown from the Titanic while helping to lift women and children into the small boats, Mr Whitely finally swam to a small boat and was helped in. It was while there that he heard a conversation between the two lookouts [Jewell and Hogg], neither of whom he recalled having seen before, but who, he is confident, were on board the steamship.'[17]

The only lifeboat to carry two lookouts was Number 7, but for some unaccountable reason nobody aboard this boat mentioned picking anyone up from the sea. Some time later Whitely was on the upturned collapsible B with Lightoller. Quite how he accomplished this is unexplained; all we know is that when Whitely went over the side of *Titanic* he was helping to load another boat.

Seeing that the situation was indeed critical and likely to deteriorate, Lowe promptly went and fetched his revolver, or more likely a Browning automatic pistol. At the American Inquiry Senator Smith was somewhat surprised to learn of Lowe's actions and asked, 'What for?' Lowe replied, 'Well sir, you never know when you'll need it.'

Lowe then returned to duty and helped out wherever he could. The first boat he assisted with was Number 5, on the starboard side of *Titanic*. (He told the British Inquiry that he helped with boats 1, 3, 5 and 7.[18]) He did not know the names of any of the crewmen or others who helped him prepare and lower Number 5. One helper, however, did stand out in his mind. This individual had stood by the boat, his arms windmilling, shouting, 'Lower away, lower away!' Unable to tolerate this affront to his authority, even from an obviously first class passenger, the fifth officer shouted back, 'Get the hell out of the way, and I'll lower away. Do you want me to drown the lot of them?' Completely crushed by this outburst, the passenger turned, and without a word walked away to assist in the loading of boat Number 3. There were to be repercussions from Lowe's outrageous behaviour toward none other than the chairman and managing director of IMM and the White Star line, J. Bruce Ismay himself.

At about 1am Fred Fleet, who was helping with boat Number 6 noticed a ship's lights on *Titanic's* port side.[19] (This boat was, in fact, lowered slightly before Number 7 as will be shown by McGough tossing Molly Brown into it before leaving in 7 himself.)

It was only when he was working to load this boat that Lightoller first noticed that the ship was listing heavily to port and was down by the head.[20] Once the boat's complement of 24 women, two male passengers and two seamen were aboard, it began its descent to the water. Number 6 was designed to carry 65 persons. Lightoller estimated that there were about 42 people in the boat,[21] precisely 50% more than was actually the case. He was well aware that there were plenty of third class women and children on the Boat Deck and he said that he even helped some into the boat.[22] Although the second officer would only allow women into the boats, he didn't press any that had qualms. When Mrs Constance Willard refused to get into Number 6, Lightoller shrugged and said, 'Don't waste time — let her go if she won't get in.'[23] Robert Hitchens, when he looked around for more women passengers moments before Number 6 began lowering saw only two.[24]

Mrs James Joseph Brown, better known as Molly, was walking away after persuading some of her less adventurous companions to board. Unable to contain her curiosity, the optimistic Mrs Brown was off to see what was happening elsewhere. Suddenly she was seized by two acquaintances, James McGough and Edward Calderhead, and tossed over the side into the descending lifeboat, falling about 4ft. As the boat was descending, Molly heard Captain Smith ordering them to row to the ship's light showing in the distance.[25] Robert Hitchens said that Lightoller ordered Number 6 to steer toward a light about two points on the starboard bow and about five miles away. He thought that this mysterious light might be a fishing smack.[26]

Once in the water, disagreement broke out between the two crew members aboard the small boat. Hitchens, the helmsman at the time of the collision and the most important witness to events on the bridge leading up to the catastrophe, refused to row. Coincidentally the other crew member was Fred Fleet, the lookout who had first reported the iceberg's presence 25min before the collision, and the most important witness to events in the crow's-nest prior to the collision.[27]

Luckily Molly Brown possessed a particularly powerful voice, which she now used to demand that another sailor be sent down to the boat. Maj Arthur Godfrey Peuchen volunteered and his declaration that he was a yachtsman was cynically accepted by Second Officer Lightoller:

'If you're seaman enough to get out on these falls and get down into the boat, you may go ahead.' Peuchen was indeed seaman enough (or desperate enough) and he safely negotiated the ropes and arrived aboard the lifeboat. It seems that, just before Lightoller had suggested that Peuchen shin down the falls, the Captain had told him to go below and break a window in order to reach the boat. Peuchen had not been enamoured of the Captain's idea.[28] Of the six lifeboats that Colonel Gracie watched Lightoller load, this was the only one that a male passenger was allowed to enter.[29]

John Jacob Astor was the only male passenger that Gracie saw make any attempt to get into a boat being loaded by Lightoller and that attempt failed.[30] It would appear that Colonel Gracie was a little inattentive at times. At least five male passengers escaped in boats loaded by the second officer.

Aboard lifeboat Number 6 was an Italian boy with a broken arm, generally believed to have been a stowaway, who had been ordered into Number 6 by Captain Smith. Mrs Candee had seen the whole thing.[31]

Even now Fleet and Peuchen were not strong enough to row the heavy lifeboat alone. Removing her life-jacket, Molly Brown took an oar, other women followed her example and soon Number 6 was moving safely away from *Titanic*. Major Peuchen, the only male passenger aboard the boat, was later to say that Lightoller should have allowed more men into the boats as there was plenty of room.[32] The major was undoubtedly correct.

A crowd had gathered on deck near to Number 5, where Fireman Alfred Shiers was already aboard[33] preparing the boat to receive its passengers. J. Bruce Ismay helped women and children into the boat. Among them Miss Marguerite Frolicher, aged 20. A total of 30 women and children were put aboard the lifeboat but then no more could be found.[34] By this time Lowe was supervising the loading of the boat. With no more women and children available, Third Officer Pitman, commanding the small boat,[35] allowed four male passengers, among them Edward P. Calderhead (proving that this boat left after Number 6 as Calderhead put Molly Brown into Number 6) to enter, along with five crew members. Pitman had been ordered to take Number 5 by Murdoch, although he was assigned to Number 1.[36] This was a lucky break for the third officer, as events aboard his assigned boat, as we shall see, were later to become infamous. At 12.55am Number 5 was lowered away with 39 persons aboard, less than two-thirds filled.

As the boat was being lowered, Dr H. W. Frauenthal and his brother decided that it was high time they escaped the doomed liner and joined the good doctor's wife in Number 5. Both men jumped from the Boat Deck into the descending lifeboat.[37] One of them landed on Mrs Annie May Stengel, a first class passenger, dislocating two of her ribs and knocking her unconscious.

Once Number 5 was in the water, Lowe moved forward to assist in the loading of Number 3, which was being directed by First Officer Murdoch. Murdoch instructed Able Seaman George Moore to help the women and children to board. In order to comply, Moore had first to get into the boat himself; this he accomplished without difficulty and so ensured himself a place. All the 25 women and children who could be gathered were put into the lifeboat, some against their better judgement, among them Mrs F. O. Speddon and her six-year-old son

Robert Douglas. Male passengers helped this meagre complement into Number 3 before standing back in the forlorn hope that more might be forthcoming. Among these heroes were Messrs Charles M. Hays, Howard B. Case, Roebling, Davidson and Speddon. Murdoch, on realising that no more women and children were to be found,[38] then allowed a limited number of male passengers and crew members in.[39] Mr Frederick O. Speddon was amongst the happy band of 10 male passengers invited to join the ladies in the small boat. Mrs Speddon noticed that the lifeboat was marked with Numbers 3 and 5 so she asked a crew member, probably Seaman George Moore, what it meant. She said, 'Our seaman told me that it was an old one taken from some other ship.'[40]

Fifteen crew members were also aboard when, at about 1am, Murdoch ordered Number 3 lowered. Samuel Rule, who was working at the aft falls, described the lowering of Number 3. He said that the boat was lowered directly into the sea from the Boat Deck. No people were taken from A Deck because of the closed promenade windows.[41]

Murdoch next turned his attention to boat Number 1.

Number 1, unlike the other wooden lifeboats except its twin, Number 2 on the port side of the ship, was not a proper 30ft lifeboat at all. It had no buoyancy tanks built in and was designed to carry less than two-thirds the number of people. It was what was known as an emergency boat, 25ft long and having a total capacity of only 40 persons, not that it was to be called upon to serve even that number on this occasion. Both emergency boats 1 and 2 were kept swung out and ready for instant use at all times. Lights and compass should have been kept aboard. One wonders why, with no preparations necessary and with their davits needed to deal with the collapsible lifeboats stored inboard, these two emergency boats were not the first filled and lowered. According to Samuel Rule, Number 1 was indeed the first starboard boat away,[42] but his evidence is unsupported except by common sense.

Waiting close by Number 1 were a small group of passengers made up of two women and three men. Sir Cosmo Duff-Gordon approached Fifth Officer Lowe and asked, 'May we get into that boat?' Lowe replied, 'With the greatest of pleasure,'[43] and then helped Lady Duff-Gordon and her secretary, Miss Francatelli, who had recently come running up, into the boat.[44] Sir Cosmo needed no such assistance and was soon comfortably seated, along with two American acquaintances. Murdoch, who was also overseeing the loading of lifeboat Number 1, realising that these three first class males would be unable to manage the boat alone, then allowed seven crewmen to board.[45] Fireman John Collins, one of these fortunate crewmen, later said that the male passengers were ordered into the boat.[46] At the British Inquiry Sir Cosmo admitted that he knew that it should have been, 'Women and children first,' even though he hadn't heard an order to that effect.[47] There were no more women or children on the Boat Deck at the time,[48] as Murdoch and Lowe ascertained, so the officers decided to proceed.[49] Lady Duff-Gordon heard orders given for Number 1 boat to '… row forward, away from *Titanic* for about two hundred yards.'[50] Rule heard a similar instruction. Number 1 was to 'Stand off the ship and come back if ordered.'[51]

In a letter dated 28 April 1912, Miss Francatelli says, 'After all the lifeboats had gone from the starboard side all the people seemed to rush to the other side of the boat, leaving the starboard side vacant.'[52]

At 1.10am, about 3 or 4min after the Duff-Gordons had entered the boat, Number 1 was lowered with 12 people, in a boat designed to carry 40. At the helm was George Symons, who was to give evidence at the British Inquiry which still appears to make no sense whatsoever. He said that before Number 1 was lowered he never noticed a list to starboard, but a slight list to port helped to keep the boat clear of the ship's side when it was lowered. He also said that boats 7, 5, and 3 all left the ship before Number 1,[53] which lends some credence to Duff-Gordon's statement that he thought all the women and children had already gone. Not only did Symons say that *Titanic* was not listing to starboard when Number 1 was launched, but that the ship foundered within about a half hour of the boat leaving.[54] Before he had even entered the small boat, Symons had noticed a white light a point and a half on *Titanic's* port bow and about five miles away.[55]

Loaded to 30% capacity, Number 1 was the most extreme example of the inefficiency of the officers dealing with the loading and lowering of the boats during the early part of that operation. Harold Lowe assisted Murdoch in the lowering of all four of the forward starboard side boats,[56] he said, but George Symons said that the only people directing operations on the Boat Deck were Murdoch and the bosun, Nichols.[57] Etches didn't notice Lowe when he was helping to load Number 5.[58] We have only Mr Lowe's word that he was really involved in many of the good works he claimed for himself.

On the port side of the ship, boat Number 8 was loading at about the same time as Number 1. Supervising the loading was Second Officer Charles Herbert Lightoller who is to figure so prominently later assisted, whenever they had a spare moment, by Chief Officer Wilde and the captain. Although Lightoller later said that he was only looking after the forward boats,[59] the records show him to have been present at the loading and lowering of aft boats 10, 12 and 16. Number 8 was hanging quite close to the ship's side so there was no difficulty getting the ladies into it.[60] Close by Number 8, were Isador Straus and his wife Ida with their maid Ellen Bird, whom they persuaded to enter the lifeboat. Isador was denied access to the boat by Lightoller. His wife, who was offered a place, refused, choosing to remain with her husband. Subsequently Colonel Gracie persuaded an officer to allow Isador Straus into a boat on account of his age, but he refused on the grounds that he wanted no special treatment that wasn't available to all male passengers.

Steward Hart brought a group of about 30 third class passengers to Number 8[61] but few, if any, were allowed to board. While he was on the Boat Deck, Hart noticed what he believed to be the masthead light of another ship.[62] Shortly before the boat was ready to leave, Captain Smith ordered Steward Alfred Crawford to row to a steamer which could be seen about five to seven miles away on *Titanic's* port side.[63] 'He pointed in the direction of the two lights and said, "Pull for that vessel, land your people and return to the ship." Those were Captain Smith's words,' Crawford said.[64] Mrs White overheard the order but said that it came from the officer in charge of loading the boat,[65] but perhaps Captain Smith was overseeing the loading. The captain gave this instruction to at least two inadequately manned lifeboats, showing that he thought that these boats could complete the round trip in the time remaining to *Titanic*.

Crawford was sure that there were not enough people about to have filled the lifeboat properly.[66] Seaman Thomas Jones had the same impression. He couldn't see many women on the Boat Deck.[67] At 1.10am Lightoller ordered Number 8 lowered away with just 28 people aboard. Four of them were crewmen and the rest female passengers and children[68] — mute testimony that Hart's group of third class passengers had been excluded; 37 more people condemned to death. Able Seaman Tom Jones particularly remembered one lady passenger, Lucy-Noel Martha, Countess of Rothes. 'She had a lot to say and I put her to steering the boat.' The Countess was to prove invaluable as the night wore on.

Mrs White, a first class passenger who escaped in Number 8, later made the point that the enclosed Promenade Deck was the main reason for the boats being so badly under-filled. It was too dangerous to lower them the 70ft from the Boat Deck with a full complement. If the lower decks had been open then more people could have got into the boats from there, but the lower decks were not open.[69] '*Titanic* was like a rat trap,' she said.[70]

Mrs White may well have been at least partly correct, but there were no windows barring access to the aft lifeboats. There could be no such excuse for these leaving the ship with anything less than a full complement.

We know that:

- Incredibly, during the early part of the evacuation of the ship, not enough women and children could be found to fill the lifeboats;
- Sir Cosmo Duff-Gordon assisted by seven crewmen left *Titanic* in boat No 1 with just his wife and secretary, and two friends. Was No 1 a private hire boat?

Going …

First Officer Murdoch had boat Number 9 lowered until it was level with the deck where, with the assistance of Sixth Officer Moody, Quartermaster Wynne, Steward Wheat and J. Bruce Ismay,[1] they began to cram the passengers in. Sited aft of the third funnel, this was the most forward starboard boat that could be reached from the second class Promenade Deck. Second class passengers had not been encouraged onto the forward, first class areas of the Boat Deck to compete for lifeboat places. Now, third class women were allowed onto the aft, second class areas of the deck, resulting in very few second class male passengers finding places in the boats there.[2]

Purser McElroy stationed three crewmen aboard Number 9 to assist the women and children to board. One elderly lady took fright and refused to enter the small boat, despite the best efforts of Murdoch, Moody, the crewmen present and other passengers. After holding up the proceedings for a few moments, this venerable female fled below deck and was not seen again. A French lady fell into the boat, slightly injuring herself.

It seems that, at this time, the ship was listing to starboard as McElroy had the crewmen help the women to bridge the widening gap between the boat and the ship.[3] The novelist, Jacques Futrelle, escorted his wife to the boat, but she refused to leave his side. 'For God's sake, go! It's your last chance. Go!' Still Mrs Futrelle was undecided, but an officer took hold of her and forcibly placed her in Number 9. By the time that this boat was almost full there were no more women on the deck, said Seaman Haines, one of the crewmen aboard the lifeboat. He made a quick search of the lifeboat, looking for a lantern or compass but found neither.[4] Purser McElroy called for more women to fill the empty spaces but none were forthcoming.[5] Murdoch then ordered Number 9 lowered away, instructing the crew to pull clear of the ship.

Colonel Gracie had attempted to find himself a place in the boat, but had been turned away by Moody.[6] This appears to have discouraged the colonel from further attempts to leave the ship by lifeboat for he seems to have remained aboard right to the end.

Orders were issued to move all the passengers over on to the port side of the ship in an effort to correct the list. Moving three hundred people from one side of the ship to the other would incline the vessel a mere 2°.[7] The resultant surge of water across the open areas of the ship would tend to magnify this effect somewhat.

Thirty-five minutes after the first one had been launched, rockets still hurtled up from the bridge wing and exploded high overhead, adding their eerie light to the dance of the damned being played out below.[8] Number 9 left the Boat Deck with 56 people aboard: eight crewmen, six male passengers and 42 women and children, at 1.20am[9] — the best effort yet.

Wheat and Brice both said that Number 9 was loaded from A Deck[10] and this was certainly the first boat that could have been reasonably dealt with from there.

According to Assistant Second Class Steward J. Wheat, when there were no people left on the Boat Deck, Boat 11 was lowered to A Deck to be filled.[11] Although second and third class passengers seem to have been discouraged from entering the forward boats, which were located on the first class and officers' Promenade Decks, the reverse does not seem to have been the case with the aft boats, sited on the second class and engineers' promenades. Three first class passengers found their way into Number 11 where at least one of them made her presence felt by complaining about men smoking in the boat. Murdoch and Moody were once again directing operations: by this stage they had learned at least some of the rudiments of abandoning ship and this boat was filled beyond capacity with 69 or 70 people aboard.[12] In all probability the boat would have carried another 20 with no problems. 'No women that tried to get into Number 11 were unable to do so,' said Able Seaman W. Brice, describing his last moments aboard *Titanic*.[13] At 1.25am Number 11 was ordered away, just 5min after Number 9. At last a sense of urgency had crept into the proceedings. First class Stewardess Mrs Annie Robinson noticed that the band was still playing as the boat left.[14]

Steward Frederick Dent Ray, who was present at the loading and lowering of boats 9, 11 and 13 and who left the stricken liner in the latter, said that there was 'no crowd whatever on A Deck' while these boats were being loaded.[15] Washington Dodge, who also made his escape in Number 13, watched all of the starboard side boats launched before his own. He said that 'not a boat was lowered that wouldn't have held from 10 to 20 more people. There were never enough women or children to fill the boats before they were launched.'[16]

Frederick Scott, a greaser, was followed up onto the Boat Deck by eight of the vessel's 36 engineers, or so he believed, although Hart who happened to be on deck at the time didn't see them.[17] Scott thought that all of the starboard side boats had gone, but that there were still boats on the port side of the ship at this time. The time was about 1.40am and it had taken the greaser 20min to find his way up from the engine room.[18]

On the port side, Second Officer Lightoller was loading boat Number 10, assisted by Sixth Officer Moody who seems to have been everywhere at once, and with the occasional help of Mr Murdoch, who also seems to have moved about with considerable alacrity. Also helping out was Chief Baker Joughin, who had taken a drink or two and seems to have been enjoying himself immensely. He had first come up to the Boat Deck at about 12.30am. Joughin had been assigned to command Number 10[19] but thought that there were already enough crewmen aboard to handle her and so left that job to Able Seaman Edward Buley.[20] Joughin declined to leave with the boat saying, 'To go with it would have set a bad example.'[21] He obviously didn't consider that getting as drunk as a lord was setting a bad example.

By this time the ship had taken a considerable list to port and a gap of between 2½ft and 5ft had opened up between the boat and the ship's side.[22] Joughin said that 'Number 10 was hanging a yard and a half away from the ship's side. If *Titanic* had been on an even keel the gap between the ship and the boat would have been, 'just enough to step in'.[23]

Number 10 was loaded on the Boat Deck,[24] which makes Murdoch and Moody's involvement with the loading and lowering of this boat and Number 11 simultaneously all the more extraordinary. However, despite their inevitably breathless condition, the officers managed to fill this boat to within a reasonable margin of its capacity: five crewmen to manage the boat, 42 second and third class women and children and the inevitable contingent from first class, five ladies. Baker Joughin and Officer Murdoch helped the women to board the boat by telling them to jump across the gap and then threw the children in after them.[25] No more women were visible on the Boat Deck by the time the officers were ready to lower the boat. There had been considerable difficulty in finding enough women for this boat[26] otherwise it would probably have been completely filled.

Unknown to the officers, two stowaways had found their way into the lifeboat, one a Japanese and the other an Armenian. At 1.20am

Number 10 was lowered away, reaching the water with 55 people aboard.[27] A foreigner, who looked like a 'crazed Italian', jumped into the boat as it was lowering.[28]

Immediately aft of Number 10, boat 12 was also loading from the Boat Deck[29] supervised by Lightoller and Lowe. Speed was a priority with them but not, unfortunately, numbers. Wilde herded the passengers toward the boat while Fred Clench and Lightoller stood on the gunwale of Number 12 helping the women and children to board.[30]

Discipline had begun to break down, and a group of passengers tried to rush the boat and were only kept at bay by the determined efforts of Lightoller and Poigndestre.[31] Lightoller allowed only two crewmen to board the boat, both of them able seamen, Poigndestre and Fred Clench. Only one first class passenger managed to find a place, a Miss Phillips. Forty women and children from second and third class were put into Number 12. When there were no more women and children to be found on the Boat Deck, Lightoller ordered 'lower away'.[32] As the boat was lowering, a French man jumped in[33] from B Deck, which goes to show how determined this individual was; B Deck was supposedly enclosed at that point. Also on B Deck, but on the starboard side, Steward Edward Wheelton met Thomas Andrews who was looking into cabins to ensure that they were empty. Bathroom Steward James Widgery had already checked that all the passengers were out of their cabins and on deck before he went up himself.[34] Wheelton noticed that boats 7, 5 and 9 were gone but that Number 11 was still hanging in its davits. As only about 5min elapsed between the launching of boats 9 and 11, the encounter between Wheelton and Andrews must have occurred shortly after 1.20am. Wheelton's statement also tells us that the boats were visible from the corridor on B Deck, which of course they would not have been if the cabins on that deck extended right out to the sides of the ship.[35] This argues that the internal layout of B Deck more closely resembled *Olympic's* configuration than that of *Titanic* and is yet another pointer toward a switch having taken place.

Number 12 had left the Boat Deck less than two-thirds filled with 43 people aboard. This calls into question Mrs White's theory that *Titanic's* boats left the ship underfilled because of the enclosed forward end of A Deck. That deck, at the point where Number 12 passed it, was open to the elements.

Fifth Officer Lowe moved to the next boat aft, Number 14, which he loaded with the assistance of Chief Officer Wilde. Although there were plenty of third class women on the Boat Deck shortly after 12.30am,[36] 'First and second class would have had more chance of getting into 14 than third,'[37] observed Joseph Scarrott.

Panic had now broken out in earnest and a group of unruly passengers tried to board the boat without waiting for instructions to do so. 'Lowe threatened to shoot passengers if there was any more trouble,' said Seaman Scarrott.[38] Steward Crowe thought that those who attempted to rush the boats were Italian or some other foreign nationality other than English or American.[39] Crowe's racist attitude was fairly typical of the time. A youngster, 'hardly more than a school boy', had found his way into Number 14 where he was spotted by the eagle-eyed fifth officer. Entering the boat himself, Lowe threatened to shoot the boy if he did not leave. Another two men attempted to slip in but Lowe chased them back out.[40] After allowing another seven crew members (Steward James Herbert Morris among them[41]), 56 women and children to enter the boat, Lowe ordered it lowered with a total of 63 persons aboard, or so he believed. Hiding in the boat was the obligatory Italian stowaway, bringing the total saved by Number 14 to 64. Joseph Scarrott, who was aboard, believed that there were only 58 people in the boat[42] while Colonel Gracie, merely an observer, made it 60.[43] Cool and collected as ever, Lowe fired three shots from his revolver, along the side of the ship, one as it passed each deck from which passengers might be expected to try to jump into it,[44] A, B and C respectively (on *Titanic* only A Deck should have posed a threat, both the others ostensibly being enclosed). Left on deck, doomed to a watery grave, was the young boy Lowe had forcibly removed from the boat, while in Number 14 was that officer. There was one unoccupied place in the lifeboat. Another of the heroes of the *Titanic* had shown his true colours.

As Number 14 reached a point about 5ft above the freezing black water of the North Atlantic, the boat's descent was abruptly halted. Colonel Gracie noticed that the boat tackles were giving trouble and not working at all smoothly. There was also a desperate shortage of trained seamen to lower the boats[45] but I suspect that the hold-up was caused by the men on the falls being somewhat less than sanguine about the blaze of gunfire coming from the boat below. Not to be thwarted in his escape bid at this late stage, Lowe pulled the lever of the 'Murray's Patented Release Gear', releasing both ends of the lifeboat from the falls ropes simultaneously.[46] The 30ft lifeboat with its 64 passengers, plummeted to the surface of the flat calm sea with an impact which must have resembled landing on concrete and which impressed the passengers far more than the gentle grating vibration of the ship's original encounter with whatever she struck. The shock was too much for the lifeboat and it sprang a leak. For the rest of the night it had to be constantly baled. As there were no balers in the boat, the men threw the water overboard using their hats.

Male passengers were now beginning to realise that the ship really was sinking and, more importantly, that there would be no place in a boat for them. When first alerted by his steward, Henry Etches, Benjamin Guggenheim and his manservant Victor Giglio had donned heavy sweaters beneath their life-jackets, on Etches' advice. Now the magnate and his servant returned to their cabins to change into evening dress, discarding their life preservers. Guggenheim was probably well aware that if they went into the freezing sea then life-jackets would be of no help whatsoever. While they might not drown they would still freeze. Coming back on deck the two men came upon Etches. 'We've dressed up in our best and are prepared to go down like gentlemen,' Guggenheim explained to the steward.

Aft of Number 14's davits on the port side, Moody, assisted by Lightoller, was loading Number 16. At first Number 16 had been loaded from the Boat Deck, but when there were no more women to be found there, it was lowered to A Deck to collect any that might be waiting there. Three male members of the crew were put into the boat, Master at Arms Bailey, Seaman Archer and Steward Andrews. Two stewardesses were also aboard, Mrs Leather and Miss Violet Jessop (who was also to survive the sinking of the third sister ship *Britannic*). A fireman had stowed away on this boat in place of the more usual Frenchman or Italian, possibly the only crew member to leave the sinking liner surreptitiously. Lightoller allowed 50, mostly second and third class women and children, into the boat,[47] then when there were no more female passengers to be had the boat was lowered with 56 aboard at 1.35am.[48] Mrs Leather heard the band still playing just before Number 16 left the *Titanic*.[49]

Meanwhile, on the starboard side, Moody was also loading boat Number 13. It was loaded from A Deck,[50] which would be unremarkable except that to have achieved this Moody would have had to circumnavigate the Veranda and Palm Court restaurants each time he visited one or other lifeboat, a distance of about 50yd. We can only assume that Moody was not only extremely fit but was also an Olympic-class sprinter! However, Dr Washington Dodge confused things even more when he said that he was on the Boat Deck where he couldn't see what was happening on the port side because his view was obstructed by the officers' quarters, gymnasium and staterooms.[51] Nine crewmen were put into Number 13 along with three stewardesses. Three first class passengers, Dr Dodge, Mrs Caldwell and her child Alden, also managed to find a place in 13.[52] The 49 second and third class women and children allowed into the boat by Moody were all that could be found on A Deck. The officer then allowed a couple of men aboard, Mr Caldwell and a Japanese. There were only three or four men left on A Deck seconds before Number 13 began its descent to the sea. These made their way aft to boat 15,[53] which had been swung from its davits at about the same time as 13.[54] On the Boat Deck, Lawrence Beesley looked over the side, down into the small boat. A crewman looked up at him (probably Fred Barrett) and asked if there were any more women or children on the Boat Deck. Beesley looked around but could see none; this information he passed on to the crewman in the lifeboat. 'Then you had better jump in,' said the crewman. Beesley did as he was bid, bringing the numbers in Number 13 up to a respectable 64.[55] Beesley thought that the last of the rockets had been fired by the time he left the liner.[56] (Curiously Lawrence Beesley died on 14 April 1967, aged 89, exactly 55 years after the disaster.[57])

As Number 13 was lowered it passed through a 'huge jet of water, 3 or 4ft in diameter, being thrown with great force from the side of the ship,'[58] which was probably from the condenser (water used to cool the steam after it had been used by the engines). According to Fireman George Beauchamp, this discharge was the only problem that arose during the launching of 13.[59] We must assume that Beauchamp simply did not notice the other hiccups in the proceedings. Among those making their getaway in Number 13 was the second member of the crow's-nest team which had first spotted the ice. Reginald Robertson Lee (Henry Reginald Lee?) should have left in Number 11 but had found his way into 13.[60] Number 13 was lowered from *Titanic* at the same time as Number 16, 1.35am. Years later Lee told his family that he saw one lifeboat overturned and another sunk, but never mentioned these at the official inquiries into the disaster.[61]

Boat 13's problems were by no means over when they had negotiated the water jet. Once in the water, nobody knew how to release the boat from the falls and the boat was swept backwards until it was directly beneath boat number 15, which began to descend immediately.[62] Only much frantic shouting from the occupants of Number 13 saved the day. Number 15's descent was halted until the boat below could be cut free from the ropes which held it and moved safely out of the way.

Moody was also supervising the loading and lowering of boat Number 15. He allowed 14 crewmen into this boat, among them firemen Diamond, Cavell and Taylor, and stewards Rule and Hunt. One first class male passenger managed to sneak aboard, the aptly named Mr Haven.[63] Some of the 53 third class women were loaded from the Boat Deck, but before all of those present could enter the boat, it was lowered to A Deck to continue loading there.[64] Once on A Deck, a group of foreign passengers tried to rush Number 15, but were beaten off by the crew.[65] All of the women on A Deck were crowded aboard. To be absolutely sure no one had been overlooked, scouts were sent around the deck but no more women or children could be found.

Liners of the day were built in such a way that third class passengers were shut out from the Boat Deck and it would be difficult for them to find their way there unless they were shown. Even with assistance it would have taken almost 5min for third class to reach the deck.[66] Able Seaman William Lucas described the situation: 'There would have been time for third class passengers to reach the boats if anybody had bothered to show them the way.'[67] J. E. Hart, one of the stewards aboard 15, was one of the few *Titanic* crewmen to 'have bothered' to make any attempt to help the third class passengers find their way from the bowels of the ship to the boats, not that it helped in the long run.

To avert a panic, Hart told people that the ship was not in any danger. As a result many of them refused to go up to the deck[68] when they had the chance. There were no closed barriers or other obstructions to stop them from reaching the Boat Deck[69] at least along the route he chose[70] to guide two small groups to A Deck.[71]

Bathroom Steward Samuel Rule saw the interpreter taking third class passengers aft on E Deck,[72] probably making for their staircase, which would bring them up to the entrance below the Poop Deck, well away from the boats. Baker Joughin saw that the emergency door allowing third class access to the second class main stairway was open.[73] There were four emergency doors linking the working passageways of the ship to the third class areas.[74] Only crew members with experience of this class of ship would have known this route to the comparative safety of the deck. Crew members who had not served on the *Olympic* would be as helpless as the passengers. Fireman Alfred Shiers had to ask a quartermaster the way to the Boat Deck.[75]

Hart took one group of about 25 to boat 15 while it was on A Deck.[76] There were already a large number of people in Number 15, but he was told to get into the boat by Murdoch.[77] Hart said that 'the boat was then lowered'. He went on to say that when 15 was lowered, 'there were still women and children on the Boat Deck'.[78] Some first class women were still on the deck with their husbands.[79]

Samuel J. Rule had a slightly different tale to tell of the loading and lowering of Number 15. He said that when the boat left the Boat Deck there were no more passengers there, but that the boat did not stop at the third class deck on its way down.[80] Trimmer George Cavell was also of the opinion that there were no more women remaining on the Boat Deck when they left it.[81] The boat was then lowered to A Deck where there were five women, three children and a man with a baby. These people got into the boat but there were more people on A Deck who didn't, for whatever reason. Scouts were sent out to scour the deck for more passengers but none could be found.[82]

There can be little doubt that third class were discriminated against. The men were kept below decks until about 1.15am. Some were allowed to make their way to the Boat Deck only as the last boat was pulling away.[83] A junior officer was posted at the head of the companionway leading up from the third class accommodation to prevent the steerage passengers swarming up on to the decks above. While still barring the way of the steerage passengers this officer noticed the boat he was assigned to being lowered. Dutifully he remained at his post saying, 'There goes my boat! But I can't be in two places at the same time and I have to keep this crowd back.'[84]

While he was on the Boat Deck delivering his third class charges, Hart noticed the masthead lights of another ship.

At about 1.35am the boat was ordered to 'lower away', only to be halted almost immediately by the cries of those in Number 13 trapped below them. The incident was obviously almost too much for Fireman Diamond who, despite the presence of ladies and children, cursed and swore profusely, a mode of communication of which he was a master, as he demonstrated continuously for the rest of the night.

Finally, Number 15 reached the water safely, slightly overloaded with 68[85] or 70 people aboard, nearly all of them second and third class men, according to Rule.[86] (Which clearly demonstrates that, under the circumstances, the boats could and should have been overloaded, quite safely.) All of the starboard wooden lifeboats had been launched.[87]

It was Fred Barrett's understanding that boats 13 and 15 were supposed to be exclusively for third class passengers. He noted that all the women were taken off the deck before 15 was lowered.[88]

By the time another 5min had elapsed, the starboard side of the Boat Deck was deserted.[89] If Fred Dent Ray was correct when he said that all of the starboard aft boats were loaded from A Deck[90] then a deserted Boat Deck was only to be expected.

We know that:

- People were getting into lifeboats from B deck, which they could not have done if that deck had been laid out as it should;
- Fourth Officer Lowe ordered a boy out of boat No 14 at gunpoint before leaving in that same boat himself;
- There was panic aboard which the officers were attempting to control by threatening passengers with their revolvers.

... Going ...

The officers supervising the launching of the starboard boats were altogether more efficient than those on the other side of the ship. All four of the starboard, forward boats were dealt with by Murdoch and Lowe whilst the port boats were handled by Lightoller with the assistance of Chief Officer Wilde. All of the starboard, forward boats went into the water within the space of 25min and with 130 persons aboard. On the port side it took an hour to get the forward boats away with 148 people. Each group of boats should have carried 235 persons. All of the starboard wooden boats were away one and a quarter hours after the order to swing them out and begin lowering had been given,[1] with 381 persons in them. It took those loading the port side boats an hour and 35min to launch them[2] with only 335 people aboard. John B. Thayer Jr noticed that the starboard boats were got away more efficiently than those on the other side of the ship.[3] The ship's list to port must have hampered the lowering of the starboard boats as they would have rubbed on the ship's hull on their way down. This disadvantage did not stop Murdoch and Pitman from getting an appreciably larger number of people away in a quicker time than Lightoller and Wilde.

According to Mrs Stephenson and Miss Eustis there was an order given for 'Women and children to the Boat Deck, and men to the starboard side.'[4] This would appear to indicate that no men would be allowed to enter the port side boats, but only starboard boats after all the women were loaded.[5] There doesn't seem to be much to support any such order except the simple fact that almost no male passengers were allowed into the port side boats, but this we already know to have been Lightoller's interpretation of the 'women and children first' convention.

After seeing the aft boats away on the port side, Mr Lightoller returned to the forward section where boats Numbers 2 and 4 were still suspended, while on the other side of the forward Boat Deck Murdoch had already got collapsible C under the davits vacated by Number 3 boat. The Englehart collapsible boats were described by Harold Sanderson as proper lifeboats because they were fitted with buoyancy tanks[6] which made them almost unsinkable. Murdoch put six crewmen into boat C under the command of Quartermaster Rowe.

Rowe said that when he got into C there were already 'three women and children in it; there were no more about'. There was a bright light visible about five miles away, about two points on *Titanic's* port bow. By this juncture, the ship had taken on a 6° list to port,[7] which was steadily increasing. To begin with *Titanic's* list to port had been quite small, but was constantly growing more pronounced making it increasingly difficult to launch the starboard boats.[8] In one respect, at least, conditions favoured those aboard the sinking liner. Under normal conditions lifeboats could be launched only from the lee side of a ship on the high seas[9] — a point conveniently overlooked today when lifeboat places for all aboard are advertised.

Pantryman Albert Pearcey, who had been directing third class male passengers through the first class saloon toward the Boat Deck, made his own way on deck. His own boat, Number 3, had gone so he made a beeline toward C, where Murdoch told him to get in.[10]

A group of 'Italians and foreigners who had sneaked into C', were cleared out by Murdoch, who fired his pistol in the air to drive home his argument. Four Chinese or Filipinos managed to hide from the watchful Murdoch in the bottom of the boat. William Mellors saw more than one officer threatening to shoot male passengers if they could not control themselves.[11] Seamen Jack Williams and William French saw for themselves that the threat was not an idle one: as they watched six men were shot down.[12]

Third class passenger Eugene Daly tried to get into a lifeboat and was threatened by an officer with a gun. Looking round he saw two men lying on the deck and was told that they had been shot.[13] No doubt Mr Daly did as the officer bid because he survived the incident.

Just about all the women and children on the Boat Deck were ushered into the collapsible, 27 in all, almost all third class. There were no more women and children visible when third class Pantryman Pearcey and Barber Weikman scrambled into the boat on the instructions of Murdoch.[14] Not only were the passengers conspicuous by their absence, so were the ship's officers. The only officer that Pearcey saw on the Boat Deck while C was being loaded was Murdoch,[15] who was in charge on the starboard side assisted by the bosun[16] and Lamp Trimmer Samuel Hemmings who said that he had put lamps into all of the starboard side boats still on the ship when he came on deck.[17] One can't help wondering where everybody had gone.

Gatti's secretary Paul Mauge described how about 60 people, employees of Signor Gatti — cooks, waiters, wine waiters, scullions, etc — were confined in the second class dining saloon and were not allowed to proceed to the Boat Deck.[18] Of this predominantly Italian contingent there were no survivors, although their confinement below decks undoubtedly made room in the few remaining boats for what *Titanic's* officers obviously considered were more deserving British and American passengers. It is a great pity that the officers on both the Boat and A Decks did not take more advantage of this selfless act on the part of restaurant staff by filling up the lifeboat places which they might have occupied.

When asked, at the British Inquiry, 'Why did they let you pass?' Mauge replied, 'I think it was because I was dressed like a passenger. I told the stewards who were barring the way that I was secretary to the chef, and they let me pass.' Mauge did not see any passengers prevented from reaching the Boat Deck,[19] but he doesn't mention seeing any helped either.

It seems that the last two passengers on the Boat Deck, just before boat C was lowered, were J. Bruce Ismay, who had been on the deck the whole time,[20] and a first class passenger, Mr Carter. Steward James Johnson had earlier seen the company chairman, dressed in 'slippers and dustcoat' trying to get women and children to enter lifeboats.[21] In the one and a half hours between learning that the ship was mortally damaged and getting into boat C, Ismay had made no attempt to identify himself to any of the ship's senior officers,[22] nor had he used his unique position as head of both the line that ran the ship and the company that owned her to secure himself a place in a boat. He left *Titanic* in the last lifeboat launched.

Ismay said that there were 'no passengers or crew on deck when [he] left the ship,'[23] which leaves one wondering just who lowered boat C. Quartermaster Rowe, who was in charge of boat C, corroborated Ismay's story inasmuch as he said that there were no more women and children about when the boat was lowered,[24] as did the ship's barber.[25] On the other hand, First Class Steward Edward Brown, who had helped with boats 5, 3 and 1 before lending a hand with C,[26] said that Ismay was far from being the last to enter C. He was in the boat relatively early, calling for and helping women and children climb aboard.[27] Mrs Charlotte Cardeza said that not only was Ismay in the boat long before it was full but that he selected his own crew to row it.[28] John Thayer said that there was a large crowd of men around the last of the forward boats and that it was every man for himself. He also said that Ismay pushed his way through this crowd to reach the boat.[29]

As there were only 37 people in a boat designed for 47, Ismay and Carter, understandably, stepped into this boat as it began to be lowered, or so Ismay asserted.[30] Carter later said that he and Ismay were advised to get into a boat by Chief Officer Wilde as they were first class passengers.[31] Lightoller testified that Ismay had been bundled into the boat by Wilde, but Ismay denied that this had happened.[32] Lightoller's statement was almost certainly intended to protect the company chairman's reputation but Ismay didn't think that he had done anything from which his reputation needed protection.

Murdoch ordered boat C lowered from the deserted deck at 1.40am with 39 people aboard,[33] swinging from the davits formerly occupied by boat Number 3.[34] It took a good 5min to lower C as the rubbing strip on the boat kept catching on the rivets of the ship's hull plating because of *Titanic's* 6° list to port.[35] To deter would-be jumpers Purser Herbert McElroy fired two shots into the air from the boat.[36]

The collapsible boats had been surveyed by Mr Peacock, Surveyor to the Board of Trade at Glasgow, and he had found them to be perfectly satisfactory.[37] His findings were about to be tested.

Lightoller still toiled manfully on the port side boats. When he reached Number 2 he found it full of 'dagoes' whom he removed at gunpoint[38] before loading it with a more suitable complement. Three crewmen — Seaman Frank Osman, Steward James Johnson and a cook — were allowed to board, to manage the boat under the command of Fourth Officer Boxhall.[39] Boxhall had the foresight to have a box of pyrotechnic signals put into the boat.[40] Eight first class female passengers were loaded along with one elderly third class man and his family.[41] No more women would get into the small boat.[42] Luckily Boxhall knew that 'There is always a lamp in the emergency boat.'[43] This obviously applied only to Number 2 emergency boat as there was no lamp in Number 1. At 1.45am, Number 2 descended to the surface of the sea. There were 25 people in a boat which should have held 40.[44] Boxhall believed that his boat was the last port side boat away[45] but Number 4 and collapsible D were still on the ship, as well as A and B, which we will look at later.

Next Lightoller returned to boat 4, which he had first attempted to load almost an hour earlier. Four crew members were put into this boat under the command of Quartermaster Perkis. The A Deck windows had at last been opened to allow access, and the sounding spar which had projected below the boat had been removed. Because of the ship's list to port the boat swung well clear of the ship's side and had to be hauled close alongside and lashed there. Makeshift steps were constructed to allow the waiting first class female passengers to enter the boat with some decorum. Colonel Gracie said that Second Officer Lightoller took up station with one foot in the boat and the other on the deck of *Titanic*.[46] Quite probably this made Lightoller's eyes water as the sill of the A Deck windows was 4ft above the deck itself.[47] Gracie probably meant Lightoller had one foot on the sill. The rail was too high for Miss Edith Evans to clamber over. Some of the other women in the boat tried to pull her in but were unable to do so. Unfortunately for Miss Evans there were no crewmen close enough who were prepared to lend a hand and obviously such a menial task was beneath the Second Officer.

Lightoller tried to stop 13-year-old Jack Ryerson from getting into the boat but was outvoted by the rest of the passengers. Even after the boy was in the lifeboat the second officer was heard muttering, 'No more boys.'[48] When Colonel Gracie later asked Lightoller about this, the second officer could offer no explanation.[49]

By this time Lightoller thought that the ship's list had decreased somewhat.[50]

Among the passengers waiting to board were John Jacob Astor and his wife. Astor asked Lightoller if he might be allowed to accompany his young, pregnant wife into the boat. Permission was refused so Astor tamely put his wife into the boat and left. Neither the second officer nor Colonel Gracie saw John Jacob Astor again, not even on the Boat Deck later.[51] Thirty-six women and children, all that remained,[52] were loaded into Number 4 from A Deck.[53]

Then, at 1.55am, this the last wooden lifeboat to leave *Titanic*, was lowered with 40 people aboard, one of them a French stowaway.[54] Twenty-five seats which could have been used to advantage by any of the more than 1,500 people still aboard the stricken liner were vacant. As the boat left the ship, Greaser Thomas Granger heard the band still playing.[55]

There was only one more boat which could easily be got under davits still aboard — collapsible D. Both collapsibles A and B were kept on top of the officers' quarters, either side of the forward funnel. They would have to be manhandled from there down onto the Boat

Deck, negotiating the funnel rigging on the way before either collapsible could be put under the forward davits. Originally put aboard purely as ostentation, these two Englehart collapsibles were to do sterling service as we shall see in a chapter devoted entirely to events surrounding them.

Only three crewmen were available to man boat D: Quartermaster Bright, in command, Seaman Lucas and Steward Hardy. Lightoller had great difficulty finding enough women and children to fill the collapsible.[56] He hadn't bothered to fill most of the others he had loaded for this same reason, or so he said. Luckily, Quartermaster Bright had been the third man in the group which had fired the distress rockets from the bridge[57] and it is to him that we are indebted for information regarding the numbers of rockets taken to the bridge and to the numbers fired. He had remained on the bridge firing rockets until all the lifeboats had gone and only collapsible boats remained,[58] which tells us that the rockets were still being fired at 1.55am when Number 4 left.[59]

All the women that could be found on the Boat Deck, about 40,[60] were hustled aboard the collapsible. Lucas noticed that there were hardly any third class on the Boat Deck as D was filled.[61] When there were no more women to put into the boat on that deck, first class passenger Hugh Woolner made his way down to A Deck to see if he could find any there. A Deck was deserted[62] except for the Strause's, Astor, Edith Evans, three sisters and H. Bjornstrom Steffanson,[63] as was the Boat Deck. Hardy noticed that, by the time D was ready for lowering, there were no women or men on deck. He did not know where all the people had gone but thought that they might have gone over to the other side of the ship.[64] His main concern was that there didn't appear to be enough people left to lower the boat.[65]

Unable to delay any longer — the forecastle was just going under the surface of the sea[66] — Lightoller ordered collapsible D lowered at 2.05am.[67] To the best of the second officer's knowledge, there were 37 women and children, mostly third class,[68] and three crewmen in a boat designed to carry 47. Lurking in the bottom of the boat was third class passenger Joseph Dugemin, a stowaway. Lightoller had allowed no male passengers to board boat D while it hung at the Boat Deck, even though he had the utmost difficulty finding enough women to fill it to his satisfaction.[69] But when, at the last moment two young girls were found, he considered that the boat was laden as heavily as was prudent and so they were left behind.[70] As the boat descended past A Deck it swung about 9ft from the ship's side, not far enough to discourage Hugh Woolner and H. B. Steffanson from making a jump for it. Both men landed safely in the boat.[71] Obviously encouraged by their success, Frederick Hoyt, whose wife was already safely in the boat, leapt from the deck of the sinking liner, missed the lifeboat and landed in the sea, whence he was hauled aboard the lifeboat. Even after this brief immersion Hoyt had to row hard for the rest of the night to keep from freezing to death.[72]

Time had run out for those attempting to get the lifeboats away. No more would be swung from the davits, at least as far as the normally accepted version of events is concerned.

It is a curious fact that, as a result of the *Titanic* disaster, new regulations were brought in ensuring a place in a lifeboat for everybody aboard all passenger ships. While this is undoubtedly a step in the right direction, it does not address the main reason for the exceptional loss of life in the disaster. *Titanic* had 20 boats of which 18 were successfully launched, most of them hopelessly under-filled. Had there been 40 boats it is still virtually certain that only 18 would have been launched, most of them only partly filled. Under the prevailing conditions, the lifeboats could, in all probability, have been safely overloaded by as much as 25%, perhaps more. The problem lay not in the numbers of boats but in the inefficient way in which those available were used.

Officially, no rafts were constructed (although one witness was quite certain that a raft was used). No organised search of the ship, for women and children, was instigated and no system or organisation existed on the Boat Deck or anywhere else. Lack of training and inefficient leadership were amongst the causes of the unacceptably high percentage lost. Had the available boats been overloaded and lowered in reasonable time, had proper rafts been constructed from floatable objects such as deck chairs, lifebuoys and cabin trunks, almost everybody could have been saved of the approximately 2,168 aboard. Even if the officers were unaware that it was safe to lower the boats fully loaded, Captain Smith should have known and Thomas Andrews and the rest of the Harland & Wolff guarantee party certainly would have.[73] There can be no possible excuse for lowering them less than one-third filled. In fact the falls 'were good for something like 60 tons'.[74] They were not only capable of handling four boats in rapid succession but were capable of taking the weight of four fully laden boats at any one time.[75]

Second Officer Lightoller's insistence that male passengers were not to be allowed into the boats under any circumstances, even if there were not enough women and children available to fill those boats, undoubtedly contributed more than a little to the loss of life. At this point in the story, Lightoller stands head and shoulders above the rest of the cast, with the exception of Lowe, for sheer pig-headed, self-opinionated, mindless adherence to imperfectly understood orders.

Until this time Lightoller's conduct had left much to be desired, but, although he had made mistakes, they had at least been honest ones. Self-glorification had not been his aim, but that was about to change. Lowe, on the other hand, had successfully looked after himself at the expense of at least one young boy, and who knows how many others.

There is another aspect of the loading and lowering of the boats that requires consideration. One of the lookouts, Reginald Lee, talking to his family long after the event, told them that he saw one of *Titanic's* lifeboats hang suspended by only one end during launching.[76] Had this statement been unsupported it would have been meaningless, but it is not. Mrs Lillie Renouf, a second class passenger, also saw a boat being so badly lowered that it was almost vertical.[77] Perhaps both witnesses were mistaken. Anyway, this boat was not mentioned at either official inquiry.

Now we know that:

- Officers were actually shooting passengers in an attempt to keep some sort of order on the boat deck;
- The predominantly Italian restaurant staff, employed by Gatti and not the White Star line, were detained in the second class dining saloon and given no opportunity to reach the lifeboats; all were lost.

… Gone …

All hope for most of those still aboard *Titanic* left with collapsible D at 2.05am. It must have been apparent to even the most optimistic that the ship could not last long. The forecastle was under water and the roaring seas were pouring into the ship through every opening before the bridge.[1] Ever faster the water crept inexorably up the forward part of the main superstructure until it reached the Boat Deck. The vessel had minutes to live and so had most of the people still on her.

In the first class smoking room Archie Butt, Arthur Ryerson, Francis D. Millet and Clarence Moore sat at their usual table enjoying a last drink and hand of cards together. They gave up the pretence and left the smoking room at about 2.10am. Thomas Andrews remained, lost in thought, his arms folded across his chest, staring at the painting above the fireplace. Different sources identify this painting as either Approach of the New World or Plymouth Harbour, both by Norman Wilkinson. Approach of the New World was commissioned specially for *Olympic*.

A painting, identified as that from *Olympic*, now hangs in a Southampton museum. However, there seem to be several differences between the Southampton painting and the one shown in photographs of *Olympic's* first class smoking room, taken in 1911.

Some time round about 2am, Harold Bride said that Jack Phillips sent him to see if there were any boats left. 'I saw a collapsible boat near a funnel and went over to it. Twelve men were trying to boost it down to the Boat Deck. They were having an awful time. It was the last boat left. I looked at it longingly a few moments. Then I gave them a hand, and over she went. They all started to scramble in on the Boat Deck.'[2] Bride's evidence doesn't quite tie up with the accepted record.

In this version from Bride both collapsibles A and B were safely moved from the deckhouse roof to the Boat Deck and at least partially filled well before the water reached them.

At about 2.05am Captain Smith went to the wireless cabin to release Bride and Phillips, who were still hard at work trying to summon help.[3] The junior operator described their release thus:

'Then came the Captain's voice, "Men, you have done your full duty, you can do no more. Abandon your cabin." '[4]

Bride lost no time gathering up his clothes and money, and Phillips' money as well.[5] Phillips was still operating the wireless, hoping to contact some other vessel much nearer than the *Carpathia*. Right to the end Phillips never wavered, continuing to send at a consistent 15 words a minute.[6]

A little earlier the junior operator, instead of remaining with Phillips, had left the wireless room for a look around. He had seen people searching for lifebelts in the gymnasium and officers' quarters.[7]

According to Bride, a stoker found his way into the wireless room and tried to steal Phillips' life-jacket but Bride brained him with a spanner, leaving him for dead before he and Phillips left the wireless room for the last time.[8] As they left, water was just beginning to find its way into the cabin. They climbed onto the roof of the officers' quarters[9] where Phillips ran aft[10] and Bride went forward to help with the preparations to launch collapsible B. In one version of his story this was the last Bride saw of Phillips. In another version, Phillips walked aft only to turn up later on boat B. In yet another, Bride and Phillips were on A Deck when Phillips went aft and was swallowed up by the crowd. None of these stories, told by the junior wireless operator, was true.

Whether or not Captain Smith ever released the wireless men from their duty is debatable. That Phillips remained at his post right to the end is indisputable, as is the fact that Bride left the cabin in time to reach collapsible B before it was washed overboard.

The ship was going down fast now. Panic had set in with a vengeance. More than a hundred passengers had gathered on the after end of the Boat Deck where Father Thomas R. Byles was hearing confessions and giving absolutions.

Wallace Hartley and the rest of his small orchestra also knew that the end was near. They stopped playing the lively ragtime music with which they had been trying to keep up the spirits of the passengers and no doubt themselves, and began to play hymns. As the bows sank deeper and the water crept back along the sloping Boat Deck, Hartley led the band in a final hymn, Nearer My God to Thee.

Struggling to release the collapsible when Bride arrived were Chief Officer Wilde, First Officer Murdoch, Second Officer Lightoller, Sixth Officer Moody and greaser Walter Hurst. At 2.10am the water swept over the forward end of the Boat Deck and carried the boat and those working on it over the side. Bride was holding on to a rowlock as B went overboard, he said. Again the Marconi man came up with a variety of stories of his escape from the ship. In one version he said that he then swam away from the boat as fast as he could to avoid the suction as the ship sank.[11] Obviously he didn't swim that far away because he ended up on that same collapsible B.

The ship was listing heavily to port[12] when B was washed overboard, which would mean that boat A, which was also on the Boat Deck, would have been carried over the side by the rushing water at about the same time or slightly after. At least boat A was the right way up when it went into the water, which was more than could be said of B, at least in the official record.

Efforts had been made to launch boat A earlier, but the collapsible had become entangled in the funnel rigging and the attempt had been abandoned. Everyone's attention was turned toward B.[13]

Nonetheless, Steward Edward Brown said that he helped with Boat A and that they 'had no difficulty in getting it off the roof of the officers' quarters and that they slid it down planks'. He did not know where the planks came from.[14] That A was suspended from davits is evinced by Brown having to cut the aft falls to release the boat.[15] He probably used Colonel Gracie's penknife, which had been borrowed to cut the boats free from their lashings on the deckhouse roof.[16]

Lightoller told a slightly different story. He said that he 'was unable to loosen A from the ship in time' and that he and his men were compelled to abandon it, still tied down on board *Titanic*. He thought A had gone down with the ship.[17] A slight variation on the Lightoller story was provided by Steward Mellors who said that he was standing by boat A while one of the crew was trying to cut it free. The onrushing water eventually tore the boat free.[18]

The different versions are completely incompatible.

Brown's version is certainly the more believable, simply because this boat left the ship the right way up and undamaged, with both passengers and crew aboard. Lightoller's account of his further exploits being somewhat beyond belief also tends to colour one's view of his explanation of events while still aboard the ship.

Had boat A been washed overboard with the canvas sides down but otherwise undamaged there would have been no reason why those sides could not be raised once the boat was afloat. The raising of the sides and bailing out of any accumulated water would have made the lifeboat seaworthy and considerably increased the chances of survival for those aboard. The fact that this was not done suggests that A was damaged to the point where it could not be made seaworthy.

In fact, the sides of A were raised before the boat went into the water. Only after *Titanic* sank, when scores of people tried to climb into the boat, were the sides collapsed and the boat flooded. It had been overturned by the weight of people struggling to get aboard, before righting itself and drifting, barely afloat, supported by the tin buoyancy compartments and the cork railing around it.[19]

Consequently, all of those who found their way into A had been in the freezing sea, which meant that their chances of survival were somewhat reduced. Of the 30 or so people who collected either in or around A, there were only 14 aboard come morning; three of those had frozen to death during the night but remained in the boat. Others had been thrown over the side once the cold had killed them. August Wennerstrom had been in the boat before the swimmers had overturned it, at which time he had been knocked unconscious. When he came round he found his way back to boat A, finding it in the condition described above. He was allowed back on board and surprisingly survived.

R. N. Williams, who was also lucky enough to find a place in A, sat for most of the night in water up to his waist. O. Abelseth, who remained standing for the greater part of the night, described the water in his part of the boat as about 12–14in deep.

While more than 1,500 people died from cold in the water about them, the small group in Boat A remained huddled in their semi-submerged lifeboat until dawn. Allowing for the condition of collapsible A, there was nothing else that they could have done. It is a curious fact that moving about under extremely cold conditions, either in the water or out of it, but in still air, shortens life expectancy dramatically.

Only the fact that those in A sat or crouched, huddled up and practically motionless for the hours of darkness, allowed them to survive. Even so they were all suffering from the effects of frostbite and exposure and would need hospital treatment.

Survival time for a swimmer in water at 28°F is a matter of a very few minutes, even with a life-jacket. Most of the people who went into the water from the ship, where they had been relatively warm, would have died instantly from a condition known as hydrocution, the effects of hydrocution being very similar to electrocution. The shock of the intensely cold water stops the heart instantly. Those who avoided the effects of hydrocution, who were cold before they entered the water, would have been suffering from the effects of hypothermia within 1 or 2min, the effects of swimming greatly magnifying the problem. The cold water passing over thrashing limbs would carry the body heat away in no time, resulting in paralysis, loss of consciousness and death. Nobody could have survived for as much as half an hour, most for less than 5min. Which brings us to the impossible scenario of collapsible B and that redoubtable mariner Charles Herbert Lightoller.

As we know, collapsible B was washed off the Boat Deck at about 2.10am, with second wireless operator Bride hanging on like grim death to a rowlock. As he told it in this version, Bride found himself underneath the upturned boat where he estimated he remained for between half and three-quarters of an hour,[20] which is impossible. Being beneath the collapsible, Bride did not see or hear anything in the last 10min of the life of the ship.

Second Officer Lightoller, seeing that B had been swept overboard, hurried across to the other side of the Boat Deck. He thought that he saw Chief Officer Wilde working on the falls for Number 1 boat. Lightoller then calmly walked into the sea[21] where he was promptly sucked down and pinned against a grating by water pouring into the stokehold blower. Suddenly a blast of air escaping from the grating blew him to the surface but he was instantly sucked down again by water entering the ship through the fiddley gratings, immediately abreast of the funnel.[22] He again broke surface and espied the upturned collapsible. According to the second officer, he had been under water for 3 or 4min. At the British Inquiry Lightoller said that he came up near the collapsible that they had failed to launch but which had been thrown into the water.[23] Such was Lightoller's familiarity with this class of ship it seems that he was never disorientated and was always sure of exactly where he was, even while submerged!

Quite how collapsible B now came to be on the starboard side of the ship Lightoller omits to explain. In no time this extraordinary seaman hauled himself onto the upturned boat and took up position at the bow. More members of the crew began to arrive and struggle aboard, blissfully unaware of the wireless operator beneath their feet.

The ship buried her bow ever deeper. Reports rang out 'like a volley of musketry'. The submerged forecastle was shuddering, 'shaking very much', as the water roared into the upper decks.

Further aft Father Byles and a German priest were now dispensing absolution on a wholesale basis. As the waters rushed toward them

Byles cried, 'Prepare to meet God.' Many of the third class passengers who had emerged onto the deck only moments before, fell on their knees and prayed. Others struggled to companionways and ladders in a bid to reach the still dry stern, before the sea reached them.

Alcoholic beverages and spirits had been 'on the house' for some time and available to the crew and all classes of passengers, which might go some way toward explaining a few of the more bizarre events aboard.

Belfast firemen Paddy Dillon and Johnny Bannon had 'made for the whiskey and got our share'. They had made a healthy start on somebody else's share when the ship lurched forward. Before making for the open deck, Dillon rammed a bottle of brandy into his jacket pocket. Together the two Irishmen staggered out onto the deck. Paddy Dillon, undoubtedly adversely affected by the fresh air, not to mention the whiskey, staggered across the deck and over the side of the ship into the sea.

Colonel Gracie's hurried sternward progress was halted by the mass of humanity which had erupted onto the Boat Deck from the third class accommodation far below only moments before.[24] Curiously, the colonel didn't see any women among the crowd. In fact, neither he nor Lightoller saw any women on the Boat Deck in the interval between the lowering of the last boat and the ship foundering.[25]

This mass of humanity did not affect the progress of the water as it rushed aft, like a tidal wave. Riding this wave like a surfer, Gracie managed to reach the roof of the officers' quarters where he grabbed a handrail and was promptly dragged under by the ship:

'I was taken down with the ship. I was hanging on to the railing, but I soon let go. I felt myself whirled around, swarm under water, fearful that the hot water that came up from the boilers might boil me up … I swam, it seemed to me, with unusual strength and succeeded finally in reaching the surface and in getting a good distance away from the ship.'

He said that he could tell when he was nearing the surface by the increase in light.[26] The colonel omitted to mention where this light which illuminated the surface of the sea was coming from. Certainly, if the colonel's story is accurate, not from the *Titanic*.

Gracie did not know how far he was from the ship when he surfaced, '… because I could not see the ship. When I came up to the surface there was no ship there. The ship would have been behind me, but all around me was wreckage. I saw what seemed to be bodies all around … There was a sort of gulp, as if something had occurred behind me, and I suppose that was where the water was closing up where the ship had gone down.'[27] The colonel also said that he never, 'for an instant,' suffered from any exhaustion. 'I kept my presence of mind and courage throughout.'[28]

The ship had barely reached the point where the stern was lifting clear of the water (when the water in the bow section weighed more than the heavy machinery in the stern) when Gracie was dragged under. At that time it would have had between 5 and 10min left on the surface. The ageing colonel, who was to die a year later, must, if his story is to be believed, have swum under water for more than 5min — clearly an impossibility. Nobody could have made the swim described by Gracie, under the conditions prevailing. If he left *Titanic* how and when he said, then the ship must still have been on the surface when he came up. Or he might have been much further aft than he thought when he was carried under water, but if that was the case then he was still aboard when it became impossible to stand on the sloping decks, something he would certainly have recalled. Much more likely is that Gracie didn't leave the ship as he described at all. His story bears an uncanny resemblance to that of Second Officer Lightoller's, which is not surprising, as neither is likely to be true.

The main reason for Gracie and his friend Clinch-Smith having difficulty making their way aft would have been the people coming onto the Boat Deck by the forward companionways. These people panicked on seeing the seawater rushing back along the Boat Deck and fled aft only to run full tilt into the iron railings separating the first and second class promenade space. This means that Gracie was caught by the water forward of that dividing fence; just aft of the third funnel, well aft of the officers' quarters mentioned by the colonel, but not far enough for him to have spent less than 6 or 7 min under water at the very least.

Jack Thayer and another male passenger sat on the starboard rail abreast number two funnel, facing outward. 'You're coming boy, aren't you?' the fellow passenger asked Thayer. 'Go ahead, I'll be with you in a minute.' The other passenger let go and slid down the sloping side of the ship, down into the water. He was swallowed up by the torrent of water rushing into A Deck. Thayer never saw him again. About 10sec after his friend had vanished Jack Thayer leapt from the Boat Deck, hurling himself as far from the ship as he possibly could.

The shock of the freezing water knocked the breath out of Thayer. It took him some moments to recover but then he swam furiously away from the ship. Stopping about 40yd off, he turned and rested, buoyed up by his life-jacket, watching *Titanic*. 'The ship seemed to be surrounded with a glare and stood out of the night as though she were on fire. I watched her. I don't know why I didn't keep swimming away. Fascinated, I seemed tied to the spot.'

The young, fit Thayer had the breath knocked from his body on contact with the freezing sea. For a while he was completely immobilised by the shock and could do nothing to help himself. Only after he had recovered from this initial shock could he swim away from the sinking ship. This reaction is entirely normal and shows just how unlikely are the stories of Lightoller and Gracie, who must have suffered the same shock on entering the freezing water. It should be remembered that Colonel Gracie was by no means a young man.

Some of the people in the lifeboats were watching the doomed ship. As the bows sank deeper, the whole vessel steadily tilted forward. By this time her first funnel was partly submerged. Apparently there was no sound coming from the ship except the music of the band who were now playing Nearer My God to Thee.

In boat 14 Mrs Charlotte Collyer watched. To her, *Titanic* looked 'like an enormous glow worm, for she was alight from the rising waterline, clear to her stern,' she said, '… electric lights blazing in every cabin, lights on all decks, and lights on her mastheads' (sic). Below the rising water, in cabins submerged for some time now, the lights continued to burn, imbuing the normally dark water around the submerged forward part of the vessel with a turbid, unhealthy green glow.

Suddenly, the huge forward smoke stack seemed to lift away from the decks supporting it,[29] the steel cables which had braced it tearing their fixings out of the ship, taking large sections of deck planking with them. The port side cables giving way first allowed the starboard braces to influence the gigantic funnel's direction of collapse. Instead of falling directly forward, the funnel struck the starboard bridge wing, crushing it in its descent before smashing into the water, squashing the life out of any and every swimmer in its path. The surge caused by the falling smoke stack pushed water-logged Collapsible A away from the ship, eliminating any possibility that the unmanageable boat might be sucked toward the foundering giant.

Those in collapsible A were so close when the funnel broke loose with a shower of sparks, that they thought the entire forward part of the ship had exploded. As visits to the wreck more than 80 years later have shown, something may well have exploded in the forward part of the vessel.

The ship was sliding forward now as the bows sank ever deeper, water pouring into every opening. The second funnel was partly submerged when the forward motion ceased and the huge stern began to rise slowly into the air. Explosions deep under water were heard by those in the lifeboats. Possibly boilers that had been maintaining pressure to supply steam for the electricity generators had been reached by the icy seawater, which was 4° below freezing.[30]

Still people scrambled toward the stern of the doomed behemoth, among them Chief Baker Joughin. Having imbibed of the free spirits on offer throughout the ship, and with his own supply to hand, Joughin wasn't thinking along quite the same lines as everybody else trapped aboard. Unable to make any progress through the struggling mass of humanity intent on prolonging their lives by a few seconds (as was the baker), Joughin had a novel idea. Because of the ship's heavy list to port the starboard side of the hull was not vertical. Joughin climbed over the rail on that side of the deck and proceeded to walk, or climb, his way aft along the outside of the hull, thus avoiding those on deck. The strategy worked and the chief baker made it all the way to the extreme aft end of the Poop Deck. Whatever else happened, Joughin was now sure of being amongst the very last to get his feet wet. With perfect equanimity the baker awaited the end.

In boat 2, a seaman watched in amazement, seeing steam, smoke and what he took to be lumps of coal emptying from *Titanic's* funnels.

Aboard the ship, all was bedlam. Carl Jansen knew from the shrieks and cries coming from forward and from the people scrambling past him, trying to reach the stern, that the end was not far away.

In boat 13, schoolteacher Lawrence Beesley watched and noted everything:

> 'And then, as we gazed awe-struck, she tilted slowly up, revolving apparently about a centre of gravity just astern of amidships, until she attained a vertically upright position and there she remained motionless! As she swung up, her lights, which had shone without a flicker all night, went out suddenly, came on again for a single flash, then went out altogether.[31] And as they did so, there came a noise which many people, wrongly I think,

have described as an explosion; it has always seemed to me that it was nothing but the engines and machinery coming loose from their bolts and bearings, and falling through the compartments, smashing everything in their way. It was partly a roar, partly a groan, partly a rattle, and partly a smash, and it was not a sudden roar as an explosion would be; it went on successively for some seconds, possibly fifteen to twenty, as the heavy machinery dropped down to the bottom (now the bows) of the ship: I suppose it fell through the end and sank first, before the ship. But it was a noise no one had heard before, and no one wishes to hear again; it was stupefying, stupendous, as it came to us along the water. It was as if all the heavy things one could think of had been thrown downstairs from the top of a house, smashing each other and the stairs and everything in the way ... When the noise was over the Titanic was still upright like a column: we could see her now only as the stern and some 150 feet of her stood outlined against the star-specked sky, looming black in the darkness, and in this position she continued for some minutes — I think as much as five minutes, but it may have been less. Then, first sinking back a little at the stern, I thought, she slid slowly forwards through the water and dived slantingly down; the sea closed over her and we had seen the last of the beautiful ship on which we had embarked four days before at Southampton.'

Charles Lightoller agreed with Beesley that the noises coming from the ship were not explosions but the boilers breaking loose.[32] Pitman distinctly heard four reports, but again thought that they were caused by boilers leaving their bedplates.[33]

Jack Thayer, who you will recall had leapt from the ship some minutes before when the water had first swept along the Boat Deck, had managed to reach collapsible B. He climbed onto the upturned lifeboat and watched. The stern of the liner was still rising but had almost reached a vertical position. 'Her deck was turned slightly toward us. We could see groups of the almost fifteen hundred people still aboard, clinging in clusters or bunches, like swarming bees: only to fall in masses, pairs or singly as the great after part of the ship, two hundred and fifty feet of it, rose into the sky.'

She now stood perpendicular and motionless, 'looking like a gigantic whale submerging itself head first'. The ship remained 'in this amazing attitude' for what seemed to Thayer to be five minutes. (It is interesting that both Beesley and Thayer gave similar estimates for the time that *Titanic's* stern was perpendicular.)

Passengers Phillip E. Mock, Martha Stevenson and Mrs Thayer all said that *Titanic's* stern reached a vertical attitude before the ship sank.[34] Mock also noticed a huge column of black smoke hanging over the sinking liner.[35] Reginald (Henry) Lee noticed what he took to be underwater explosions as *Titanic* sank.[36]

Watching the final moments of the vessel, Dillon and Rule could see no people on the Poop Deck.[37] They obviously thought that this was worthy of comment in light of other testimony to the contrary.

There is, of course, one problem with all eyewitness accounts of the actual sinking. The instant that the ship's lights went out, the whole area would have been plunged into impenetrable darkness. With eyes unaccustomed to this Stygian blackness, the watchers would have seen nothing at all. Charles Hendricksen, who was watching from boat 1, said that he could not see the ship clearly, only her outline. When she sank they were left in total darkness.[38]

With young Jack Thayer on the upturned collapsible boat was Second Officer Lightoller, who was also watching the ship's final moments. He described what he saw from the moment he first scrambled aboard the small boat: 'At this time the whole of the third funnel was, I think, still visible, and the vessel was slowly raising her stern out of the water. The ship did not break in two and could not be broken in two.[39] The ship was at about 60° when the lights went out, but the stern continued to rise until it was vertical.'[40]

John Collins, who was washed overboard from somewhere amidships also noted that the ship's lights stayed on even after the stern lifted clear of the water. He was under water for about 2min and when he surfaced the lights still blazed.[41]

Both of the other two surviving officers, who claimed to have actually watched the ship sink, Pitman and Lowe, agreed with Lightoller inasmuch as the ship did not break in two at the surface.[42] The technical journals of the day were in full agreement with the ship's officers.

Nonetheless, several surviving crew members did believe that the huge hull had snapped in two during the final moments. Joseph Scarrott said, 'When she sank the after part broke.'[43] Frederick Scott thought that she broke behind the aft funnel.[44] Poigndestre thought that the ship had broken at the forward funnel.[45] Thomas Granger

(Ranger) said, 'The forward end went underneath and seemed to break off.'[46] George Symons thought that the ship snapped in two between the third and fourth funnels.[47]

Whether or not the ship had broken in two was immaterial to those people either in or on the lifeboats, or to those struggling in the icy water. The ship had gone and they were alone and in the dark. Those in the water who could reach either collapsibles A or B fought to get aboard.

The people in boat 4, which was still relatively close to the ship when it sank, managed to haul seven people from the water, two of whom died in the lifeboat from the effects of even a couple of minutes' immersion in the bitterly cold sea.

We know:

- The variety of ways that, according to his own accounts, Second Wireless Officer Harold Bride escaped from the sinking ship;
- How unlikely are the stories told by many of those who supposedly were saved by collapsible boat B.

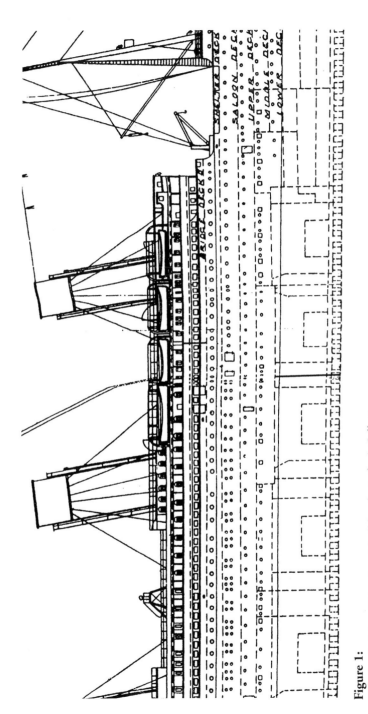

Figure 1:
Showing height of Number 6 bulkhead. *Author's Collection*

Figure 2:
Showing position of the fireman's passage beneath the forward holds. *Author's Collection*

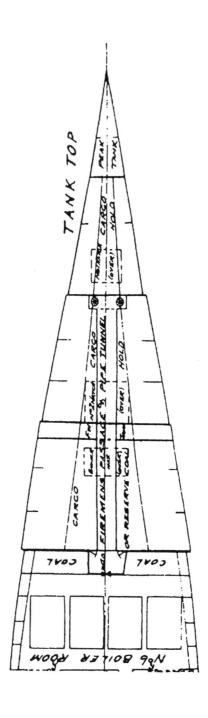

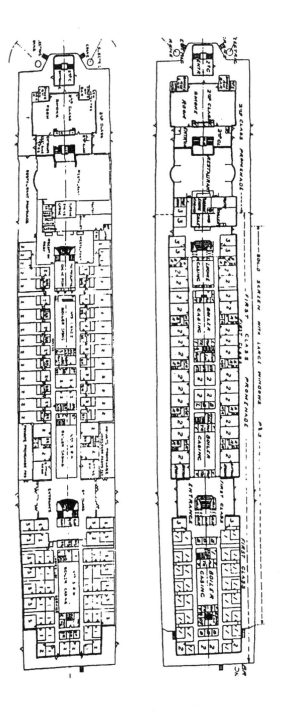

Figure 3:
B deck plans showing difference in layout between *Titanic* and *Olympic* (*Olympic* at top). *Author's Collection*

Figure 4:
Olympic in 1911 with *Titanic*-style forecastle deck C and aft promenade deck B. *Harland & Wolff*

Figure 5:
Titanic with alterations to B and C decks complete. Harland & Wolff / Ulster Folk & Transport Museum (H1712)

Figure 6:
Titanic (background) and *Olympic*, October 1911 or March showing later C deck. *Harland & Wolff*

Figure 7:
Olympic on maiden voyage, showing original forecastle deck C layout. Not officially changed until 1914.
National Maritime Museum London (P1514)

Figure 8:
Titanic with forecastle deck cowling and unique C deck porthole layout. *David Hutchings Collection*

Figure 9:
Titanic in 1911, without joint in hull plates. *Harland & Wolff / Ulster Folk & Transport Museum (H1712 — detail)*

Figure 10:
Olympic in 1911, with joint in hull plates. *Harland & Wolff/Ulster Folk & Transport Museum (H1515)*

Figure 11:
Olympic in 1912, without joint in hull plates. *Harland & Wolff /
Ulster Folk & Transport Museum (H1825)*

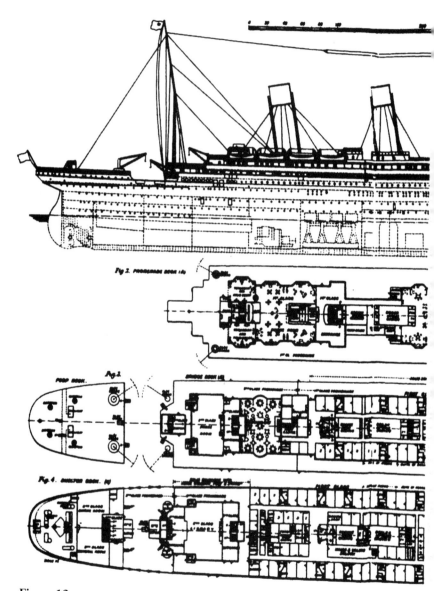

Figure 12:
Plan of *Titanic* in 1911. Note that the B deck was altered. *Author's Collection*

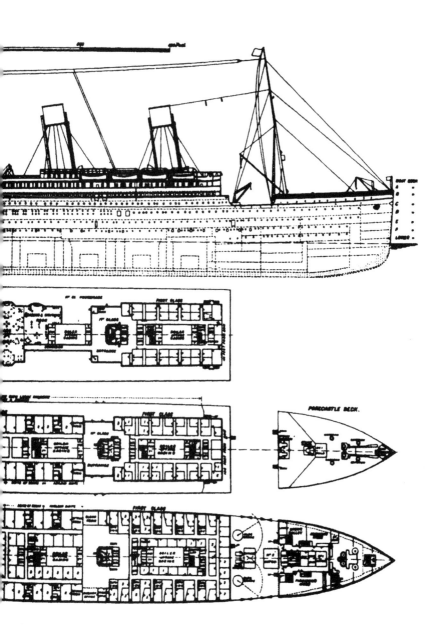

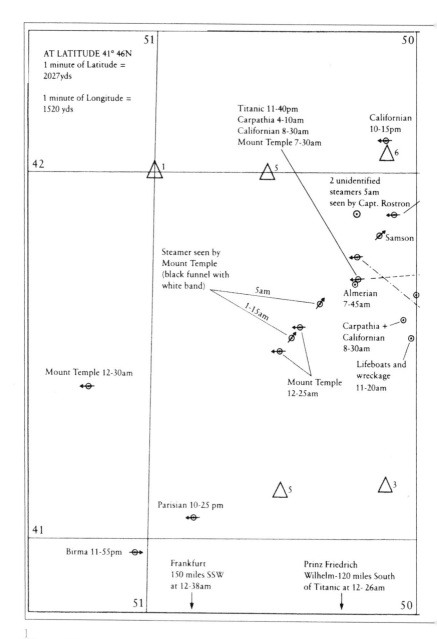

AT LATITUDE 41° 46N
1 minute of Latitude =
2027yds

1 minute of Longitude =
1520 yds

51

50

42

Titanic 11-40pm
Carpathia 4-10am
Californian 8-30am
Mount Temple 7-30am

Californian
10-15pm

6

1

5

2 unidentified
steamers 5am
seen by Capt. Rostron

Samson

Steamer seen by
Mount Temple
(black funnel with
white band)

5am

1-15am

Almerian
7-45am

Mount Temple 12-30am

Carpathia +
Californian
8-30am

Mount Temple
12-25am

Lifeboats and
wreckage
11-20am

5

3

Parisian 10-25 pm

41

Birma 11-55pm

Frankfurt
150 miles SSW
at 12-38am

Prinz Friedrich
Wilhelm-120 miles South
of Titanic at 12-26am

51

50

Figure 13:
Map showing position of ships between 10.15pm and 11.20am on the night
of 14/15 April 1912. *Amended from* The Riddle of the Titanic

5

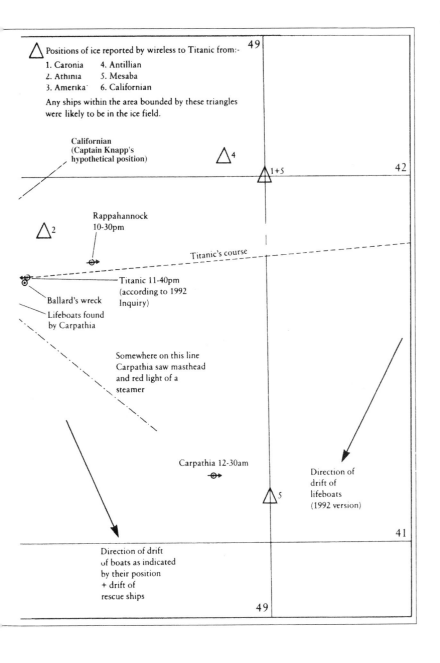

△ Positions of ice reported by wireless to Titanic from:-

1. Caronia   4. Antillian
2. Athinia   5. Mesaba
3. Amerika   6. Californian

Any ships within the area bounded by these triangles were likely to be in the ice field.

49

Californian
(Captain Knapp's
hypothetical position)

△4

△1+5   42

Rappahannock
10-30pm

△2

Titanic's course

Titanic 11-40pm
(according to 1992
Inquiry)

Ballard's wreck

Lifeboats found
by Carpathia

Somewhere on this line
Carpathia saw masthead
and red light of a
steamer

Carpathia 12-30am

△5

Direction of
drift of
lifeboats
(1992 version)

41

Direction of drift
of boats as indicated
by their position
+ drift of
rescue ships

49

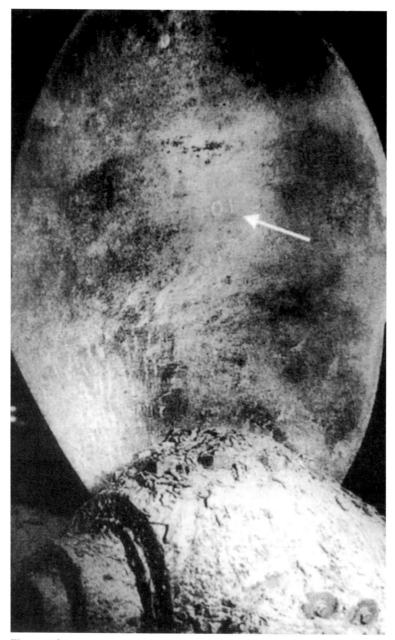

Figure 14:
Titanic's starboard main propeller as fitted to *Olympic* following the *Hawke* collision in October 1911.

20

Heroes and Villains

One cannot help wondering why Captain Smith kept the ship under way while the lifeboats were being loaded and lowered. Could it have been an attempt to reach the mystery ship whose lights were visible and at whom Boxhall's rockets were directed? Lightoller even expressed a wish that he might have a 6in gun so that he might attract the mystery ship's attention by putting a shot into her.

How many rockets were fired from *Titanic* and what colours were they? Both inquiries seemed to think that eight white rockets were fired, but the evidence of the witnesses suggests otherwise. The helmsman, who was on the bridge and later in a lifeboat and was in a position to see everything to do with the rockets, said that red, white and blue socket signals were sent up.

The ship's rockets came in boxes of a dozen and at least two boxes were brought to the bridge. Boxhall said that when he finished firing rockets there were still some left in the box. The inquiries took this to mean that between 6 and 10 rockets were fired (in the mistaken belief that only one box was used instead of the two, possibly three suggested by the evidence). A couple of rockets left in the box really means that at least 18, more likely 22 and perhaps more than 30 were expended in the vain hope of bringing the mystery ship to the rescue.

The inquiry findings were obviously brought in to implicate the *Californian*, laying stopped almost 20 miles to the north, and thereby provide a name for the mystery ship seen from *Titanic*. *Californian* and Captain Lord were completely innocent of the charges suggested by the courts of inquiry as was finally proven by Dr Robert Ballard's discovery of the wreck in 1985. However, there is a quite simple explanation for events aboard *Californian*, from which a mystery vessel was also seen, this one firing exclusively white rockets. This explanation, while exonerating Captain Lord from failing to go to the aid of the *Titanic* after seeing her distress signals, suggests that he may have been guilty of a far more serious crime, which we shall look at in the next chapter.

Why did Captain Smith order some of his lifeboats to row to the mystery ship, unload their passengers and return to the sinking liner? The only possible explanation is that he expected the stranger (if she was a stranger) to close the gap between them. Under the circumstances it is entirely understandable that Smith might have mistaken the stranger for another vessel he expected to see at the time. Unless he was completely out of touch with reality and his wireless operators, the captain must have had some idea of what ships were in the area. He must also have been aware that at least one nearby vessel — the *Rappahannock* — was in no condition to render any assistance having more than enough problems of her own: she had had her steering gear damaged that night. Later her owners wrote to the Board of Trade denying that they had any vessel in the area at the time.

More unsettling is the apparent lack of people on the Boat and A Decks — an absence so noticeable that many survivors mentioned it before, during and after the inquiries.

We know that the vast majority of Signor Gatti's employees were held prisoner in the second class saloon until the boats had gone — as they were only Italian waiters they didn't matter anyway, was the attitude at the time. We also know that a vast number of passengers appeared on deck very shortly before the ship sank. These are the people who obstructed Thayer's and Gracie's passage aft. Why these people only found their way onto the deck at such a late stage has never been satisfactorily explained. Crew members testified that all the passageways which would have allowed those in third class to find their way to the Boat Deck were open. This does not agree with the stories told by surviving third class passengers who tell of closed gates and crew members actively obstructing their way up. By far the most likely explanation for the lack of third class passengers on the Boat Deck until the last of the boats had gone is the one put forward by those third class passengers who survived. They stayed below because they had no choice in the matter. In the sentiment of the day, third class were no more important than the Italian restaurant staff.

Much the same feeling would have applied to the 'black gang', the crewmen who slaved in the engine and boiler rooms of the ship. However, these crew members, notoriously the most unruly element aboard, were at least able to help themselves to some extent; they knew their way about the ship, most of them having served aboard *Olympic*. At least some of these crewmen found their way to the boats, seemingly despite the best efforts of the officers who ordered them below after they first came up from the stokeholds or other nether regions of the ship.

Not so fortunate were the engineers, who were lost to a man.

Whether they stayed at their posts through a sense of duty or whether armed officers stood over them is not known, but we do know that the officers were not only armed but quite prepared to use their weapons.

That there was panic aboard is certain, although many witnesses at both inquiries said otherwise. Other witnesses said that passengers were shot down and even the officers testified that groups of passengers attempted to rush the boats. Again we see that the testimony of the surviving officers is suspect. Why would the officers say that there was no panic when there was, if not to show themselves in a better light than perhaps they deserved?

We know, from his own statement, that Lowe ordered a boy at gunpoint to vacate his seat in a lifeboat, before taking that seat himself. Ironically, when Lowe's boat was launched there was room for one more passenger. The boy could have gone anyway and Lowe need not have shown himself for the self-seeking individual he was.

Lightoller, instead of waiting for orders from his superior officer Murdoch, repeatedly left his post to badger Captain Smith into allowing him to swing out the boats before the captain and other senior officers were ready. This officer then made an unholy mess of loading the boats in his charge, preferring to send those boats away badly under-filled rather than allow any male passengers to go with them. Lightoller, too, would not allow boys to enter the boats and threatened one who had managed to find a place. Only the intervention of first class passengers still aboard, possibly John Jacob Astor among them, and female passengers in the boat saved the boy from being hauled from the boat at gunpoint and possibly shot. It is a sad reflection of events aboard that these officers, so demonstrably inadequate, managed to save their own lives while others, who performed their duties to the end, went down with the ship.

Events in the wireless cabin followed this typical pattern. From the time the captain gave the orders for a general distress call to be sent out, Jack Phillips, the first wireless operator, stuck to his duty, which is rather more than can be said of the second operator Harold Sidney Bride. At about 12.15am Captain Smith had gone to the wireless cabin. 'You had better get that assistance,' he said. He had put his head round the door earlier to warn the operators that a distress signal might be required. Bride had been off duty until midnight, but, soon after the collision, he had got up to help Phillips, or so he said. Phillips was in the bedroom when the captain made his second visit. When he heard the captain he came back into the wireless room and asked the skipper if he wanted them to use a distress call. 'Yes, at once,' the captain replied. As the sole surviving witness to events in the wireless cabin, we have to rely on Harold Bride's all too fallible memory.

Thirty-five minutes after the accident Jack Phillips sent the first distress call from the *Titanic*. In morse it was –.–. —.– –. . (CQD).

Bride went on to say that the captain left but then came back to the wireless room and asked Phillips what he was sending. 'CQD,' Phillips replied. Bride was then struck by 'the humour of the situation'. What he found humorous about being aboard a sinking ship, crying for help in the middle of the icy North Atlantic is baffling! 'Send SOS,' Bride suggested, 'It's the new call, and it may be your last chance to send it.' Phillips found the remark amusing and chuckled. The operators then indulged in light banter saying 'lots of funny things to each other'. Phillips had obviously taken Bride's remark about it being his last chance to send the new signal seriously and began sending ... – – – ... (SOS).

That first distress call was heard by the French steamer *La Provence* and the Canadian Pacific vessel *Mount Temple*; the latter tried to reply, but it was said that her wireless was not powerful enough to reach *Titanic*. The position given in this first call for help was incorrect and, as we have seen, given as 41º46'N, 50º24'W. Three minutes later *Ypiranga* received a CQD from *Titanic* saying that she required assistance and was in position 41º44'N, 50º24'W. This same message was received about 10 times by *Ypiranga*. Just 7min later, at 12.25am, the Cunard liner *Carpathia* received *Titanic's* CQD. This message said, 'Come at once. We have struck a berg. It's a CQD, O.M. [old man] Position 41º46'N, 50º14'W'. At the same time as *Carpathia* received the distress call, it was also picked up by the shore wireless station at Cape Race and relayed. A minute later a slightly longer message was heard from MGY (*Titanic*). 'CQD. Here corrected position 41º46'N, 50º14'W. Require immediate assistance. We have collision with iceberg. Sinking. Can hear nothing for noise of steam.' This message was received by *Ypiranga* and was repeated about 15 times over.

Then MGY (*Titanic*) sent, 'I require assistance immediately. Struck by iceberg in 41º46'N, 50º14'W.'

At 12.30am *Titanic* contacted *Frankfurt* saying, 'Tell your Captain to come to our help. We are on the ice.' At the same time, *Caronia* contacted *Baltic* informing her of *Titanic's* plight. Also at 12.30am *Mount Temple* heard MGY (*Titanic*) still calling for assistance and reversed course toward the stricken vessel.

This radio traffic continued unabated until 12.45am when for the first time *Titanic* called SOS. This signal was directed at *Olympic*, more than 500 miles away.

The ether was alive with wireless messages flashing between the vessels in the area. *Titanic* to *Celtic* at 12.50am. *Caronia* to *Baltic* at 12.50am. At 1am *Cincinnati* and *Olympic* both answered the distress call. *Titanic* replied to *Olympic* giving her position 41°46'N, 50°14'W.

Then, at 1.02am, *Titanic* called up *Asian* requesting assistance. At the same time *Virginian* called up *Titanic* but got no response because *Titanic* was already occupied. For the next almost quarter of an hour *Titanic* exchanged signals with *Olympic*. At 1.15am *Baltic* signalled *Caronia* requesting that they relay a message to *Titanic* saying that *Baltic* was on her way to the rescue. It took *Caronia* 10min to get the message through. In the meantime *Virginian* heard Cape Race inform *Titanic* that she was going to her assistance from 170 miles away.

From 1.25am *Titanic* and *Olympic* again worked together for about 15min. At 1.40am the shore station at Cape Race called *Virginian*, saying:

> 'Please tell your Captain this: The Olympic is making all speed for Titanic, but his [Olympic's] position is 40°32'N, 61°18'W. You are much nearer to Titanic. The Titanic is already putting women off in the boats, and he says the weather there is "calm and clear". The Olympic is the only ship we have heard say, "Going to the assistance of the Titanic." The others must be a long way from the Titanic.'

Five minutes later *Carpathia* received its last signal from *Titanic*. 'Engine room full up to the boilers.' At the same time *Mount Temple* heard *Frankfurt* calling *Titanic*. There was no reply.

Titanic's signals were growing weaker, indicating that the main generators were either failing or had failed. The emergency generators were able to power the emergency lighting and wireless under ordinary circumstances but they drew their steam from the main boilers. If steam pressure failed then so, automatically, did almost everything else. The Marconi equipment would continue to function for a while, as long as the back-up batteries lasted, if the operator had the opportunity to switch over to them. It would appear that Phillips' signal saying 'Engine room full up to boilers' actually meant that the remaining, working boiler rooms were filling up. There were no boilers in *Titanic's* engine rooms.

At 1.47am *Caronia* heard *Titanic*, but the signals were weak and unreadable. Then just a minute later *Asian* heard an SOS from *Titanic*. *Asian* replied but could get no response from the liner. At 1.50am *Caronia* heard *Frankfurt* and *Titanic* working together. This was the last time that *Caronia* heard *Titanic's* signals. At 1.55am Cape Race signalled *Virginian*, 'We have not heard *Titanic* for about half an hour. His power may be gone.' Then 5min later at 2am Virginia heard *Titanic* calling very faintly, power greatly reduced. Then silence.

This would be the time when, according to Bride, the captain released them from duty. When he collected up their money. When a stoker crept into the wireless room and attempted to steal the life-jacket off Phillips' back, whilst the operator continued to transmit the distress call. This unfortunate stoker reckoned without the lightning reactions of Bride and his murderous aptitude with a spanner!

Then, at 2.10am, *Virginian's* operator caught two 'V's very faintly '... – ... –'. The spark was similar to *Titanic's* and the *Virginian's* wireless man thought that Phillips was adjusting his spark, but it was almost certainly an intermittent signal. A badly distorted and partially missing SOS '... – – – ...'.

At 2.10am the water should have reached the wireless cabin. This would be the moment when, again according to Bride, Phillips and he abandoned the wireless room, leaving the unconscious stoker to his fate.[1] Yet again, according to Bride, after leaving the cabin Phillips walked or ran aft[2] either on the Boat Deck or on the roof of the officers' quarters while the heroic second wireless man went forward. As we know, water was apparently entering the wireless room when Bride left. He went forward to where he had seen crew members struggling to get collapsible B off the roof of the officers' quarters. Much to his surprise, the boat was still there.[3]

Still following Bride's record of events, that was the last he saw of Phillips except when he saw him later on collapsible B where Phillips confessed to failing to pass the *Mesaba* ice warning to the bridge, amongst other minor irregularities. Bride's story is a tissue of half truth and falsehood throughout. He endeavoured to cover his own mistakes and pass the buck onto his friend and colleague Phillips and so appear in a far more heroic light than he deserved. As we are about to see, Jack Phillips could not have been on collapsible B.

At the American Inquiry Bride told a similar story when he said that he and Phillips left the wireless room together as water started coming in. They then climbed onto the roof of the officers' house and

Phillips went aft. Bride went forward and assisted in pushing collapsible B off the roof of the officers' quarters onto the Boat Deck[4] where, a few moments later, it was taken overboard by the sea.

As the wireless room was situated on the Boat Deck and filling with water, we can be sure that the spot where collapsible B would have landed, some way forward of the wireless room on the same deck, was already submerged when Phillips and Bride left their cabin. If Bride helped to get collapsible B off the deckhouse roof then he must have done so well before the sea reached the wireless cabin.

At about 2.15am, *Titanic's* bridge submerged[5] and her mighty stern began to swing upwards into the night sky, where, as we know, it remained for about 5min[6] before the ship dived beneath the sea. As the rear end of the ship approached the vertical the lights went out, flashed on and were then extinguished forever as the power finally failed. The exact time was 2.17am.

At 2.17am *Virginian* received the last CQ from *Titanic*. *Virginian's* wireless operator had great difficulty reading the signal because Phillips' spark was blurred and ragged, hardly surprising as the *Titanic's* wireless cabin must have been almost full of water by this time, with more pouring in by the second. The signals ended abruptly as *Titanic's* power failed. 'It thus appears that the Marconi apparatus was at work until within a few minutes of the foundering of the *Titanic*,'[7] complete and independent evidence that even when *Titanic's* wireless room was below the surface of the sea, Jack Phillips was still at his post, trying to summon aid. In all sense, it could be no other hand on the Morse key but Phillips'. Bride had already left the ship. The only other occupant of the wireless room, according to Bride, was the unconscious fireman, whose knowledge of Morse code would be rather sketchy at best, I suspect. The CQ received by *Virginian* at 2.17am is conclusive proof that Bride lied about what had happened aboard *Titanic*, as he lied about how and when he left the vessel and events thereafter.

As with most of those credited with hero status after the *Titanic* disaster, Bride's reputation as one of the more noble creatures aboard is entirely undeserved. That there were heroes from amongst the crew is undeniable, but unfortunately none of them seem to have made their escape aboard collapsibles A and B, or any other lifeboat.

The true heroes of the *Titanic* were those who helped others to save themselves or gave up their place in a boat to someone whose need they considered greater; people like the young lady who gave up her seat in a lifeboat to a married woman with children.

Officers like Wilde, Murdoch and Moody could easily have made their escapes but did not, preferring to put their passengers' safety above their own. Moody refused to leave even when ordered to by Murdoch, saying, 'There is plenty of time yet.'

Wallace Hartley, band master, and the rest of the orchestra, whose names should be recorded so that all may know them, continued to play their instruments in the finest tradition until the angle of the deck made it impossible for them to keep their feet. The effect on morale aboard the sinking liner of the band's selfless dedication is incalculable. What tune they played at the end is unimportant. The fact that they were playing at all is what counts.

The only reason there is any doubt as to what was being played is Bride's dubious testimony, he being the only survivor to remember *Autumn* as the last hymn. If Bride was telling the truth about his escape, then he was underneath collapsible B when the band played their last tune and if he wasn't telling the truth about his escape, and he wasn't, then how can we believe his account of what tune he heard? The general consensus of opinion appears to be that the band played Nearer My God to Thee, which just happened to be Hartley's favourite hymn. This was the tune played at the funeral of Reginald Robertson Lee (Henry Reginald Lee), *Titanic's* starboard lookout at the time of the collision, who never forgot the band's conduct.[8]

The ship's engineers, who kept the lights, pumps and generators running right to the end,[9] were all lost. This group of crew members made no attempt to leave the ship but remained at their posts, keeping the vital power supply going until the need for power had gone.

The postal workers tried so desperately to save the mail entrusted to their care. These men went with that mail to the bottom of the North Atlantic.

The male passengers stood back so that the women and children could be saved, many lying to their families in order to persuade them to leave.

These, and many more like them, were the heroes of the *Titanic*. Not a few self-seeking officers and passengers who mendaciously talked their way into the history books.

We know now that:

- The number of rockets fired from *Titanic* is virtually certain to have been greater than the eight usually believed;
- The vast majority of third class passengers only reached the boat deck after the last of the lifeboats had gone;
- Thanks to the last wireless signal from the liner being picked up by the *Virginian*, the story told by Bride, describing his escape, is untrue.

21

Californian

Almost 20 miles to the north of *Titanic*, in 42°5'N, 57°7'W, the Leyland vessel SS *Californian* lay with her engines stopped, drifting with the ice.

To begin to understand what happened aboard the *Californian* we must go back to shortly before she began her voyage from London to Boston.[1] But first a brief description of the vessel and her captain.

Launched at Dundee in Scotland on 26 November 1901, the *Californian* was 447ft 6in long by 53ft 6in broad. As yard number 159, she was built to the specifications set out by her prospective owners, Frederick Leyland & Company Ltd (the Leyland Line) and had a gross registered tonnage of 6,223. Designed primarily for the cotton trade, the vessel was constructed with cavernous cargo holds specially to contain such extremely bulky cargo.

During construction the Leyland Line was taken over by J. P. Morgan's IMM company. To make the new ship more versatile and useful to the new owners, the upper bridge deck was lengthened and 19 staterooms were included. Although certificated to carry 47 passengers, a more normal complement would be 35. The passenger accommodation was on the port side of the ship, while the starboard cabins were for the ship's officers, engineers and stewards. The remainder of the crew were housed under the forecastle head, in the usual manner. Although primarily cargo vessels, ships of this sort were not uncommon during the great age of ocean voyaging. Nor were they any less well appointed, with a view toward passenger comfort, rivalling the best passenger liners of the day. *Californian's* passengers' dining saloon was handsomely panelled in Hungarian ash and satinwood with teak frames. The seats were upholstered in moquette (deep loop pile wool on cotton).

The smoking room had oak panelling and was upholstered in tooled leather. On the floor were non-slip rubber tiles. Electric lighting was standard throughout the ship. The maiden voyage of the *Californian* began on 31 January 1902.

In 1911 the *Californian* was taken over by her fourth captain to date, Stanley Lord. Lord was born in Bolton on 13 September 1877[2] and had joined the West Indian & Pacific Steam Navigation Company in 1897 after first going to sea as a cadet in 1891. He had served as second officer on the *Lurlie* and then, when Leyland took over the line in 1900,[3] Lord was taken over as well. Within the year the Leyland Line itself was swallowed up by IMM.[4] He obtained his Master's Certificate in February 1902 and his Extra Master's three months later, on 3 May. He served in *Antillian* from August 1904 until January 1906, mainly as chief officer, but in 1906 he took over as captain and remained as such for a further five months.[5] He then skippered a series of Leyland Line vessels, first *Antillian* then *Louisiana* and the *William Cliff* before assuming command of the *Californian* in March 1911[6] at a salary of £240 per annum.[7]

On 20 February 1912 *Californian* had left New Orleans with a cargo of cotton, bound for Le Havre, France. On her arrival on 20 March it was discovered that 55 bales were 'country damaged'. *Californian's* owners would have been less than pleased at finding these bales had arrived at their destination in less than perfect condition. Captain Lord, although probably blameless, would as master of the vessel have been held responsible for the damaged cargo.

The Leyland Line had something of a reputation for squeezing the very most out of their ships and their masters. There was a joke on this subject going the rounds at about the time of the *Titanic* disaster. A ship at sea passes another so heavily laden that almost the entire hull is below water. The captain radios 'Have just passed four funnels heading west, presumed Leyland steamer.'[8] While not being particularly humorous, the gag does tell us that it was common knowledge that Leyland Line steamers regularly sailed heavily, if not overloaded. This then was the line which Captain Lord served.

During the early days of April 1912 vast numbers of ships languished in port for want of fuel, owing to the coal strike. Would-be transatlantic travellers champed at the bit, unable to find a ship. Passengers and seamen alike searched for any vessel with enough coal to make the passage and enough room for either passengers or crew.

Californian was one of those ships which lay idle for the first part of that month. Some sort of general cargo had come aboard; what it was is of no importance at this point. Without warning *Californian* was ordered to put to sea at once. From somewhere the coal for her hungry furnaces was found at short notice. (It can only have been stockpiled against just such an emergency.) There was no time to lose. Cyril Evans, *Californian's* wireless operator, hurried ashore to collect the latest Marconi Telegraph Communication Chart for the North

Atlantic of April 1912. This chart should have showed the approximate positions of ships at sea for the month and allowed wireless operators to work out what vessels could be contacted at whatever point in the voyage. This was a vital piece of paper as far as the wireless operator was concerned if he was to be able to carry out his duties with any efficiency. In his haste Evans picked up the wrong chart. When he returned to the ship he discovered that he had the Marconi chart for the South Atlantic — a disaster. However, so great was the urgency with which *Californian* was preparing for sea that the unfortunate Evans had not the time to fetch the correct chart from the offices ashore.[9] He would have to improvise.

At the time, the Leyland Line normally offered a second class passage every Saturday from London to Boston for £10, or a west to east passage for $50.[10] Despite the number of people who must have been prepared to take passage on the *Californian*, the passenger accommodation remained empty. There was a healthy profit to be made from carrying passengers, so this in itself is highly suspicious.

Californian sailed from London on 5 April 1912 with the wrong wireless chart and no passengers, clear indication that they were about some very urgent business that could not wait, no matter what it cost the company in lost fares. What could possibly be so important amongst the general cargo that it had to be got to sea in such a tremendous hurry but seemed to be in no such hurry to arrive at its destination? Events surrounding the *Californian* were to grow steadily more mysterious.

At a steady 10 or 11kts *Californian* made her way out onto the cold grey waters of the North Atlantic until by noon on 14 April she had reached position 42°5'N, 47°25'W.[11] At that time *Titanic* was about 40 miles to the north and 100 miles to the east, travelling at more than double *Californian's* speed.

During the afternoon *Californian's* course was altered so that longitude 51°W would be crossed in latitude 42°N. This was done in response to ice reports received on 9 and 13 April. Earlier, at about 6.30pm, she had passed three distinctive, flat-topped icebergs which had been reported to her by the *Parisien*. The bergs were about five miles to the south of *Californian*. The ship had then been in position 42°5'N, 49°9'W.[12] As this sighting took place more than 5hr before *Titanic* supposedly struck the berg, there can be no question of Captain Lord preparing an alibi[13] and it firmly establishes that his vessel was in latitude 42°5'N.

Captain Lord had taken what he considered to be normal precautions by doubling the lookouts and placing a man at the very front of the ship.[14] His attitude to ice was very different from that of *Titanic's* Captain Smith.

Californian hurried onward until, at 10.15pm, a brightness was detected along the western horizon. Captain Lord assumed, rightly, that this glow was caused by ice ('ice blink' as it was known).[15] As the *Californian* neared the ice the captain decided that it would be imprudent to attempt to navigate a passage through it before dawn. Captain Lord's sense of urgency seems to have deserted him completely at this time. At 10.21pm (10.33pm *Titanic* time) the captain rang down to the engine room for full astern and the helm was ordered hard a-port. The ship swung toward the northeast (east-north-east by compass) and slowed to a stop. Captain Lord then ordered the engines stopped but steam to be kept up throughout the night. For the remainder of the hours of darkness, the *Californian* would drift safely with the ice. The extra lookouts were sent below.[16]

With the field ice, icebergs and ship all drifting slowly in the same direction, all possibility of a serious collision had been averted. The master of the *Californian* should have been able to look forward to a good night's sleep. It would probably have been better for Captain Lord if he had done just that. However, that is not quite what happened.

Having stopped the *Californian* about half a mile from the edge of the ice field, Lord calculated the ship's position. To do this he used the ship's previous course, S89°W (true), the distance she had travelled since the noon position of 120 miles and a stellar observation taken at 7.30pm. Third Officer Groves told that they got perfectly good sights all day.[17] The position worked out by Captain Lord was 42°5'N, 50°7'W.[18] This position has been argued over ever since the latter part of April 1912, but it was worked out from sights taken by all of the officers, which agreed with one another, and was reinforced by sights taken the following day.[19]

Lord was just about to leave the bridge when he pointed out a light[20] on the starboard quarter,[21] to the eastward, to his third officer. The captain thought it was an approaching vessel, but Third Officer Groves thought it was merely a star.[22] Groves changed his opinion as the night wore on — so much so that he was later sure that the vessel in sight at 11.25pm, on their starboard quarter, had two masthead lights[23] (*Titanic* had only one[24]), was a passenger ship and showed her port side light.[25] At the time he reached this conclusion *Californian* was heading northeast and the mysterious vessel was coming toward them from a direction slightly to the west of due south.[26] If this unnamed vessel were *Titanic*, then at that time she was heading north-northeast. There is no record of the White Star liner ever being on this course.

It was a flat calm night with no moon, making it difficult to be sure where the horizon lay. Lord had already been fooled into thinking that stars, low on the horizon, were ships' masthead lights.[27] It was bitterly cold, the temperature having dropped to 27°F (-3°C).[28]

Lord made his way down to the Saloon Deck where he sent for the chief engineer, W. S. A. Mahan. When the engineer arrived, the skipper pointed out the light he had drawn to Groves' attention minutes earlier, which now clearly appeared to be a steamship approaching from the southeast. While the engineer was still on deck, the captain confirmed his instructions that steam should be kept up during the night in case the engines should be needed in a hurry.

At about 10.50pm the wireless operator met the captain on deck. Lord asked Evans, the operator, if he knew of any other vessels in the vicinity. 'Only the *Titanic*.' If only Evans had possessed the correct radio communication chart then he might conceivably have had some idea of what other ships were close by. As it was he could only guess how close another vessel might be from the strength of its wireless signals.

Pointing out the approaching steamer, Lord said, 'That's not the *Titanic*, she's a vessel close to us in size. You'd better contact *Titanic*, however, and let her know we're stopped in ice.' Evans left immediately to transmit the required message, which he did at about 10.55pm. The chances of confusing a small tramp steamer with a large liner were minimal simply because of the blaze of light emitted by the passenger vessels,[29] as Captain Lord well knew.

Evans managed to get the first half of his message through to the liner, 'We are stopped and surrounded by ice,' before *Titanic's* operator angrily cut him off with, 'Keep out! Shut up! You're jamming my signal. I'm working Cape Race.' Evans gave up and just listened to the traffic coming from the liner for a while. He wasn't put out by Phillips' apparent rudeness, it was normal practice for operators to talk to one another in this offhand manner. The larger, faster and more prestigious a vessel happened to be, the higher its rating as far as priority was concerned. Evans would have been quite familiar with wireless procedure as practised aboard White Star ships as he had served on the *Cedric* before transferring to *Californian*.[30]

As usual, Evans switched off his equipment at 11.30pm. (11.42pm *Titanic* time) and prepared for bed. It had been a long day, as usual, for the *Californian's* wireless operator; he had been on duty since 7am.[31] A 16.5hr day was quite normal Marconi routine aboard ship, especially ships which only carried one operator. For such devotion to duty Evans was paid the magnificent sum of £4 a month, and board. Senator Smith, at the American Inquiry, could not resist making a sarcastic comment, 'You have your board on the ship, and room? Four pounds a month and all this for a 105 hour week!'[32]

By the time that Cyril Evans switched his equipment off, the mystery vessel approaching *Californian* from the southeast, which had been only a white masthead light and what appeared to be white deck lights, was now showing her green (starboard) light as well.[33] Captain Lord estimated the mystery ship to be about five miles from the slowly drifting *Californian*, bearing southeasterly, broad on *Californian's* starboard bow.[34]

Californian's bridge was about 49ft above the waterline. Using the rule, V (distance in miles) = the square root of the height in feet above the waterline multiplied by 1.14, we see that the visible horizon (had there been one) would have been about eight miles from *Californian*.[35] The mystery ship's lights would be clearly visible to the master and officers of the Leyland steamer. Applying the same rule, *Californian's* lights would have been clearly visible to the lookouts in *Titanic's* crows-nest for a distance of about 12 miles.

Captain Lord ordered the officer of the watch, Third Officer Groves, to signal the stranger with the Morse lamp, but he could get no response.[36] Allowing for the 12min time difference between *Titanic* and *Californian*, this signalling was going on at just about or very slightly after the time of the collision, 11.40pm.

Ship's time changes with the vessel's longitude and clocks are usually set at midnight for the approximate position at noon the following day. The clocks aboard *Titanic* were to be put back by 47min during the first watch. As a westbound ship reached 40°W, the time recorded on wireless messages changed from GMT to NY time, and vice versa.[37]

Groves noted that this strange passenger vessel put her lights out and came to a halt at 11.40pm but failed to notify the captain,[38] although Captain Lord had noticed that she had stopped at about 11.30pm.[39] It was only after the deck lights had gone out that the stranger's red light became visible to Groves.[40] We know that *Titanic's* lights continued to burn brightly until after two o'clock the following morning.

At about five to 12 (11.55pm *Californian*, 12.5am *Titanic*) Ernest Gill, a donkeyman on the 8 to 12 watch, came on deck to smoke a cigarette. There was no smoking allowed between decks because of the combustible nature of the incredibly urgent cargo, whatever it might have been. Looking over the starboard rail Gill saw a 'very large steamer, about 10 miles away'. From the deck of *Californian* the visible horizon would have been about seven miles away. How the donkeyman managed to see a ship, by his own estimate at least three miles over the horizon, he never explained. Gill watched this steamer for a full minute (obviously it didn't take him long to smoke a cigarette). Going below, he told a mate, William Thomas, who was in bed, that he had seen a steamer 'going full steam'. Thomas later denied that Gill had mentioned a steamer or rockets, but said that they had only talked about the ice.[41] Gill was very precise about time, but even if *Titanic* and *Californian* had been keeping the same time, which they were not, then Gill sighting a large steamer going full steam happened at least 16min after *Titanic* struck.[42]

'After midnight, we slowly blew round and showed him our red light' said Captain Lord,[43] describing how his ship was drifting.

About half an hour later, at 12.30am (12.42am *Titanic*), unable to sleep the donkeyman went on deck again. He had been there for about 10min when he first noticed a white rocket, 'about 10 miles away on the starboard side. I thought it must be a shooting star (there was a meteorite shower that night.) In seven or eight minutes I saw distinctly a second rocket in the same place.' Gill didn't attach a great deal of importance to the pyrotechnic signals, saying 'I do not know if anyone else did who saw them, but I did not.'[44] 'It was not my business to notify the bridge or the lookouts …' Shortly after seeing the second rocket Gill turned in for the night.

According to Gill's statement, he had seen just two rockets, one at about 12.52am (*Titanic*) and the second at approximately 1am (*Titanic*). He said that he saw the white stars thrown out by the rockets but he didn't hear the reports as the rockets exploded, nor did he hear the roar of escaping steam, even though on such a night the sounds could well have carried. Although he was watching the mysterious vessel for the better part of 20min, Gill did not notice any flashing Morse lamp as perhaps he might have done if the ship was the *Titanic*. Interestingly, Groves said that he saw the mystery ship's lights go out at 11.40pm, but Gill says that he saw this same ship with lights all ablaze after 12 o'clock.[45]

Californian's carpenter, McGregor, told a somewhat different story to the Clinton Daily Item while the ship was in America following the disaster. The paper ran an article based on McGregor's story:

'… That the Californian was within 10 miles of the Titanic when she sank. At the time the Californian was sailing just ahead of the Titanic but had seen a big field of ice and in order to avoid it had turned south and went round the big mass. It was also said that the wireless operator on board the Californian notified the Titanic and all other vessels in the vicinity of the presence of the big ice field.

'It was shortly after the Californian had gone by the ice field that the watch saw the rockets which were sent up by the Titanic as signals of distress. The officer on watch, it is said, reported this to the boat (sic) (captain) but he failed to pay any attention to the signals excepting to tell the watch to keep his eye on the boat. At this time the two boats were about 10 miles apart. It being in the night the wireless operator on board the Californian was asleep at the time.

'It is said that those on board the Californian could see the lights of the Titanic very plainly, and it is also reported that the Titanic saw the Californian. Finally the first mate on the Californian, who with several of the officers had been watching the Titanic, decided he would take a hand in the situation and so roused the wireless operator and an attempt was made to communicate with the Titanic. It was then too late, as the apparatus on the Titanic was out of commission. The operator did, however, catch the word "Titanic" which was probably being sent from the Carpathia or some other boat, and this information was given to the Captain. He immediately ordered the boat to stop and was very much concerned as to the fate of the Titanic after that, but it was far too late. The Californian had during this time continued ahead under full steam and by the time the name of the boat was ascertained it is believed to have been about 20 miles away.

'The Californian turned back and started for the scene but it is a very slow boat as compared with the Carpathia and several others, and although the Carpathia was about 50 miles away when it first learned of the accident it was able to get there much sooner than the Californian. The next morning the Californian learned from the Carpathia that it had reached the scene and that the Titanic had gone down and that all the survivors had been picked up. According to McGregor, the captain of the Californian had the appearance of being 20 years older after the news reached him. It is the belief of McGregor that the captain will never be in command of the Californian again and he told Mr Frazer [his cousin] that he would positively refuse to sail under him again and that all the officers had the same feeling. Mr Frazer says that according to the story as told him, that had the captain of the Californian turned back when the rockets were first seen, hundreds of the Titanic's passengers could have been taken off on that boat.'[46]

The newspaper article bears very little resemblance to what really happened, but it is fairly typical of the sort of scurrilous attacks that Captain Lord was subjected to.

We know that:

- Captain Lord of the *Californian*, instead of turning in for the night, was clearly expecting something to occur that would require his immediate attention;
- Only white rockets were seen from the *Californian* (*Titanic* sent up red, white and blue signals)

Californian — Officers' Evidence

Second Officer Herbert Stone came on duty at about midnight and found the captain at the wheelhouse door. Lord pointed out the steamer, which by this time was a little astern of *Californian's* starboard beam. The captain also pointed out the field of dense ice to the south of the *Californian*. Lord then told Stone that he would not be going to bed but that he intended to rest, fully dressed, on the chart room settee. He then left the bridge at 12.15am.[1]

Captain Lord was a little over 6ft tall, while the chart room settee was only 5½ft long. Clearly the skipper was not anticipating a good night's sleep. The best he could hope for was a night of fitful dozing in the steam-heated chart room.

Californian was in no danger from the ice, as she was drifting with it. The watch officers on the bridge would be well able to handle anything which might arise without disturbing the captain's rest. There is no apparent reason for Lord to have subjected himself to the rigours of a night on the chart room settee rather than in his own bunk.

Second Officer Stone took over the watch from Third Officer Groves shortly before 12.10am (about 12.20am *Titanic*). All times from *Californian* are imprecise because there was no clock on the upper bridge and times must therefore be taken from individual officers' watches or be estimated.[2] The Third Officer had checked *Californian's* heading against the compass and found it to be east-northeast. In so doing, he would have allowed for the compass variation of about 24°W and deviation about 2°E, giving a known error of 22°W.[3] He appraised Stone of this and that the ship was swinging to starboard.[4] He also drew Stone's attention to the mystery ship off the starboard beam and told him that he had already tried to contact her by Morse lamp, without success. Groves had previously noted that the mystery ship was slowly changing her bearing and was coming round to the southwest.[5]

Stone took note of the stranger's position in relation to that of the *Californian*. To him it appeared to be dead abeam, on the starboard side, south-southeast of the Leyland vessel. As Stone studied the stranger, he noticed that she had only one masthead light[6] and was showing them a red (port) side light.[7] He could also see some indistinct lights which he took to be open doors, portholes, or deck lights — hardly a description of the brilliantly illuminated *Titanic*. Stone judged the mystery ship to be a small tramp steamer, about five miles off.[8] He was sure that there wasn't a second masthead light or he would have been able to see that as well.[9]

At 12.10am (12.22am *Titanic*) Stone tried the Morse lamp for himself but, even though he could clearly see the mystery ship's lights indicating that the reverse would also be true,[10] there was no reply to his signals. *Californian's* Morse lamp was visible at up to about 10 miles and the mystery ship was only about half that distance away.[11]

The *Californian's* apprentice officer, James Gibson, joined Stone and Groves on the bridge at approximately 12.15am (12.27am *Titanic*). He, too, tried to attract the attention of the mysterious and peculiarly uncommunicative stranger with the Morse lamp.[12] At first he thought that the other vessel was answering, but when he studied her through his binoculars he saw that the flickering light he had taken for a Morse lamp now appeared to be a masthead light,[13] and was probably an oil lamp. The apprentice did notice that there was a flash on the deck as a rocket was launched from the mystery ship,[14] but he heard no report as the rocket exploded, releasing its shower of stars.[15]

Gibson described what he saw of the mystery ship through his binoculars. He, too, was sure that she had a single masthead light,[16] but he thought that she looked 'queer'. He was convinced that the tramp steamer he was observing had a heavy list to starboard because her port light 'seemed to be higher out of the water than it was before'.[17] He, like Stone, was quite certain that it was not a passenger ship.

We know that Boxhall did use *Titanic's* Morse lamp in an attempt to contact a mystery ship visible from the stricken liner, with results not unlike those of Stone, Groves and Gibson. The red light seen by all three officers, to the south of *Californian*, indicates a ship steaming west to east, the reverse of *Titanic's* heading.[18] While it is possible that the officers on the bridge of the *Californian* were looking at the same vessel as those on *Titanic*, it is not likely. The watchers aboard the White Star ship saw no rockets fired by their mystery ship.

About 20min later, at 12.35am (12.47am *Titanic*) Captain Lord, who had been resting in the chart room, blew up the voice-pipe connecting his own cabin with the bridge, sounding the whistle. When Stone replied, Lord enquired whether the mystery ship had moved. Stone told him that it had not and that, despite repeated attempts with the Morse lamp, the other ship maintained a stubborn silence.

Ten minutes after his conversation with the captain, Stone noticed a flash of light in the sky in the direction of the anonymous steamer.[19]

'[It was] just above that [nearby] steamer. I thought nothing of it as there were several shooting stars about, the night being fine and clear with light airs and calms. Shortly after, I observed another [light] distinctly over the steamer: in fact, it appeared to come from a good distance beyond her. Between then and about 1.15 I observed three more, the same as before, and all white in colour ...'[20]

He did not think that all of the lights he saw were rockets.[21]

Californian's second officer saw five white rockets over a 15–20min period, the last at about 1.10am[22], which he reported to Captain Lord.[23] According to Gibson, however, Stone told him that he had seen the five rockets at 12.55am.[24]

Stone heard nothing of the rockets detonating with a sound that 'seemed to split the night in two', above those on *Titanic*.[25] He was so sure that the rockets might have come 'from a greater distance' than the vessel they had in sight that he said as much to the captain 'the next day' and 'to the chief officer and to the third officer in conversation'.[26] By soon after one o'clock the stranger had changed her bearing from *Californian* and was steaming away to the southwest.[27] The rockets seen from *Californian* rose to no more than half the height of the stranger's mast and must therefore have been ordinary rockets or Roman candles[28] and not the much more powerful socket signals *Titanic* was sending up. All of the signals seen from *Californian* were white.[29] (Remember that *Titanic* fired an assortment of red, white and blue signals.)

The second officer whistled down the speaking tube to the captain's cabin. Lord must have left the chart room and crossed to his own cabin (next door) to answer, which tells us that he was wide awake. The time was 1.15am (1.27am *Titanic*).[30] Lord asked if the rockets were private signals, to which Stone replied, 'I don't know. But they are all white.' Captain Lord then ordered the second officer to keep signalling the mysterious stranger, saying, '... when you get an answer let me know by Gibson.'

Stone continued to try, with the Morse lamp, to raise the nearby steamer without success, while the captain returned to the chart room settee.

Why would the captain again leave his own comfortable cabin with its full-size bunk and direct communication via the voice-pipe to the bridge, to take his ease on the uncomfortably short chart room settee? He could with equal if not more direct availability to the bridge have remained in the comfort of his own cabin. A possible explanation might be that Lord was well aware that resting in a warm room after exposure to the cold night air might lull him to sleep and was doing his best to avoid that happening.

The Leyland vessel continued its clockwise swing through south until by 1.50am she was heading west-southwest. The mystery ship was now over the port bow bearing southwest by west. By 2am (2.12am *Titanic*) she began to steam away, changing her bearing to southwest ½ west.[31] In the time she had been in sight, this vessel had moved between five and eight miles[32] and her bearing from *Californian* had altered by more than six points (more than 70º).[33] Her red (port) light disappeared and only the stern light remained visible. In his report to the captain, Stone wrote 'the vessel was steaming away fast …' The apprentice agreed that the mysterious ship had steamed away to the southwest.[34]

Remembering his orders, Second Officer Stone dispatched Gibson to the chart room to let the captain know what the stranger was doing. Stone, describing the incident, said:

> 'I told Gibson to go down to the master and be sure and wake him up and tell him that altogether we had seen eight of these white lights, like white rockets, in the direction of this other steamer; that this steamer was disappearing in the southwest, that we had called her up repeatedly on the Morse lamp and received no information whatsoever.'[35]

Captain Lord was dozing on the settee when the apprentice put his head around the chart room door. Gibson thought that the captain was wider awake than was actually the case when he delivered his message, as ordered by Stone. He said that Captain Lord acknowledged his report, saying 'All right,' and then enquiring about the rockets: 'Are you sure there were no colours in them?' He then asked what time it was. The apprentice returned to the bridge and reported the conversation to Stone.

There is an important deduction to be drawn from Captain Lord's continual attention to the colour of the pyrotechnic signals seen from his ship.

Gibson told Lord Mersey at the British Inquiry that Captain Lord was awake when he delivered his message about the rockets at 2.05am. Notwithstanding this, he had told Stone on his return to the bridge that he had wakened the captain up,[36] as instructed by the second officer.[37]

Although Captain Lord had answered the apprentice, Gibson, he had not been fully awake and had no recollection of the junior officer's visit to the chart room. This is hardly surprising as the captain must have spent a good deal of the day on the bridge of the *Californian* exposed to the biting cold. As a direct result of this he was likely to be suffering from the onset of hypothermia (a general lowering of the body temperature). Very shortly after going from the cold exposed bridge to the warm chart room the captain would inevitably have begun to doze (a well-known effect of mild hypothermia suffered by most who spend a good deal of time exposed to extremes of cold; and we know the evening of 14 April 1912 was extremely cold in that area). As far as Captain Lord was aware, no one had entered his cabin between 1.30 and 4.30am.

Cyril Furmstone Evans, *Californian's* wireless operator, had turned in for the night at 11.30pm. However, a final ironic twist of fate was still to take place. Third Officer Groves went off duty at midnight, although he didn't actually leave the bridge until at least 12.10am. Instead of going directly to his own cabin, he stopped off at the wireless room at about 12.15am (12.27am *Titanic*). Evans was in his bunk, half asleep, when the third officer disturbed his well-earned rest.[38] Groves was interested in the new, electronic marvel invented by Mr Marconi, and had taken the trouble to learn the basics of Morse code. Although not up to the standards required by the Marconi Company, the Third Officer could get the gist of what he heard. He spent a considerable amount of time in the wireless room listening to the traffic and Evans was used to these nocturnal visits. Groves asked Evans what ships he was in contact with. Evans replied, 'Only the *Titanic*.'[39] Evans thought that, judging by the strength of her signals, *Titanic* was about 100 miles away at 11 o'clock.[40]

Had Evans been wider awake he might well have reminded Groves to wind up the clockwork mechanical signal detector. Groves put on the headphones and switched on the wireless receiver, but, because of the disabled signal detector, he heard nothing.[41] After a few minutes he gave up, switched off the set, removed the headphones and left the cabin. When Groves tried the wireless, a mere 19.5 miles to the south and west, *Titanic* was already transmitting her call for help. How differently might events have turned out if only the *Californian's* Third Officer had known that the clockwork signal detector required winding.

At the British Inquiry Lord was asked why he hadn't had the wireless operator wakened when rockets were first reported to him. Lord replied, 'When? At 1 o'clock in the morning?'[42] Lord would have known that it was all but useless to attempt to contact another ship with but a single operator. He appreciated that even Marconi employees had to sleep sometimes.

Stone and Gibson remained on the bridge where they kept an eye on the strange vessel to their south. The apprentice had already noted that the stranger had a heavy list to starboard. It will be recalled that *Titanic* listed heavily to port.

At the British Inquiry, Lord Mersey asked Stone why he had reported the disappearance of the mystery ship to the captain, as if there were some significance to it. 'Why could you not have told him in the morning? Why wake the poor man up?' Stone answered correctly, 'Because it was my duty to do so, and it was his duty to listen to it.'[43]

Stone described the disappearance of the mystery ship as gradual, the stern light slowly fading as if the vessel were steaming away from them. He did not think that the disappearance of the lights had in any way the appearance of a ship foundering.[44]

At exactly 3.40am, the apprentice saw first one and then two more white rockets.[45] He was sure of the time (3.52am *Titanic*) as it was shortly before dawn and he was to go off duty at 4am. They were a long way off[46] and were almost certainly rockets fired by *Carpathia* as she raced up.

Although Gibson was so sure of his timing it was disputed by Second Officer Stone. At the British Inquiry Stone said that 'At about 3.20am just about half past three, as near as I can approximate, Gibson reported to me he had seen a white light in the sky to the southward of us, just about on the port beam. We were heading about west at that time. I crossed over to the port wing of the bridge and watched its direction with my binoculars. Shortly after, I saw a white light in the sky right dead on the beam.' Two more lights quickly followed the first seen by Stone. He did not believe that these lights were rockets and did not report seeing them to the Captain.[47]

Second Officer Stone testified that during the earlier part of the watch, he saw a single masthead light[48] and a red side light about five miles off to the south-southeast, which was substantially the same as Gibson said. Stone also said that he only saw a possible five rockets before 2am but saw the three later ones which Gibson reported and which Stone agreed appeared to come from a different vessel from the first batch. Stone did not think that all of the first five rockets he saw, if they were rockets and not shooting stars, came from the ship he could see. On the contrary, he was of the opinion that only the third rocket he saw came from the vessel visible to the southward. He thought that the others came from another ship further off.[49] The reason he thought this was because the rockets only appeared to reach half as high as the masthead of the mystery ship.[50] Stone wondered if the 'rockets' were not rockets at all but Roman candles, which were used as company night signals between ships. These Roman candles only threw a star or ball of light to a height of about 50ft. However, the Second Officer did notice that as the bearing of the light changed, so did the bearing of the rockets.[51] Stone was also quite sure that the ship to southward had only the one masthead light and not the two that the apprentice thought he saw when asked about events that night on later occasions. At the British Inquiry both men agreed that they saw only one masthead light.

At about 4am *Californian's* chief officer, G. F. Stewart, came onto the bridge to begin his watch. Stone and Gibson reported the rockets and light that they had seen. Stewart looked out toward the south-southwest and saw a four-masted steamer.[52] 'There she is!' he said, believing that he was looking at the same ship that had been visible earlier and which had moved off and then returned.[53] 'There is that steamer. She looks all right.'

Stone replied, 'That's not the same steamer. She has two masthead lights.'[54]

It was Stewart's opinion that the mysterious rocket-firing ship that Stone and Gibson had told him of was replying to yet another vessel further to the north.[55]

As it began to grow light at about 4.30am the chief officer left the bridge to awaken the captain, who was still dozing in the chart room.[56] Stewart first mentioned that the ship which had fired the rockets was still to the south of them when he woke Lord.[57]

Even after he reached the bridge Captain Lord did not order the *Californian* under way immediately but waited until it was fully light before deciding in which direction lay the safest way through the ice.

Eventually he saw clearer water to the west and ordered the engines to stand by, which was entirely superfluous as the engines had been standing by all night.

It was about 5.15am when *Californian* got under way.[58] At about the same time, Chief Officer Stewart drew the captain's attention to a four-masted steamer with a yellow funnel, to the south-southeast of them, about eight miles away.[59] Stewart told Lord he was concerned that this vessel might be in distress, damaged by the ice. He then told the captain that Second Officer Stone had told him this ship had fired several rockets during his watch. When, at the British Inquiry, it was suggested to Stewart that the ship might possibly have been the *Carpathia*, he strenuously denied it.[60]

For the very first time Captain Lord had reason to believe another ship in the area might be in trouble. He ordered Stewart to wake the wireless operator, which he did at about 5.40am,[61] and find out if the vessel needed assistance.

Stewart said that when he woke Evans, 'I told him to get out and see what the ship was to southward.' Evans had a slightly different recollection of what Stewart said: 'Wireless, there is a ship that has been firing rockets in the night. Will you come in and see if you can find out what is wrong — what is the matter.'[62] All Captain Lord wanted Evans to signal the other vessel for was to 'get an idea of what kind of ice field we had gotten into'.[63] If Evans was roused from a sound sleep then it is possible that he would have no clear memory of what was said to him immediately on waking.

Evans transmitted his first wireless signal of the day, 'CQ', the standard Marconi signal meaning, 'All stations, someone answer.' Almost immediately the *Frankfurt* replied, saying, 'Do you know that the *Titanic* has sunk during the night, collided with an iceberg?' Even as Evans was acknowledging *Frankfurt's* message *Virginian* joined in. It was from her that *Californian* received the official news that *Titanic* had sunk, and the position of the disaster. Evans wrote the details on a piece of paper, including the position and handed it to the chief officer, who took it straight to the captain, on the bridge.

Upon receiving the news that *Titanic* had sunk Captain Lord kept a cool head and ordered the chief officer to verify the position saying, 'You must get me a better position, we don't want to go on a wild goose chase.'[64]

Before this early morning exchange of wireless messages, a very strange incident had occurred. *Mount Temple* had informed everyone else that *Titanic* had sunk. *Mount Temple's* wireless operator was later to confirm this.[65] What he could not explain was how he could possibly have known the White Star liner had sunk when the only people in possession of that fact were on board *Carpathia* or in *Titanic's* lifeboats. The information was not broadcast until some time later. One possible explanation is that *Mount Temple* was close enough to see the liner sink.

Captain Lord worked out a course to *Titanic's* last known position, 41°46'N, 50°14'W. To reach the site of the sinking, *Californian* would have to steer S16°W for about 19.5 miles. Once Captain Lord was sure of what direction to move in he made no mistakes. If anything, he was even more coldly efficient than Captain Rostron. *Californian* got under way and had no difficulty in finding *Carpathia*, indicating that either both positions were accurate or adrift by the same amount.[66] For the first three or four miles of the journey to *Titanic's* last reported position *Californian* was 'Just crawling through the ice.'[67] It would take her two and a half hours to reach the wreck site.[68]

As the Leyland vessel headed south, at 6.30am[69] the captain ordered a lookout, Benjamin Kirk, to be hauled up the foremast in a coal basket, where he would have a better field of vision than from the crow's-nest. Kirk, unlike *Titanic's* lookouts, was issued with a pair of binoculars and instructed to keep a sharp lookout for wreckage, boats or survivors. *Californian's* lookouts were not supplied with binoculars in the ordinary course of events.[70]

Slowly at first, the *Californian* pushed through the ice until she reached open water at about 6.30am or soon after. She then increased speed until she was moving at her top speed of about 13kts,[71] 70rpm. At the British Inquiry, Groves said that at about this time he was wakened by the chief officer, who told him he was wanted on deck. When he got on deck he 'saw some lifeboats with people in, ahead of us'. He then went to the bridge and noticed that their lifeboats were swung out. *Carpathia* was abeam of them, about five miles off on the port side.[72] We can only assume that Groves was mistaken as to the time.

In another version of his story, Groves was wakened by the sound of ropes being thrown onto the deck above him and realised that the boats were being prepared. Before he had time to wonder why, Stewart came into the cabin and told him to get up and go to the bridge. According to Groves in this version, Stewart said, 'The *Titanic* has sunk, and the passengers are all in the water ahead of us.'[73]

Californian made her way down the western edge of the ice field. At about 7.30am they came up to, and passed, the *Mount Temple*, laying stopped.[74] *Californian* pressed on and quickly passed the pink-funnelled *Almerian*,[75] another Leyland vessel but one with no wireless and therefore unaware of the disaster. Shortly after passing *Almerian*, another four-masted steamer was sighted to the south and east, laying stopped on the other side of the ice field with her derricks rigged over the foremost hatch.[76] Evans, after a certain amount of difficulty, had made contact and was able to verify that this newly sighted vessel was the *Carpathia*.[77]

Captain Lord continued southward until he saw a way through the ice and then altered course towards *Carpathia* when she was abeam of *Californian*, which is exactly how Captain Rostron described her approach from the southwest.[78] *Californian* came to a halt almost alongside *Carpathia* at about 8.30am just as the last of *Titanic's* lifeboats were being hauled aboard the rescue ship.

The facts, as we know them, paint a very different picture from that normally accepted. They certainly do not show the stationary *Californian* moving to within a few miles of the, at best, slowly moving *Titanic* before moving off again. Nor do they suggest that *Californian* and *Titanic* were, at any time, visible to one another. The mysterious vessels seen from both IMM ships were moving while neither *Titanic* nor *Californian* was under way at the time. Obviously the ship seen from *Titanic* was some vessel that has never been identified, as was the ship seen from the *Californian*. Where do these facts lead us?

That Cyril Evans had no time to correct his mistake in picking up the Marconi communication chart and that the ship sailed with no passengers argues that she left harbour with quite considerable urgency.

That coal was available to fill her bunkers, even though other, more prestigious, vessels lay idle because of the coal strike, indicates that the owners were well prepared for this pressing departure, before it became urgent.

Given that *Californian's* departure and subsequent voyage were urgent, it seems more than a little odd that Captain Lord would halt his ship for the night at the first sign of field ice. It will be remembered that *Californian* stopped before entering the ice field and that no icebergs were in sight at the time. Despite the apparent alacrity in leaving London, there does not appear to have been any great sense of urgency about reaching Boston.

Could it be that *Californian's* haste was at an end because she had reached her primary destination? Fantastical as it first appears, that conclusion is supported by further evidence regarding Captain Lord's actions on that fateful night.

When Lord stopped his ship, at 10.21 pm, he ordered that steam pressure be kept up and that the engines maintain a state of readiness for immediate use. *Californian* was in no danger; she was not in the ice, merely drifting with it. There was absolutely no danger of colliding with an iceberg, or anything else that was not moving under its own power. There was no wind, no icebergs in sight[79] and *Californian* was showing all the necessary lights. Why on earth would the captain have given the order to burn precious coal uselessly? The answer is frighteningly simple: he wouldn't. The only reason the order was given was because Captain Lord expected to have to make use of the engines before dawn.

This supposition is sustained by yet another of the captain's actions. That he elected to spend the night, fully dressed, on the chart room settee rather than his bunk in the cabin next door also argues that he expected a disturbed night. The choice of the 5½ft settee by the 6ft skipper tells us that his intention was to remain awake throughout the night, as anyone who has tried to sleep on a bed that is too short will appreciate.

Repeatedly, when white rockets were reported to him, Captain Lord asked if there was any colour in them, or were they company signals, effectively the same thing. Even when the apprentice reported to him when he was all but asleep (and had no recollection of the event), Lord asked the same question. Leslie Reade, in his book *The Ship That Stood Still*, suggests that Stone should have been curious about Captain Lord's obsession with 'colour' in the rockets.

Lord asked Gibson '… were there any colours in the rockets, at all?' or, according to Stone's report of what Gibson told him, 'If he were sure there were no colours in them, red or green.' Telling of his own last call to Lord, Stone described the master as being even more pressing. The captain 'again asked me if I was certain if there were no colours in those lights whatsoever. I again assured him that they were all white. Just white rockets.'[80]

Obviously coloured rockets were on the skipper's mind; he expected them to be seen. Not only did he expect coloured rockets to be seen, but he also expected to have to move his ship. Did he expect to have to go to the assistance of another vessel, which would fire coloured rockets to summon him?

The officers on watch on the *Californian* saw only white rockets, so Captain Lord waited where he was for the expected coloured signals to appear. That these multihued pyrotechnic signals never came was hardly Captain Lord's fault. Nineteen and a half miles is a very long way to expect to be able to see a rocket or socket signal, even one of the powerful shells exploded 800ft in the air by *Titanic*.

Robert Hitchens, *Titanic's* helmsman at the time of the collision, testified at the British Inquiry that the liner sent up red, white and blue rockets.

Quartermaster Olliver, who assisted Quartermaster Rowe in fetching the rockets (socket signals) from the poop to the bridge, testified that they took a box each. The signals came in boxes of 12, making a total of 24 on hand for immediate use. The British and American inquiries both missed this point completely and, basing their judgement on the idea that only a dozen rockets were available and that some remained in the box when the fireworks display was over, concluded that only eight were fired.

As a grand total of eight rockets were seen from *Californian*, during the earlier part of the midnight to 4am watch, the inquiries concluded that the rocket-firing ship was the *Titanic*, despite all the evidence to the contrary. It is much more likely that something like 20 rockets were sent up from the stricken liner, making a mockery of the findings from both inquiries.

Captain Lord did not react to white rockets because he expected to see coloured ones.

As far as is known, only one ship fired coloured rockets that night, in that general area. It is surely reasonable to believe that these were the rockets which Captain Lord was waiting for. That the captain was thrown into some confusion by the news that the *Titanic* had sunk while he dozed on the chart room settee is illustrated by his order after daybreak on the 15th that the engines be got ready. He forgot, or chose not to remember, that those same engines were already standing by, awaiting his orders, and had been all night.

The rockets seen from *Californian*, which the second officer was certain were not distress signals, were in all probability just that, ordinary company signals or Roman candles. Company signals do not go as high as rockets, nor do they explode,[81] which is a reasonable description of what was seen from the Leyland vessel. Captain Lord himself said, 'I didn't think it possible for any seaman to mistake a company's signal for a distress signal. So I relied on the officer of the watch.'[82] Captain Lord did not think that the rockets were distress signals because he believed that they were being fired close enough to the *Californian* for their detonations to be clearly heard.[83] Second Officer Stone told Lord that he would have roused the captain himself if he had thought the rockets he saw were distress signals.[84]

The captain certainly did not believe that the signals were of any import as is revealed by a line from a letter written after the event. Knowingly to ignore a distress signal was unthinkable and, 'There was everything to gain and nothing to lose,' by responding.[85] Late in his life Captain Lord had simplified the whole case to a three word, unassailable issue '*Californian* never moved.' Therefore *Californian* could not have been the mystery ship seen from *Titanic*.

Although Captain Lord may well have been innocent (as he always maintained) of not going to the assistance of a vessel sending up distress signals, it now appears that he might have been guilty of a more serious offence.

Could Captain Lord have been expecting to see coloured rockets and to have to go to the assistance of another vessel because he was party to a conspiracy to sink her?

We know that:

- Officers aboard the *Californian* confirmed that only white rockets were seen on the night of 14/15 April;
- Captain Lord, on every occasion that the sighting of rockets was reported to him, asked if there were any coloured ones seen;
- *Californian's* wireless operator told of how *Mount Temple* was transmitting the information that *Titanic* had sunk before anyone except the people in her boats and aboard *Carpathia* should have known.

In the Boats

In case of accidents, lifeboat Number 7, with possibly as many as 28 people aboard but more likely only 19 or 20, waited close to the sinking liner until all of the starboard boats reached the water,[1] pulling away only when the ship began to settle more quickly. The crewmen aboard, lookouts Hogg and Jewell, and Able Seaman Weller, quite reasonably moved clear of the vessel at that time to avoid any suction which might result from her sinking.

There was no lantern or compass in Number 7,[2] but a dining room steward had the foresight to bring a green flare with him when he entered the boat. The name of the steward is not recorded, nor is whatever happened to the green flare, but Mrs Helen Bishop was in no doubt that he and the flare were aboard. Mrs Bishop also had nothing but praise for two of *Titanic's* crew members who were in boat 7, Jack Edmonds and George Hogg.[3] There is no Jack Edmonds on the crew list, so Mrs Bishop may have been mistaken but, as the crew list is notoriously unreliable, it is much more likely that she is correct and the official list faulty. Nevertheless, the conduct of both passengers and crew in boat Number 7 appears to have been superior to some, as we shall see. The only criticism which can, in fairness, be levelled at Number 7 is that they, with perhaps as many as 45 empty seats in the boat, did not go to the assistance of those souls struggling in the water after the ship foundered. Notwithstanding, that criticism can be levelled at almost all of the boats. At least in Number 7 there doesn't appear to have been any heated discussion as to whether a rescue attempt should be mounted or not.

First class passenger William T. Sloper watched the ship sink and took note of what followed. He described seeing people floating on bundles of deck chairs and others on hastily inflated pneumatic life-rafts, which ties up with what Joseph Scarrott saw later. He neglects to mention why these rafts were hastily inflated when there had been about 2hr from the time that the order came to fill the boats until the vessel foundered.

Sloper also describes how a large ship came within a few hundred feet of his lifeboat while hundreds of people who were in the water supported only by their life preservers were still alive. This ship was strangely silent and was darkened so as to make identification impossible.

Mr Sloper believed, in the light of the subsequent governmental inquiries, that this mysterious vessel was the *Californian*, but there is a far more likely candidate in the shape of the *Mount Temple*. Crew members from the Canadian Pacific liner later described how, at one point, they were close enough to *Titanic's* boats to look down on them.

During the course of the night, boat Number 7 joined up with Number 5 and two passengers from the latter transferred. It seems that Mrs Washington Dodge and Mr Edward P. Calderhead were so disgusted with the conduct of the crew in Number 5 that they took the earliest opportunity to distance themselves. We will see why in a moment. One thing above all others impressed itself upon the survivors in boat Number 7 — the intense cold. Even though they were in the comparative shelter of the lifeboat,[4] people who had not even been wet were on the verge of dying from the cold!

Well before dawn *Carpathia's* rockets were seen and heard. As it began to grow light, the rescue ship came into view. Shortly after 4 o'clock *Carpathia* stopped to pick up the first survivors from boat Number 2 who thought that they had been in the lifeboat for about 8hr.[5] It took the undermanned boat Number 7 over 1hr to reach *Carpathia's* side, arriving there at 5.10am. Once alongside the Cunard liner, the lifeboat was hoisted aboard.

Boat Number 5, under the command of Third Officer Pitman, assisted by four other crew members, had a somewhat less quiet night than Number 7. First Officer Murdoch had ordered Pitman to keep the boat close to the stricken ship. 'Hang around the after gangway', seem to be the words he used before finishing with, 'Goodbye and good luck.'

Murdoch obviously thought that many more than the 41 people already aboard could be squeezed into the lifeboat once it was in the water, which has to be why he ordered Pitman to wait by the after gangway.

Pitman totally ignored his superior officer's orders and had boat Number 5 rowed away from *Titanic* immediately. Pitman, to his credit, never claimed to be one of *Titanic's* heroes and, unlike that of many who did, his story has the ring of truth.

Pitman may well have been disconcerted by the actual lowering of the boat. Mrs Warren, a passenger, said that the boat was lowered 'very jerkily' and she thought that 'she was going to be dumped out'.

Little wonder if Pitman thought that he had taken enough risks for one night. Mrs Warren and Mr George A. Harder noticed that there was no light or compass to be found in the lifeboat.[6]

After *Titanic* had foundered Mrs Dodge and Mr Calderhead suggested that they should go back and try to save some of those in the water. Pitman and the other passengers believed that this would be too dangerous and refused. A little later they came upon boat Number 7 and tied up to her. This was when the two passengers, unable to tolerate the company of the other occupants of their small boat, risked their lives by climbing into the boat tied alongside.

In Pitman's defence, it must be said that to have gone back into the mass of struggling humanity immediately after the sinking might well have ended in disaster for them all. On the other hand, they might have been able to save as many as another 35 lives, perhaps more. In the event Pitman was guided by the opinions of the majority in the boat. That, in hindsight, his decision appears to have been the wrong one, doesn't alter the fact that he acted as he did to try to ensure the safety of those already in Number 5, including himself.

As we have already seen with Lowe and the launching of boat Number 14, Pitman was not the only officer aboard *Titanic* to put his own safety above that of the passengers. After reaching *Carpathia*, boat Number 5 was taken aboard the Cunarder.

Helmsman Quartermaster Robert Hitchens in command of boat Number 6 was assisted by Lookout Frederick Fleet (probably the two most important witnesses to the events leading up to, during and immediately after the collision). They were so short-handed that they had to have a volunteer male passenger added to the otherwise all female occupants of this boat. Not until the boat had been lowered did it become apparent to passengers and crew alike that there were not enough men aboard to manage it. Major Peuchen had to swarm down the lifeboat falls in order to reach it at all. He believed that an Italian boy, with a broken wrist or arm, was a stowaway, but Mrs Helen Candee had seen Captain Smith himself order the boy into the boat. The major, not content with falsely accusing the young Italian, then tried to usurp command of the lifeboat, but he reckoned without the determination of Robert Hitchens. The welfare of those in his boat had been entrusted to him and he was not about to pass that responsibility on to Major Peuchen, of whom he had no prior knowledge.

Later, possibly in a malicious attempt to get back at Hitchens, Peuchen said that he, Hitchens, called to another boat asking if they knew of any buoy around there. The major thought that this showed just how little Hitchens knew about navigation, expecting a buoy in the North Atlantic.[7] Hitchens as a quartermaster and helmsman must have gleaned some knowledge of navigation, even if that knowledge was a little sketchy. He was experienced as far as serving on a ship's bridge was concerned and must, at some time in the past, have served as an ordinary seaman. Seen from this viewpoint his remarks to the other boat make little sense unless he was joking and trying to raise the spirits of those in both lifeboats. Or perhaps he knew that there should be buoy, of some sort in the vicinity, released by *Titanic* to act as a collection point for the boats.

Hitchens took the tiller while Fleet and Peuchen rowed. Throughout most of the night he stuck to his post, although well aware that he would be much warmer if he allowed somebody else to man the exposed tiller and took an oar himself. To operate the tiller it was necessary to stand in the stern of the boat. For a short time he did allow one of the women passengers to take over while he rowed, but she allowed the boat to wander off course, which alarmed the other passengers.[8]

When boat Number 6 was loading, Captain Smith had ordered the crew to row towards the lights of another ship in the distance. Second Officer Lightoller had repeated the order, indicating a light visible about two points on *Titanic's* starboard bow and about five miles away. How Hitchens and Fleet were supposed to propel a 30ft lifeboat with about 26 women in it for a distance of five miles has never been explained. Perhaps Smith and Lightoller had reason to believe that this mysterious vessel would close the gap between herself and *Titanic*. In the event they were hopelessly wrong. Even with the assistance of the redoubtable Major Peuchen, it was a hopeless task. Among the female passengers was Mrs J. J. Brown, better known today as 'The Unsinkable Molly Brown', who after distributing articles of her own clothing to those whose need was greater than her own, took an oar. Thus encouraged, other women followed her example and Number 6 was under way.

Try as they might, the passengers and crew of Number 6 could not get any closer to those lights, which they could clearly see, and it soon became obvious that the stranger was moving away.[9] Somewhat discouraged, Hitchens ordered the women to rest on their oars and let the boat drift, but it was so cold that they couldn't stand it and insisted on rowing to keep warm.[10] As the night wore on, it grew steadily colder.[11]

When *Titanic* sank, the passengers tried to get Hitchens to turn back, hoping they might pick up some of the people in the water. The helmsman refused,[12] saying that there were 'only a lot of stiffs there'.[13] Indelicately put maybe, but undoubtedly true. Hitchens afterwards said that he only heard one or two cries for help after the ship went down,[14] which probably meant that Number 6 was some considerable distance from the site.

Number 6 had been rowing away from *Titanic* for about 1hr when the liner finally sank. It would have taken a similar amount of time to make the return journey. Hitchens would have been well aware that nobody could survive in the freezing water for that long a period.

Quartermaster Hitchens was not popular with the rest of the people in his boat. Even Fred Fleet said that it was Hitchens who refused to return to the wreck site, although the women thought that he should. (Hitchens was obeying the orders of Captain Smith and Second Officer Lightoller.)

Mrs Edgar J. Mayer accused Hitchens of drinking brandy and of taking a woman's wrap or a blanket for his own use.[15] Hitchens denied this as well as an accusation that he used bad language. Bad language is a relative thing; words considered acceptable in conversation among the crew might well have offended the sensibilities of the cosseted and sheltered women from first class. As we have seen by Hitchens' remarks regarding the suggestion that he return to the site of the sinking to seek survivors, he was not a man to mince words. Hitchens had more than enough to contend with — the insubordinate pair, Peuchen and Fleet, passengers who disputed his every decision, and Madame de Villiers who constantly called for her son who hadn't even been aboard the *Titanic*. However, despite all these distractions, he still managed to take notice of *Titanic's* red, white and blue distress signals.[16]

As seems to be the norm with *Titanic's* lifeboats, there was no light or compass in boat Number 6, so it would have been all but impossible to tell who was where in the boat, or what anyone was doing. During the night they came up to lifeboat Number 16 and the two boats were tied together to ride out the hours of darkness. Before parting company, a stoker was transferred from Number 16 to help with the rowing.

At about 3.30am, or just after, Miss Norton noticed the first of *Carpathia's* rockets to be seen from number 6 and Hitchens changed course toward the newcomer. The report of the rockets had first been heard a few minutes before,[17] which tells us that a rocket could be heard over a greater distance than it could be seen under the conditions prevailing that night. This must support Captain Lord's contention that the signals seen from the *Californian* were not rockets at all but company signals, Roman candles.

The lifeboat had been in the water for just over 2½hr, for the greater part of which it had been heading towards the lights of a mystery ship, possibly to the northwards, because they did not reach *Carpathia's* side until about 8am, about 1hr longer than it had taken to row the first leg.

There are several possible explanations for the time difference between the outward and return journeys. Quite possibly the people at the oars were simply more tired by the time Number 6 started toward the rescue ship, or *Carpathia* may have stopped somewhat to the south of the position in which *Titanic* foundered. However, if the lifeboat had rowed away from the liner towards the south or southwest, then the return journey would have to have been against the Labrador current, which flows from north to south. This line of reasoning places the mystery ship to the south of the doomed liner and there is more evidence to support this conjecture.

From whatever direction Number 6 approached *Carpathia*, Robert Hitchens was still taking his responsibilities seriously. He saw everybody else off the boat before leaving himself[18] and watching as the lifeboat was hoisted aboard *Carpathia*. The quartermaster helmsman had performed at least as well as, and probably a good deal better than, some of his superior officers.

The confusion really begins with lifeboat Number 3, or was it Number 5? Mrs Frederick O. Speddon saw both Numbers 3 and 5 marked on this boat. 'Our seaman told me that it was an old one, taken from another ship,' she explained. J. Bruce Ismay later testified that 'all boats were new and none were transferred from another ship'.[19]

As many as 15 crew members found their way into Number 3 along with 10 male passengers and 25 women and children, 50 people in all, or so the British Inquiry would have us believe. Colonel Gracie spoke to many of the survivors soon after the disaster and worked out that there were only 40 people in the boat[20] and that the actual number might have been as low as 32.[21] As usual, there was no light or compass in the boat.[22]

Soon after reaching the water, two oars were lost overboard in the confusion.[23] Among those aboard were Miss Elizabeth Shutes and Lookout Reginald Lee: both noticed a peculiar smell before and after the accident — icebergs. As the night wore on, the composure of those in Number 3 began to break down. The women bickered about anything and everything, while their husbands sat in embarrassed silence. Regardless of the extreme conditions prevailing at the time, Miss Elizabeth Shutes found time to complain about people smoking in the boat. No doubt the arrival of the *Carpathia* was greeted with as much relief by the crew and male passengers at being able to finally escape the women in the boat as anything else. Not until 6am did Number 3 ultimately reach the side of the rescue vessel and disgorge its passengers, before the boat was hoisted aboard.

Boat Number 1, containing Sir Cosmo and Lady Duff-Gordon, long a source of amusement or irritation to those who study the loss of the *Titanic*, was ordered by First Officer Murdoch to 'Stand off the ship's side and come back if ordered.'[24] This boat, designed to carry 40 persons but with only a dozen on board, seven of whom were crew members, was surely the obvious choice to pick people from the water after the ship foundered. That may well have been what Mr Murdoch had in mind when he lowered Number 1. It was not, however, what was in the minds of the boat's occupants, who rowed away from *Titanic* with alacrity.

Even before this lifeboat was lowered, Sir Cosmo and fellow passenger C. E. Stengel had already spotted the lights of another vessel between one and two points off *Titanic's* port bow. According to Seaman Lyons, a member of the crew, Sir Cosmo and Mr Stengel did not get on, but they seem to have been agreed on what to do once their boat was in the water: ignore Murdoch's instructions and row toward the light of the mystery ship.[25]

The fifth passenger aboard Number 1, Mr A. L. Saloman, said that he, Mr Stengel and Sir Cosmo Duff-Gordon decided which way the boat should go between them.[26] They waited for about quarter of an hour before making off, well before the ship sank,[27] and were a safe distance away, the occupants all agreed.

After the *Titanic* had foundered they did return to the site, but not until the cries of those in the water had died away and it was safe to do so. Collins, another crew member aboard Number 1, said that the cries of those in the water went on for about 10min,[28] while Pusey thought 15–20.[29] The noise from those in the water slowly died away as the cold killed everyone off.[30]

The crewmen in the boat had wanted to return sooner, while there were still people to be saved, but Sir Cosmo and Lady Duff-Gordon had persuaded them that it was too dangerous (which it undoubtedly was).[31] Lady Duff-Gordon later denied this, but another of the seamen from Number 1, Hendricksen, was sure that it was Lucille[32] (Lady Duff-Gordon's trade name) and her husband who raised the objections, nobody else.[33] Collins, however, said that Hendricksen had never said anything about going back for survivors.[34] Sir Cosmo reinforced his expressed disinclination to return to the wreck site by helping Fireman Taylor pull on an oar[35] as they headed in the opposite direction, toward the other boats.[36]

Fireman J. Taylor told a very similar story. He agreed that the crewmen in the boat had wanted to go back for survivors but that the passengers had objected.[37] He added that as a result of the objections, they never went anywhere near the people struggling in the water.[38]

Lady Duff-Gordon claimed that although 'she heard terrible cries before the ship sank' from those in the water, her impression afterwards was of absolute silence.[39] Anyway, the boat had been ordered to row towards the lights. The cries of those people who went into the water after the ship sank are too well attested to be imaginary, which throws more than a little doubt on Lady Duff-Gordon's denial.

Hendricksen said that when *Titanic's* lights went out they were left in darkness and that from the lifeboat he could not see the ship at all clearly, just her outline. This is exactly what one would expect on a moonless night. With only a myriad stars to illuminate the scene, it is surprising that Hendricksen could see anything at all, although night blindness does affect some people more than others. Having said that, almost total darkness means almost zero visibility. Symons said that it was so dark that he could not even make out who shared the boat with him; they were invisible.[40]

When Number 1 finally returned to the wreck site all was quiet. Symons, in charge of the boat, said that they found nothing but floating wreckage.[41] By the time he gave evidence at the British Inquiry his story had changed. There he said that they found nothing at all.[42] This is hardly surprising as by the time witnesses were being called for the Mersey Inquiry, bribery seems to have been widespread and evidence tailored to fit in with what the inquiry wanted to hear, as we shall see.

The movements of boat Number 1 after leaving *Titanic's* side are a little vague because nobody from the boat could later remember the same events. Sir Cosmo said that they were about 1,000yd from the ship when it sank. Fireman Collins thought that they were about

100yd away. Lady Duff-Gordon's secretary, Miss Francatelli, estimated the distance at nearer to 200yd. Symons guessed that they were about a quarter of a mile from the ship when she sank, but Fireman Taylor supported Miss Francatelli. They all agreed that emergency boat 1 did not, 'Stand off the ship's side and come back if ordered.'

While Number 1 was drifting, about half an hour after the ship had foundered but before the arrival of the *Carpathia*, Fireman Robert W. Pusey began to bewail his lot.[43] He complained that the crew members had lost everything in the wreck. Sir Cosmo, being of a kindly disposition, took pity on the crew members. He told them not to be downhearted and that he would give them all a cheque for £5 apiece in order that they might purchase new kit.[44] Then out of the goodness of his heart the baronet offered to write to each of their wives to let them know that they were safe.[45]

If the money that Sir Cosmo Duff-Gordon offered was a bribe, as has been suggested on more than one occasion, who can blame him for using his money and influence to best ensure the well-being of his family and friends? The unremarkable story of boat Number 1 was to cause a storm at both American and British inquiries, chiefly because of the £5 that Sir Cosmo offered the crewmen but also because the boat left *Titanic* with so few people.

Had Sir Cosmo left well alone, then it is more than likely that he would have been forgotten amid the much louder outcry over Captain Lord and J. Bruce Ismay. The baronet was not a man to sit idly by while there was any likelihood of his being able to incriminate himself further. One wonders if, perhaps, he had been tasting a little of the London Dry Gin which was the basis of his family fortune. Even as the British Inquiry was getting under way, Duff-Gordon's agent approached seamen who had been with Sir Cosmo in boat Number 1. These seamen were offered inducements, by the agent, as they freely admitted when giving their evidence. There is some reason to suspect that many more of the witnesses at the British Inquiry may have been persuaded, one way or another, to tell a story that might not have been the whole truth, or even part of it!

Boat Number 1 reached *Carpathia* safely and was taken aboard to join others already there.

Boat 8 left *Titanic* with perhaps 28 people aboard, 24 women and children and four crew members. Steward Crawford seems to have been in charge, assisted by Able Seaman Jones, Steward Hart and a cook. There were no male passengers in this boat, but that hardly worked to disadvantage. Very few of the women could have been described as shrinking violets. One of them had so much to say for herself that Steward Crawford put her to steering the boat, so releasing all four crew members to man the oars. It was a good idea in theory, but, as one of the crew admitted to Mrs White, 'he had never had an oar in his hands before, in his life'.[46] There would never be a better time for the crewman to learn how to row!

Lucy-Noel Martha, the Countess of Rothes, remained at the tiller for most of the night, leaving it only to comfort Signora de Satode who was screaming for her husband, or to take a turn at an oar. She was not the only female passenger prepared to take a turn at rowing the heavy boat: Miss Marie Young, Miss Gladys Cherry, Mrs F. Joel Swift, Mrs William R. Bucknell, Albina Brazzani and Miss Maloney all took an oar for part of the night.

Throughout most of the night the occupants of boat Number 8 could see the two masthead lights of another ship, about 10 miles away, thought Mrs White.[47] They rowed toward the lights and had covered three or four miles before they gave up, because the mystery ship seemed to be drifting away from them. This resulted in them being the furthest from *Carpathia* when she came up in the morning.[48]

Mrs White had to stand in the boat all night because the seats were too high for her to climb onto. As she was suffering from a bad foot this made standing more of an imposition than it might otherwise have been. To add insult to injury, Mrs White believed, the four crewmen smoked in the boat, something she complained about bitterly.[49]

Seaman Jones and the Countess of Rothes were the first in the boat to see *Carpathia* when she appeared in the morning. The Cunarder picked up the people from Number 8 and then hoisted the boat aboard. Crawford noticed that there was no field ice around *Carpathia* when she arrived.[50] Jones was so impressed by the Countess of Rothes that he removed the lifeboat's number, which was on a detachable plate, and had it mounted before presenting it to her as a token of his appreciation. They remained friends for many years.

Boat Number 9, under the command of Able Seaman Haines assisted by seven other crew members and with 48 passengers, eight of them male, got away from *Titanic* at about 1.20am. As seems to have been normal, there was no light or compass in the boat. Quartermaster Wynne saw a steamer's lights about seven or eight miles away.[51] He saw the red light first and later a white one. About 10–15min after the red and white lights disappeared he saw another, different, light in the same direction. Wynne was not the only person to see more than one mystery ship in the immediate area that night and many of those who did see only one, disagreed as to what sort of vessel was nearby.

Boat 9 reached *Carpathia's* side some time between 7 and 8am and the passengers and boat were taken aboard. Wynne, in contrast to all other crew members, but not necessarily passengers, had managed to take his kitbag with him into the lifeboat. He got it as far as the deck of *Carpathia*, 'where it was pitched off the ship'.[52] One wonders why.

Boat 10, with ex-Royal Naval seaman Buley in charge, left *Titanic* with perhaps 53 people officially aboard. Lurking in the bottom of the boat were a Japanese and an Armenian, both stowaways.[53] Assisting Buley in managing the lifeboat were Seaman Evans, Fireman Rice, Steward Burke and one other.

The lifeboat was rowed away from the ship where it later joined up with boats 12, 14 and D, under the command of Fifth Officer Lowe. Buley was taken out of Number 10 to become part of the 'all volunteer' crew of Number 14, assembled by Lowe to take that boat back to the wreck site in the hope of finding survivors.[54] Buley described how they picked up four survivors from the freezing sea. All the others he saw were, 'dead, frozen, not drowned'.[55] Of over 1,500 people who went into the sea when the ship sank, only 13 were picked up by the lifeboats.[56]

Mrs Imanita Shelley said that a ship's baker was among the crew of Number 10.[57] Only three of the 14 bakers aboard were saved: Joughin, Burgess and Neal.

Lifeboat Number 10 was amongst the 13 boats picked up by *Carpathia*. Why Captain Rostron chose to salvage only 13 of *Titanic's* boats,[58] he never explained.

Boat 11, under the command of Able Seaman Humphries, assisted by Seaman Brice and Stewards White, MacKay and McMicken, left the ship overloaded, with 70 people aboard. No other boat saved more lives than Number 11. This lifeboat spent a relatively quiet night as the occupants awaited rescue, except for a woman who repeatedly set off an alarm clock. Whether or not the alarm clock survived the night is not recorded, but one has one's doubts!

As usual, there was no light or compass to be found in the boat. Nor were the almost obligatory stowaways in evidence. Number 11 was another of the boats taken aboard the rescue vessel.

Boat Number 12, under the command of Able Seamen Poigndestre and Fred Clench, left *Titanic* with 43 people. With the exceptions of the crewmen and a French man who jumped into the boat as it was being lowered, all aboard were women and children.[59] Undermanned as it was, Number 12 could do little to help those unfortunate enough to find themselves swimming after the ship went down. Like boat Number 6, which also had only two crewmen to manage it, Number 12 was almost completely at the mercy of wind and wave. The lifeboat was in dire need of assistance itself and in no position to offer help to anyone.

As one has come to expect, there was no light or compass in boat 12.[60] It should be remembered that the BoT inspector, Captain Maurice Clarke, had inspected all the boats less than five days previously, at Southampton. At that time they were found to be fully equipped. Boats' compasses were not stored in the lifeboats but in a locker on the Boat Deck. Lanterns, however, should have been there, hanging from a hook beneath the thwarts (seats running from one side of the boat to the other).

Poigndestre explained that there were not enough crewmen in boat 12 to risk picking up survivors, and even if they had the necessary hands, it was too dark to see them anyway![61]

Number 12 joined up with the flotilla assembled by Fifth Officer Lowe, where we can only assume that the officer assigned more oarsmen to the badly undermanned lifeboat. Later, Lowe in Number 14, having removed all of his own passengers and distributed them throughout the other three boats in the group, set off to return to the site of the sinking in search of survivors.

Fred Clench said that while Lowe was away in 14 looking for swimmers, he saw a group of men on a raft. Then he heard two whistles blown. Clench shouted to the officer on the raft who had blown the whistle: he turned out to be Lightoller. At Lightoller's request boat Number 12 was pulled (rowed) over toward him, 'and found it was a raft – not a raft exactly but an overturned boat'. All of the people from the capsized lifeboat were taken into Number 12 among them were Second Wireless Operator Harold Sidney Bride and the baker, Charles Joughin. Joughin noted that, apart from fellow cook Maynard and the wireless operator, most of the occupants of the boat were women.[62] This information is important because it bears out the evidence of Joseph Scarrott who was in lifeboat 14 and who also describes how that boat came across a raft supporting survivors.

It was at about 6.30am that Number 12 picked up the people from what turned out to be collapsible boat B; supposedly Charles Joughin the baker had remained in the water until this time.[63] *Carpathia* was not far away, taking aboard survivors from other boats and in most cases the boats as well.

While Number 12 had been tied up with the others of the flotilla they had taken aboard some of the passengers from the overloaded collapsible boat D. Now, as they set off towards *Carpathia*, this lifeboat was itself overloaded with no less than 70 people aboard it. Under anything like normal conditions, and with a competent commander, the lifeboat would have been perfectly well able to manage with a substantially greater overload than this. But no sooner was the second officer aboard than he took command. In his own inimitable fashion he had the boat trimmed to ride high by the bow and thus made the craft unseaworthy. Thanks to this master mariner's efforts, the boat was almost swamped at the last moment.[64] Eventually passengers and boat were taken onto the Cunarder. Given Lightoller's notion of a well-trimmed boat, one can't help wondering how many others of those that found their way to collapsible B might have had a better chance of survival without his assistance.

We have seen that:

- There were people on inflatable life-rafts in the sea after *Titanic* had foundered although the liner never carried this type of raft;
- A large ship, blacked out to avoid identification, came to within a few hundred feet of boat No 7 soon after the sinking;
- At least one of *Titanic's* lifeboats had more than one identification number on it.

24

In the Boats (2)

Boat 14, under the command of Fifth Officer Lowe, with Able Seaman Joseph Scarrott, two firemen, Stewards Crowe and Morris and a volunteer passenger, C. Williams, carried 50 women and children, and, of course, the almost inevitable Italian stowaway.

The fifth officer's boat had been experiencing problems ever since it had left *Titanic's* Boat Deck. For some unexplained reason, while being lowered its descent had been arrested while it was still some 5ft above the water. Rather than wait for the problem to be rectified, Lowe pulled the lever which operated the Murray's Patented Release gear and dropped the final 5ft into the sea. From that point in time, the boat leaked like a sieve, which is hardly surprising, and had to be baled continuously.[1]

Lowe's actions while lowering Number 14 must throw considerable doubt on the statements of the other surviving officers. These all agreed at the inquiries that the reason so many boats were lowered under-filled was that they did not know if the boats were strong enough to stand lowering with a full complement without buckling. Lowe seems to have been quite confident that his boat, with about 60 people in it, could withstand a 5ft drop without serious harm. I would be dubious about dropping an empty lifeboat this distance into unbroken water.

Miss Compton, a passenger aboard Number 14, said that there were no balers in the boat and that the men had to bale out the water 'using their hats'.[2] (Another hint that Captain Clarke's inspection at Southampton, may not have been quite as exhaustive as we have been led to believe.) Miss Compton went on to say that the women in 14 wanted to get well away from the sinking ship.[3]

As we have already seen, during the night Lowe collected a small group of boats together. Miss Compton had left *Titanic* in collapsible D,[4] one of the boats Lowe had rounded up, which tells us that these boats were brought together before the liner foundered. Miss Compton also tells of men baling her lifeboat but we have already seen that Number 14 left *Titanic* with only female passengers aboard except for one volunteer male passenger and a stowaway.[5] She must have been talking about the period after joining up with Lowe's party.

At its largest, the group of boats assembled by Lowe comprised Numbers 4, 10, 12, 14 and collapsible D. Lowe redistributed the people until all the boats, with the exception of his own Number 14, were equally laden. The people from Number 14 he distributed between the other four boats. When Number 14 was empty he picked a crew of oarsmen for it and raised the mast.

Until this time Lowe had been heard swearing and being generally blasphemous by a passenger, Miss Minahan. Now that *Titanic* had sunk, the passengers had to persuade the officer to return to the site of the sinking to look for survivors.[6] Once persuaded, Lowe set about attempting a rescue in a businesslike manner.

Having made his preparations, he set off in Number 14, after having waited for about 1hr in order to allow the icy water to thin out the swimmers to more manageable numbers, to collect whoever he might.[7] As it turned out, he had waited too long. Only four living persons were plucked from the frigid clutches of the North Atlantic. Among the survivors, one of whom died in the boat shortly after being rescued, was a steward, J. Stewart.[8]

One of the more fortunate individuals was a Japanese gentleman, whom Lowe found lashed to a door.[9] Initially the fifth officer was disgusted that the man had managed to survive and said that he would like to 'throw him back'. A few minutes later Lowe was ready to eat his words when he saw the same Japanese survivor rowing with the best of his hand-picked crew in a forlorn attempt to save more lives. From that moment Lowe had nothing but praise for the oriental. Graceless, arrogant, self-opinionated and thoroughly unlikeable Lowe may have been, but he knew a hero when he saw one.

Even as they searched the wreck site Lowe noticed that there didn't seem to be a single female corpse floating among the bodies and how little wreckage there was.[10] There were so many bodies that Number 14 had trouble rowing through them, Lowe said.[11] As always, there was apparently no light or compass in Number 14,[12] so until dawn Lowe could not be sure of what direction he was heading or even see where he was in relation to the other boats. Before long he gave up the search because he knew it was impossible for anyone to have survived in the freezing water;[13] except the baker and any number of others on or in boats A and B — or so they would have us believe.

When day began to break Able Seaman F. O. Evans, who was now in Number 14, saw icebergs as high as *Titanic* itself around them.[14]

It grew lighter and, as visibility improved, those in Number 14 spotted a number of people on a raft. Lowe took the lifeboat to the rescue. Joseph Scarrott described the incident saying that they picked up about 20 people from this raft, 'constructed of air boxes. It was not a collapsible boat,' he asserted.[15] Scarrott's statement, although ignored at the time, is one of the more significant pieces of evidence to come to light. He was obviously describing a life-raft and he stated quite categorically that this raft was not a collapsible boat, capsized or otherwise. Joseph Scarrott, as an able seaman, would be an experienced hand and would recognise a collapsible boat when he saw one. We must therefore assume that the raft he described was just that, a raft. There are no rafts listed amongst *Titanic's* life-saving equipment, but there is mention of them from other survivors, notably Mr William T. Sloper.

This information, coupled with Mrs Marian Thayer's statement, which as we shall see in the next chapter is corroborated in no uncertain manner, suggests the close proximity of another vessel. The presence of upturned lifeboats and life-rafts also suggests that this other vessel was in no condition to render assistance to *Titanic* as she was putting her own passengers or crew off in small boats and anything else that floated.

It may be significant that Lowe, or any other survivors with the exception of Scarrott, failed to mention this raft at either official inquiry. However, a great many things were carefully not mentioned, or ignored, at these inquiries.

We also know that people were picked up from an upturned collapsible by boat Number 12, but at the British Inquiry Lowe said that these people were rescued by himself in Number 14. Number 12 was the last boat to reach *Carpathia* simply because it had stopped to collect the people from collapsible B.[16] Lowe had heard about the upturned collapsible by the time he gave evidence, and it is more than likely that he confused this boat with the raft, whose passengers he did save. The simple fact that boat 12 picked up those people from collapsible B while Lowe picked up people from another boat, that he thought was B, shows that there were at least two rafts in the area which could be, and were, mistakenly identified.

As dawn, and *Carpathia*, approached a breeze sprang up and the sea began to grow choppy, people in the boats could see icebergs in every direction.[17] Lowe took advantage of the breeze by raising the sail in Number 14. Returning to his flotilla he took the heavily-laden collapsible D in tow — it was still desperately short-handed when it came to oarsmen. Even as he towed this boat towards the rescue ship Lowe spotted yet another, in an even more parlous state.

Collapsible A was floating with its canvas sides down and awash with water. There were 15 people aboard, 11 men, one woman and three corpses who had expired during the night, victims of the intense cold.[18] As Number 14 and its dependant collapsible D approached the swamped Englehart lifeboat, Lowe fired four shots into the air to alert the bedraggled occupants to his arrival. Having picked up the living from the waterlogged boat[19] and distributed them between his own boat and D, he set sail directly towards *Carpathia*, which by this time was on the scene and picking up survivors. As far as Lowe knew at the time, only three collapsibles got away from the ship.[20] After the people from 14 and D, possibly more than 100, were taken aboard the Cunarder, both boats were cast adrift to sink. Presumably the badly leaking 14 would founder in the foreseeable future, but the collapsible, which had served so well, was still in good condition and could well present a hazard to the numerous fishing boats which worked the Grand Banks, for some weeks to come. That these collapsible boats could withstand the ravages of the North Atlantic for a considerable time is proven by the fact that boat A was found and picked up by the *Oceanic* on 13 May, almost a month after the disaster.[21]

Boat 13 left *Titanic* under the command of Fireman Fred Barrett, referred to by Lawrence Beesley as 'the captain', with Lookout Reginald Lee, Fireman George W. Beauchamp and at least six other crew members aboard. This boat and Number 9 both had more men, mostly crew, aboard than perhaps they might have done.[22] Fifty-five passengers had managed to find a place in the boat, among them first class passenger Mr Washington Dodge and second class Messrs Beesley and Caldwell. All the rest were third class with the possible exception of the almost inevitable Japanese stowaway. That *Titanic's* officers automatically assumed that all non-Caucasians or English-speaking persons were Armenian, Italian or Japanese and also stowaways illustrates the widespread racism of the period. As usual the light and compass were missing from the lifeboat.[23]

The only vessel coming to their rescue, as far as the occupants of boat 13 were aware, was the *Olympic*. Coming from more than 500 miles away, she was expected to arrive at about two o'clock the following afternoon.

Almost immediately after boat 13 left the stricken liner, a ship's lights were seen, close to the horizon and on *Titanic's* port side. These lights drew away and finally disappeared below the horizon. Fireman Beauchamp said that at the time he didn't know what the light was that Number 13 tried to reach. The lights turned out to be those of the *Carpathia*.[24] After *Titanic* foundered, the people in boat 13 sang at the top of their voices to drown out the cries of those freezing to death in the water.

For most of the night the boat drifted aimlessly, although at one time they did try to follow the light of another lifeboat. The occupants of boat 13 were often fooled into believing that stars, down on the horizon, were ship's lights. The night was so dark and the stars were so bright that this mistake was all too easy to make.[25] Beesley's description of conditions agrees exactly with that of the watch officers on the *Californian*. The schoolmaster said that he could not be sure of exactly who was in his boat because in the darkness he could see only a few feet.[26]

According to Lawrence Beesley, the plan, if there was one that night, was simply to try to keep the boats together until daybreak. At about 3.30am, the people in the boat heard and saw one of *Carpathia's* rockets for the first time. Towards dawn a ship's lights were seen, Beesley thought, to the northwest. Number 13 was rowed slowly in that direction. What Lawrence Beesley believed to be the northwest appears to have been, in reality, southeast.

Beesley thought that some of *Titanic's* boats had white lights in them but there is no other evidence of this except for Mrs Stuart White in boat 8. She had a cane with an electric light built into it. She waved the illuminated cane aloft throughout the night as a beacon for the other lifeboats to home in on. The other lights recorded are the green flares which were shown from Number 2. These had been put aboard the boat by Fourth Officer Boxhall and were seen from *Carpathia* guiding her to the lifeboats.

According to Beesley, Number 13 was the eighth or ninth boat to reach *Carpathia*, arriving there sometime between 4.30 and 4.45am. The boat and its occupants were taken aboard the Cunard vessel.

Lifeboat 15, with about 70 people squeezed into it, left *Titanic* under the command of Fireman Diamond.[27] Only one first class male passenger, Mr Haven, appears to have found his way into this boat, but three third class male passengers were lucky enough to happen upon room for themselves. About 53 third class women and children were crowded in, and the boat was overloaded by the addition of another dozen or so crew members.[28] Samuel Rule initially believed that there were only four female and three male passengers in the boat and testified that this was the case when he gave evidence on day six of the British Inquiry. When he was recalled on day nine he changed his story and said 'Those in the boat were mainly women and children.'[29] Clearly Rule had been talking to representatives of the White Star line.

Once again there was no light[30] or compass in the boat. Compasses were not general issue to all lifeboats and would have been of little use to crewmen inexperienced in their use, but every man should have been familiar with the workings of a lantern had there been any provided. Boat 15 spent a fairly uneventful night. The most remarkable discovery as far as most aboard were concerned was Fireman Diamond's impressive proficiency in Anglo-Saxon profanity.

This lifeboat rowed away from the sinking ship for a distance of 500–600yd. From there Samuel Rule watched events as far as he was able. He could see no people still aboard the liner.[31]

Number 15 was one of only three wooden lifeboats cast adrift by *Carpathia* after her passengers had been taken aboard the Cunard liner. Just what criteria Captain Rostron employed when deciding which of *Titanic's* lifeboats to salvage is unrecorded. Presumably this highly efficient master mariner had a very sound reason for taking some boats aboard while casting others adrift. Understandably perhaps, none of the Englehart collapsible boats were collected, but to discard three of 16 brand-new (only used once) lifeboats appears incomprehensible, unless these three were damaged or showed something else that the good captain would rather not be made public. Numbers 4 and 14 we know leaked like sieves and both of these boats formed part of Lowe's flotilla, but there seems to be no common factor linking number 15. All we can be sure of is that Captain Rostron did not cast these boats adrift because he had no more room.

Lifeboat 16, under the command of Master at Arms Bailey assisted by Seaman Archer and Steward Andrews, spent an uneventful night afloat. Other members of the crew aboard this boat included two stewardesses, Mrs Leather and Violet Jessop. Miss Jessop was to go through the whole performance of abandoning an 'Olympic' class vessel at sea again when *Britannic*, the third sister ship, struck a mine and sank in the Aegean Sea on 21 November 1916. As a variation on a theme, instead of a Japanese, Armenian or Italian stowaway, one of *Titanic's* firemen was found aboard the lifeboat.[32] Number 16 was taken aboard *Carpathia*.

Collapsible C, commanded by Quartermaster Rowe with Steward

Pearcey, Barber Weikman and three firemen to help, left *Titanic* at about 1.40am, with perhaps as many as 39 people aboard, including four Chinese or Filipino stowaways.

Before leaving the liner, Rowe had seen a bright light about two points (22.5°) on *Titanic's* port bow, about five miles away. Once clear of the sinking ship, the occupants of collapsible C rowed towards this mysterious light, but never seemed to get any closer to it.[33]

This was the boat that J. Bruce Ismay and Mr Carter had quietly stepped aboard: in so doing Ismay had ruined the remainder of his life — although this remainder was considerably longer than it would have been had he not stepped into the boat. This must have been some consolation for the managing director of the shipping line in the years that followed.

Ismay said that collapsible C was pulled (or pushed, depending on which way round one was sitting because of the peculiar system employed to propel a lifeboat through the water) toward a light, which appeared on *Titanic's* starboard side.[34] This light is another mystery vessel as the steamer's lights seen by the majority of witnesses were on *Titanic's* port side.

Ismay described 'the lights of another vessel, not the *Californian*, but a sailing ship'.[35] He didn't see *Titanic* sink because he was one of those employed in pushing an oar rather than pulling and therefore had his back toward the sinking ship as the lifeboat headed away.

Needless to say, the efforts of the oarsmen in collapsible C were unavailing and the mysterious sailing vessel was never reached, nor identified. When it grew light, this boat rowed to *Carpathia* where all the occupants were taken aboard and the boat cast adrift. Ismay did not see *Carpathia's* lights before daylight,[36] which is explainable simply by Number 13 heading towards the north. The IMM executive would then have his back to the approaching rescue vessel.

Emergency boat 2 with Fourth Officer Joseph Groves Boxhall commanding left *Titanic* at about 1.45am with about 25 people in a boat designed to carry 40. Assisting Boxhall were three crew members, Able Seaman Osman, Steward Johnson and a cook. All passengers, with the exception of one old third class man and his family, were first class women and children. Seaman Osman described how a box of rockets had been put aboard the boat in the mistaken belief that they were biscuits. He also told how, throughout the night, Boxhall had fired these rockets.[37] Mrs Walter Douglas said that the, 'box of green lights, like rockets, had been put aboard Number 2 by Boxhall'.

After launching, Boxhall had Number 2 rowed around to *Titanic's* starboard side before rowing away towards the southeast.[38] Osman said that it was impossible for their boat to get close to the liner's starboard side because of the heavy list.[39] *Titanic* was listing heavily to port at this time. As they rowed away Boxhall both felt and saw the suction caused by the liner as she settled, about 200yd away.[40]

Boxhall was fortunate enough to find a lantern in Number 2, possibly the only one of *Titanic's* boats so well equipped. He testified that there was 'always a lamp in the emergency boats,' but this seems to be doubtful testimony because emergency boat 1 had to manage in the dark.

Instead of taking the tiller Boxhall contented himself with alternately rowing the boat and lighting flares. Mrs Walter Douglas had the tiller in Number 2 when *Titanic* sank, while Boxhall was pushing an oar. Consequently the fourth officer did not see the vessel sink even though the lifeboat was only about half-a-mile from the scene.[41]

Able Seaman Osman said that 'not until morning did we see an iceberg',[42] which tells us just how dark the night was and how poor the visibility. When daylight came, icebergs were visible all around, some of them towering over 200ft from the surface of the sea. Until the rising of the sun these monstrous mountains of ice had not shown themselves, even as darker silhouettes against an almost jet black sky. Boxhall said that in the sunlight the icebergs around them looked white but when he first saw them at first light they looked black.[43] Lightoller's assertion that icebergs were easier to spot at night from low down, rather than from a ship's crow's-nest, doesn't seem to have held true in this instance.

Boat 2 was the first to be picked up by *Carpathia*, reaching her side at about 4.10am. Seeing that there was an officer in the boat Captain Rostron sent instructions that he was to report to the bridge immediately on coming aboard. A few minutes later *Titanic's* shivering fifth officer reported, 'My God sir, they've gone with her. They couldn't live in this cold water. We had room for a dozen more people in my boat, but it was dark after the ship took the plunge. We didn't pick up any swimmers.'[44] Boxhall's few simple words sum up what must really have happened. It was too cold for people to last for more than a few minutes in the water and too dark to find them in the time that they remained alive.

The rest of the boats were scattered over a four-mile area at the time and it would take Captain Rostron and *Carpathia* more than another four hours to collect all of the 706[45] people to be taken aboard.

Lifeboat Number 4, under the very capable command of Quartermaster Perkis, assisted by Able Seaman McCarthy, Storekeeper Foley and Fireman Smith, with 36 women and children aboard and the inevitable stowaway, this time French, was one of the very few boats on hand to assist those left in the water when *Titanic* foundered.

Six persons were plucked from the wintry sea, all of them crew members. Hemmings, Prentice, Dillon and Scott all lived to tell of their experiences. Seaman Lyons and Steward Siebert died in the lifeboat, overcome by the cold.[46]

Dillon described how he was taken down about two fathoms when *Titanic* foundered and then had to swim for what he thought was about 20min before being picked up. Dillon's estimation of the time he spent in the water is unlikely to say the least, but even a few minutes in the icy seas could well have seemed much longer. He was unconscious when lifted from the water and when he came round in the boat he found Seaman Lyons and Steward Siebert lying on top of him.[47]

Among the almost exclusively first class passengers was Mrs Marian Thayer. Mrs Thayer wrote her version of the night's events some years later, but the passage of time does not appear to have dimmed the memory. In her written statement she says, 'We passed an overturned boat shortly after reaching the water.'[48] At that time, judging from what other witnesses had to say, there should not have been any upturned boats in the water, or anywhere else for that matter. However, we do know that Mrs Thayer's recollection of the capsized lifeboat is accurate as this same boat was seen and recorded by both Captain Rostron of the *Carpathia* and Captain Lord of the *Californian*. If contemporary accounts are to be believed, then all of *Titanic's* 16 wooden lifeboats and all four collapsible boats are accounted for.

Of the two collapsibles which were washed overboard as the forward end of the Boat Deck disappeared beneath the sea, collapsible B did finish up upside down. The Englehart boat was washed overboard more than 15min after boat Number 4 left the liner, so it was not this boat that was seen by Mrs Thayer soon after her lifeboat left.

Mrs Ryerson, who was also in Number 4, definitely saw collapsible B later during the night, or early the following morning. She described how the people were standing back to back on the upturned boat. Mrs Thayer did not mention there being anybody at all on the boat that she saw.

During the night boat Number 4 joined Lowe's flotilla, which was made up solely of boats from the port side of the liner. The supposedly brand-new lifeboat leaked so badly that it had to be baled out continuously.[49] Mrs Thayer rowed all night with water up to her shins. She was still at an oar when the boat reached *Carpathia* at about 7am. She said that they had to row to the rescue ship's side because Number 4 was leaking so badly that it would have sunk before *Carpathia* came to them.[50]

Before *Carpathia* came into view Mrs Jean Hippach had been watching the shooting stars which criss-crossed the sky above the slowly sinking lifeboat. She had never seen so many.[51] One wonders if she had heard the old wives' tale about somebody dying every time a shooting star is seen. If she had, then the superabundance of meteoric activity should have come as no surprise. Only with the coming of the morning sun did the occupants of Number 4 see icebergs for the first time.[52]

Collapsible D, under the command of Quartermaster Bright and with two other crew members, Able Seaman Lucas and Steward Hardy, to assist him, left *Titanic* with a total of 44 people aboard, among them a third class stowaway, Joseph Dugemin, and two first class passengers who had leaped into the boat as it was being lowered. It seems that first class passengers who made their way, one way or another, into lifeboats, without first obtaining permission from an officer, were regarded as heroes, while third class passengers who did the same thing were stowaways. No male passengers were allowed into D while it was still aboard the ship, but Frederick Hoyt, whose wife was in the boat, jumped into the sea close by and was picked up.

During the night boat D joined Lowe's flotilla where Lowe took all of her crew members to man his own boat, Number 14. Seaman Lucas described how 36 people were taken off an overturned collapsible boat but this must have taken place while he was assisting the fourth officer.

With no light, compass or crew members aboard, collapsible D drifted helplessly while Lowe was away from the group of boats, looking for survivors at the wreck site. Undoubtedly the passengers aboard D would have felt a great deal better about their situation if Lowe had had the foresight to tie their boat to one or more of the others.

Heavily laden as it was when it left *Titanic*, only three short of capacity, collapsible D had been obliged to accept many more people from Number 14 when Lowe had emptied his boat in preparation for his rescue attempt. Overloaded to the point where it could not sustain any more passengers, the canvas-sided boat awaited the return of Number 14. When Lowe returned to take D in tow, the people in the collapsible were afraid that the fourth officer was going to unload even more passengers into their boat. They were mistaken and Lowe merely towed them towards the *Carpathia*, which had arrived on the scene and was picking up survivors by this time.

On the way to the rescue ship they came across waterlogged collapsible A with its 14[53] survivors. Picking up these people, Lowe distributed them between his own boat and the collapsible before carrying on toward *Carpathia*. They reached the Cunarder at about 7am, much to the relief of those in the amazing and ridiculously overloaded Englehart boat. Lowe, throughout the ordeal, had not once overloaded his own boat, although it was rated to carry 65 persons. When it reached *Carpathia* there were still five empty places in boat 14.

Before proceeding with the impossible stories of collapsible boats A and B, perhaps we should try to make some sense of what had happened aboard the other 18 of *Titanic's* lifeboats.

We know the night was so cold that even in the relatively sheltered environment of the lifeboats people were dying from the effects of hypothermia; even those that had escaped a soaking were suffering. We also know that it was not possible for anybody to survive for long in the icy water before they froze to death.

It is also apparent that certain of *Titanic's* officers and crew, particularly some of those who had charge of a lifeboat, put their own safety before that of the passengers who remained on the ship. Certain male passengers, who later represented themselves as heroes of the disaster, were nothing of the kind but acted solely out of self-interest.

We know that the lifeboats were not properly equipped, many having no light or compass, although these same boats were supposedly rigorously inspected immediately before the voyage began. It also seems that not all of the boats were quite as seaworthy as they might have been; at least three of them leaked badly and one had at least two different numbers on it, indicating that it could well have come from another ship.

That another ship was in the vicinity is undeniable. The number of witnesses that saw a ship's lights is more than sufficient to dispel any doubt. From the evidence of those witnesses it is virtually certain that more than one ship was close by and possibly even a third and fourth.

The upturned lifeboat, which, if the great majority of witnesses are to be believed, cannot have come from *Titanic*, also points to the close proximity of another ship, as does the life-raft seen by Joseph Scarrott.

The night was so dark that visibility was effectively nil as was demonstrated by the people in the lifeboats, who not only couldn't see the large number of immense icebergs surrounding them, but also the person next to them in the boat until it grew light the following morning.

Robert Hitchens' statement that he saw red, white and blue rockets, or socket signals, sent skyward from *Titanic* as he watched from his place in boat number 6 is probably the most important evidence regarding the activities of other vessels in the area, particularly *Californian*, as we have seen. From the evidence already presented, it is apparent that the heroic story of the loss of the *Titanic* that we all know bears little or no resemblance to what really happened.

Now we come to the most outrageous and misleading stories of them all: those told by the people who escaped the disaster in or on collapsibles A and B.

We know that:

- Fourth Officer Lowe, in boat No 14, picked people up from a life-raft although *Titanic* did not carry such rafts;
- A first class female passenger saw another ship, possibly damaged, close by;
- This same passenger also describes seeing an upturned lifeboat at the scene well before *Titanic* sank, before collapsible B was supposedly washed off the ship.

Collapsibles A and B

It is some measure of the gullibility of the ordinary man in the street, that the stories recounting the adventures of those survivors from the *Titanic* who made their escapes aboard collapsibles A and B were given any credence at the time, let alone have been accepted for over 80 years.

The received scenario covering events in *Titanic's* collapsible boat A after the sinking is extremely unlikely to say the least, while that of collapsible B is utterly impossible.

Extract from the British Sub-Aqua Diving Manual (author's notes in brackets):

'The Effects of Cold and Hypothermia.

'Hypothermia occurs when the core temperature falls below 35ºC. People immersed in water are more likely to experience hypothermia than any other group. People who fall into very cold water without adequate protective clothing may die within seconds or minutes. At between 25º and 30ºC the casualty will appear to be dead. Water is a very good conductor of heat so people who fall or jump into very cold water may experience a very severe shock, sufficient to stop the heart immediately. The effect is so instantaneous that it has been likened to electrocution and is called "hydrocution." It is found in people who fall overboard in Arctic seas and those swimmers who jump into icy lakes. If a person survives the initial impact of falling into cold water, he will gradually cool down. If he has no buoyancy and no thermal protection, after about 10 to 15 minutes in very cold water he will be unable to remain afloat. He will sink and drown. If he has a means of remaining afloat, he will not sink but will become hypothermic and unconscious. He will eventually die from hypothermia. Even after rescue the problems are not over. It is quite common for people suffering from hypothermia to die at the moment of rescue or soon afterwards. Re-warming deaths are due to; as the casualty warms up his skin and peripheral blood vessels dilate allowing warm central blood through. The cold peripheral blood is returned to the centre. This sudden surge of cold blood* *through the heart may be enough to stop it. In addition, cold has a number of other serious effects. Cold may produce spasm in the arteries of the heart itself and cause a heart attack.*

'MAXIMUM SURVIVAL TIME for an unprotected swimmer in water at 0ºC is one hour. [The water temperature around Titanic was -2ºC.] At 5ºC this survival time is extended to 2.5 hours. The rate of heat loss is related to body surface area, small people cool more quickly than large ones. Clothing worn by someone who falls into water should not be discarded as it helps to maintain an insulating layer of warm water. Movement of the water, produced by swimming will disrupt the insulating layer. Generally it is not advisable to swim if one falls into cold water, unless safety is very close. Evaporation of water from wet clothing can produce rapid cooling. By the time shivering has started, significant body cooling has already occurred. After immersion a person should get himself as warm as possible. A hot high energy drink will help to warm him up.

'People who are cold, or likely to become cold, should not drink alcohol. Alcohol increases heat loss by dilating the blood vessels of the skin and reduces heat production by lowering the amount of sugar in the blood. The treatment of hypothermia requires urgent admission to hospital. About 20% of those people rescued alive from the sea die on their way to hospital. The casualty should be removed from the water and protected from wind, rain and spray. Even if the person is conscious he must be made to lie down, preferably with his legs slightly raised. This will reduce the possibility of a drop in blood pressure and shock. The person should be kept still. Muscular activity will increase the risk of an after drop in temperature. Handling the person should be kept to a minimum. Rough handling may cause cardiac rhythm problems. [Climbing from boat to boat, rowing and clambering up the side of a ship by means of a cargo net hung over the side obviously didn't constitute rough handling to the stalwarts from boats A and B.] It is essential that heat of friction is not applied to arms and legs, this will cause an after drop. He must never be given alcohol.'

The diving manual has another relevant passage, which deals with the effects of prolonged under-water swimming, without benefit of breathing apparatus. As this pastime seems to have been indulged in by some of those who found their way to A and B. I will include the pertinent material here.

> '*HYPOXIA. Swimming under water, particularly at any depth, for any longer than a breath could normally be held at the surface causes a serious reduction in the amount of oxygen in the blood and a corresponding increase in carbon dioxide. The symptoms are, progressively, blue lips and ear lobes, poor co-ordination and fatigue, convulsions, unconsciousness, heart stops.*'

Small wonder that some of the survivors from the last two collapsible boats to leave the *Titanic* appeared so colourful.

Furnished with the above knowledge we are, at last, in a position to examine the ludicrous evidence of some of the people from boats A and B.

Colonel Archibald Gracie, who supposedly made his escape on collapsible B, described the shape of the clinker-built lower hull of an Englehart lifeboat: 'The collapsibles had round bottoms, like a canoe.'[1] Gracie was certainly not describing a flat-bottomed boat here and his discription differs somewhat from Lightoller's who described the boats as flat-bottomed.[2]

In his account of the last few minutes of *Titanic's* life, the colonel mentions only one collapsible being still aboard. Second Officer Lightoller told Gracie that collapsible A never left the ship[3]; Lightoller believed that A had been taken down with the ship because it had become tangled in the rigging of the forward funnel and in its own lashings. This impression was shared by Steward Whitely who said that, 'A became entangled and was abandoned while everyone's attention was turned toward B'.[4] Lightoller and Whitely both eventually found their way onto B.

Steward Edward Brown told a very different story. He said that there was no difficulty in getting boat A off the roof of the officers' quarters and that to do so those persons involved in the task slid it down planks. He did not know where the planks came from. Once again, Lightoller's story does not tie up with other evidence. This time the other evidence comes from people who actually got away in boat A.

From the evidence it appears that Lightoller gave up on A prematurely and consequently had no idea what had happened to it. If the passengers and crew had time to find planks and get the boat from above the officers' quarters[5] down onto the Boat Deck then Lightoller must have left quite some time before A went into the water.

When Boat A originally left *Titanic*, it was the right way up, but was turned over by people trying to get into it after *Titanic* sank, said August Wennerstrom. He also said that he had been on A until that point but was thrown out and knocked unconscious. When he come round he found his way back to the boat, which was now filled with water and held up (kept afloat) only by the cork railing around the boat.[6] That Wennerstrom was unconscious and therefore not struggling when he went into the water would have improved his chances of survival immensely. Insensibility would also have lessened the shock to the system of suddenly being immersed in the freezing water. The evidence of both Brown and Wennerstrom is, so far, totally believable, but Brown then said that he was in the water for about 2½hr,[7] which must raise some doubts.

One passenger, Abelseth, said that he swam for about 20min before he found boat A,[8] which is extremely unlikely but not impossible.

Abelseth's estimate of the time he spent in the water could be a long way from being accurate. When he did finally manage to board the boat he said the people there were standing in about 12 or 14in of water. He had been pulled into the boat from the water and must have been fairly close to the bulwarks, where the hull was at its shallowest.[9]

Mr R. N. Williams Jnr who was closer to the boat's centreline said that the water came up to his waist.[10]

Also plucked from the icy clutches of the North Atlantic by boat A were Mrs Rosa Abbott and Mr P. D. Daly.[11] Mrs Abbott was the only female to be saved from the sea after *Titanic* sank.

Not long after the liner had foundered there were about 30 people either in or clinging to A but as the night wore on, the cold steadily killed them one at a time, until by morning there were only 11 or 12 remaining.[12]

A. Bright, who was in charge of boat D when Lowe in boat 14 towed them up to the waterlogged collapsible, said that 13 men and one woman were transferred to D. Either way, over half of the people that had managed to reach this boat succumbed to the cold before morning,[13] which is exactly what one would expect. Only those actually inside the confines of the boat's hull would have had any chance of surviving the night as the temperature steadily dropped.[14]

That anybody survived aboard collapsible A is nothing short of amazing. From what we know of the effects of extreme cold, one would have expected all aboard to have perished. But, if they had huddled together, kept still and supported each other generally, then it is just possible that they could have survived. Nowhere in the evidence of those from A is there any hint of dissension or selfishness. On the contrary, most of those taken from the sea were hauled aboard by the people already in the boat. None of them seems to have been in the water for any length of time, with the possible exceptions of August Wennerstrom and Olaus Abelseth, whom we have already looked at. As I said earlier, the exploits of the people in collapsible A are only just believable. This cannot be said of the exploits of those in the last of *Titanic's* boats that we shall examine, which were totally impossible. Nonetheless, the evidence of the survivors from boat A needs to be treated with a certain amount of suspicion. While their story could be true, it could also be a tissue of lies.

Collapsible B was supposedly washed overboard as *Titanic* buried her bow beneath the water. Clinging on to it at the time was the second wireless operator, Harold Sidney Bride, among others. In one version of his story Bride said that he finished up underneath the upturned boat where he remained for a half to three-quarters of an hour. Then he swam away from the boat for about three-quarters to an hour before returning.[15] We know that this is impossible in water at 28°F (-2°C).

In another version of his story Bride said that he got out from under B immediately after it was washed overboard. He swam away from the ship as quickly as he could.[16] While he was swimming he saw other men in the water, swimming and sinking.[17] Why men would be sinking if they were wearing life-jackets he does not explain. There were plenty of life-jackets for all aboard.

In yet another version Bride said, 'I saw a boat of some kind near me and I put all my strength into an effort to swim to it. It was hard work. I was all done when a hand reached out from the boat and pulled me aboard. It was our same collapsible.'[18] None of Bride's stories makes sense.

When he reached the collapsible, he said, the wireless operator estimated that there were between 30 and 40 people on it.[19] Among those on the upturned boat, said Bride, supported by Whitely, was his friend and superior officer Jack Phillips,[20] which we already know must be a lie. It was while Phillips was supposedly on boat B that he allegedly told Charles Lightoller about the *Mesaba* ice warning,[21] which again must be a deviation from the truth. Curiously, Lightoller never mentioned this message to the American Inquiry. Lightoller admitted that he did not see Phillips himself but was reliant on Bride for the information that he had been aboard the capsized boat. Bride told him that Phillips had died during the night from fear and cold.[22]

Fireman John Collins was washed overboard as *Titanic's* stern began to lift out of the water, by the same wave that had carried B off the ship. When he first saw collapsible B there were already more than 15 or 16 people on it.[23] The boat was about 4 or 5yd away from him.[24]

Second Officer Lightoller was also washed off the ship by the same wall of water that took boat B. Or alternatively he walked or dived into the sea. Instead of being immediately washed clear he was sucked down by water pouring into the ship and pinned against a grating. Just when he thought there was no escape, a blast of air escaping from the ship blew him clear. Surfacing, he swam toward the foremast, which was still sticking up out of the water, but realised that the apparent safety offered by this seemingly solid structure was illusory and turned away. Spotting B he then swam toward that. When he reached it there was nobody aboard, but there were a lot of people in the water around it.[25]

John Hagan (not the John Hagan who appears on the crew list but another with the same name, who was working his passage) left *Titanic* holding onto the keel of boat B at the stern, when it floated off. When the forward funnel fell, he said it missed him and the boat by about 1yd. He noticed that there were a number of planks floating nearby which he thought were deck planking from the forward part of the ship. This was the planking which was to provide collapsible B with makeshift paddles and clubs.

Col Archibald Gracie was another who was sucked down by the ship. Gracie's story is really exceptional. He left the ship at about the same time as the second officer. Drawn under water he was held captive by the suction for some moments before being blown clear. He then proceeded to swim, still under water, away from the ship. By the time Col Gracie finally broke surface the ship had gone.

We know that *Titanic's* stern remained in a vertical attitude for almost 5min. If we allow another minute for it to have reached that position after Col Gracie was swept, or dived, or jumped, overboard, then he was swimming under water for approximately 6min. If we reduce the colonel's outrageous claims to one quarter they are still patently impossible. It is at this point that what little credibility Gracie still retained disappears.

When Gracie reached B, Second Officer Lightoller was already on the bow and Wireless Operator Bride was on the stern of the boat.[26]

After the colonel had been on the boat for a while he noticed that his hair had frozen stiff.[27] Looking about him the colonel believed that he saw lights in other lifeboats.[28]

A. H. Barkworth went into the sea wearing a large fur coat over the top of his lifebelt. He eventually reached collapsible B[29] and supposedly climbed aboard unaided.[30] Anybody who has fallen into the water, or been swimming fully clothed, will already know how likely that story is to be true!

Fireman Harry Senior, a relative latecomer to B, said that Lightoller, Gracie and J. B. Thayer were already on the lifeboat when he tried to get on, 'but some chap hit me over the head with an oar'.[31] At the time Senior thought that there were about 35 people on the boat, but no women, he noticed. It is from Senior that we get the story about Captain Smith reaching boat B and being pulled aboard but slipping off again saying, 'I will follow the ship.'[32] Entrée Cook J. Maynard also told of the captain reaching the boat but being unable to maintain hold, sliding off again.[33] As Senior was one of the last people to reach collapsible B after *Titanic* had gone, he would have been too late to have seen the captain even if he had reached the boat, which he most likely did not. Assistant Cook John Maynard said that the captain had swum alongside B just before *Titanic* sank. He went on to say that the captain could not maintain his hold on a lifebelt. He did not explain how he recognised the captain in the inky darkness or why the skipper had been unable to put on his life preserver. Walter Hurst was certain that Smith never reached B.[34]

Steward Whitely was another who was discouraged from attempting to board B before managing to secure himself a place. He described his experience: 'I drifted near a boat, wrong side up. About 30 men were clinging to it.[35] They refused to let me get on. Somebody tried to hit me with an oar.'[36]

As the cold indiscriminately killed those aboard the upturned boat, and those in the water, the surviving members of the latter group managed to scramble aboard. Not that they were very much better off, dressed in soaking wet clothes and exposed to the freezing air. As their clothes either dried or froze on them, their plight would have been exacerbated. Nevertheless they stood on the upturned boat in two rows, back to back,[37] in an effort to keep the unstable craft steady, Lightoller on the bow calling orders as to which way they were to lean next. For the next 4hr, until about 6.30am, they kept this up, while one by one, men toppled off the boat, victims of the inexorable cold.[38]

Gracie explained that part of the reason for standing on the boat was to avoid the icy water,[39] which seems unlikely as the air was even colder.

Had they been dressed in warm dry clothing and with only their feet in the water, the survivors on B would still almost certainly have been unable to do what they described themselves as having done. Dressed as they were in mostly flimsy waterlogged clothing and having been immersed in the icy cold water of the North Atlantic, their story stops being merely impossible and becomes laughable. But there is yet more to come.

Charles Joughin, ship's baker, told a story so incredible it is astonishing that nobody actually called him a liar at the time. According to the baker he had returned to his cabin on more than one occasion and taken a drink or two of whisky before the ship sank. Between drinking bouts Joughin had usefully employed himself by throwing deck chairs out of the open windows on B Deck.

It was 'like threading a needle', he said.

Returning to the upper deck shortly before the ship began to rotate about its axis and lift the stern toward the heavens, he saw that the route aft was obstructed by a mass of humanity obviously intent on exactly the same course as himself, namely to reach the extreme rear of the ship. With a typically drunken flash of inspiration Joughin decided to walk up the outside of *Titanic's* heavily listing hull. Suiting the action to the thought, he hopped over the ship's rail and actually walked up the sloping side, steadying himself with the handrail. In this fashion he managed to reach the very highest point on the sinking ship, when she had assumed a vertical attitude. Standing on the outside of the stern he awaited the end. As *Titanic* slipped slowly beneath the water Joughin calmly stepped off and swam away, without even getting his hair wet.

Up until this point the baker's story, bizarre though it is, has a believable quality about it, but not for much longer.

After being in the water for over 1hr, the whisky-fortified chief baker saw the upturned collapsible, floating on its side. It was just growing light as he paddled his way towards it. When he tried to get onto the boat those already aboard pushed him back off again.[40] Not being easily discouraged, Joughin tried again, and again. At long last he succeeded in scrambling aboard. Another cook, Maynard, helped the baker to hold onto the lifeboat and eventually to get partly onto it. He had been in the water for 2½hr.[41] After getting onto the boat,

Joughin found it even colder than being in the water.[42] This impression was borne out by the evidence of Fireman James McGann who was also on B. 'All our legs were frostbitten and we were all in the hospital for a day at least.'[43]

Col Gracie gave an alternative, if equally incredible, scenario for how those on the capsized boat passed the night. He said that the water came up to their waists as they reclined on the bottom of the boat.[44] Col Gracie freely admitted that he relied, for corroboration, on those who also claim to have escaped on boat B.[45]

It was fully light[46] at about 6.30am, with *Carpathia*'s or some other steamer's lights already in sight,[47] when boats 4 and 12 picked up the people from the collapsible and finally lifted the baker completely out of the water. Gracie said that he, Lightoller, Barkworth and Thayer were taken by boat 12.[48] He is supported by Hemmings in boat 4 who said that only 4 or 5 survivors got into Number 4; the rest went into the other boat.[49] Lightoller thought that between 28 and 30 people were saved on the overturned boat,[50] but other sources put the figure closer to a dozen. But then Lightoller does seem to have viewed the entire event through rose-tinted glasses, doesn't he?

Fred Clench, commanding boat 12, said that when he picked up the survivors from B they were wet through.[51] The chances of anybody surviving for 4hr with their clothing soaked through in a temperature of 27ºF are negligible, particularly with the added factor of wind chill, which came with the breeze, shortly before dawn.

The upturned boat had been steadily sinking lower and lower in the water throughout the night. Even early on, very few of those aboard were able to find themselves a place completely clear of the water. As the boat settled ever lower, more and more people found themselves standing in the water, some up to their waists. Joughin, as such a relative latecomer, would have been lucky to have found himself a spot as desirable even as this.

As can clearly be seen from his own testimony, Joughin was actually in the water, if only partially, for at least 4hr, two of them exposed to the wind as well. Remembering that he had imbibed more than a little alcoholic spirit, his resistance to the effects of the biting cold would have been considerably reduced. (This supposed feat of endurance is quite impossible as is shown at the beginning of this chapter in the extract from the British Sub-Aqua Club manual.) Exactly the same conditions were supposedly endured by the others on B with the exception that they were merely standing, only partially immersed in water, for the full 4hr and were not necessarily drunk. They also were exposed to the wind which sprang up just before dawn. It is beyond the boundaries of possibility that anybody could have survived for this length of time under these extreme conditions.

For some reason as yet undetermined, the people from collapsible B told a story which bore very little, if any, resemblance to the truth. For the sake of completeness, it might be as well to mention here that when collapsible B was found a few days later by a vessel which was searching the area for the bodies of victims, the side of the lifeboat was smashed. Strangely, there were no marks on the bottom of the boat from the polished shoes of those who had supposedly scrambled aboard it during the night, boot polish being waterproof. Around the damaged boat floated the corpses of several passengers, heavily clad in warm clothing, and with their pockets stuffed with food and tobacco. Obviously not a group who had intended to take a swim, these people were ideally dressed and provisioned to withstand a night in an open boat. With this extra information to hand it is possible to put together a purely speculative scenario for collapsible B.

Could this boat have actually been launched very late in the proceedings aboard the sinking liner? That at least would account for the attempts to launch it supposedly being abandoned in favour of boat A. If the boat was in the water then there would be no point in spending any more time on it.

Logic dictates that as the ship was sinking by the bow then the forward boats should be the first attended to. In fact, there was no reason why all the boats could not have been lowered at the same time except that the crew were untrained. Having said that, most of the crew were fully experienced seamen and would know what was required. If the sequential system was used simply to keep the lowerings under the supervision of an officer, then where was the logic in sending those officers off in earlier boats while their services were still required? All four collapsibles were stowed at the forward end of the main superstructure, A and B on the roof of the officers' quarters and C and D on the Boat Deck. Crew members could certainly have been found to prepare these boats for launching while the officers saw to the standard wooden boats. If this is indeed what happened (and there is no evidence to support it at present) then it is possible that collapsible B was filled from the Boat Deck and went into the sea the right way up just like boat A.

We also know that aboard the doomed *Titanic* first class passengers had a far greater chance of survival than those from the other two classes. Is it not possible that these last two collapsible boats, or perhaps only B, were held back intentionally, to take off certain selected first class passengers and probably the ship's senior officers? Or is it possible that it was loaded and lowered with that same group of selected people fairly early on in the proceedings? This would account for the ship's log not being put aboard any of the other lifeboats. With over 2½hr between the collision and the ship sinking, it is inconceivable that not one person aboard thought to save this invaluable document. If the log book was put aboard A or B then the mystery is explained.

We know that collapsible A was overturned and swamped by the mass of people struggling in the water after the ship had sunk. Could the story of B have been similar?

If collapsible B was somehow set afloat with a crew and loaded with first class male passengers, well wrapped up against the cold, then we have a possible explanation for the group of corpses found floating near the smashed lifeboat. Launched during the last few moments before *Titanic* adopted her stern in the air attitude, the lifeboat would have had no time to get clear before the water was full of kicking, struggling and screaming humanity. What would be more natural than these people should try to climb aboard the collapsible, floating so conveniently nearby?

The people in the boat would have tried to fend them off, but there would have been too many and they would have had the strength of desperation. In the struggle the boat must have turned turtle. The more lightly dressed swimmers would to some extent have been able to clamber up onto the overturned boat while the heavily clad millionaires, with the added weight of their waterlogged clothing, would not. The extra warm clothing, which was to protect them from the cold air during the night was little protection from the icy sea water. It would have been these people's own addiction to comfort which condemned them to death. Strangely, the crew members aboard the upturned boat outnumbered passengers by a ratio of about three to one. As there were more passengers than crew still aboard the liner when it sank, a somewhat different ratio might have been expected.

Throughout the night the upturned boat merely drifted, surrounded by the people who had once been its occupants. Even if the cold killed them relatively quickly, they would still have remained close to the drifting boat. After all, the same winds and currents affected them more or less equally. There is a phenomenon well known to scientists, commonly called 'the cluster effect'. This effect is demonstrated by the tendency of articles floating freely to congregate in groups or clusters.

We have seen how:

- More than half of the people who made it into collapsible A, after being in the sea, died from the cold before morning;
- Baker Charles Joughin, after drinking heavily, supposedly survived in the sub-zero sea water for more than four hours;
- Collapsible B was later found surrounded by the heavily-clad bodies of what would appear to be its original occupants.

The Rescuer

Carpathia was launched on 6 April 1902. She was 540ft long, 64.5ft wide and weighed 13,603 gross register tons (8,660 net tons). As first constructed she had passenger accommodation for 204 people in second class and 1,500 in third. During 1905 the internal layout was altered so that 100 first class, 200 second class and 2,250 third class passengers could be carried. This was still the layout on the night that the *Titanic* sank and *Carpathia* achieved immortality as the ship which raced to the rescue, saving the lives of over 700 persons.

Carpathia's captain at the time of the *Titanic* disaster was Arthur Henry Rostron. Born in Bolton, Lancashire, in 1869, he had joined Cunard in 1895 after serving with other lines aboard both sailing vessels and steamers as a junior officer. Twelve years after joining Cunard he was given his first command, the cargo steamer *Brescia* in the Mediterranean trade. As his career progressed he commanded *Ivernia*, *Saxonia* and *Pannonia*. He took over his sixth command, *Carpathia*, in January 1912. His senior officers were: Thomas William Hankinson, Chief; Horace Dean, First; James Bisset, Second; Eric Res, Third; and Geoffrey Barrish, Fourth.[1]

At midday on Thursday, 11 April 1912, *Carpathia* left New York's pier 54, bound for the Mediterranean. Aboard were 128 first, 50 second and 565 third class passengers. The early part of the voyage was uneventful. Day by day the weather grew colder, and by Saturday it was raining. The following day, Sunday 14 April, dawned cold, bright and clear. Just as on *Titanic*, far to the east and north of *Carpathia*, the captain held a mid-morning divine service. All the crew attended and according to Mrs James Fenwick, a first class passenger, it was 'most impressive'. Sunday passed slowly, especially for Harold Cottam the overworked wireless operator.

Cottam had been on duty since 7am, in the 'wireless shack'. Unlike more modern vessels, which were constructed with a wireless cabin, *Carpathia* dated from a time before wireless was carried by merchant ships. Consequently, the 'wireless shack' was a later addition to the main superstructure of the vessel in the shape of a white-painted, box-like cabin, perched atop the main deckhouse, above the second class smoking room and aft of the single funnel.

Carpathia carried only one wireless operator, which was completely normal for the period. Only the largest and most modern liners carried two. Wireless operators on these smaller ships had no fixed hours of duty: they were expected to be available throughout the day to handle passenger and commercial traffic, as well as being on call should the captain require their services at any other time. However, most captains realised that even a lowly wireless operator had to have some sleep and so did not call upon them after about 11pm, except in cases of dire necessity. This is the most likely reason that Cyril Evans of the *Californian* was not called upon to contact the mystery ship seen late on Sunday evening from that vessel.

It was close to midnight, as usual, when Cottam decided to retire for the night. He was awaiting acknowledgement of an earlier message he had sent to the Allen liner *Parisien*, so instead of switching off, he kept the earphones on his head as he undressed. Still no message came from *Parisien* so he switched to the frequency of the Cape Cod land station, planning to listen in to a few messages before tuning back into *Parisien's* wavelength. He heard a batch of messages, mostly commercial or personal, intended for the *Titanic*. These Cottam wrote down, intending to forward them in the morning.

Curiously, Cottam had received no warnings of ice in their vicinity although *Carpathia* was well within the co-ordinates given in the *Mesaba* ice warning. The ship had been within wireless range of the shore station at Cape Race for some time, as well as being in contact with other vessels. How the wireless operator had managed to miss all of the warnings transmitted that day is unknown. *Carpathia* was certainly within wireless range of *Californian* when that ship sent a warning to *Titanic*. Perhaps Cottam merely neglected to pass these vital navigational messages on to his captain, just as Phillips and Bride neglected to pass on the ones that they received aboard *Titanic*.

More than ready for bed, *Carpathia's* wireless operator was having trouble with a knotted shoelace, which delayed him and kept him on the air for a few minutes longer than he would otherwise have been. Then, on a whim, he decided to call up *Titanic* and let her operator know that Cape Race was trying to contact them.

'MPA [*Carpathia*]: I say, old man, do you know there is a batch of messages coming through for you from MCC [Cape Cod]?'

Cottam was cut off with, 'MGY [*Titanic*]: Come at once. We have struck an iceberg. It's a CQD, old man. Position 41°46'N. 50°14'W.' This signal was received by *Carpathia* at 12.35am.[2]

Cottam was taken aback by the unexpected call for help from the *Titanic* and replied, 'MPA: Shall I tell my captain? Do you require assistance?'

'MGY: Yes. Come quick.'

Realising that this was a real emergency, Cottam delayed only as long as it took him to put on his jacket before scurrying forward to the bridge. The officer of the watch was H. V. Dean, *Carpathia's* first mate. The wireless operator blurted out his message. Dean, at first was inclined to believe that Cottam had either made a mistake or was pulling his leg, but soon realised that he was serious. Marching Cottam before him, the first officer set off to alert the captain. They hurried down the steep companion-way (staircase) which led to the captain's quarters. This not being a time to stand on ceremony, they burst in on the skipper.

Captain Rostron had just gone to bed and was not yet asleep. Understandably, he was not pleased by the unheralded arrival of his first officer and the Marconi man. He angrily demanded an explanation for the intrusion into his privacy. Dean stood by as Cottam reported to Rostron, 'Sir, I have just received an urgent distress call from *Titanic*. She requires immediate assistance. She has struck an iceberg and is sinking. Her position is 41°46' North, 50° 14' West,' he said hurriedly, fearing that his master's wrath might be about to fall upon his head.

Even as Cottam spoke, Captain Rostron threw back the bed covers, swung his feet to the floor and was out of bed reaching for his clothes. 'Are you certain?' he asked.

'Yes, sir.'

'Absolutely certain?' Rostron checked as he dressed.

'Yes, sir.' Cottam assured him.

Within a very few minutes the captain was in the chart room examining the navigation chart and working out the precise position of *Carpathia* in relation to the position given by *Titanic*. The distance between the two ships was 58 miles and the course he would have to steer, the now famous N52°W, was calculated in short order.

The bosun's mate was passing the chart room window on his way to supervise the men detailed to wash down the decks when the captain spotted him. Rostron called him into the chart room and told him to get all of *Carpathia's* boats ready for lowering. These instructions caused the bosun's mate some alarm and the captain was forced to explain that *Carpathia* was in no danger. They were going to the assistance of another vessel.

Captain Rostron sent for Chief Engineer Johnson with instructions that he was to report to the bridge, which the engineer quickly did. The captain instructed him to put on extra stokers and to squeeze as much speed out of the ship as he possibly could. So that none of the extra energy produced by the stokers should be frittered away on anything other than increased speed, Rostron ordered the hot water supplies to passenger and crew quarters alike shut down. The same applied to the steam heating systems throughout the ship. *Carpathia's* normal top speed was 14kts but Johnson and his crew managed to exceed that by 25%. The whole vessel shuddered and the engine bedplates shook as the engines struggled to meet the demand for more and more speed. Black smoke belched from the single funnel as *Carpathia* raced towards *Titanic's* given position at 17.5kts.[3]

The ship's doctors were sent for next — three of them, English, Hungarian and Italian. Each was assigned a group of survivors to look after. The English doctor would see to the first class, the Italian to the second and the Hungarian, third.

By this time the rest of the ship's officers had assembled on the bridge. Rostron issued orders to cover all eventualities. Chief Steward Hughes and Chief Purser Brown were to have all of their men at the gangways to help survivors as they came aboard and send them, according to their class, to the appropriate dining saloon.[4] All of the crew were called and, after a cup of coffee, set to work preparing the ship for its new load of passengers. Tea, coffee and hot soup were prepared. Blankets were readied and stacked to hand. All of *Carpathia's* 565 steerage passengers were to be placed in just one section of the third class quarters while the remainder, 1,685 berths, were to be given over to the third class survivors from *Titanic*. Extra lookouts were detailed to watch for any sign of ice from the bows, bridge wings and crow's-nest.[5] James Bisset said, 'There were at least 13 lookouts on *Carpathia* that night.'[6] *Carpathia's* crew set to work with a will.

While all of this was going on, Cottam remained at his wireless set. So as not to have to leave the Marconi apparatus, even for a moment, he had a steward to help him and to carry messages to the captain. A copy of every message received was sent straight to the bridge where Captain Rostron was controlling operations. The information, what there was of it, coming from *Titanic* was not encouraging.

At 12.50am (*Titanic* time) *Titanic* called *Olympic*, 'I require immediate assistance.'

At 1.10am, again to *Olympic*, 'We are in collision with berg. Sinking, head down, come as soon as possible. Get your boats ready.'

At 1.25am, 'We are putting the women off in small boats.' Cottam was later to deny that he ever received any message to the effect that *Titanic* was putting people off in small boats.[7]

At 1.35am, 'Engine room getting flooded.'

At 1.45am, 'Engine room full up to the boilers …'

In *Carpathia's* wireless diary is an entry: '12.20am. [2.10am *Titanic* time] Signals very broken.' Until then *Titanic's* signals had been good.[8]

In the meanwhile Captain Rostron, with unparalleled efficiency, had ordered all the ship's gangway doors (doors in the sides of the steel hull) opened and lights to hang from the sides of the ship and above all the gangways. A chair was hung from ropes at all of the gangways so that the sick and injured could more easily be hauled aboard. Canvas bags were readied to lift the children from the small boats. Lines were hung from *Carpathia's* sides for the crews of the lifeboats to catch onto. Engine oil, to be poured down the forward lavatories to smooth the water around the ship, was prepared. Chief Officer Hankinson reported that all was in readiness at 2.30am.

Rostron had already ordered that decks, companionways and public areas of the ship were to be kept clear of passengers, but the activity outside their doors began to arouse suspicions that all was not as usual. Passengers began to ring for their stewards and demand to know what was going on. Heads began to appear around cabin doors as curiosity overcame the inmates, many of whom had been first alerted by the sudden drop in cabin temperatures. The stewards, politely but firmly, assured passengers that there was no cause for alarm and advised them to stay in their cabins. In the main the passengers did what they were told, thus allowing *Carpathia's* crew to complete their preparations.

Carpathia ploughed on through the unnaturally smooth, flat calm sea. The sky was ablaze with stars and the air, bitterly cold, carried the faint but unmistakable odour of icebergs. The time was about 2.45 am.[9] Captain Rostron described the situation later:

'Almost at once the second officer reported the first iceberg. It lay two points on the port bow and it was the one whose presence was betrayed by the star beam. More and more now we were all keyed up. Icebergs loomed up and fell astern; we never slackened, though sometimes we altered course suddenly to avoid them.[10] It was an anxious time with the Titanic's fateful experience very close in our minds. There were 700 souls on the Carpathia; these lives, as well as all the survivors of the Titanic herself, depended on a sudden turn of the wheel.'

As *Carpathia* raced toward the scene of the sinking, the lights of yet another unidentified westbound steamer were seen.[11] Captain Rostron said, 'We saw the masthead lights of another steamer quite distinctly between us and the *Titanic,* two points on the starboard bow, and one of the officers saw her red light.'[12]

As soon as Captain Rostron thought that there was any chance that they would be in view of *Titanic,* he ordered rockets to be fired[13] at about 15min intervals. When they got even closer to Boxhall's position, Cunard Company's night signals were fired — a blue light and two Roman candles, each throwing out six blue balls to a height not exceeding 150ft — to let the people in the boats know that *Carpathia* was approaching. 'Occasionally we caught sight of a green light; we were getting pretty near the spot.'

When a green light had first been sighted, a little off the port bow,[14] it had raised the hopes of Captain Rostron and the officers on the bridge of *Carpathia.* They at first thought they were seeing *Titanic's* starboard riding light, but now they knew better.

It was about 3.35am and they were getting close to the position worked out by *Titanic's* navigating officer but there was no sign of *Titanic* herself. '… had the great liner been afloat we should have seen her'. At 4 o'clock Captain Rostron stopped engines '… we were there'.

Then another green light was seen,[15] just ahead and low down. Rostron knew it must be a lifeboat and began to ease *Carpathia* forward, to bring the small boat alongside. Suddenly, out of the darkness a large iceberg loomed up, directly ahead and less than a quarter of a mile away.[16] The captain and the second officer both saw it at the same time. Until that moment Captain Rostron had intended to bring the boat alongside on *Carpathia's* port side. Although there was very little, if any, wind or waves, this was the lee (sheltered) side of the ship. The intervention of the iceberg caused an abrupt change in plan, not for the first time that night, and Captain Rostron swung his ship round to collect the lifeboat on his starboard side.[17] Captain Rostron had taken a calculated risk and it had paid off. His own words best describe how he felt at that moment:

'Devoutly thankful I was that the long race was over; every moment had brought its risk — a risk that only keen eyes and quick decisions could meet — but with that feeling was the veritable ache which the now certain knowledge of the liner's loss brought. No sign of her — and below was the first boat containing survivors.'

Captain Rostron had found the boats exactly where he expected to.[18] A former shipmate of Captain Rostron who had served under him in several vessels wrote, 'The great thing about Rostron was, he was a great navigator. There was nothing slapdash about Rostron and the navigators around that night and I would certainly place Rostron and his team at the top of the list.'[19]

If Captain Rostron had made for the position worked out by Boxhall, allowing for the known currents, then it follows that Boxhall's position was accurate. As the wreck was found some distance from this position, it is evident that *Titanic* moved a considerable distance after the signal giving her position was sent out, some of it probably as she dived toward the sea-bed.

Captain Rostron later said, 'I may state this, that the position given me by the *Titanic* was absolutely correct and she was absolutely on her track, bound for New York.' Seventy-four years later Captain Rostron's conclusions were confirmed by Robert Ballard who stated that, 'the *Titanic* was exactly on course'.[20] Boxhall himself told the American Inquiry that soon after he met Captain Rostron the Cunard skipper said to him, 'What a splendid position that was you gave us.' When asked what that position had been, Boxhall answered, '41° 46' N, 50° 14'W.'[21]

Captain Lord said, 'We also checked up in regard to the position, and found it to be what had been reported by the *Virginian*.'[22] Lord presumably worked this out from his own dead reckoning position and the course he steered on his way to the wreck site. This would, of course, have been impossible if either position had been very far out.

A cry came from the boat below, 'We have only one seaman aboard and cannot work very well.'

As the boat was still a little way from *Carpathia's* gangway, Rostron manoeuvred the ship until they were right alongside. The passengers began to climb aboard. Captain Rostron observed, 'Obviously they had got away in a hurry, for there were only 25 of them and the capacity of the boat was fully 40.' Even at this early stage in the rescue Rostron had noticed how badly under-filled the lifeboats were. He had also noticed that there was an officer in the boat and sent word for that officer to report to him as soon as he came aboard.

Joseph Groves Boxhall told Captain Rostron that the *Titanic* had sunk at about 2.30am, a mere 1½hr before the rescue ship arrived at the scene. 'Alas that we had not been nearer!' Rostron commented later. All of the millionaries had gone with the ship.[23]

It was just growing light and the new day revealed an awe-inspiring sight to the people on *Carpathia*[24] and in *Titanic's* lifeboats. Everywhere were icebergs. Less than half of a mile from *Carpathia's* starboard beam was the frozen monster that had faced them only a few minutes before. Less than 100ft off the port quarter was a growler — a broken-off lump of ice 10–15ft high and about 25ft long. Describing the event, Rostron said, 'When we had stopped and daylight broke I found it [the iceberg] was something like a quarter of a mile off.' He added that he had not seen that particular berg before.[25]

The ice-field stretched as far as the eye could see. The captain instructed a junior officer to go up to the wheelhouse deck and count the bergs. He counted 25 that stood about 200ft in height and dozens more ranging in height from 150ft down to 50ft, all between one and two miles off.[26] Floating pathetically amid this awesome display of nature were *Titanic's* small boats.

Charles Lightoller was obviously not quite as observant as Captain Rostron's lookouts. When it grew light he couldn't see any icebergs closer than 10 miles away. 'There was no packed ice and no growlers,' he said. It is sometimes difficult to believe that Lightoller was there at all.

Carpathia continued with the business of picking up survivors. As they came aboard, Rostron noticed, 'Their thankfulness for safety was always mingled with the sense of their loss and the chattering cold that possessed them.' By the time they were taken aboard *Carpathia*, some of the passengers had been in the open boats for as much as 6hr. Few of them were dressed for the prevailing conditions, many having nothing more than an overcoat thrown over their night-clothes to protect them from the Arctic cold. Captain Rostron believed that this unpreparedness on the part of the passengers showed the urgency with which they had left the ship. However, Mrs Rene Harris said that an English lord and lady had not only saved themselves but their luggage as well.

According to Mrs Harris this lord and lady were later seen aboard *Carpathia*, sometimes in sports clothes and at other times in evening dress. These aristocrats even had a couple of *Titanic's* crewmen put on life-jackets and pose for photographs until Lowe stopped them.[27]

While aboard *Carpathia* the crew from lifeboat Number 1 were assembled for a group photograph and all seven signed their names on Lady Duff-Gordon's life-jacket.[28]

Obviously not everyone left the liner in haste. At least one of the crew reached *Carpathia* with his kit, which he was not allowed to keep, but he must have had time to pack.

Slowly *Carpathia* moved from lifeboat to lifeboat picking up first the people and then, in most cases, the boat itself until all the survivors and 13 of *Titanic's* lifeboats were aboard the Cunarder. Captain Rostron was sure that he had picked up the people from all of the boats within a range of four to five miles. Some boats were stored on the forecastle deck while others remained hanging from *Carpathia's* davits. Robert Hitchens thought that only two of the liner's lifeboats were cast adrift by *Carpathia*.[29] This almost agrees with what Lawrence Beesley had to say about which boats reached the Cunard vessel. He said that only 17 of *Titanic's* lifeboats ever reached *Carpathia*.[30] As we shall shortly see, Captain Rostron didn't quite agree with either estimate.

Toward the end of the rescue operation, Rostron couldn't help noticing that there was very little wreckage. 'Except for the boats beside the ship and the icebergs, the sea was strangely empty. Hardly a bit of wreckage floated – just a deck chair or two, a few lifebelts, a good deal of cork; no more flotsam than one can often see on a seashore, drifted in by the tide.'[31] Where the cork might have originated is another of the mysteries surrounding the loss of the White Star liner. Despite some written information to the contrary, *Titanic's* bulkheads were not lined or filled with cork; neither was cork part of her cargo. Perhaps, like the extra boats, it came from a different ship.

Titanic's surviving wireless operator thought that he saw the corpse of his superior in the lifeboat as he was leaving it to board the Cunarder. He believed that Phillips 'had died on the raft of exposure'.[32] Why Bride thought anybody would bother to transfer a corpse from the upturned lifeboat into an already overloaded one is anybody's guess, but it is inconceivable that he didn't notice Phillips aboard the lifeboat until the last moment.

Captain Rostron searched the wreck site but saw only one body floating in the water, '… the intense cold made it hopeless for anyone to live long in it'.[33] His second officer, James Bisset, also only saw the one floating body.[34] Maj Arthur Peuchen, and all of *Titanic's* surviving officers, saw no bodies at all, just a little wreckage.[35] Over 1,000 people wearing life-jackets had gone into the water when *Titanic* sank. The cork jackets should have kept them all afloat, even if the terrible cold had killed them. Where all of the floating corpses had got to is yet another of the unexplained phenomena connected to the loss of RMS *Titanic*, as is the curious absence of the vessel's lifebuoys. Board of Trade Inspector Carruthers testified that the ship carried lifebuoys which lit up when they went into the water.[36] Nowhere in the record is there any mention of these lifebuoys being seen by either survivors or rescuers.

We have seen that:

- As *Carpathia* steamed to the rescue she passed an unidentified vessel;
- Captain Rostron, on arrival at the site of the sinking, was surprised at just how little wreckage there was;
- Captain Rostron saw only one body floating in the water.

Aboard *Carpathia* and New York Arrival

At about 8am the men on the bridge of *Carpathia* saw another vessel coming up: the *Californian*. *Carpathia* signalled the Leyland Line vessel, asking her to continue searching, because Captain Rostron had decided to make for New York. A breeze had come with the dawn and the sea was rising. The captain of the *Carpathia* wanted to get well clear of the dangerous, ice-filled area before darkness began to fall again.

At the British Inquiry Captain Rostron described the boats from which *Carpathia* rescued people and those he saw at the scene of the disaster. In answer to the Attorney General's question, 'Altogether, how many boats did you pick up?' Rostron said rather more than anybody expected, or seems to have taken in.

'We got 13 lifeboats alongside, and we picked up 13 lifeboats, two emergency boats, and two Berthon [collapsible] boats. One lifeboat we saw capsized, and one of the Berthon boats was not launched from the ship. There was also a collapsible boat which we saw capsized. This made a total of 20.'[1]

Captain Rostron was describing a full-sized lifeboat, at the scene, which he saw capsized as well as an upturned collapsible. We know that all of *Titanic's* wooden lifeboats were floating the correct way up and had all carried survivors. So where did this overturned lifeboat come from? Certainly not from *Titanic*.

While Captain Rostron's arithmetic is faultless, he was misinformed about what boats had actually left *Titanic*: quite possibly he never saw collapsible A. He had, however, confirmed Mrs Thayer's statement that there was an upturned lifeboat, not a collapsible, at the scene. According to Captain Rostron's statement he actually got 17 boats alongside, 13 full sized lifeboats, two emergency boats and two collapsibles, exactly as Lawrence Beesley described. One extra full-sized lifeboat remains unaccounted for.

This capsized lifeboat is possibly one of the more important items we have when it comes to unravelling the morass of misinformation encircling the loss of the *Titanic*. If the information on the upturned boat came only from Captain Rostron or Mrs Thayer then perhaps it might be dismissed, but not when the story of its existence comes from both of these sources. And definitely not when its presence is confirmed by the pariah of the story, Captain Stanley Lord, where it did nothing to help his case.

Captain Rostron also noticed something else that should have excited considerably more interest than it did. He saw, 'two steamers to the North, seven to eight miles away, neither of them was the *Californian*'.[2]

Even as *Carpathia* left the scene of the disaster, *Californian* began searching for swimmers who might have beaten the odds and survived the cold. Some dark shapes were seen on an iceberg and for a moment the officers of the *Californian* thought that they might be people, but they turned out to be seals. As the ship slowly steamed in ever-widening circles, so as to cover as large an area as possible without missing anything, the officers on her bridge noted the peculiar lack of floating wreckage and bodies.

Captain Lord, however, did take note of the lifeboats he saw. 'There were about six of them, the remainder having been picked up by the *Carpathia*. One was capsized, and there were two smaller boats with collapsible canvas sides.'[3] Lord's statement is, characteristically, clear and precise. The capsized boat he saw was not a 'smaller collapsible' but a full-sized wooden lifeboat. The flatter-bottomed, smaller collapsible boats with their dark flotation ring around the top of the solid wooden part of their hull would have been difficult to confuse with a conventional lifeboat, even upside down. The conclusion is inescapable. As all of *Titanic's* lifeboats are accounted for, there was an upturned lifeboat from another ship at the location.

Needless to say, *Californian's* search for more survivors was fruitless and at about 10.30am she resumed her interrupted voyage to Boston. When *Californian* left the site on the Monday morning the wreckage had drifted another 11 miles, which is exactly where it should have been allowing for the 1kt current from west-northwest. Captain Lord had ascertained the direction of the current from observations taken that evening.[4] The position was 30 miles from *Californian's* reported position at 11.40pm the previous evening.[5]

At 10.25am the following day, a wireless signal was received aboard *Carpathia* from *Californian*: 'Searched vicinity of disaster until noon yesterday, saw very little wreckage, no bodies, no sign of missing boat, regards Lord.' This showed that both Lord and Rostron knew that all of *Titanic's* boats were not accounted for, which makes later evidence appear a little bizarre.

After logging about 56 miles, *Carpathia* broke free of the ice and shaped a course toward New York. Other ships that had diverted toward *Titanic's* radioed position also resumed their voyages.

The suggestion had been made that the survivors from *Titanic* should be transferred to *Olympic* when she rendezvoused with the Cunard vessel, but this idea did not seem advisable to Captain Rostron. He discussed the suggestion with Ismay but the conversation may have been a little one-sided as Ismay was under the influence of opiates. He was being treated for shock.

At about 3.10pm on the 15th Rostron sent a signal to Captain Haddock, commanding *Olympic*, saying that he did not think it a good idea for *Titanic's* people to see *Olympic*. A quarter of an hour later another signal was sent to *Olympic* saying, 'Mr Ismay's orders. *Olympic* not to stand by *Carpathia*, no transfer to take place.' The matter was settled in Rostron's favour. No doubt he had made the right decision. The appearance of *Titanic's* almost identical sister ship would certainly have brought back painful memories for the survivors.[6]

The officers on *Carpathia* had given up their cabins to *Titanic's* survivors. Captain Rostron's cabin was occupied by three ladies, all the widows of millionaires who had gone down with the ship. 'Survivors were accommodated wherever room could be found.' (Which hints at there being rather more than 705 of them as *Carpathia* had accommodation for considerably more than this.) Most of the people from the White Star vessel had only the clothes they were wearing when they came aboard *Carpathia*, which in many cases did not amount to very much. *Carpathia's* passengers and crew rifled their own belongings for anything that could be spared. In this way *Titanic's* survivors were clothed, some of them in a remarkable variety of garments.

Four men from *Titanic* had died aboard *Carpathia*, or been brought aboard already dead and needed to be buried. They were Able Seaman Lyons, Bedroom Steward Siebert, a fireman and one other, so far unidentified. *Carpathia's* engines were stopped at 4pm and her flag was lowered to half mast. Passengers were below because it was quite cold and windy. An Episcopal monk, Father Roger B. T. Anderson, conducted the burial service and the four unfortunates, who according to some accounts had actually made it to *Carpathia* before succumbing, were committed to the deep.

J. Bruce Ismay, on boarding *Carpathia*, was observed to be in a state of shock. He refused any food or hot drink and was taken to the cabin of *Carpathia's* English doctor, McGee, where he would remain, eating nothing solid for the remainder of the voyage.[7] Some time after Ismay had come aboard Captain Rostron visited him, suggesting that the chief executive of the White Star line might like to notify his New York office of the fate of the *Titanic*. Ismay wrote a note and handed it to the captain for delivery to the wireless room: 'Deeply regret advise you *Titanic* sunk this morning after collision with iceberg, resulting in serious loss of life. Full particulars later. Bruce Ismay.' Rostron took the note to the wireless cabin himself, but the message was not transmitted until two days later and was received in New York at 9am on 17 April.[8]

No satisfactory explanation for this delay has ever been put forward, but it is difficult to believe that the wireless operator would ignore a direct order from the captain. Nor is it credible that the alarmingly efficient Rostron would have been unaware that his instructions had not been carried out.

This delay in informing New York or Liverpool of the true fate of the *Titanic* was the direct cause of much unnecessary suffering on the part of those with friends or relatives aboard the lost liner. Despite repeated attempts by other vessels, shore establishments, President Taft and even Marconi himself, the wireless operators on *Carpathia* refused to broadcast any details of the disaster.

Various excuses were put forward later, such as Bride's assertion that the naval operators aboard USS *Chester* were hopelessly inefficient and were using the wrong version of the Morse code. Another excuse was that they were too busy sending survivors' messages and lists of names.[9] None of these excuses holds water[10] because it would have taken less than 5min to transmit a concise account of the tragedy. However, this delay in sending out any information did give the survivors time to agree on what story they were going to tell.

Commenting on *Carpathia's* unnatural silence regarding news of the disaster, the *Springfield Sunday Union* said, 'Four days of terrible suspense breeds wild rumours.' *The New York Evening News* said, '*Carpathia's* silence baffled everyone.'[11]

One message from Ismay, however, was transmitted and it was to cause him no little inconvenience later. On Lightoller's prompting he sent a cable to his New York office asking that the White Star ship *Cedric* be held there so that *Titanic's* crew members could be returned to England without delay.[12] Why Lightoller persuaded Ismay to make this blatantly obvious attempt to avoid an American Inquiry has yet to be established.

At 8.23am on 18 April 1912, Phillip Franklin received another curious message from the White Star chairman. This message was to the effect that a responsible ship's officer and 14 crewmen were to be on hand, in two tugboats, to take charge of all of *Titanic's* lifeboats as soon as *Carpathia* reached New York. This message had been sent at the request of Captain Rostron.[13] Why the Cunard Captain and Ismay were so keen to get the boats off *Carpathia* also remains unexplained.

Families and friends of those who had been aboard the liner besieged the White Star offices. Even the very rich were not content to keep in touch by telephone or telegraph; they too made their way to the company offices.[14] J. P. Morgan's son, J. P. Morgan Jr, unaware that his father had decided against travelling on the doomed liner at the last moment, turned up at the White Star offices seeking news.[15]

Aboard *Carpathia*, *Titanic's* surviving officers knew that there would be an inquiry and so they met for a consultation.[16] No doubt they had also realised that things would go that much smoother for them if they all told a similar story.

Meanwhile the *New York Times* had contacted Frederick M. Sammis, Marconi's Chief Engineer in New York, requesting an interview with any wireless operators aboard *Carpathia*. The newspaper intimated that they were quite happy to pay for the privilege of being first to interview the Marconi employees. Sammis was enthusiastic about the idea and promptly sent a wireless message to Cottam.

In total four Marconigrams were sent to Cottam instructing him to keep quiet until *Carpathia* docked and a personal interview with a *New York Times* reporter could be arranged. A four-figure sum was promised if the wireless man would provide an exclusive story. He was instructed to go to the Strand Hotel as soon as the ship tied up in New York. All of the Marconigrams setting up this exclusive interview were signed by Sammis, although there is no doubt that Marconi knew of them.[17]

Soon after clearing the ice-field *Carpathia* ran into that other great danger to shipping around the Grand Banks — fog. This thick, wet, grey blanket was to remain with them almost all of the way to New York. 'The dismal nerve wracking noise of the whistle every half minute must have been particularly distressing to the survivors, and I was sorry for their state of mind, having encountered this after all their other experiences,' wrote Rostron later.

During Wednesday afternoon wireless communication was established with the American scout cruiser USS *Chester*. Through her, *Carpathia* was able to send names of survivors. This had been happening whenever *Carpathia's* wireless operator managed to find a few spare minutes from the moment that the first survivors' names were known.

Cottam had been on duty, almost without a break, since the first distress call from *Titanic* had been received. After repeated requests from Cottam and Captain Rostron, *Titanic's* surviving wireless operator, Harold Bride, was eventually persuaded to assist the *Carpathia's* own exhausted Marconi man.

Bride had to be carried to the wireless shack because his injured feet would not allow him to walk. Certainly he himself could offer no explanation as to what was wrong with his feet. All he knew was that he couldn't walk.[18]

Working now as a team the wireless operators managed to transmit a fairly comprehensive list of survivors. So complete was the list that it contained the names of almost a hundred more people than had actually been picked up. Who these people were and where they came from is another little puzzle as they do not appear on *Titanic's* passenger or crew lists. Could they have come from the same ship as the upturned lifeboat?

It is only reasonable to assume that Captain Rostron had the survivor list checked before the names of those he had taken aboard were transmitted, so such a glaring error is almost impossible. A simple head count should have been enough to show that the list was faulty and in need of correction before it was sent out. Unless a head count of people picked up was taken and somehow agreed with the number of names on the survivor list.

Despite Cottam and Bride's reluctance to send out any details of the disaster, at least one man in New York seems to have had more than a vague idea of what had happened. Carr Van Anda, editor of the *New York Times*, was handed a wireless bulletin, received by David Sarnoff, whose radio room was situated at the top of Wannamaker's department store. The bulletin described *Titanic's* CQD and request for assistance. From this scanty information Van Anda supposedly deduced what had really happened.

Monday morning's edition of the *New York Times* carried the story of *Titanic's* sinking, while other papers confined themselves to the known facts and simply printed the information in the bulletin.

That there were close ties between the *New York Times* and the Marconi company is undeniable: Van Anda and Marconi were acquaintances.[19] There had been an arrangement between the newspaper and Marconi, covering transatlantic news, for seven years,[20] but how information reached the newspaper editor without being overheard we simply do not know.

Still *Carpathia* headed westwards until, on Thursday afternoon, the fog-horn of the Fire Island lightship was heard. At about 6 o'clock the *Carpathia* stopped near the entrance to the Ambrose channel and picked up a pilot. Captain Rostron was surprised by the number of press boats that had come out to greet them. 'Press boats literally surrounded us!' he said.

With the comfort of the survivors uppermost in his mind, the captain refused to allow any reporters aboard: 'To have them interviewed by dozens of alert young newspaper men eager to get the most lurid details, would cause endless distress.'

When the ship stopped at quarantine one enterprising newsman made a death-defying leap which brought him onto the deck of *Carpathia*. His arrival was reported to the bridge. The captain put the reporter on his honour not to leave the bridge, having explained that he could not allow the passengers to be interviewed. 'I must say, he was a gentleman,' Rostron later said of the reporter. Of course, after the ship docked and the reporter was allowed to go ashore he became something of a celebrity himself.

Before the *Carpathia* got to quarantine, the weather made a violent change, bringing the tragedy to a dramatic ending. First a violent wind sprang up, and the rain poured down. Then the sky was split by flashes of lightning and the air reverberated to the heavy crash of thunder.

Slowly *Carpathia* made her way up the channel, picking up the port doctor, Joseph J. O'Connoll, from the *Governor Flower* on the way. She steamed past the Cunard pier and moved on until she came to White Star's. Once there, *Titanic's* boats were lowered, each with two of her crewmen aboard, where they were taken in two by the harbour tug *Champion*. Only then did *Carpathia* move to her own dock. The time was 9.35pm.[21]

On the dockside, hundreds of photographers' flashlights twinkled and all around *Carpathia* there were dozens of tugboats. Eventually *Carpathia* was secured to the dockside and first her own passengers and then the survivors from *Titanic* could be disembarked. 'After 9 o'clock at night they left us — those that had come out of the terror of shipwreck — and no one was more glad than I to see them passing on to the land.' Captain Rostron was understandably relieved that his responsibility towards the survivors was at an end. As he put it himself, 'The job was done.' The 30,000-strong crowd began slowly to disperse. Although many of the survivors refused to tell the waiting reporters anything, they were quoted anyway.[22] The press then, as now, used its collective imagination to fill in the lurid details, accurate and otherwise.

In New York plans were made to greet the survivors and to ease their entry into America. The United States Secretary of the Treasury sent a telegram to the New York Surveyor of Customs instructing him to suspend all customs regulations where *Titanic's* passengers were concerned. The usual examination of steerage passengers, normally carried out at the infamous Ellis Island establishment, was also to be waived.

Only the closest relatives of survivors were to be allowed onto the Cunard pier, and no more than two for each expected survivor. Forty inspectors checked all applications for pier passes before issue. Newspaper men were not welcome.

The New York Police Force under the direction of Commissioner Waldo and Mayor Gaynor was to mount a massive exercise in crowd control. Streets leading to the dock were barricaded, only authorised pedestrians and vehicles being allowed through by the 150 patrolmen, 12 mounted officers and 25 detectives who manned the barricades. A special squad of burly policemen, under the control of Lt Charles Becker, were to roam through the crowds, dealing with pickpockets and petty thieves.

The choice of Lt Becker for this vigilante group was truly inspired. Three months later Becker was convicted of heading an underworld gang specialising in murder, graft and corruption. Becker was also convicted of the murder of gambler Herman Rosenthal on 15 July 1912 and was subsequently executed for the crime.

Even the precautions so far described were considered insufficient and the pier itself was roped off for 75ft either side of the main entrance. The authorities really did not want anybody talking to *Titanic's* survivors until they had been briefed regarding exactly what to say — at least that is what it looks like. Green lanterns were hung from this rope to advertise its presence. Even with such deterrents at least one reporter was to surmount all obstacles and make it aboard *Carpathia* soon after she docked.

Mr Marconi himself came to visit *Carpathia*, in compliance with Van Anda's wishes,[23] shortly after she tied up. Accompanying him was a *New York Times* reporter, Jim Spears. Van Anda had telephoned the inventor from the *Times* office and encouraged him to take the reporter along.[24]

For part of the journey Marconi and his companions were advised to avoid the traffic by taking the elevated railway, but this did not take them the whole way. They arrived at pier 54 in a taxicab laid on by the newspaper.[25] Because of Marconi's unique status he was allowed aboard, but with only one companion.[26] Of all his entourage he chose Jim Spears.

Marconi and the reporter went straight to the wireless room where the *New York Times* man interviewed Harold Bride, who was still at work.[27] Once again, with Marconi's connivance, the *New York Times* had stolen a march on its rivals.

Even before Marconi and the reporter reached *Carpathia*, wireless operator Cottam had left the ship and was making for the Strand Hotel. Despite the traffic congestion he must have arrived there by about 10pm. The *New York Times* had taken a suite at the hotel as a newsroom specifically to deal with information coming from *Carpathia*. Although he was a prime target for the reporters, Cottam was kept waiting for 1½hours before he was interviewed, or so he said. The interview lasted about half an hour and was over by midnight.[28] For granting the interview Cottam was paid $750, which he received within the month.[29]

The news the world had been waiting for was published in the *New York Times* not as a result of a general press release but as two exclusive interviews with Cottam and Bride.[30]

At about 2am Cottam telephoned his employer, Mr Marconi. He never satisfactorily explained why. All we can be sure of is that he was not seeking permission to give the interview.[31] That a lowly wireless operator should make a telephone call, in the middle of the night, to an international celebrity of Marconi's standing is an enigma in its own right. Whatever the reason it must have been compelling.

The first thing that J. Bruce Ismay did on reaching his New York hotel was to issue instructions that no White Star vessel was to put to sea without enough lifeboats for every person aboard.[32]

Many of *Titanic's* 174 surviving third class passengers had lost everything in the disaster and were destitute. The White Star line and private relief organisations provided some support, including enough money to enable many to make their way to friends or relatives in distant parts of the country. The Pennsylvania Railroad provided a special train, on which any survivor, regardless of class, could travel free of charge to Pennsylvania and points west. The railroad company went so far as to provide cabs to convey passengers from the Cunard pier to the railway station.

The last survivors to leave *Carpathia* were 210 members of *Titanic's* crew. After filing down the sternmost gangway, they were led along the almost deserted pier, down a flight of narrow stairs to where the United States Immigration Service tender *George Starr* awaited them. The tender transported them six blocks to the north, to White Star pier 60, at the foot of West Twentieth Street.

After leaving the *George Starr* the crew members were marched across the pier, which had been cleared of all but essential personnel, and shepherded aboard the Red Star Line vessel *Lapland*. (The Red Star line was also a part of the IMM combine.) The 206 ordinary crew members were assigned to cabins in *Lapland's* third class, while the four officers were accommodated in first. In a carefully planned and executed operation, White Star and the US Immigration Service had managed to keep all of *Titanic's* surviving crew well away from the eager reporters. What were they afraid some member of the crew might say, that could not equally well be said by a surviving passenger? Whatever it was, it almost certainly dated from before the accident, as afterwards ordinary crew and passengers mixed and exchanged information freely until they reached New York.

Although the White Star pier had supposedly been cleared of all but a few company employees, souvenir hunters managed to reach *Titanic's* lifeboats during the night. Wooden markers bearing the name SS *Titanic* were stolen, along with most of the motifs identifying the boats as White Star property. Might not these souvenir hunters have been those self-same company employees who remained on the pier when the crew of *Titanic* were marched past?

One lifeboat nameplate, at least, was removed by J. J. Kirkpatrick, a quartermaster on *Carpathia*, as a souvenir. It now rests in Liverpool Maritime Museum.[33]

On the following morning, Friday, men were put to work sanding the ship's name and other identifying marks from the boats' wooden markers.[34] While this work was going on, more company employees stood guard on the boats, supposedly to keep other souvenir hunters away but effectively keeping everybody except White Star employees at a safe distance.

On 20 April the lifeboats were lifted out of the water and stored in a loft between piers 58 and 59, well away from the public gaze. They were still there, on chocks and covered by tarpaulins, on 16 May when they were joined by collapsible A, which had been picked up by *Oceanic* on the 13th. Later the boats were moved to the yard of C. M. Lane Lifeboat Company, King and Dwight Street, Erie Basin, Brooklyn, New York. From this time they seem to disappear from the pages of history.

We now know that:

- Both Captain Rostron of the *Carpathia* and Captain Lord of the *Californian* saw a full-sized wooden lifeboat floating, upside down, at the site of the disaster, when all of *Titanic's* wooden lifeboats were found the right way up and at least partially occupied;
- Captain Rostron saw two steamers to the north of where he was collecting survivors, between where *Titanic* and *Californian* would have been while the liner was sinking.

The American Inquiry

The hastily convened United States Committee of Commerce Inquiry into the loss of the *Titanic*, suggested by Senator Smith,[1] ostensibly ran for 17 days, between 19 April and 25 May, but it actually began on 18 April, aboard the SS *Carpathia*.

Senator William Alden Smith, who also headed the American Inquiry, arrived at the White Star dock well before the third class passengers disembarked. Boarding the Cunard vessel, he was directed to the surgeon's cabin where J. Bruce Ismay was waiting, with Phillip A. S. Franklin, IMM's Vice President. Pushing past Franklin, Smith engaged the grief-stricken Ismay in earnest conversation. The discourse lasted almost half an hour. Then, after observing, for a few minutes, third class passengers being interrogated by Immigration Officers, he left the ship – so much for waiving of all immigration formalities for survivors.

Smith's fellow committee members were: Senator George C. Perkins, California; Jonathan Bourne Jr, Oregon; Theodore Burton, Ohio; Furnifold M. Simmons, North Carolina; Francis G. Newlands, Nevada; and, Duncan W. Fletcher, Florida. The members of the committee might have presented a well-balanced political front but their maritime expertise was minimal. These, then, were the men who were expected to unravel one of the most complex disasters in modern history. Or might their purpose have been simply to cloud the issue yet further? At any rate, that is what they succeeded in doing.

Senator Smith was a vehement opponent of John Pierpont Morgan and his giant trusts, and this plainly dictated the course of the American investigation. He wanted to use the inquiry as a weapon.[2]

Smith's primary objective wasn't to discover what had caused the disaster and thereby guard against the same thing happening again. He wanted to show that the officers and crew of the *Titanic* had been negligent and that the company was aware of this negligence, which, of course, it was. He failed hopelessly.

The senator was a politician first and foremost. He undoubtedly realised that heading this inquiry would bring him to the attention of the voting public. He didn't fool President Taft who told British Ambassador Brice that he thought the inquiry would last as long as it kept William Alden Smith in the headlines.[3] The secretary of state was in agreement, believing that the inquiry was self-advertisement by Smith.[4]

Initially *Titanic's* surviving officers, particularly Boxhall, were extremely indignant that an inquiry was to be held in the United States at all. They were of the opinion that as the ship was registered in Britain and the accident had occurred in international waters, an American inquiry was an unjustifiable interference.[5]

Although close to exhaustion, J. Bruce Ismay proved to be more than a match for Senator Smith on the first day of the inquiry. Try as he might, the senator could get no indication that Ismay had any knowledge of negligence. He was to run into this same stonewall attitude with the other White Star officers, and he fared little better with the crew members, even though Ismay had asked the surviving officers to co-operate with the inquiry. According to Ismay, White Star had nothing to hide.[6]

Meanwhile, in an effort to maintain an already disrupted schedule, *Carpathia's* water tanks and bunkers were refilled; blankets and linen were replenished from another Cunard vessel as the ship prepared to resume her interrupted voyage to the Mediterranean. One unavoidable hold-up was Senator Smith, who required that Captain Rostron gave evidence at the inquiry. So as to inconvenience Rostron as little as possible, Smith managed to arrange affairs so that the captain could give his evidence very early on in the proceedings. Captain Rostron's statement was taken on the very first official day of the inquiry, in private.

The surviving crew members of *Titanic* bitterly resented their virtual imprisonment aboard the *Lapland*, but curiously fewer than half of them attended a memorial service held ashore. The service, held at the Institute of the Seaman's Friend Society, 5507 West Street, New York, on the 19th was open to all.

On 20 April federal subpoenas were served on 29 of *Titanic's* crew members aboard *Lapland*. These men were taken off the ship and, on the 21st travelled to Washington, when the inquiry moved there, where they were lodged at the Continental Hotel. The United States Government was now paying their expenses. Shortly afterwards these 29 men were joined by five others who had been snatched off *Lapland* after she had sailed.

Titanic's officers were also lodged at the same hotel, a circumstance which caused some friction. Neither officers, or crew were happy with the arrangement and said so. The officers complained about being quartered so close to the more lowly crew members and were subsequently moved to another floor. The crew complained about having to share rooms, something that they would have been obliged to do aboard ship. As a result of their complaints the crew were moved to a somewhat less ostentatious hotel, the Hotel National, where a separate room for each man was surprisingly provided. No doubt the members of the toiling classes felt more at home in these more austere surroundings.

During the session on Monday, 22 April, Fourth Officer Joseph Boxhall made the first mention of a mystery ship. Still demonstrating their uncanny ability to sniff out newsworthy interviewees, the *New York Times* immediately dispatched a reporter to see Captain Lord.[7]

Phillip Franklin and IMM's Boston agent both tried to stop Captain Lord and his wireless operator, Cyril Evans, going to the American Inquiry, even though both men had been subpoenaed. Despite the pressure brought to bear by his owners, Captain Lord was quite happy to give evidence. His only concern at that time was whether or not *Californian* would be able to sail from Boston on time.[8]

Before leaving Boston to attend the inquiry, Lord made a statement giving no indication that he thought he might be accused of refusing to go to the assistance of the stricken *Titanic*. If he had thought of it, then a simple suggestion that Boxhall's position was adrift or that the *Californian* had encountered fog, a not uncommon occurrence on the Grand Banks, would have provided a way out. When he got to the American Inquiry Lord met Phillip Franklin and J. Bruce Ismay. Captain Lord immediately struck up a rapport with them and sat chatting for more than 10min.

On the Wednesday, Fifth Officer Lowe, for the first time, put forward the excuse for the boats being lowered sometimes less than half filled. He said that the officers did not know that the lifeboats could be lowered with a full complement of passengers and believed that full boats would break in half while being lowered. This was, of course, absolute nonsense. *Titanic's* senior officers were all experienced seamen who must have been involved in more than one boat drill in their time.

Second Officer Herbert Lightoller had been shipwrecked several times before and must, therefore, have known how strong lifeboats really were. Thomas Andrews, who had helped to design and build the ship, was also aboard. His company had tested the boats by lowering them filled with weights to simulate overloading. The boats had passed the tests with flying colours. Andrews must have been aware of this and equally must have passed the information on as soon as it became apparent that the boats were to be required in earnest. Although the excuse originally put forward by Lowe is patently absurd, it has been accepted as fact ever since the disaster. The only question remaining to be answered is, why was it accepted?

Ismay had requested leave to return to England after giving evidence on the first official day of the inquiry. The request was denied. He tried again on the 23rd, with the same result. The following day Ismay and his attorney, Charles Burlingham, arrived at Smith's office an 10am and tried yet again. Again his request was denied.

Had Senator Smith extracted all of Ismay's evidence on day one then there could be no possible objection to the White Star chairman going home. If, on the other hand, Smith had not found out all that he needed to from Ismay, then why not? Ismay was recalled to give further evidence on day 10 of the inquiry, but again Smith failed to elicit any information that showed negligence.

The more lowly members of the crew, although still incensed at having to remain in America, were making the best of their stay in Washington. Having to make do on two shillings a day did nothing to improve their somewhat jaundiced view of the United States judicial system. To supplement this meagre amount of pocket money, several crewmen appeared at a local theatre, The Imperial, where they related their experiences to rapt audiences. These crewmen received the entire proceeds of the show, but just how much that amounted to is not recorded.

Two days before the theatre appearance by the crewmen, they had been awarded an extra 10 shillings a day witness fees. This extra cash came as a direct result of Senator Smith's intervention on their behalf. Smith, by this time, was on first-name terms with all of the surviving ordinary crewmen.

On Thursday 25 April, 23 of *Titanic's* crew were interviewed by individual members of the subcommittee, three at a time and in a hurry.[9] This was a serious mistake if the committee were really trying to get at the truth the evidence was fragmented as a result.

Senator Smith interviewed Evans, Haines and Hemmings at 10pm to conclude the day's evidence. It might well be because the evidence was so fragmentary that Senator Smith did not notice the way that the seamen's statements were leading.

As usual, far too much attention was paid to the evidence given by the officers and first class passengers while not enough notice was taken of what the ordinary crewmen had to say. No notice whatsoever was paid to third class survivors, none of whom were called as witnesses.

On the day preceding this display of haste in the American Inquiry an ordinary crew member from the Leyland Line's *Californian* took steps to see that his voice would be heard. Donkeyman Ernest Gill sold his story to a Boston newspaper for $500. As we have already seen, Gill's story implicated the *Californian* as the mystery ship visible from the *Titanic*. Gill stated that shortly before midnight he saw a large liner steam up, lights blazing, then stop. According to Gill this vessel then proceeded to fire two rockets from about 10 miles away. He was called to give evidence on the 26th and swore that the affidavit he had given two days previously was true. The donkeyman recounted his story for the benefit of the subcommittee. They drew the obvious, but erroneous, conclusion that *Californian* had failed to go to the assistance of the *Titanic* despite seeing her distress signals.

In the interests of fair play the captain and watch officers from *Californian* were called to give evidence, as well as the ship's apprentice, who had also seen the rockets.

Captain Lord gave *Californian's* position at the time of the disaster as 19.5 miles from the point worked out by *Titanic's* navigating officer. He also told of the repeated attempts by his officers to contact the mystery ship by Morse lamp. The other *Californian* witnesses told of what we have already looked at in the chapter dealing with *Californian's* role in the affair. None of Lord's officers made any attempt to deny that a ship and rockets were seen at about the time *Titanic* was sinking. However, they could not agree on what sort of ship the mystery vessel might be. They agreed, in the main, that this mysterious vessel was under way while it was in view from *Californian*. For the sake of completeness, I will reproduce Captain Lord's statement to the American Inquiry in full:

'When I came off the bridge, at half past ten, I pointed out to the officer that I thought I saw a light coming along, and it was a most peculiar night, and we had been making mistakes all along with the stars, thinking they were signals. We could not distinguish where the sky ended and the water commenced. You understand, it was a flat calm. He said he thought it was a star, and I did not say anything more. I went down below. I was talking with the engineer about keeping the steam ready, and we saw these signals coming along, and I said: "There is a steamer coming. Let us go to the wireless and see what the news is." But on our way down I met the operator coming, and I said: "Do you know anything?" He said: "The Titanic." So then I gave him instructions to let the Titanic know. I said: "This is not the Titanic; there is no doubt about it." she came and lay, at half past 11, alongside of us until, I suppose, a quarter past one, within four miles of us. We could see everything on her quite distinctly; see her lights. We signalled her at half past 11, with the Morse lamp. She did not take the slightest notice of it. That was between half past 11 and 20 minutes to 12. We signalled her again at 10 minutes past 12, half past 12, a quarter to one, and one o'clock. We have a very powerful Morse lamp. I suppose you can see that about 10 miles, and she was about 4 miles off, and she did not take the slightest notice of it. When the second officer came on the bridge, at 12 o'clock, or 10 minutes past 12, I told him to watch the steamer, which was stopped, and I pointed out the ice to him; told him we were surrounded by ice; to watch the steamer that she did not get any closer to us. At 20 minutes to 1, I whistled up the speaking tube and asked him if she was getting nearer. He said: "No; she is not taking any notice of us." So, I said: "I will go and lie down a bit." At a quarter past one he said: "I think she has fired a rocket." He said: "She did not answer the Morse lamp and she has commenced to go away from us." I said: "Call her up and let me know what her name is." So, he put the whistle back, and apparently, he was calling. I could hear him ticking over my head. Then I went to sleep.'

Senator Smith then asked Lord, 'You heard nothing more about it?'

'Nothing more until about something between then and half past four, I have a faint recollection of the apprentice opening my room door; opening and shutting it. I said: "What is it?" He did not answer and I went to sleep again. I believe that the boy came down to deliver the message that this steamer had steamed away from us to the southwest, showing several of these flashes or white rockets; steamed away to the southwest.'[10]

Smith asked Lord to imagine that if *Titanic* had used her Morse lamp and fired rockets, 'for a half to three-quarters of an hour after she struck the ice, would you, from the position of your ship on a night like Sunday night, have been able to see those signals?'

Lord said that her Morse lamp was 'an utter impossibility' and he didn't think there was much chance of seeing a rocket either. 'It would have been way down on the horizon.[??227] it might have been mistaken for a shooting star, or anything at all.'[11]

Captain Lord also said that if *Titanic's* distress call had been received then *Californian* could have gone to the rescue at any time. 'I gave instructions to the Chief Engineer, and told him I had decided to stay there all night. I did not think it safe to go ahead. I said "We will keep handy in case some of these big fellows come crunching along and get into it." '[12]

Cyril Evans, *Californian's* wireless operator, was the last witness from the Leyland vessel. He testified that he had told Captain Lord that the closest vessel he had contacted by wireless was *Titanic*. This merely confirmed Lord's guilt in the eyes of the subcommittee. Evans also confirmed that the apprentice had informed the captain of the existence of the rockets on no less that three separate occasions. He did not remind Smith's committee of Captain Lord's repeated questions regarding colour in the pyrotechnic signals, or Senator Smith might have drawn a somewhat different conclusion, at least as potentially detrimental to Lord's career as the conclusion that he did reach.

By the last weekend in April both Captain Lord and Donkeyman Gill had given their evidence. The press had accepted Lord's version of events and dismissed Gill's. As far as they were concerned the issue of the *Californian* was finished. Lord had been the better witness and the American public were convinced.[13] Senator Smith's summing up was to change all of that.

Senator Smith presented the Report of the Committee of Commerce on the 28th, making it abundantly clear that he believed that the *Californian* was closer to *Titanic* than the 19.5 miles that Lord had calculated.[14] Curiously, Captain Lord never received any official communication relating to the findings of the American Inquiry.[15]

On Monday, 29 April, *Titanic's* crewmen were released from the jurisdiction of the Senate Inquiry. One day later J. Bruce Ismay was also released. He left Washington and immediately made his way to New York where he boarded *Adriatic*. The ordeal of the British crew members, officers and the chairman of the company owning RMS *Titanic* was over, at least in America. On the other side of the Atlantic a far more searching and technical inquiry was being prepared.

In the meantime the Smith Inquiry attended to a few loose ends, notably a signal from the Marconi Company to Bride instructing him to keep quiet until he could sell his story for a handsome sum. Bride was to make at least $1,000 for his version of events, although he was to tell the British Inquiry that it was only half that amount.[16] It will be remembered that the great inventor had himself taken a *New York Times* reporter aboard *Carpathia* for an exclusive interview with *Titanic's* second wireless operator. Marconi testified that he had authorised Bride to accept payment from any newspaper, not specifically the *New York Times*, but he neglected to mention the preferential treatment he had already shown to that newspaper. He denied that there was any deal between his company and the newspaper.[17]

Sensing that all was not what it might be, Senator Smith tried to ascertain just what was the relationship between the *New York Times* and the Marconi Company.[18] The senator believed that information which should have been available to friends and family of those aboard *Titanic* had been suppressed for the benefit of the newspaper.[19]

On the penultimate day of the hearings Capt John J. Knapp of the US Hydrographic Office removed any lingering doubt that might have remained in Senator Smith's mind as to the guilt or innocence of Stanley Lord. He testified that the ship seen from the *Titanic* could have been no other but *Californian*, and conversely, that the ship seen from *Californian* must have been *Titanic*. He supported his evidence with convincing looking charts, which might well have fooled the nautically inexperienced Smith. In any case, Captain Knapp was wrong as was finally and irrevocably proven by the position of the wreck, discovered in 1985. To have reached the position postulated by Knapp, and later Lord Mersey, between taking a 7.30pm star sight and stopping at 10.20pm *Californian* would have had to steam right through the ice-field at a speed of 14.7kts, of which she was incapable, and in a direction 10° to port of her intended course.[20]

According to one Knapp chart there was no evidence of any mysterious third ship: no such steamer could have been seen either from *Titanic's* lifeboats or from the rescue ships the following morning.[21] Even a cursory examination of the evidence from the boats and rescue vessels should have caused Smith to discard the charts for what they really were, useless. Captain Rostron clearly saw two mystery ships to the north of the lifeboats as dawn broke.

The American Inquiry officially dragged on until 19 May, but in reality it was still continuing on the 25th, when Senator Smith paid a visit to *Olympic*. *Titanic's* sister ship was in New York as part of her regular scheduled Atlantic service.

Smith interviewed Captain Herbert J. ('Pappy') Haddock, who gave the Senator a conducted tour of his vessel. In the stokehold Smith came across a familiar face, Stoker Fred Barrett. The fireman pointed out where the iceberg had smashed through the side of *Titanic*, and where he had been standing at the time. Suitably impressed Smith left the ship. He returned to Washington to write up his entirely predictable report.

The report contained a description of *Titanic*, her owners, and the complicated arrangements of holding companies. It went on to describe the ship's trials and inspection certificates handed out by the British Board of Trade. A highly suspect description of the passenger list was also thrown in. The voyage prior to the collision was described in some detail, including ice warnings received, along with course, speed, weather and conditions.

The collision, progressive flooding and eventual foundering of the liner were explained in detail, but the report merely summarised the wireless traffic after the collision, and a list of ships in the area was included.

Captain Lord of the *Californian* was condemned for failing to go to the assistance of a vessel which was sending up distress signals. Although Senator Smith had some justification for his condemnation of Lord, he was censuring him for entirely the wrong reasons and for the wrong offence. In the light of the available evidence, Captain Lord was guilty of a far more serious crime than simply failing to respond to a distress signal, to which many ships in the area that night also failed to respond — Conspiracy to Barratry is an extremely serious crime. At a blow, Senator Smith had started a controversy, which rages to this day, but has absolutely nothing to do with the central issue confronting his inquiry: what caused the loss of the *Titanic*?

The report took the British Board of Trade to task for allowing regulations to get so far out of date that a passenger vessel of *Titanic's* size and capacity could be constructed and certified with so few lifeboats. The conduct and performance of the crew were also summarised, none too flatteringly. 'Some crewmen never reported to their boat stations but deserted the ship in earlier boats,' he said. 'The organisation of the escape was haphazard.'[22]

E. J. Smith came in for his share of criticism from the senator who said that Captain Smith's indifference to danger was a direct cause of the disaster.[23]

Captain Rostron and *Carpathia* came in for no faint praise for their part in the rescue. Although Captain Rostron was exonerated from imposing any sort of censorship after the rescue, the two wireless operators aboard his ship were rebuked for keeping back information and selling it later, for profit. The delay in sending Ismay's 15 April message, stating that *Titanic* had sunk, was not explained.

Marconi said that he was as surprised as everybody else by *Carpathia's* wireless silence. He had sent two messages inquiring why no news was coming out, but they were never answered.[24]

In his recommendations Senator Smith suggested sweeping changes in regulations governing lifeboat structure and capacity for passenger vessels. Regular boat drill for both passengers and crew as well as adequate manning of lifeboats was also recommended, as was the installation of wireless with operators in attendance 24hr a day.

Twenty-three years later, *Titanic's* senior surviving officer gave his written opinion of the American Inquiry: it was 'incomplete and incorrect'. He also said that its only aim was to, 'Make our seamen, quartermasters, and petty officers look ridiculous. It was a farce.'[25]

We have now looked at how:

- *Titanic's* surviving crew members were held incommunicado when they first reached New York;
- No third class passengers were called to give evidence at the American Inquiry;
- William Alden Smith gave history a scapegoat in the shape of Captain Lord, despite there being nothing to base this on.

Home!

Shortly after 7am on Monday, 29 April, *Lapland*, with her cargo of 172 *Titanic* crewmen, entered Plymouth harbour. Something over half an hour later she dropped anchor in Cawsand Bay, far from the dockside. Three tenders immediately set out to collect the passengers from the ship. The first two collected *Lapland's* first and second class passengers and carried them to Millbay docks, whence they departed by train for London. The third tender, *Sir Richard Grenville*, had two White Star directors aboard, Harold Sanderson and E. C. Grenfell, and four other officials and was reserved for *Titanic's* crew members. The officials were a solicitor for the White Star line, Mr Furniss; the local Receiver of Wrecks and Collector of Customs, Mr W. Woolven; White Star's Southampton Victualling Superintendent, Mr J. Bartholomew; and the company's Plymouth Agent, Mr Frank Phillips.

It must have been immediately apparent to *Titanic's* crew members that they were not going to be allowed to go straight home. How they were treated would today be called illegal imprisonment. The Board of Trade had hoped to begin taking statements straight away but were thwarted right at the outset.

The President of the British Seafarers' Union, Mr Thomas Lewis, and the Secretary, Mr Cannon, had requested that they be allowed to accompany the White Star officials and Board of Trade representatives on their visit to the *Lapland*. The request was denied. Not being so easily deflected from their purpose, the two union officials hired a small boat to take them out to the *Lapland*. Once close enough to be heard through a megaphone, they advised *Titanic's* crewmen not to make any statement until they had union representation.

The crew took notice of the advice and refused to say anything to the Board of Trade officials. Eventually, after following a tortuous route around the harbour for hours, Lewis and Cannon were allowed to board the *Sir Richard Grenville*. Now with their trade union representatives to hand, the people from *Titanic* were prepared to talk.

The 17 surviving stewardesses were the first to give their statements, followed by first and second class cashiers Miss R. Bowker and Miss M. Martin.

Not until just before midday did the survivors finally reach the quayside and step ashore, most fondly imagining that their ordeal was at an end and that they would, at last, be allowed to go on their way. This was not to be, however. Despite protests, they were taken to the third class waiting room. This normally public room was sealed off from the outside world by the high dockyard fence. On the inside were *Titanic's* crew, while on the outside were their loved ones, the general public and the ever-present and vociferous press. Dockyard police and a contingent from the local constabulary insured that the division between crew members and the outside world was not breached. People with a predilection for smelling conspiracies might be led to believe that this rigidly enforced imprisonment suggested that the jailers had something to hide! They could well be correct!

More statements were taken and subpoenas issued, requiring the presence of the recipients at the Board of Trade Inquiry, about to be held in London. All of the survivors were interviewed by the Board of Trade and White Star representatives.

As if the survivors had not already had enough to put up with, before they could be released from custody they each had to appear before the Receiver of Wrecks. An overnight stay in the docks had already been foreseen and the necessary steps taken. Mattresses were laid out in neat rows; blankets, pillows, etc, were provided. Long tables were set up in order that the crew could be fed and watered. Watchers, outside the dockyard gates, could see the piles of bread and bedding through the waiting room windows. Words were exchanged through the bars of the gate between the crowd outside and the crew inside, but these were few and far between, being actively discouraged by an over-zealous constabulary.

Even after they had been interviewed, the detainees were given no indication as to how or when they might be released, nor was any information forthcoming as to how they were to make their departure. Each crew member was asked to give his, or her, word of honour that, on release, they would not make any public statement.

Clearly the officials representing His Majesty's Government didn't consider the word of honour of an ordinary member of *Titanic's* crew binding enough. Before leaving the dockyard the survivors were compelled to sign what they believed to be the 'Official Secrets Act'.[1] Again we see clear evidence of suppression. Of what was it that the general public were to be kept in ignorance?

Sometime about one o'clock, survivors began to leave the waiting room and congregate outside in the fresh air. Despite their pledge of secrecy, some managed to exchange a few words with friends, relatives and reporters outside the gate. These people complained bitterly about their treatment and confinement. To some extent they also related their various versions of events on the night *Titanic* sank. The reporters were only too glad to receive these titbits of information, which they inflated with varying degrees of embellishment into newspaper articles. Then, about half an hour after the first survivors had appeared, the dockyard gates were opened and a crowd of crewmen poured out. The reporters, as usual, reacted instantly by pouncing on whoever they could get to, causing a scene more resembling a rugby scrum than a civilised interview.

About 85 seamen, firemen, lookouts, etc, had been released. These were put on a special train which left Plymouth for Southampton at 6pm. Still detained in Plymouth were the stewards, stewardesses and catering staff who had survived the wreck. These were the people who were detained overnight, to be released the following day, Tuesday, 30 April. Why this group was singled out and kept isolated from the rest of the world for the extra 24hr is obscure.

On the evening of the 29th, hundreds of people began to gather at Southampton West railway station to welcome home the first of *Titanic's* crew. The train arrived three-quarters of an hour before expected, slowly steaming into the station. So great was the press of the crowd, pushing forward to catch a glimpse of the survivors, that the station porters found it all but impossible to control them.

As the train drew to a halt, carriage doors were wrenched open by members of the crowd. Survivors were literally dragged from their carriages by overjoyed friends and relations.

Slowly the crowd began to disperse as the disappointed relatives of those still detained at Plymouth drifted away. Then all that remained on the platform were small groups, each clustered around a survivor. Frequently the whole scene was illuminated by photographers' flash guns.

Meanwhile the train pulled out for the short journey to its terminus, Southampton Docks station, where the scene was re-enacted.

The following day the second batch of survivors arrived at Southampton from Plymouth. Their train, expected to arrive a little before 8pm, didn't turn up until after 9pm, at Southampton West station. The scene was much as it had been when the first contingent had arrived the day before: massed crowds, cheering and relief when loved ones were found — or bitter disappointment and despair when survivors confirmed that the awaited reunions would never take place.

The train went on its way to the Docks station where yet another large crowd awaited its arrival. Here, however, the atmosphere was very different. There was no cheering; the crowd waited in silence to see who would emerge from the carriages. They knew that these would be the last to arrive for some time. There was still room for hope: after all 43 members of *Titanic's* crew were still in America giving evidence before the Senate subcommittee. As their evidence was completed, in dribs and drabs they were allowed to leave the United States and return home.

A week later, on 6 May, similar scenes were re-enacted at Liverpool when *Celtic* arrived with another small batch of *Titanic* survivors. The first of the witnesses had returned to their native shores — among them were three of the most important witnesses to give evidence at either inquiry: Lookouts Fleet and Lee, and Quartermaster Helmsman Robert Hitchens.

Mrs Florence Ismay and her maid, along with J. Bruce's brother, Bower, sailed for Queenstown aboard the *Oceanic* on 9 May, to await the arrival of the White Star chairman.

J. Bruce Ismay duly arrived aboard the *Adriatic*, which must have diverted to the Irish port specially to pick up the other waiting Ismays, before proceeding to Liverpool, where she arrived at the Princess landing stage at 7.30am on 11 May. A White Star manager, Mr Henry Concannon, had accompanied the Ismays to Queenstown, but had returned to Liverpool before them to distribute a written press statement:

'Mr Ismay asks the gentlemen of the press to extend their courtesy to him by not pressing for any statement from him. First he is still suffering from the very great strain of the Titanic disaster and subsequent events.

'Again because he gave the American Commission a plain and unvarnished statement of fact, which has been fully reported; and also because his evidence before the British Court of Inquiry should not be anticipated in any way. He would, however, like to take this opportunity of acknowledging with full heart, the large number of telegraphic messages and letters from public concerns and businesses and private friends to him and confidence in him, which he very much appreciates in this, the greatest trial of his life.'

This press release was more than a little successful, for when the *Adriatic* docked a large group of well-wishers were on hand to welcome Ismay home. Nearly all of the first class passengers had already departed the ship when the Ismays appeared. J. Bruce was highly gratified by the applause and cries of concern and support from the crowd. Both he and Florence smiled at this reception, so very different from the chairman's treatment in the United States. Also arriving aboard *Adriatic* were most of *Titanic's* surviving officers — Lightoller, Lowe and Pitman — all of whom were to serve the White Star company so well at the coming British Inquiry.

On the 12th the body of Wallace Hartley reached Liverpool aboard the *Arabic*. The body was taken by hearse on the 60-mile journey to the orchestra leader's home town of Colne, in Lancashire.

On 18 May, Harold Sidney Bride, *Titanic's* surviving second wireless operator, arrived in Liverpool aboard the *Baltic*. He was met by his father.

All but one of *Titanic's* surviving crew were home and the truant was not absent for long. Fireman Thomas Hart turned up at his home in College Street, Southampton, about a month after the disaster. As he had not been among the survivors picked up by *Carpathia*, he had a certain amount of explaining to do. He managed to convince the gullible authorities that he had lost his discharge book during a drinking bout in a Southampton pub shortly before *Titanic* sailed. His place aboard, he said, had been taken by whoever had stolen or found his papers. To account for the missing month, Hart explained that he had been living rough, afraid to return home because of the uproar caused by the disaster.

Although accepted at face value at the time, and since, Hart's story is nonsensical, simply because an impostor among *Titanic's* crew would have been discovered immediately. No fewer than 34 other crew members lived close by Hart's home, most of them members of the 'black gang', as was Hart himself. In the closer knit communities of 1912 it is inconceivable that Hart would be unknown, at least by sight, to the vast majority of his neighbours who happened to be aboard. It is equally inconceivable that somebody impersonating the fireman would not be recognised and challenged. Unless Thomas Hart's impersonator bore an uncanny physical resemblance to the man from College Street, then he cannot have existed. If the impersonator did not exist, and Thomas Hart's name is not on *Titanic's* list of defaulters, then Hart must have been aboard, with all of the ramifications which that brings. If *Carpathia* did not rescue him, then some other vessel must have done so.

The British Board of Trade was keen to conduct the official British Inquiry into the loss of the *Titanic* itself, quite probably because it was the body which set out the rules governing the construction of such vessels as *Titanic* and what life-saving equipment was to be installed. The shortage of lifeboats aboard the ship had already become a matter of public debate.

On 16 April, Horatio Bottomley MP, gave notice that he intended, two days later, to ask Sidney Buxton, President of the Board of Trade, 'whether he can state the exact lifeboat accommodation which was provided on the *Titanic*, and what proportion it bore to the authorised number of passengers and crew'. Bottomley, as proprietor of the popular *John Bull* magazine, had frequently published articles embarrassing to the Government. For some time before the *Titanic* disaster his magazine had been running a series of features pointing out the deficiencies of lifeboat accommodation aboard modern British liners.

On the 18th, the *Daily Mail* ran an article in which they quoted Alexander Carlisle as saying that the Board of Trade's lifeboat regulations were 'archaic'. The article went on to relate how, although the number of boats aboard *Titanic* exceeded the board's requirements, they had proved to be hopelessly inadequate. Carlisle, adopting the tactics of HMS *Hawke's* Commander Blunt, namely getting his answer in before any questions were asked, also mentioned that his original plan had provided for more than 40 boats. Carlisle might well have saved his own reputation by his remarks, but he had put a lot of others at risk, most notably those of the Board of Trade, White Star and his former employer, James Pirrie. While giving his evidence at the British Inquiry, Ismay denied that any plans were ever submitted to him showing four lifeboats per davit, 40 boats in all.[2] While this denial was undoubtedly truthful enough as far as it went, the reason that Ismay could so confidently say he had never seen a design showing 40 boats was because there had never been any such drawings. *Titanic's* lifeboats had always been envisaged in multiples of the available davits, ie 16.

Under the circumstances it is only too obvious why the Board of Trade was so keen to conduct this inquiry. One of the main issues was bound to be its own regulations. What safer way to cover up its own shortcomings than to investigate them itself, although such an inquiry could hardly be called impartial.³ How could it, when the same Board of Trade had certified as safe a ship that had so spectacularly proved itself otherwise on its maiden voyage?⁴

This barefaced piece of self defence by the Board of Trade didn't go unnoticed. Only a few days after the British Inquiry began, *John Bull* ran the headline '*Titanic* Trickery. Another Whitewashing Inquiry? — The Farce of the Proceedings — The Board of Trade As Both Defendant and Plaintiff!'⁵

Mr Martin MP, put a question to the Prime Minister: 'Since the Board of Trade must necessarily be itself on trial, would it not be more appropriate if the inquiry was conducted by a select committee of the House?'⁶

Clearly, from the Board of Trade viewpoint, the man to chair the Inquiry Committee would be John Charles Bigham, Baron Mersey of Toxteth, who had already proven his worth when it came to shady Government dealings. He had been party to the Governmental inquiry and cover-up of the infamous Jameson raid that had effectively sparked off the Boer War. He was familiar with maritime law and the shipping business. In a long legal career he had experienced every kind of litigation with the exception of murder cases, which he had assiduously avoided.⁷ It is a curious irony that the man presiding over an inquiry into the causes of over 1,500 deaths should have so marked an aversion to murder trials.

Mersey had served the bench faithfully and, as Mr Justice Bigham, was now president of the Probate, Divorce and Admiralty Division of the High Court. On 23 April 1912 a warrant was issued by the Lord High Chancellor of Great Britain, the Right Honourable Robert Threshire, Earl Loveburn, appointing Lord Mersey Wrecks Commissioner for the United Kingdom. Names of the assessors who were likely to assist Lord Mersey were submitted to the Home Secretary also on the 23rd.

Capt Arthur Wellesley Clarke, an Elder Brother of Trinity House, had served for many years as Trinity House Master in Admiralty Court, was extremely knowledgeable about the merchant service and was eventually to receive a knighthood; John Harvard Biles, Professor of Naval Architecture at Glasgow, a leading authority on ship construction and bulkheads, received a knighthood in 1913. In a letter to Sir R. Chalmers, a senior civil servant at the Board of Trade, Professor Biles had already written that 'the public outcry about the boats is likely to obscure the real cause of the trouble: the neglect to carry the bulkheads as high as possible'.[8] Rear Admiral, the Honourable Somerset Arthur Gough-Calthorpe, representing the Royal Navy, was one of the youngest men ever to have achieved his rank; Cdr Fitzhugh C. A. Lyon had already acted as assessor in many inquiries and he had a great deal of experience with passenger vessels, having commanded P&O liners; Mr Edward Catmore Chaston, senior engineer assessor on the Admiralty list for appointment to Board of Trade inquiries, was a prominent member of the Northeast Coast Institute of Engineers and Shipbuilders.[9] Lord Mersey would not be short of expert opinion, it would seem.

The following day, 3 May, the 'Order for Formal Investigation' was approved by the Board of Trade and signed.

On or about the same date, the Board of Trade received a letter from Mr Gerard J. G. Jensen, written on 29 April.[10]

Jensen was a civil engineer who operated from premises at 14 Victoria Street, London SW, or so he said! Supposedly, he was associated to a long-established company who had been in business since the last quarter of the 19th century. Mr Sidney Herbert Marshall was the firm's manager and A. S. Everett was secretary. The company specialised in sewage disposal and drainage. Jensen apparently had both a telephone number and a telegraphic address, 'Cloucalis, London'. Little or nothing else seems to be known about this shadowy figure, who was to make such an impact on the career of Capt Stanley Lord. The Institution of Civil Engineers has no record of him. He does not appear on the Electoral Register, and most unbelievable of all, his name is missing from the Roll of Rate Payers. This individual, whose profession should have made him well known to a wide range of organisations such as borough councils, large estates and builders, seems to have left no more trace of himself than a letter and his name. That a sanitation engineer should choose to involve himself in the official British Inquiry into the loss of the *Titanic* is, to say the least, surprising. Nevertheless, in his capacity as a friend of a friend of *Californian's* carpenter, he did.

As we know, the *Lapland* with most of *Titanic's* surviving crew and some mail from America, arrived at Plymouth on Sunday, 28 April. In one of those mail bags was a letter posted by *Californian's* carpenter, W. F. McGregor, in Boston, on the 19th. The letter was addressed to a friend of the carpenter's. By the following day this friend, whoever he might have been, had received the letter and communicated its content to Jensen. Why he chose the mysterious sanitation engineer is a puzzle, but evidently Mr Jensen was not a man to waste time. That same day, 29 April 1912, Jensen posted a letter of his own to 'The President of the Board of Trade, Whitehall, SW.' The Jensen letter is postmarked, 'London SW. 6.30pm.' The full text of the letter follows:

'Sir.

'*Titanic* Inquiry: I think I am discharging a public duty in bringing the following matter to your notice and to suggest that at the forthcoming inquiry witnesses should be called and closely examined from the Leyland Co's SS *Californian*. My information is from a letter written by the carpenter of the *Californian* to a friend of his but I should be obliged if you would consider the source of your information as confidential.

'Briefly stated the facts are:

1) That while the *Californian* was lying in the ice with engines stopped, the *Titanic's* signals of distress were seen by various members of the crew.
2) That the matter was reported to the captain of the *Californian* on at least three occasions.
3) That the *Californian's* captain took notice of the matter.
4) That the signals were reported to the first officer when he relieved the captain in the ordinary course.
5) That the first officer then set the Marconi operator to work and got in touch with the *Titanic* — but then it was too late to be of service.
6) That the *Californian* was within 10 miles of the *Titanic* and could have saved every soul, had her captain responded to the call for help.
7) That Newfoundland fishing boats are occasionally run down by the *Californian* and other liners and no attempt is made to save the lives of the fishermen in the endeavour to keep time in crossing the Atlantic.

Yours faithfully.

Gerard Jensen.'[11]

A formal acknowledgement was sent to Jensen on 1 May but there was no comment on the content of his letter. The Jensen letter was taken at face value by Sidney Buxton who passed it on to Sir Walter J. Howell, the Assistant Secretary and Chief of the Marine Department of the Board of Trade, and their solicitor, Sir R. Ellis Cunliffe. The Receiver of Wrecks in Liverpool was also informed of the accusations that had been brought against Captain Lord.[12] Unsurprisingly, the documents in the Receiver's office were destroyed by Luftwaffe bombers during World War 2,[13] as were so many other papers relating to the *Titanic*!

We have now seen that:

- *Titanic's* surviving crew were detained upon returning to England and effectively sworn to secrecy before being released;
- Thomas Hart turned up at his home in Southampton some weeks after the sinking claiming that his certificate of continuous discharge had been lost, or stolen, and that somebody had been impersonating him aboard *Titanic*, and just how likely his story is to be true.

30

British Inquiry

The venue selected for the British Inquiry was the Drill Hall of the London Scottish Regiment.[1] Responsible for this inspired choice was the Honourable Clive Bigham.

The cavernous, echoing Drill Hall, large enough to accommodate 300 people, was entirely unsuitable for the purpose, even with heavy draperies festooning the walls and a sounding board strategically placed above the members.[2] The acoustics were abominable, to the extent that sound was dispersed so much that it came to the assessors and public alike as a muffled echo. The search for a more suitable room was begun at once, but it was not until the hearing had only two more days to run that one was discovered, and by that time the witnesses had all been heard. Although Lord Mersey complained bitterly about the choice of venues, he never once mentioned that the hall had been booked by his son.[3]

Lord Mersey sat on a raised platform, flanked by his assessors. The witness stand was to the left of the platform and had its own sounding board to improve the acoustics, which still, 'left much to be desired'.[4]

Behind the witness box was a 20ft-long model of *Titanic*, mounted on a geared display board which could be rotated to simulate the actions of the ship as she filled with water. There was a white mark below the first funnel to indicate where the first point of contact between the ship and the iceberg had occurred.[5] The model was supplied by the builders, Harland & Wolff.

To the left of the model was a huge chart of the North Atlantic, to show exactly where events occurred. A large scale side view plan of the vessel, almost 40ft long, was also on display. The purpose of the plan was to illustrate the maze-like layout of the ship and allow witnesses, assessors and the public alike to understand the complex series of events that led to the sinking. It could also be used to portray the difficulties involved in evacuating a vessel of this magnitude.

Facing Lord Mersey were rows of seats to accommodate spectators, and there were yet more seats in the galleries. Curiously, on the first day of the inquiry there seemed to be very little public interest. Shortly before 11 o'clock, when the hearing was due to start, some 50 counsel and 60 pressmen had taken their places, but the seats reserved for members of the public were only about one-third filled. The gallery, which was reserved for ladies, had only three occupants. One of these was Mrs Sylvia Lightoller who attended every single one of the 36 sessions.[6]

Representing the Board of Trade was the Attorney General, Sir Rufus Daniel Isaacs KC, who even while the inquiry was in progress was insider-dealing in Marconi Company shares, which had been given a considerable boost by the part wireless had played in the disaster.

When Isaacs' brother, Godfrey, had taken over the business side of Marconi in 1910, share prices were 10 and 12shillings (50p and 60p). As a result of the part played by wireless in the *Titanic* disaster, those share prices had risen sharply to £9 and £10.[7] Godfrey Isaacs offered to sell Marconi shares to his brothers Rufus and Harry on 9 April 1912. Harry accepted the offer but Rufus refused, at that time, to invest. However, on 17 April, while the newspapers were full of praise for Marconi's contribution to saving *Titanic's* passengers and crew, Harry offered Rufus some of his shares. This time Rufus saw that he could be on to a good thing and bought 10,000 of the shares at £2 each (about £700,000 at today's prices). Of these he transferred 1,000 each to Lloyd George and the Master of Elibank, keeping a mere 8,000 for himself.[8]

Sir Rufus was to question the inventor during the inquiry[9] and in doing so undoubtedly managed to improve his investment. Both Rufus Isaacs and Lloyd George denied having any interest in the English Marconi Company, which was technically true, but neither thought it expedient to mention their American holdings.[10] By buying when he did, Sir Rufus Isaacs actually made money out of the disaster he was supposedly, impartially, investigating.[11] Isaacs' involvement with the Marconi Company only became general knowledge on 18 January 1913.[12]

Alongside Sir Rufus were the Solicitor General, Sir John Simon KC, Mr Butler Aspinall KC, Mr S. T. Rowlatt; and Mr Raymond Asquith.

In the other corner, representing the White Star line, was the Right Honourable Sir Robert Finlay KC, MP. Assisting Sir Robert were Mr F. Laing KC, Mr Maurice Hill KC, and Mr Norman Raeburn. Instructing the lawyers were the solicitors, Messrs Hill Dickinson & Company.

Instructed by Capt Smith's widow, Eleanor, her solicitors had enlisted the services of Mr Thomas Scanlan MP, to appear on behalf of the National Sailors' and Firemen's Union. Mr Clement Edwards represented the Dockers' Union. Mr D. W. Harbinson, appeared for the third class passengers, instructed by a solicitor, Mr Farrell. Looking after the interests of Sir Cosmo Duff-Gordon and his spouse was Mr Henry Duke KC.

Captain Lord and the officers and owners of *Californian* were not actually represented at all. Mr C. Robertson Dunlop was allowed only to watch the proceedings and act in an advisory capacity on their behalf. Even in this modest endeavour Mr Dunlop does not appear to have pushed himself unduly. Despite this apparent lethargy, on the odd occasion when he did try to present a clear and reasoned case for the *Californian* he was faced with an almost continuous barrage of interruptions from Lord Mersey and the Attorney General.[13] Although Dunlop was nominally counsel for Captain Lord and the *Californian*, he had already received instructions from elsewhere to do nothing that might lead to the identification of any other ships involved,[14] presumably from the owners of the Leyland Line.

Dunlop was to have appeared for the *Californian* and his application was the first thing heard by the inquiry but Lord Mersey turned the application down, saying that the question at issue was between the *Californian's* captain and Donkeyman Gill and that he, Mersey, was not going to go into the matter at any length.[15] As we shall see, Lord Mersey soon forgot that he had ever said anything of the kind.

Dunlop wasn't the only counsel not allowed to take an active part in the proceedings. Lord Mersey refused to hear counsel for the Shipwrights' Association, the Dockers' Union, and the Imperial Service Guild. He also excluded counsel for the radical Seafarers' Union in favour of the more conservative Sailors' & Firemen's Union. Whether the cable of warm sympathy from the secretary of the Sailors' & Firemen's Union, Havelock Wilson, already received by J. Bruce Ismay[16] had any bearing on Mersey's decision is unknown.

On the first day of the hearings Sir John Simon presented the list of 26 questions to which the inquiry would attempt to furnish answers. In its original form these questions fell naturally into four groups:

- First, they would provide a description of the ship as she left Southampton on 10 April and of her equipment, crew and passengers.

- Second, there would be an account of the journey across the Atlantic, of the messages she received and of the disaster.
- Third, a description of the damage to the ship and its gradual and final effect, with observations thereon, would emerge.
- Fourth, an account of the saving and rescue of those who survived.

Question 24, however, was to change the whole thrust of the inquiry when, some days after the last witness had been heard and the doors closed to the public, while the board met in private conclave, an extra sentence was inserted between the two sentences of the original question. In their original form the questions were judged acceptable by the representatives of the White Star line (but not, one would imagine, as acceptable as the revised version).

Right from the outset Mersey controlled the witnesses with consummate skill, only allowing them to say what he wanted to hear. Or when, like Scarrott, they said something he didn't like, he either misinterpreted or ignored it. On more than one occasion the Wrecks Commissioner even badgered a witness into changing a statement in such a way that it no longer said what he intended it to.

When Scarrott mentioned his 'raft' made of 'air boxes' Lord Mersey chose not to hear him. Scarrott was asked by Scanlan, 'Would lamps be necessary for the safety of the boat on a dark night?' Mersey interrupted, 'That is not a proper question to ask. You can ask me that at the proper time, and very likely I shall not answer it.'[17] There can be no doubt that Mersey was being selective as to what testimony he was prepared to hear because he then allowed Scanlan to ask if eight men would have been necessary for the safety of the boat in a storm, even though there had only been two crewmen in Number 14[18] and no storm.

On Monday, 6 May, the commission's members had a day out. They went to Southampton to inspect *Titanic*'s sister ship, *Olympic*. After touring the ship and seeing such things as the operation of the watertight doors Mersey and his assessors watched as a lifeboat was lowered.

Shortly after lunch, which was taken aboard, Lord Mersey, his son the Honourable Clive and Professor Biles returned to London on a special train. The other members remained aboard *Olympic* over night, where they undoubtedly made the most of the facilities offered by the sumptuous liner and the hospitality of the White Star Co. Even at this early stage much of the outcome of the inquiry was already predictable.

During the days that followed, *Titanic's* crewmen filed through the witness box, only to have much of what they said ignored by the omnipotent Wrecks Commissioner. Fireman George Beauchamp testified that water entered Number 10 stokehold through the bunker door, showing that the bunker was filling but not the stokehold itself. This indicates that either the bulkhead had failed or that the hole in the ship's side did not encompass the whole of the forward boiler room.

Beauchamp went on to say that the lights which his lifeboat tried to reach turned out to be *Carpathia*. Mersey completely ignored both these parts of his evidence.

Robert Hitchens, who was helmsman at the time of the collision, said that the wheel was still at hard a-starboard when the ship struck and that at no time immediately before or after the collision was the ship under a port helm. He also said that *Titanic* was firing red, white and blue rockets. Mersey failed, or appeared to fail, to grasp the significance of Hitchens' fundamentally momentous evidence.

Able Seaman William Lucas said, 'There would have been time for third class passengers to reach the Boat Deck, if anybody had bothered to show them the way,' implying that nobody did bother.

Fireman Fred Barrett testified that water came through the bulkhead separating Numbers 5 and 6 boiler rooms, showing that the bulkhead had failed. To be fair to Lord Mersey, he did appear to take this information on board but still did not grasp its importance.

Lookout Reginald Robertson Lee (Henry Reginald Lee) said that the iceberg struck the ship just forward of the foremast. Mersey failed to recognise that this point of impact is further aft than he believed, although nowhere near as far aft as Captain Smith told the wireless operators.

According to Lee, he had not seen the iceberg sooner because it was obscured by mist; Fleet also reported this mist. Mersey said that he thought Lee was making up the story of the mist as an excuse for not having seen the berg in time to avert the disaster.[19]

Trimmer Robert Patrick Dillon said that he was ordered forward from the engine room, where he was on duty, to instruct the firemen not to draw their fires but to keep steam up. Dillon visited four stokeholds where he passed his instructions on.

Trimmer George Cavell testified that the boilers in Number 4 boiler room were working at a pressure of 225lb/sq in. *Titanic's* engines were designed to work at 215lb/sq in, indicating that they were exceeding their maximum design revolutions. Mersey once again missed the importance of what was being said.

Fireman Alfred Shiers said that 5min after the collision *Titanic* was still moving slowly forwards.

Greaser Frederick Scott, who had been on duty in the turbine engine room, said that the engines were ordered slow ahead 10mins after the collision.

Baker Charles Joughin said that the crew had closed the watertight door in the 'Scotland Road' alleyway, and that a great many of the crew came from *Olympic*, 'which would have helped them in the matter of boat drill and so forth'. Mersey missed the significance of all these items of evidence.

On day 7 Captain Lord of the *Californian* stepped into the witness box, and into the pages of history. One very interesting piece of information to come from Captain Lord was that his ship carried four lifeboats and two emergency boats with a capacity of 280 people, more than double the number of persons that his vessel was certified to carry.

Lord gave the position where the *Californian* had stopped for the night. He described the mysterious vessel that he had seen and how he was sure it was not a large liner. Having noticed that the vessel stopped at about 11.30pm he had taken special notice when the third officer informed him that it had moved by 1.15am.

Lord also explained that he had only the haziest of memories regarding Gibson's later visit to his cabin. He explained that he had fallen asleep and that the apprentice had failed to wake him properly. The Attorney General said that he found it impossible to believe that Lord was actually asleep at 2 o'clock in the morning.[20] Quite what he thought sea captains did all night he never divulged. Nor did the Attorney General query what Captain Rostron was doing in bed when *Titanic's* distress call was received by the *Carpathia*.[21]

Captain Lord explained that he did not believe the rockets seen were distress signals because the mystery vessel was close enough for the report of their bursting to be heard aboard *Californian*. He described how it was a general rule to double the lookouts in the presence of ice. This simple precaution had been observed on both *Californian* and *Carpathia* but not on *Titanic*.

Lord went on to describe how he received news of the disaster, how he reached the wreck site, and what he saw there. He might just as well have said nothing at all for all the difference that his testimony made to Lord Mersey.

Californian's apprentice, James Gibson, was next onto the witness stand. He too described the mystery ship and the rockets seen from *Californian*. In Gibson's version the mystery vessel had a heavy list to starboard (*Titanic* listed to port). The apprentice also told how he had reported the rockets to the captain who was dozing in the chart room. All of the rockets he saw were throwing out white stars, which agreed with Captain Lord's evidence. Gibson's evidence is the basis of the belief that eight rockets were seen from the *Californian*.[22]

Californian's second officer, Herbert Stone, estimated the distance of the mystery ship at about five miles but he thought that the rockets might be coming from a vessel even further away. The ship he saw was moving because the bearing from *Californian* was constantly changing. Stone told Lord Mersey and the three assessors that Captain Lord had asked Gibson if there was any colour in the rockets.[23] The second officer didn't believe that all of the signals seen were rockets at all. One of the counsel for White Star, Mr F. Laing, explained to the inquiry that companies' signals were made by Roman candles, not rockets.[24]

On the eighth day of the inquiry, *Californian's* third officer, Groves, opened the proceedings. He told of seeing the lights of a mystery ship, which had first become visible at 11.25pm and which slowly changed its bearing, indicating that it was under way. Quite obviously Lord Mersey didn't know the difference between a heading (the direction in which a ship was moving or in which her bows were pointing) and a bearing (the position of a ship in relation to the position of the watcher).[25]

Groves said that the mystery ship put its lights out at 11.40pm, which was enough to convince Lord Mersey, apparently, that as this agreed with the time of *Titanic's* collision then the mystery vessel must be her. Mersey, in his enthusiasm to identify the mystery ship seen from *Californian* as *Titanic*, had managed to convince himself that stopping the ship's engines would automatically plunge the liner into darkness. It had to be explained to him that this was not, in fact, the case.[26]

If the vessel seen by Groves had been the *Titanic*, which was heading west and was to the south of *Californian*, then he must have seen her green starboard light. Dunlop asked the third officer, 'Did you see her green light at all?'

'Never,' Groves replied.[27]

Groves also described how at about a quarter past twelve he went to the wireless cabin and listened to the wireless, but heard nothing. He had to wake up the Marconi man and ask him what ships he had. This interruption of his already short night's sleep no doubt endeared the third officer to the Marconi operator. After a while he gave up and retired to bed for what he believed would be the remainder of the night.

Groves described the trip to the wreck site the following morning, but he thought *Californian* had only steamed about 11 miles to reach the scene of the disaster. Lord Mersey had another piece of testimony with which to beat the unfortunate Captain Lord.

Californian's chief officer, G. F. Stewart, was next, but as he was off duty at the time the mystery ship and rockets were seen, his evidence was, in the main, only corroborative although he did confirm that the ship had steamed due west since 9.40am.[28] This firmly established that *Californian* was in the latitude claimed by Captain Lord.

Under pressure from Mersey to admit that the signals seen from *Californian* might have come from *Titanic*, Stewart finally flatly denied the possibility.

'Do you think it may have been the *Titanic*?' Mersey asked.

'No sir,' Stewart replied.[29]

Cyril Furmstone Evans, *Californian's* wireless operator, had one or two items of interest to impart, the first being that he habitually worked a 16hr day, from 7.30am to 11.30pm. Another was that he had received information that *Titanic* had sunk early on Monday morning, when none but the survivors and people aboard *Carpathia* should have known. We have already seen just how free *Carpathia* was with the news. Evans also said that he had a good deal of trouble contacting *Carpathia* at all. This was lost on Lord Mersey.

The captain of the *Mount Temple*, Henry Moore, opened his mouth and put his foot in it when he gave his evidence. 'I got a report that the *Titanic* had struck an iceberg in 41°46'North, 50°14'West. We were then about 15 miles from where the *Titanic* foundered.'

Given that statement Lord Mersey might have been forgiven for believing that he had found the mystery ship. Almost inevitably he did not appear to take in what Moore had said; at least he never followed it up as any competent inquirer should have. Board of Trade solicitor Ellis Cunliffe later wrote a 13-page review of the case in which he dealt at some length with the allegations that the vessel seen from *Titanic* was *Mount Temple*.[30]

Captain Moore also gave a very clear description of yet another mystery ship: 'She had a black funnel with a white band round it, and some sort of device on it. She was going East.' Lord Mersey instigated a search for such a vessel, which was never found.[31] Interestingly, that description fits the Anchor Donaldson Line's *Saturnia*, which, in trying to reach *Titanic*, got to within six miles of her position before being stopped by ice.

Captain Moore seemed unsure as to how many lifeboats the *Mount Temple* carried. When asked he replied that they had '20 lifeboats when *Mount Temple* left London'. He didn't say how many remained when they reached their destination.

Mount Temple's wireless operator, John Durrant, supported Evans' evidence regarding the hours worked by Marconi employees. Durrant started work at 7.30am, the same as Evans, but he worked until at least 1am the next day, 1½hr longer than Evans.

As the days passed, evidence was presented concerning Sir Cosmo Duff-Gordon and his party's escape in boat Number 1. This caused something of a sensation and distracted the public gaze from more important issues such as the evidence of Symons, who had charge of boat Number 1, that *Titanic's* rockets were sent up at 1min intervals.

Symons also mentioned a visitor he had received at his home in Weymouth, since his return from America. This visitor was a representative of Sir Cosmo Duff-Gordon.[32] He had questioned Symons extensively, and one of the questions asked was if he were 'master of the situation'. Symons used this same expression repeatedly when describing himself during his evidence. The phrase, 'You used your discretion,' was also employed at the private interview and repeated 'Ad nauseum' during the lookout's testimony. The use of these phrases in Symons' evidence strongly suggests that he was coached as to how he was going to give his testimony by his visitor. Symons told the inquiry that this visitor had suggested that he had best say nothing about the meeting.[33]

Although Symons had made a point of bringing the interview to light, Lord Mersey made no comment and appears to have been totally oblivious to an obvious attempt to influence a witness. Scanlan kept at Symons, trying to get at the truth until he was stopped by Mersey, who said, 'Have mercy on him Mr Scanlan.'[34]

Duff-Gordon's lawyer, Duke, said that a firm of solicitors had been instructed by a friend of Duff-Gordon's to obtain statements from the witnesses. This friend had not been instructed by Sir Cosmo to tell the solicitors anything, the only communication between the friend and Duff-Gordon being to the effect that Sir Cosmo would like to attend the inquiry. Sir Cosmo had been at sea at the time of the suspect interview and had therefore not approached the witness. Nor had he instructed anybody else to do so.[35]

Symons continued his evidence by denying that lifeboat Number 1 was in reality a private hire boat. He also omitted to mention Duff-Gordon's £5 present to each of the crew of boat Number 1 at the American Inquiry as well.[36] Despite there being evidence to show that the failure of boat Number 1 to return to the site of the sinking in search of survivors had not been wholly Symons' fault, Isaacs pilloried him for not doing so.[37]

The next witness, Fireman James Taylor, another crewman from private hire boat Number 1, told how a gentleman representing Sir Cosmo Duff-Gordon met him in the White Star office at Southampton. There this gentleman took a statement which Taylor signed. He thought, he said, that he was signing for seven shillings expenses. He had been sent for by Mr Blake, the Superintending Engineer of the White Star line, to meet Duff-Gordon's representative.[38] We now have clear and corroborative evidence of an attempt to influence witnesses with the active assistance of senior officers of the White Star line. How else could Duff-Gordon's solicitor have obtained Symons' home address? Another indicator overlooked by the inquiry.

In a private conversation with a gentleman whose grandmother ran a public house in Southampton, and had been a friend of Fireman Fred Barrett in 1912, I was informed that it was common knowledge that many of the witnesses at the British Inquiry were induced to give evidence favourable to the company.

In his evidence Quartermaster Wynne told how, soon after the collision, he was ordered by the captain to get the two accident books ready. This shows that Smith intended that some sort of record of the accident was to be kept, at least before the extent of the damage became known.

On day 11 Second Officer Lightoller began his extensive evidence, such as it was. Lightoller obviously tried to look after the interests of the White Star line as well as his own while giving his evidence. Geoffrey Marcus described it as 'an amazing performance' in his account of the disaster: The Maiden Voyage.[39] This makes a good deal of Lightoller's evidence useless for anyone attempting to make sense of the events surrounding the loss of the *Titanic*, but he did allow one or two items of interest to slip out.

Lightoller stated that he had absolutely no knowledge of any ice warnings except the one received from *Caronia* that morning.

Titanic's senior surviving officer insisted that the view from the ship's bridge was the equal of that from the crow's-nest and, under the peculiar conditions that night, he would have spotted an iceberg at between 1½ and 2 miles away. When asked if he could see a growler at a safe distance, he replied, 'Yes, I could see one at 2 miles away. When there is a slight breeze you can always see a phosphorescent light, which is called 'ice blink', and you can see that before the iceberg comes above the horizon.[40] This evidence supports the lookout's evidence that the vessel's bow was already beginning to swing to port when the alarm bell was sounded as it shows that the bridge officers should have seen an iceberg before the lookouts did and reacted accordingly.

The great Antarctic explorer Sir Ernest Shackleton also gave evidence supporting the notion that the iceberg might have been seen from the bridge at least as soon as from the crow's-nest.[41]

According to the second officer it would have taken the ship about 9min to travel 1½ miles at the speed she was going that night. Not unusually, Mr Lightoller was hopelessly incorrect in his estimate of the time it would take a vessel moving at about 25 miles per hour to travel 1½ miles, which would actually be between 3 and 4min. Unless, of course, *Titanic* was making only 10kts at the time, in which case his estimate would be correct.

Another interesting snippet that Lightoller let fall was that on the following morning, although he could see icebergs about 10 miles away, there was no field ice or growlers around, which does not quite tie up with what other witnesses saw. Once again one wonders if he was there at all.

When asked by Scanlan, 'Were you not making all the speed that you could?' Lightoller replied, 'No. There was a shortage of coal and a number of boilers were off, so there could not have been the desire to make the most speed we could.' He estimated the vessel's top speed would be somewhere about 24kts but we have already had some experience of Lightoller's estimates of speed.

Yet another pearl that he cast before the British Board of Inquiry was that *Titanic* was on the 'Autumn Southern Route'. This would have been a direct contravention of company standing orders but nonetheless it is almost certainly true.

When questioned about the bunker fire, Lightoller denied any knowledge of it, saying that it would be the responsibility of the engineer to see that it was put out. There is nothing more dangerous at sea than fire, so one would have expected the second officer to have adopted a slightly less cavalier attitude towards it. Lord Mersey's attitude to fire at sea appears to have been not dissimilar to Lightoller's.

When Edwards was questioning Harold Sanderson, he asked him if he was aware of the bunker fire between Belfast and Southampton. Mersey interrupted, 'Do let us confine ourselves to the real serious issues of this inquiry. That fire had nothing to do with this disaster.'[42] Because the fire didn't fit in with his preconceived ideas, Lord Mersey was doing his very best to ignore it.

Lord Mersey and Sir Rufus Isaacs were both sceptical about Lightoller's reliability as a witness and discussed this quite openly.[43]

Herbert John Pitman, third officer, denied that he even knew that the ship was going in the direction of ice. 'No, we were not.' he said. 'The course marked out at noon that day was 10 miles farther south than necessary yet at 5.50pm the commander altered the course yet more southerly.'

Fourth Officer Joseph Groves Boxhall reached the bridge shortly after the collision. The captain was there and Boxhall heard First Officer Murdoch say to Smith, 'I was going to port around it but she was too close,' he testified. This bears out Hitchens' statement that the ship was still at hard a-starboard when she struck and was never under a port helm.

Boxhall testified that the only ice warning of which he was aware was from *Caronia* and had arrived on the Sunday morning; there were none later. Boxhall had told the American Inquiry that he didn't receive any ice warnings on the Sunday, but he now told the British Inquiry that he received one that morning. He said that there were no warnings after 'the Sunday morning one'.[44]

According to Boxhall, only the fourth and fifth officers should have been on duty that night. Murdoch was keeping lookout but he only came on the bridge at gone 11 o'clock. He and Lowe were on duty from 8pm to midnight, he said, which leaves us with the question: just what was Moody doing on the bridge with Murdoch?

The position of the ice mentioned in the *Caronia* warning was not plotted on the chart, Boxhall said.

Next came possibly the most colourful of *Titanic's* surviving officers, Fifth Officer Harold Godfrey Lowe. Although his version of events was dramatic, it did not add anything to the already existing body of evidence, except a few details of his failed rescue attempt.

We have seen how:

- The Attorney General, Sir Rufus Isaacs, was insider-dealing in Marconi shares while he was supposed to be gathering impartial evidence at the British Inquiry;
- Lord Mersey was only prepared to accept what witnesses said if it happened to be what he wanted to hear;
- Everything that Captain Lord said was totally disregarded by Lord Mersey's inquiry.

British Inquiry (2)

A Marconi Company official, Mr Turnbull, told the British Inquiry that the records of the wireless traffic from *Titanic* had been lost but that they were trying to reconstitute them.[1] This was convenient for their surviving representative from the liner, Bride, as very little that he said about messages being sent or received could be verified. As we have already dealt with the second wireless operator's story at some length, it should not be necessary to delve too deeply into it here. Needless to say, Bride shifted all responsibility for ice warnings failing to reach the bridge onto his senior and friend, Jack Phillips.

According to Bride, the only ice warning he received was that from the *Californian*. Even Mersey couldn't help commenting on Bride's evidence because he didn't believe that anybody who could remember things that well would continually contradict himself. 'Does it all come to this, that his own memory is quite defective?' he said.[2]

To underline his dissatisfaction with Bride's evidence, the Commissioner directed a question to Lightoller, Boxhall and Lowe, who had already given their testimony. The three officers all agreed on the answer. The only ice warning to reach the bridge, on Sunday, 14 April, was from the *Caronia* and that message was received at 9am. Lightoller then denied that they were warned that they were running into an ice-field[3], even though he had previously stated that he had calculated when they would reach the ice!

On the 15th day of the inquiry, H. T. Cottam, wireless operator of the *Carpathia*, took the stand. Cottam gave no hint that he had been in contact with *Titanic* before the first distress call was received at 10.35pm but Durrant, of the *Mount Temple*, had already said that he heard *Titanic* and *Carpathia* working together at 9.45pm. Cottam told the inquiry that *Titanic's* signals were very good right up to the end, but in *Carpathia's* wireless diary is an entry, '12.20am signals very broken'.

Frederick Fleet was next to enter the witness box. As the man who supposedly first saw the iceberg, Fleet's appearance was eagerly awaited. In the event his evidence came as something of a disappointment. The lookout adopted a curmudgeonly attitude and as a result appeared to be of less than average intelligence. The strategy worked to the extent that even though Fleet gave evidence that Lord Mersey did not want to hear, when he said that about 10min before the collision the view ahead of the ship was suddenly obscured by mist, the Commissioner still congratulated him on completion of his testimony: 'Well, you have given your evidence very well, although you seem to have distrusted all of us.' This rare accolade from Lord Mersey was richly deserved. Who can blame Fleet for being distrustful of Mersey and his inquiry?; he had already seen enough to know that a cover-up was in progress.

Fred Fleet had told the inquiry that he first saw the ice at about 11.40pm. It now appears that he was telling rather less than the exact truth. Fleet first saw and reported ice at 11.15, a full 25min before the accident. One wonders what Lord Mersey's reaction might have been if Fleet had told the whole truth. In all probability the Wrecks Commissioner would have completely ignored the evidence, as he did so much other testimony that did not fit into the picture he was attempting to paint.

Quartermaster George Thomas Rowe, who was on duty on the Poop Deck (at the extreme rear of the ship) at the time of the accident, told the committee that the first indication he had that there was anything amiss was when he saw a lifeboat in the water, off the starboard side of the ship. Rowe telephoned the bridge to ask them if they knew a boat had been launched. An officer replied, saying, 'No — is there?' Rowe's evidence where he describes seeing a lifeboat that the officers on the bridge knew nothing of, argues that the boat did not come from *Titanic* at all.

Rowe also told how he assisted with firing the distress rockets for about 40min, an unconscionably long time to spend sending up eight rockets.

Lamp Trimmer Samuel Hemmings then gave his evidence. He said that quite early on in the drama, he heard air escaping from the top of the forepeak tank (in the extreme bows of the ship), as water entered it from below. He also said that the carpenter told him that water was entering the first, second and third holds. This shows that the point of first contact in the collision was very much further forward than is generally thought, or the inquiry believed.

On the 16th day, First Class Bedroom Steward Alfred Crawford said that he saw 'a dozen or more' rockets sent up from *Titanic*. Crawford made an attempt to describe the mystery ship that he saw from *Titanic* and later from a lifeboat. He also explained how 'Captain

Smith ordered us to make for the light, [about five to seven miles away] hand over the passengers and then come back to the ship.' Presupposing that Captain Smith was not a complete imbecile, this implies that the master expected the mystery vessel to close with the stricken liner. As the captain would have been aware that no contact had been established with the mysterious vessel he can have had no valid reason to suppose that she would approach the doomed *Titanic* — unless a previous arrangement existed whereby a vessel would come to *Titanic's* assistance, without first being signalled by either lamp or wireless. The captain's orders to Crawford's and other boats therefore makes no sense. He could not expect the small boat, with only four inexperienced oarsmen, to be rowed between 10 and 14 miles, to the mystery ship and back, in the time remaining to *Titanic*.

The members of the Board of Inquiry, in discussion amongst themselves, came up with much the same answer. They believed that Captain Smith expected the mystery ship to close with *Titanic* although they failed to find any reason for this expectation.[4]

Crawford further testified that his lifeboat did attempt to carry out the captain's instructions and in the process he saw both the red and green side lights of the stranger as she turned away.

Lord Mersey attempted to explain away the obvious implications of Captain Smith's orders by suggesting that the witnesses were wrong. He thought that what Smith must have said was, 'Go to that light, put your passengers off and return to this place.'[5] Mersey's brazen attempt to alter the evidence until it agreed with his own preconceived ideas was, in this instance, pointless. Whether or not the lifeboats returned to the site of the sinking didn't matter a jot. The freezing cold water would have killed the swimmers long before the boats could complete the 10–14 mile round trip.

In an outrageous display of 'witness leading', Lord Mersey left no room for doubt that he believed the mystery ship to be the *Californian*, and by the phrasing of his questions forced the witness into agreeing with him — questions such as, 'Your interest in the *Californian* ceased when you saw *Carpathia*?'[6]

In public conversation with the Attorney General, Lord Mersey said, 'We have heard about the mysterious light as it was called that was seen from the *Titanic*, but, dismissing that light, was there any light or any vessel seen by any witness from the *Titanic* at this time?'

The Attorney General replied, 'There is some evidence of a light being seen.'

Mersey responded, 'I know, I say, dismissing that imaginary light, is there any evidence of any ship having been seen at this time, or about this time, by the *Titanic*?'

'No, I do not think so.'[7]

Without there, as yet, even being a question to cover the possibility, Captain Lord and the *Californian* already stood condemned of a crime that they had never been, and never would be, charged with.

While Thomas Lewis, acting for the British Seafarers' Union, was questioning Crawford, Lord Mersey interceded. He asked Lewis if the questions he was asking were at random or whether he was following instructions. Lewis told the Wrecks Commissioner that he was following written instructions. Mersey then insisted that Lewis hand him his notes and took over the questioning himself (so denying witness and counsel the freedom to reveal the facts). Lord Mersey's questioning, unsurprisingly, resulted in no conclusive answers. Eventually he handed the papers back to Lewis.

Lewis, in a show of displeasure, said, 'I am obliged to your Lordship … I should like to ask whether I have to submit documents in future to your Lordship, or whether I am entitled to ask the witnesses questions?'

Also on day 16 Ernest Gill, the donkeyman from *Californian* whose statement in America had so besmirched Captain Lord, took the stand. He essentially repeated his American evidence and, as before, it was accepted by the Court of Inquiry without any serious attempt at cross-examination being made. He was never asked, for example, how he could so clearly see a vessel 10 miles away.[8] The Attorney General went so far as to declare the donkeyman's statement to be true[9] even though it is laden with inconsistencies. However, Gill did say that at the time he attached no more importance to the rockets than anyone else aboard *Californian*. When Dunlop attempted to seize upon this and point out that nobody had been particularly concerned about the rockets, Mersey intervened saying, 'I disagree with that being in accordance with the evidence.'[10]

Later that day J. Bruce Ismay took the stand. Already a pariah as far as the Americans were concerned, Ismay must have expected a similar reaction from his countrymen. He could not have been more wrong.

Ismay was at pains to explain to the commission that *Titanic* was, in fact, American-owned. Only when he explained that the liner had sailed under a British flag because 'You cannot fly an American flag over a foreign-built ship,' did Mersey understand that the vessel was not British.[11]

The inquiry attempted to establish whether or not Ismay had used his position as head of the company to influence Captain Smith. Ismay denied this saying that in all his Atlantic crossings he had never attempted to interfere with the navigation of the ship (any ship).[12] He explained that, although he didn't pay for his passage, he looked upon himself as an ordinary passenger. When Isaacs commented that his not paying 'rather disposes of the theory of your being an ordinary passenger,' Ismay replied that he would have travelled in a similar way on any other vessel, including a Cunarder.[13]

Captain Rostron supported the White Star chairman by saying, 'It would be unthinkable for any self-respecting Captain — least of all Captain Smith — to take orders from anybody while at sea.' The captain was omnipotent.[14]

Captain Hays, who had been with White Star for 14 years, also supported Ismay's assertion that he would never interfere with the navigation of a ship at sea. He said that Ismay had sailed with him before, but only as an ordinary passenger and had never interfered.[15]

Having denied that he had done anything to influence the speed of the *Titanic*, Ismay admitted that a high speed trial was planned for the Monday. This, he explained, had been arranged before the ship left Ireland and whether or not it actually took place would rest with the captain.[16]

Ismay also pointed out that as a result of the disaster the southern route had been moved 150 miles further south, but even this was no guarantee of safety as ice had already been reported on the new route.[17] As we already know, the provision of a new route would hardly have affected the *Titanic* as she was not following the correct course, for that season, anyway.

On the subject of lifeboats, particularly those that leaked or had more than one identification number on them, Ismay said, 'All boats were new and none were transferred from another ship.'[18] He also insisted that the number of boats on *Titanic* had nothing whatever to do with her relative unsinkability, but was governed by Board of Trade regulations,[19] which was at least partly true.

The White Star chairman told not of one mystery ship but of two, a steamer on *Titanic's* port side and a sailing vessel to starboard. He revealed that the light which his lifeboat had tried to reach could not have been *Californian* because it was on the wrong side of the liner.

Lord Mersey was not so easily dissuaded: 'Never mind about what side. Have you come to the conclusion that the vessel whose light was seen for such a long time was not the *Californian*?' Ismay replied, 'No, but I said the light we pulled toward was not the *Californian*.'[20]

On the following day Ismay said again that the only light he saw was the one to starboard and that he never saw one to port. He was sure that the light he did see was not that of the *Californian*.

On the 18th day, Edward Wilding, since the demise of Thomas Andrews, Chief Designer for Harland & Wolff, gave evidence regarding the structure of the ship and its watertight compartments. S. T. Rowlatt questioned Wilding about the water seen flowing into the watertight firemen's passage from the spiral stairway.

Common sense tells us that this damage, highlighted by Rowlatt and Mersey, could not have been caused by a finger of ice because the ice would have broken, not the steel ship. Only ice in considerable bulk could have smashed its way through the ship's plating and ribs with enough force to rupture the firemen's passageway at least 5.5ft from the outer skin of the ship. Such an impact would have been felt by every person aboard as the iceberg shouldered the liner aside or arrested her progress entirely.

The damage described by Wilding, Rowlatt and Mersey is not dissimilar to that inflicted upon *Olympic* by the knife-edged prow of the *Hawke*. In that accident the ship was thrown violently sideways. That a tremendous impact such as would have been required to inflict the damage described, delivered by a blunt instrument, was not felt by all aboard *Titanic*, means that it did not happen.

Edward Wilding returned to the stand to state that if only *Titanic* had rammed the iceberg head on, the front 100ft of the ship would have telescoped but she would have remained afloat. Later Wilding said that, judging from the evidence of Patrick Dillon, the damage to *Titanic's* hull extended from the forepeak, through 1, 2 and 3 holds, Number 6 and 5 boiler rooms to Number 4. Seven compartments were open to the sea, not the usually accepted four. He went on to say that the ship's officers should have known that it was safe to lower the lifeboats fully laden. The falls were each capable of handling something in the region of 60 tons.

The marine architect from Harland & Wolff then admitted that liners of the period were built in such a way that third class passengers were shut out from the Boat Deck and that it would be difficult for them to find their way unless they were shown. Just before leaving the witness stand he dropped another bombshell when he said that it would have been difficult to have carried *Titanic's* bulkheads up as far as C Deck because of Board of Trade regulations regarding third class.

Lord Mersey summed up the design and construction of the 'Olympic' class vessels when he said, 'We know how the *Titanic* was built. It was designed by Messrs Harland & Wolff and built by them without any control of the White Star line.'[21]

The next performer in the tragicomic masterpiece was Alexander Carlisle, the late Chief Designer for Harland & Wolff, who stated that he had originally intended that there be four boats per pair of davits, 64 boats in all. He said that his designs were submitted to both Ismay and Harold Sanderson.[22] Ismay denied ever seeing them.[23] As Carlisle originally designed the Boat Deck, there would have been no difficulty in stacking the larger number of boats. They could all have been attached to the falls, swung out and lowered in an hour, Carlisle averred.

After his original design was turned down he suggested that the number of boats per set of davits be reduced to three, 48 in all. This suggestion was also rejected.

Harold Sanderson said that although Harland & Wolff knew that the Welin davits were capable of handling more than one boat, the management of White Star were never informed.[24] If this statement were true then what earthly reason could there have been for putting the extra collapsible boats onto the ship when, as far as the management of the line and the crew of the vessel were aware, there was no way of launching them? Curiously, *Titanic's* crew swung out both collapsible C and D without the benefit of any special instructions from the builders, indicating that they were well aware that the davits were quite able to manage more than one lifeboat.

On day 21, Captain Passow of the American Line steamer *St Paul* gave evidence. He said, 'I have never seen an iceberg on a perfectly clear night, near enough that I could not clear it.' He was speaking from experience having more than 700 Atlantic crossings to his credit.

Mersey asked him, 'Then if you are right, and this was a perfectly clear night, why didn't they see it?'

Captain Passow replied, 'I cannot account for it my lord.'[25] He went on to say that it was the duty of the officers on the bridge to notice haze around icebergs, and report it to the captain. Not the lookouts.

Captain Steele RNR, Marine Superintendent at Southampton, said that 'On a clear night an iceberg could be seen at six or seven miles.'[26]

Stanley Howard Adams, the wireless operator on the *Mesaba*, told of the ice warning sent to and acknowledged by *Titanic* at 9.40pm. This must be where any knowledge of this message comes from, because Bride knew nothing of it and Phillips, as we know, never left the wireless room.

On day 28 Captain Rostron of the *Carpathia* gave his evidence, most of which we are already familiar with. Interestingly, he said that *Carpathia* had received no ice reports by wireless before they caught *Titanic*'s distress signals at 12.35am. This is remarkable because *Carpathia* had passed almost completely through the southern extremities of the same ice field that had proven fatal to the White Star liner.

As *Carpathia* had sped to the rescue, her lookouts had managed to spot threatening icebergs at between one and two miles distance. Once they had stopped and daylight broke they were surprised to see a 25–30ft berg only about a quarter of a mile off.

Probably the most important single piece of evidence Captain Rostron presented concerned the number of lifeboats at the scene. We have already seen that he accounted for more boats than *Titanic* carried. We also know that he saw a capsized wooden lifeboat that cannot have come from the liner because all of her wooden boats supposedly reached *Carpathia* the right way up and with survivors.

The *Carpathia*'s skipper also mentioned the peculiar lack of wreckage and floating bodies at the scene of the sinking. He must have thought that this was unusual or he would not have commented upon it.

In an affidavit Rostron stated that, as it grew light and while he was picking up *Titanic*'s survivors, he saw two ships slightly to the north of the wreck site. Neither of these vessels was the *Californian*, Rostron was sure. This affidavit, from a most reliable witness, places at least two unnamed vessels between *Titanic* and *Californian* at about, or soon after, the time of the disaster.

The British Inquiry rambled on, although the witnesses yet to come were all non-participants in the actual drama that had been enacted at sea. They could add nothing material to the evidence already before the inquiry.

However, on 14 June, a full month after Captain Lord had

appeared in the witness box,[27] and just a week before the final day of the public hearings, which was day 28, on 21 June, a new line was inserted into question 24. In its original form the question had been innocuous enough.

Question 24: What was the cause of the loss of the *Titanic* and of the loss of life which thereby ensued or occurred? Was the construction of the vessel and its arrangements such as to make it difficult for any class of passengers or any portion of the crew to take full advantage of any of the existing provisions for safety?

The new line, inserted between the first and second sub-questions was to alter the entire thrust of the inquiry and to allow it to provide the world with an officially sanctioned scapegoat, the *Californian*.

The new line read as follows: 'What vessel had the opportunity of rendering assistance to the *Titanic*, and, if any, how was it that assistance did not reach the *Titanic* before the steamship *Carpathia* arrived?'[28]

Contrary to all the principles of English justice, this question was inserted after Captain Lord and his officers had given their evidence and without their knowledge. They were given no opportunity to defend themselves even though Captain Lord made a request, through Dunlop, that he be officially charged, so that he could have his day in court. His request was denied.[29]

When the addition to Question 24 was inserted Lord Mersey asked, 'Will this involve my dealing with the *Frankfurt*?' The Attorney General told him that there would only be a brief reference to that ship and that the question was intended to 'cover the *Californian*'. Isaacs went on to say that Lord Mersey had already heard all of the evidence regarding the *Mount Temple*.[30] If that was the case then Lord Mersey was the only person, at that or any other time, who had heard all of the evidence regarding the Canadian Pacific liner.

The whole purpose of the British Inquiry should have been to establish right or wrong. It was not a court of law and had absolutely no right to determine guilt on any person's part, merely to establish what had gone awry and ensure that steps were taken to prevent a repetition. Nevertheless, Lord Mersey, in his report, published on 31 July 1912,[31] roundly condemned Captain Lord in 3½ pages of tight print.

In essence, the Commissioner's report concluded that the collision of *Titanic* with an iceberg was due to the excessive speed at which the ship was navigated and that a proper watch was not kept. Although the ship's boats were properly lowered, they were not properly manned. That the track followed was safe if a proper watch had been kept. That there was no discrimination against third class passengers in the saving of life. One out of four correct answers is not a very impressive showing from the longest British Inquiry into the loss of a ship at sea on record.

J. Bruce Ismay, Chairman and Managing Director of the White Star line and Sir Cosmo Duff-Gordon were both exonerated of improper conduct.

The inquiry also found that the Leyland Line's *Californian* might have reached the *Titanic* if she had attempted to do so.

Thanks to Dr Robert Ballard's discovery of the wreck of the White Star liner we now know this to be another incorrect judgement on the part of the inquiry.

Lord Mersey's report recommended better watertight subdivisions on ocean-going vessels, better lookouts and lifeboat places for all aboard.

Charles Lightoller did not agree that more lifeboats would have meant more people saved. He said that if *Titanic* had more boats she would have needed more seamen to man them.[32] A glance at *Titanic's* crew list shows that the liner carried only 22 able seamen,[33] which gives Lightoller's opinion some credibility — as does the inescapable fact that only 90% of the available lifeboats were launched from the sinking ship even though they had almost 2hr from the time the order to fill and lower the boats was given.

Why a recommendation for better lookouts was included remains a mystery. On day 16, Mersey himself justified Captain Smith's decision not to increase the number of lookouts as *Titanic* approached the icefield, saying, 'Two people did not see it. Three people did not see it, so I don't suppose 50 could have seen it.' He was referring to the two lookouts and the officers on the bridge.

Other recommendations included regular lifeboat drills, and round-the-clock manning of wireless installations on emigrant and foreign-going passenger ships. In conclusion, Lord Mersey took the Board of Trade to task for failing to bring the 1894 shipping rules up to date. Contrary to expectation, he had bitten the hand that fed him.

In almost every respect Lord Mersey missed the significance of evidence, which might have led him to the true causes of the disaster, as did William Alden Smith at the American Inquiry. Even Charles Lightoller, who had emerged with the status of hero, was unimpressed with the Board of Trade Inquiry, which he described as a whitewash which favoured the Board and the White Star line.[34] Geoffrey Marcus in his account, The Maiden Voyage in 1969, and Patrick Stenson in his book, Lights — The Odyssey of C. H. Lightoller in 1984, both agreed with Lightoller.[35]

The Bradford & District Trades & Labour Council quickly sent a resolution to the Home Office saying that they had, 'No confidence in the Court of Inquiry.'[36]

Lord Mersey was to continue to serve the Board of Trade. In 1913 he presided over the International Convention on Safety of Life at Sea. In 1914 he headed the inquiry into the loss of the Empress of Ireland and in the following year the Falaba. In that same year he conducted the inquiry into the loss of the Lusitania,[37] another shipwreck that remains shrouded in mystery.

To recap:

- Beauchamp, Barrett, Lee and Wilding all gave evidence indicating that the damage to Titanic was very different from that normally understood.

- The lookouts and Lightoller's evidence suggested that the iceberg was seen well before the alarm bell was rung at 11.40pm. Captain Hays reckoned that he would normally see a 60–80ft berg at 10 miles on a clear night. A normal lookout would see it at six or seven miles.[38] Captain Passow couldn't understand why the iceberg wasn't seen sooner. The answer is simple: it was seen sooner.

- Hitchens, supported by Boxhall, stated that Titanic turned to the southward, directly away from Californian's position, as she tried to avoid the collision. The helm orders were never reversed. Dillon, Shiers and Scott all indicated that Titanic's engines were kept going for some time after the accident.

- Lightoller and Cavell both gave evidence to show that Titanic had, at some point, been travelling faster than the admitted 21.5–22.5kts.

- Crawford, Rowe and Symons intimated that more than the normally accepted eight rockets were fired. Hitchens saw red, white and blue rockets sent up from the liner.

- All of the surviving officers denied seeing any ice warnings later than that of the Caronia, which was received at 9am on the fateful Sunday.

- Wilding and Lucas said that, in the event of an emergency, the people in third class would have very little chance of reaching the Boat Deck.

- Captain Smith's 'go and return' order clearly shows that he expected the mystery ship to close with *Titanic*. This ties up with *Californian's* unusual behaviour.

- Captain Lord had left England in a tremendous hurry, so much so that his wireless operator didn't have time to change a chart that he had picked up in error. One might be forgiven for assuming that *Californian's* arrival in Boston was eagerly awaited, but instead of hurrying to his destination Captain Lord stopped his ship for the night at the first sign of ice. However, he then ordered his engineer to keep a full head of steam up so that the engines would be available at a moment's notice, hinting that he may have expected to make use of them during the night.

- Instead of turning in for the night Captain Lord decided to rest, fully clothed, on the chart room sofa. This sofa being only 5½ft long could hardly be described as comfortable for the 6ft-tall captain. Here we see another indication that Captain Lord did not expect to pass an uneventful night. There is no immediately apparent reason for Lord and the *Californian* to maintain this state of readiness. The final, and most compelling, reason to suspect that the captain of the *Californian* had something far more sinister on his mind than conveying an express cargo to Boston lies in his repeated question regarding colour in the signals seen from his vessel.

- *Californian* was at the edge of a large ice-field containing any number of icebergs, a well known hazard to shipping. Knowing of this danger, so close at hand, the crew of the *Californian* might well half expect to see a distress signal, but they could have no legitimate expectation of seeing coloured rockets, except by prior arrangement. Undeniably, Captain Lord had sighting coloured rockets uppermost in his mind, to the extent that he failed to realise the significance of, or wilfully ignored, white ones. There seems little doubt that Captain Lord stopped the *Californian* where he did, and when he did, because his need for haste was at an end, he had arrived at his destination. He had only to wait until he saw the expected coloured rockets to make a rendezvous with another vessel, for whatever reason.

- The only other vessel in the area that night with any evidence to show that she fired coloured rockets is, of course, RMS *Titanic*.

If Lord Mersey and his Board of Assessors had looked for a culprit instead of a scape-goat then I suspect the name *Titanic* would have passed into the mists of time and now be nothing more than a faded memory.

In this chapter we have seen how:

- Lord Mersey altered witnesses' evidence by putting words into their mouths, forcing them to say what he wanted to hear;
- Captain Lord, of the *Californian*, was, contrary to all the principles of British justice, railroaded by the Board of Trade inquiry and given no opportunity to defend himself.

32

Discovery of the Wreck

In late summer 1985 a combined French and American expedition led by Dr Robert Ballard of the Woods Hole Oceanographic Institute and Jean-Louis Michel of IFREMER, the French National Institute of Oceanography, discovered the wreck of the *Titanic*, 2.5 miles beneath the surface of the North Atlantic. The search had been conducted using the two photographic drones, *Argo* and *Angus*, which were also equipped with state-of-the-art sidescanning sonar to help the quest. Even with all the sophisticated gear aboard the drones and parent surface ship, the discovery was finally made optically, with the ordinary video equipment.

The ship was broken in two and, while the larger forward section was essentially intact, the stern part of the vessel was shattered, almost beyond recognition. This devastated ruin was to provide another puzzle and perhaps an indication, which might one day lead to enlightenment, as to the complete reason why the *Titanic* sank.

The two main sections of the liner lay slightly more than 650yd apart. Rather inconveniently, the bow section seems to have planed down and struck the soft muddy bottom at considerable speed, partially burying the knife-edged bow almost up to the anchors, most deeply on the starboard side. The supposed damage inflicted by the iceberg is deeply buried in the silt, but for how long is anybody's guess.

A year later, in 1986, Dr Ballard returned to the wreck. This time he had the deep water submersible *Alvin* along, and a small robot submarine known as *Jason Junior*. This expedition was to explore *Titanic* for the first time. They found absolutely nothing one would not have expected.

The whole of the wreck was festooned with rivers of rust, which disintegrated if touched. Much of the once ornate woodwork had been devoured by marine life. Even the glass dome that had once covered the grand staircase was no longer in evidence. Nothing bearing the ship's name was found. The small robot *Jason Junior* explored some parts of the vessel's interior but could not be allowed to penetrate to any great depth because of the danger to it presented by the twisted steel of the liner.

Despite thousands of stunning colour photographs of the most famous shipwreck in history, little new has come from the bow section of the ship. How could it? Constructed less than a century ago, written and photographic records along with artist's impressions still exist detailing all aspects of this fantastic class of ship.

I have heard *Titanic* described as a time capsule, but if that is the case then it would have been better left for another 200 years. However, finding the shattered stern part of the ship should have finally pinpointed the exact position in which the vessel foundered, making it clear, once and for all, that Captain Lord could have done nothing to help those aboard at the time.

Possibly the most interesting points thrown up by the wreck since its discovery are:

- A hole in the starboard side of the hull, just forward of the bridge, which appears to be the result of an internal explosion and was identified as such by a French explosives expert soon after its discovery.
- An unexpected longitudinal bulkhead that Robert Ballard found. There should be no such bulkheads in this type of vessel.
- The enormous propellers, which were completely buried when Dr Ballard first attempted to film them, but which are now exposed to the hubs.

In a bid to find out what had survived inside the wreck Ballard attempted to send in the small robot *Jason Junior*. No sooner had the remotely controlled vehicle entered the ship than it ran into a bulkhead that should not have been there and that did not show on any drawings for the 'Olympic' class vessels. These ships were intentionally built with only transverse bulkheads so that in the event of serious damage they would remain on an even keel. The existence of the bulkhead discovered by Dr Ballard shows that some circumstance had caused the builders to abandon one of the basic principles behind the layout of this particular vessel.

The third item of interest, recorded on film by Dr Ballard and his team is a view of *Titanic's* rudder, seen from beneath the overhanging counter.

Robert Ballard particularly wanted to get a photograph of the ship's huge propellers, if only for a display of one-upmanship over a competitor, Jack Grimm. On the dive that this picture was scheduled to be taken, Murphy's Law played a part. No sooner had the miniature submarine *Alvin* reached the bottom, close to the broken-off stern of

Titanic, than the operator of *Jason Junior* attempted to deploy the robot vehicle. A motor that had worked perfectly well on the surface refused to run 12,500ft down. The robot was effectively useless on this dive.

Alvin's pilot, Ralf Hollis, was not to be easily thwarted. Much to Dr Ballard's consternation, he took the little three-man submarine beneath the overhang of the wrecked stern. Ballard thought for a moment that Hollis had gone crazy as he inched *Alvin* along the muddy bottom. The first rule of safe submarine piloting, as far as Dr Ballard was concerned, was, 'Never go under a man-made overhang.' What if a piece of wreckage came crashing down? However, Ballard was sufficiently keen to see the propellers that he did not immediately order Hollis to take the little submarine out from beneath *Titanic's* counter. As *Alvin* inched forward, the steel plating of the liner's stern sloped downward, coming ever closer to the top of the little submersible. Robert Ballard, veteran of many deep dives, was not normally claustrophobic but this was different, *Titanic's* hull seemed to be closing in on them from all sides.

Ralf Hollis, who didn't seem at all perturbed by the proximity of the enormous hull, reported in a matter-of-fact voice, 'I see the rudder, Bob, but I don't see any propellers,' as he stopped the submarine.

Like the bow, *Titanic's* stern was buried deep in the muddy ocean floor, to a depth of about 60ft. Only about 16ft of the enormous 101¼-ton, 78½ft-high rudder was visible. Ballard felt certain that the propellers were still there but he couldn't prove it because they were so deeply buried. Despite their disappointment *Alvin's* crew took an excellent photograph of the rudder, illustrating clearly how little of it remained above the mud and how completely the gigantic propellers were covered. It seemed that Jack Grimm would have the last laugh after all, but Robert Ballard was absolutely right, the 23½ft-diameter wing, and the 16½ft central propellers are still there.

In 1991 a new combined expedition made up of a team from the P. P. Shirshov Institute of Oceanology in Moscow, led by Dr Anatoly Sagelevitch and the Canadian IMAX film company prepared to dive on the *Titanic*. The Russians supplied the technology to reach the wreck in the shape of two small, deep diving submersibles and the research vessel *Keldysh*, from which to operate. The Canadian company provided the world's most sophisticated film imaging system.

The result of this unlikely alliance is the most incredible film ever to come from the wreck. Shown only in specially designed IMAX cinemas, on seven-storey high, wraparound screens, this film gives the watcher the somewhat uncomfortable sensation of actually being on the *Titanic*.

While filming the stern part of the wreck, *Mir 1*, a Russian submarine, repeated the dangerous manoeuvre first executed by Ralf Hollis in *Alvin*. In order to get clear shots of whatever remained beneath *Titanic's* counter the submarine crept along the bottom, beneath the overhanging stern. The marks left by the sub's skid are clearly visible in photographs, which show that the little submarine came to within a few feet of something they cannot have expected to see — a huge propeller.

On this occasion the starboard propeller was exposed to the hub. More than 20ft of mud had been removed from beneath the sunken liner's stern to uncover the propeller. A prodigious undertaking, 2½ miles beneath the surface of the North Atlantic.

In his description Dr Ballard makes no mention of having to descend an incline to reach the rudder, but the Russians are quite clear that this was the case when they visited the site. Is this evidence that the bronze propeller had been excavated from its muddy tomb?

Why on earth would anybody go to the enormous expense in both time and financial outlay to unearth this propeller? Although of considerable monetary worth, the massive bronze castings would not repay one tenth of the cost involved in raising them. So that can't be the reason for disinterring the propellers.

In an amazingly clear photograph, which appears in the companion book to the IMAX film, the thrust face of a starboard propeller blade is shown in relative close-up. Just visible in the centre of the blade are what appears to be the numerals 01, which have been taken to be a partially obliterated 401, *Titanic's* build number, but there is absolutely no sign of the missing 4.

In reality the 01, which appears on the propeller blade can be nothing more than marine growth or corrosion. The propellers on these ships did not have the vessel's build number incised, stamped or cast into their thrust faces.

In photographs taken at the time of *Olympic's* propeller replacement following the *Hawke* incident the blades are clearly marked S1, S2 and S3. However, these markings, which seem to be cast into the propeller blades, appear close to where they are attached to the hub, not in the centre of the thrust face.

Photographs of *Olympic's* propellers, taken while she was under construction, plainly show the number 400 stencilled on the reverse side of the blades. Obviously these parts were so marked only for construction purposes as the numbers shown in *Olympic's* pictures would have been erased almost immediately the propellers began to revolve under water.

Had the number 01 actually been all that remained of 401, cut into the blade, then we would have another piece of solid evidence that the vessel resting on the bottom of the sea is *Olympic* and not her sister. According to Harland & Wolff, *Olympic's* starboard propeller was exchanged for *Titanic's* following the *Hawke* collision. A spare was fitted to *Titanic* and unquestionably spares could not be given a specific ship's build number as they might be required by any of the class.

Some anomalies have appeared in the thousands of still photographs and hours of video film of the wreck. What seems to be white paint shows in various places on the hull where the top coat of black has flaked or been scraped away. *Titanic's* hull was never painted white but *Olympic's* was, to allow photographers to get clearer shots of her when she was launched.

There appears to be red lead paint around the bases of brass or bronze instruments, where they are bolted to the steel of the deck. While this was a sensible precaution against any electrolytic reaction between the ferrous and non-ferrous metals, it has long been believed that red lead was only used on *Olympic*, while white lead served the same purpose on her sister.

The hull plating around the hawse pipes housing the enormous starboard anchor is inconsistent with photographs of *Titanic* taken while she was still on the stocks, shortly before launching. This anomalous plating is a perfect match for the same area of the hull shown in a picture of *Olympic* taken in April 1911, when she was the very first vessel to make use of the specially built dry-dock at Belfast. Curiously, photographs of *Olympic* taken after 1912 show her with plating that matches the prelaunch pictures of her sister. If we were dealing with human beings then these differences in plating would be as final as fingerprints.

Harland & Wolff claim that the ships' names were incised into the steel plating on both sides of the bow of *Olympic* and *Titanic*. The French diving team scraped away the rust and paint on the bow of the wreck in an effort to reveal the name incised there. To some extent they were successful and they filmed what they discovered. The video shows part of the ship's name in raised letters that appear to be stuck to the plating. Some of them seem to have dropped off; something that is patently impossible with incised letters. Nonetheless the complete name is not visible. What is visible are the letters 'M' and 'P' that seem to have been overwritten with the raised lettering. There is no 'M' or 'P' in '*Titanic*'.

Thanks to the Americans, Canadians and Russians, a fairly extensive film archive exists, which shows most of what there is worth seeing on and around the wreck of the *Titanic*. This archive is continuously being added to.

Although objects salvaged from the wreck are of no historical value, since we already know all there is to know of the period, they do have a value as exhibition material. Collectors and enthusiasts will pay well just to see anything with a proven association with the ship, and how long will it be before some of the salvaged items begin to find their way into private hands?

Legends of great wealth carried by *Titanic* and possibly still within the crumbling carcass mean that there will always be a temptation to delve further into the wreck. To do so, however, would be wrong as *Titanic's* manifest still exists and shows that there was nothing aboard as cargo of any great value whatsoever. Only the personal possessions of passengers and crew can be of any intrinsic value, and they rightfully should be returned to the heirs and descendants of the original owners — as indeed should the personal possessions taken from the bodies recovered from the sea after the disaster. These are still presumably in a safe in some Government office in Canada.

After 73 years of dignified silence, the remains of what was 'The Greatest of the Works of Man', is being explored by businessmen and scientific researchers. Would it not be better for all concerned to allow *Titanic* to rest in peace now, along with the more than 1,500 people who died with her?

In this chapter we see that:

- When the wreck was discovered in 1985, *Titanic's* main propellers were completely buried in the mud of the ocean floor but little more than a year later these propellers were uncovered to the hubs;
- The partially obscured number '401' seems to appear on a starboard propeller blade, which, it if it were truly there, would be almost incontrovertible proof that the wreck is in fact that of RMS *Olympic*.

33

An Alternative Scenario

That the version of events surrounding the loss of the *Titanic*, universally accepted for so long, is false is amply demonstrated by the facts I have presented. What follows is my own interpretation of the evidence, as I understand it. While this interpretation may not be correct in every respect, it does have the unusual quality of fitting the known facts:

- When the helmsman of HMS *Hawke*, on hearing Cdr Blunt's order to port the helm as the cruiser and Olympic approached the Bramble Bank, turned the wheel the wrong way, swinging the warship's armoured bow towards the liner, he set in motion a chain of events that would leave more than 1,500 dead.

- With its helm jammed, the cruiser smashed into *Olympic's* starboard side with such force that both ships were seriously damaged, although just how seriously nobody knew. Only after the liner could be dry-docked would the extent of her injuries become apparent.

- The Royal Navy convened an inquiry within days. After hearing evidence wholly from naval personnel the inquiry, unsurprisingly, exonerated their vessel from all blame. This must have been seen as the 'writing on the wall' by the management of the White Star line. They quite possibly realised then and there that their chances of collecting anything from the insurance companies was practically non-existent, although they continued to fight the case until 1914.

- As it was, it took a fortnight of emergency patching to *Olympic's* hull before she was in any fit state to attempt the voyage from Southampton to Belfast for more complete repairs. Able only to use one main engine, the crippled liner made the voyage at an average speed of about 10kts, wasting the exhaust steam from the one usable engine. This steam would normally have driven the central turbine engine, which shows that this engine, its mountings or shafting, had been damaged in the collision. As this engine sat on the centreline of the vessel, immediately above the keel, which the propeller shaft ran through, we can reasonably assume that the keel itself was damaged.

- Once back at Belfast the damage could be fully assessed. A broken keel would entail expensive and extensive repairs, which would keep the ship in the yard and not earning money for months. The emergency patch had failed during the short trip back to the builders, showing that the hull was no longer structurally sound. To make matters worse, in order to repair *Olympic*, labour would have to be diverted from *Titanic* and would delay her completion. This means that White Star would be even more out of pocket due to lost fares. They had lost £250,000 (£10 million at modern rates) in fares alone during the time neither vessel had been fit for service.

- Since her launch more than three months before, in response to suggestions made by J. Bruce Ismay following *Olympic's* maiden voyage, alterations had been carried out to *Titanic's* B and C Decks. Cabins had been fitted and new portholes cut, altering her appearance slightly but not so much that she no longer looked like her sister.

- It was immediately obvious to the builders that it would be quicker to complete *Titanic* than to repair *Olympic*. Accordingly, the alterations to B Deck were torn out and the original, much simpler, layout reinstalled. At the time, the alterations to Forecastle Deck C were overlooked in the rush and the extra portholes remained.

- Otherwise *Titanic* was reconverted to *Olympic* specifications, at least outwardly, where necessary using parts cannibalised from her slightly older sister, such as instruments from the bridge, compass tower and lifeboats. Changing the ship's name would have presented no difficulties for the highly skilled workforce at Harland & Wolff.

- Almost two lunar months after the *Hawke/Olympic* collision, the reconverted *Titanic*, now superficially identical to her sister except for her C Deck portholes, quietly left Belfast for Southampton to begin a very successful 25-year career as *Olympic*.

- Back in the builders' yard, work progressed steadily on the battered hull of *Olympic*. The decision to dispose of the damaged vessel would already have been taken. It must have been obvious from quite early on that the vessel was beyond economic repair, so these repairs need not have been quite as thorough as they otherwise might have been. Instead of replacing the damaged section of keel, longitudinal bulkheads were installed to brace it.

- The torn plating and buckled ribs were straightened or replaced, a new propeller shaft and propeller was fitted and the damaged central turbine propeller shaft was patched up.

- The windows on B Deck were altered to resemble the layout of *Titanic* before reconversion. The cabins, which should have been immediately inboard of the altered windows, were never completed and B Deck remained effectively a promenade deck from which a person walking along could see the lifeboats, if they were swung out, just as Steward Alfred Crawford did on the night of the sinking.

- Parts which had been cannibalised for *Titanic* were now replaced with the ones originally intended for that ship, as they became available. These were mainly parts such as the bridge instruments, which were of a more delicate nature than the structure of the vessel and had therefore not already been fitted.

- Even as this work was going on, the ship pretending to be *Olympic* was brought back to the builders, ostensibly to have a propeller blade replaced, but in reality to have the conversion to *Olympic's* layout completed. A propeller blade change was a one-day job to the experienced workforce at the Belfast yard but, mysteriously, the work took a week. When the ship left the yard at the end of the week, the porthole layout on the starboard side of the Forecastle Deck — Deck C — appears to have been changed from the 16 portholes of *Titanic* to the 14 of *Olympic*.

- *Titanic's* maiden voyage had been set for 10 April 1912, so time was short. As a result, many things were skimped, among them the lifeboats, some of which leaked like sieves when used on the night of the disaster.

- Trials, which for *Olympic* had taken two full days, took only one working day for *Titanic*, half of which was used up by a 4hr cruise at moderate speed. Effectively the ship was not tested at all. No doubt at least some of those aboard the vessel knew just how fragile the patched up hull might be.

- The plans to dispose of the *Titanic* were, by this juncture, complete. Even as she went through her pitifully inadequate trials, word was on its way to Captain Lord of the *Californian* to put to sea.

- *Californian* was to proceed immediately to position 42°5'N, 50°7'W and there to await the arrival of the *Titanic* on the night of 14/15 April. Despite the coal shortage *Californian* was ready to depart on the 5th, but because of the inordinate hurry to leave port the wireless operator did not have time to pick up the correct charts for the North Atlantic. Captain Lord must have been instructed to await *Titanic's* signal — coloured rockets — before closing and taking off her people.

- *Californian* arrived at the rendezvous point in good time and her skipper settled down to await the liner's appearance, or at least her rockets. His engines were standing by, as was he; there was nothing more he could do.

- It is more than likely that another ship was also laid on to assist *Californian* in removing all the passengers and crew from *Titanic*. The name of this ship remains a mystery, but at least a partial description exists which gives a rough size, about 15–20,000 tons. The provision of this nameless vessel turned out to be a mistake.

- *Titanic* left Southampton more or less on time and the voyage proceeded quite normally, at least as far as the passengers were concerned. Captain Smith headed toward his rendezvous with the *Californian* and whatever other vessel or vessels were waiting. This was the reason for *Titanic's* late course change. Only the senior officers knew what was planned — Captain Smith, Chief Officer Wilde, aboard specially for this reason, and First Officer Murdoch. Murdoch took up his position on the bridge of his own volition. He was not officially on duty during the time leading up to the collision but was possibly watching for the waiting rescue ships.

- Although well aware of the presence of icebergs, the *Titanic's* officers were confident that they would see a berg in plenty of time to avoid it, which was probably correct. What lay in *Titanic's* path, however, was not an iceberg with its white fringe on top and line of phosphorescence at the waterline, but one of the rescue ships. This vessel had its lights out and had probably been damaged by the ice. For this reason *Titanic's* lookouts, who were concentrating on searching the sea ahead of the ship for ice, failed to see the darkened silhouette of the blacked-out ship until it was too late to avoid a collision.

- *Titanic* crashed into the waiting vessel, tearing at least one of that ship's lifeboats from its davits and also stripping some planking. The stranger's lifeboat crashed down into the sea where it remained afloat, now attached to *Titanic*, probably by the ropes of its own falls. The rescue ship was quite severely damaged in the collision, so badly that she took no further part in the proceedings except to confuse everybody by firing a series of white distress rockets. *Titanic*, still turning to port, swung away to the south and slowed down while the other vessel limped away to the north.

- The initial collision between the two ships must have been nose to tail which, of course, lessened the impact but did not prevent the mystery vessel's steel hull from punching a hole in *Titanic's* starboard bow below the waterline. This hole penetrated at least as deep as the firemen's alleyway.

- The impact and the vibration of *Titanic's* engines going astern shook a mass of ice free from where it had accumulated on the rigging and wireless aerials. Then, as the other ship swung around under the impact, her hull came into contact with yet more of *Titanic's* plating, starting rivets and opening seams. The damage to *Titanic* which breached the watertight integrity of the firemen's passageway could not have been caused by ice without a tremendous shock being felt throughout the ship.

- In the very best 'ram them, damn them' attitude of the day, the officers commanding *Titanic* put as much distance as possible between themselves and what they believed at the time to be their accidental victim. Momentarily the plan to dispose of their own ship was forgotten as they moved southward, away from the waiting *Californian*. By the time the required pyrotechnic signals were remembered *Titanic* was too far from *Californian* for them to be seen, but neither Captain Smith nor Captain Lord would be aware of this.

- The third vessel, damaged in the collision, was still close enough to see *Titanic's* powerful red, white and blue socket signals but not near enough for her own, more feeble rockets to be seen from the liner. It was these ordinary rockets that were seen from the *Californian*, where Captain Lord was patiently waiting for a more colourful display.

- That the officers of the watch on *Californian's* bridge should have roused the wireless operator is undeniable, if they thought that they were looking at distress signals, but they thought no such thing.

- As well as the damaged, rocket firing vessel, yet another unidentified ship lay between *Titanic* and *Californian*, as Captain Rostron saw when it grew light the following morning. This was the ship seen from the deck of the sinking liner and seen later from the *Titanic's* small boats. E. J. Smith and his senior officers, the only people aboard *Titanic* who knew of the arrangements with *Californian*, must have believed that the lights were hers.

- According to the prearranged plan, *Californian* would close the gap between the two ships and effect a rescue. This is the only possible explanation (unless Captain Smith had lost his mind) for the go and return order which was given to some of the lifeboats. The mystery ship had already demonstrated that she was oblivious to *Titanic's* signals, so why Captain Smith would make such an error of identification remains a mystery. It is possible that he was overcome by the enormity of the disaster which faced him, or perhaps he believed that the other ship would only start to round up the lifeboats once a number of them had been launched.

- Curiously, Captain Lord had, during the Boer War, demonstrated his suitability for this kind of rescue operation when he disembarked and re-embarked a large number of troops and horses in record time and without mishap. This unusual ability in a merchant navy skipper would have been well known to the management of the White Star and Leyland Lines. What more natural choice could there be?

- If the plan had worked, all aboard *Titanic* might have been saved before the ship was allowed to sink. If the collision had not occurred where, when and how it did the rendezvous would have been effected. If only First Officer Murdoch had ordered the helm put hard a-port instead of hard a-starboard then *Titanic* would have turned toward the waiting *Californian* instead of away. 'The terrible ifs accumulate.' If only Captain Lord had not dozed off in *Californian's* chart room, he might have realised that something had gone wrong much earlier.

- As it was, *Titanic* was fatally damaged in a freak accident while her officers were trying to stage a fake one. The plan, as originally conceived, was not flexible enough to take advantage of the premature damage to the ship, or even to allow a normal rescue attempt to be made by the *Californian*. Had *Californian* tried to reach the rocket firing vessel to her south then she would have come within sight of *Titanic's* signals and all might yet have been well.

The people aboard *Titanic* could hardly have been more unlucky. The ship's senior officers appear to have been crippled by their own preconceived ideas of what was to be done in the fake emergency. When circumstances changed and the danger became all too real, they could not think beyond their established plan. Had things worked out as anticipated, there would have been no hurry to evacuate the ship because it would have been in no danger of foundering until they were ready. As a direct result of this inability to think in terms of a genuine catastrophe there was no real attempt by the crew to evacuate the ship in the time available.

The people lost with the *Titanic* were not the victims of an iceberg, but of a plan that went completely and disastrously wrong. The ship sank in the wrong place at the wrong time.

The excessive loss of life was the result of a captain following his instructions to the letter. If the *Californian* had not remained at her allotted position, waiting for their coloured rockets, then the numbers who went down with the *Titanic* could have been fewer.

Lord Mersey was absolutely correct when he condemned Captain Lord for not going to the aid of the *Titanic*, but for completely the wrong reasons.

Whether Captain Lord was actually guilty is a vexed question when, after all, he was only following orders. But following orders is only an effective defence if you happen to be on the winning side. In the case of the *Titanic*, there were no winners.

Notes

Notes to the Text

Chapter 1

1. Garrett R., *Voyage Into Mystery*, Weidenfeld & Nicolson, London, 1987, p28.

Chapter 2

1. Davie, p6.
2. Oldham, p62.
3. Coleman, p48.
4. *Ibid.*
5. Jackson, p206.
6. *Ibid.*
7. Jackson, p227.
8. Davie, p10.
9. *Ibid.*
10. Davie, p8.
11. Shipbuilder, p7.
12. Oldham, p28.
13. *Ibid.*
14. Oldham, pp28–29.
15. Oldham, p29.
16. *Ibid.*
17. *Ibid.*
18. Oldham, p30.
19. Oldham, p32.
20. Oldham, p31.
21. Oldham, p33.
22. E&H FS p14.
23. E&H FS, pp14–15.
24. E&H FS, p15.
25. E&H FS, pp14 & 17.
26. E&H FS, p17.
27. E&H FS, p18.
28. E&H FS, p19.
29. E&H FS, p20.
30. *Ibid.*
31. E&H FS, p21.
32. *Ibid.*
33. *Ibid.*
34. E&H FS, p22.
35. *Ibid.*
36. E&H FS, p24.
37. E&H FS, p26.
38. E&H FS, p29.
39. E&H FS, pp29–30.
40. Oldham, p89.
41. Oldham, p71.
42. Oldham, p26.
43. Oldham, p64.
44. Shipbuilder, pp11–13.
45. Davie, p10.
46. Oldham, p140.
47. Davie, p10.
48. E&H, p13.
49. Davie, p11; E&H, p13.
50. E&H, p13.
51. Coleman, pp50–51.
52. Coleman, p51.
53. Coleman, p52.
54. Oldham, pp146–149.
55. Oldham, p143.
56. Davie, p110.
57. Oldham, p146.
58. Oldham, p145.
59. Oldham, p156.
60. Oldham, p145.
61. Oldham, p143.
62. Oldham, p148.
63. E&H, p13.
64. Oldham, p144.
65. Oldham, p152.
66. Oldham, p165.
67. Oldham, pp160–161.
68. E&H FS, pp105–118.
69. Oldham, p148.
70. E&H, p13.
71. Oldham, p167.
72. E&H, p20.
73. Shipbuilder, p17.
74. E&H, p20.
75. Sanderson, BI, day 18.
76. E&H, p32.
77. Carlisle, BI, day 20.

78. E&H, p32.
79. Archer, BI, day 25; Marcus, p32.
80. Oldham, p168.

Chapter 3
1. Lord, p134.
2. Davie, p197.
3. Wilding, BI, day 19.
4. Davie, p19.
5. Archer, BI, day 25.
6. Sanderson, BI, day 17.
7. Wilding, BI, day 19.
8. Archer, BI, day 25.
9. Pelegrino, p29.
10. Marconi, BI, day 26.
11. Shipbuilder, p120.
12. Davie, p65.
13. Reade, p23.
14. BI, p19.
15. Reade, p23.
16. Wilding, BI, day 18.
17. Davie, p22.
18. Shipbuilder, p108.
19. Sanderson, BI, day 17.
20. Shipbuilder, p32.
21. Wilding, BI, day 20.
22. Marcus, p62.
23. Shipbuilder, p157.
24. Oldham, p176.
25. E&H FS, p47.
26. E&H FS, p48.

Chapter 4
1. E&H FS, p127.
2. Shipbuilder, p160.
3. E&H FS, p127.
4. Shipbuilder, p160.
5. Shipbuilder, p159.
6. Shipbuilder, p160.
7. E&H FS, p129.
8. E&H FS, pp127–129.
9. Shipbuilder, pp160–161.
10. Shipbuilder, p162.
11. Mills, p17.
12. Shipbuilder, p161.
13. Shipbuilder, p162.
14. Mills, pp19–21.

15. Shipbuilder, p162.
16. Shipbuilder, p163.
17. Blunt, Mills, p21.
18. Shipbuilder, p160; Mills, p21, Harland & Wolff.
19. Harland & Wolff, 13 January 1997.
20. Shipbuilder, p162.
21. Mills, p22; H&W photographs.
22. Shipbuilder, p162.
23. Shipbuilder, p162; E&H FS, p130.
24. Shipbuilder, p162.
25. E&H FS, p130.
26. Boyd-Smith, p223.
27. E&H FS, p132.
28. Shipbuilder, p162.
29. Oldham, pp177 to 181.
30. E&H FS, p132.
31. Mills, p22.
32. Mills, pp22–23.
33. Mills, p23.
34. E&H FS, p134.
35. *Ibid.*
36. *Ibid.*

Chapter 5
1. E&H, p33.
2. E&H FS, p134.
3. E&H FS, p132.
4. Shipbuilder, p162.
5. Ismay, BI, day 16.
6. E&H, p38.
7. Shipbuilder, p25 and Plate III.
8. E&H FS, p50.
9. E&H FS, p137.
10. *Ibid.*

Chapter 6
1. Chantler, BI, day 25.
2. Shipbuilder, p129.
3. *Ibid.*
4. *Ibid.*
5. *Ibid.*
6. E&H, pp44–45.
7. Marcus, pp220–221.

8. E&H, p45.
9. *Ibid.*
10. E&H, pp45–46.
11. Sanderson, BI, day 17.
12. Reade, p23.
13. E&H, p44; Hutchings, p15.
14. Wade, p18.
15. E&H, p46.
16. *Ibid.*
17. *Ibid.*
18. E&H DD, p66.
19. E&H, p46.
20. Turnbull, BI, day 13.
21. E&H, p46.
22. Lightoller, BI, day 11.
23. Ismay, BI, day 17.
24. Marcus, p40.
25. Davie, p26.
26. Marcus, p39.
27. Davie, p26.
28. Bartlett, BI, day 21.
29. Davie, p37.
30. *Ibid.*
31. Marcus, p82.
32. Bartlett, BI, day 21.
33. Pitman, BI, day 13.
34. *Ibid.*
35. Bartlett, BI, day 21.
36. Reade, p32.
37. Bartlett, BI, day 21.
38. Marcus, p83.
39. Bartlett, BI, day 21.
40. Marcus, p83.
41. E&H, p72.
42. Shipbuilder, Plate V.
43. E&H, p72.
44. Shipbuilder, Plate III.
45. Lightoller, BI, day 12
46. *Ibid.*
47. E&H, p46.
48. E&H, p55.

Chapter 7
1. Lord, p140; Marcus, p48.
2. Reade, p22.
3. *Ibid.*
4. Marcus, p23.

5. Joughin, BI, day 6.
6. Oldham, p187.
7. Lightoller, BI, day 12.
8. Davie, p39.
9. Marcus, p30.
10. O'Connor, p59.
11. Archer, BI, day 25.
12. Oldham, pp185–186.
13. Oldham, p174.
14. O'Connor, pp59–60.
15. O'Connor, pp59–60.
16. Hyslop, Forsyth & Jemima, p54.
17. Hyslop, Forsyth & Jemima, pp48–49.
18. Hyslop, Forsyth & Jemima, pp49–50.
19. Hyslop, Forsyth & Jemima, p44.
20. Hyslop, Forsyth & Jemima, p53.
21. Hyslop, Forsyth & Jemima, p54.
22. E&H, p65.
23. Marcus, p52.
24. Marcus, p33.
25. Lightoller, BI, day 12.
26. Oldham, p38.
27. Marcus, pp48–49.
28. Lightoller, BI, day 12.
29. Clarke, BI, day 25.
30. *Ibid.*
31. Marcus, p33.
32. Lightoller, Titanic *and Other Ship*s, pp218–219.
33. Oldham, 933.
34. E&H, p70.
35. E&H, p71.
36. E&H, p73.
37. Davie, p12.
38. E&H, p75.
39. Marcus.
40. E&H, p75.
41. E&H DD, p74; Lord, pp145–159.

Chapter 8
1. New York Times, 16 April 1912.
2. Marcus, p74.
3. New York Times, 16 April 1912.
4. Marcus, p20.

5. *Ibid.*
6. *Ibid.*
7. Lord, pp75–76.
8. New York Times, 16 April 1912.
9. Gracie, pp4–5.
10. New York Times, 16 April 1912.
11. Marcus, p36.
12. Ismay, BI, day 16.
13. Oldham, p163.
14. E&H, p71.
15. Davie, pp213–214.
16. Lord, p75.
17. Davie, p21.
18. Gracie, p19.
19. E&H DD, p29.
20. Marcus, p37.
21. E&H, pp75–76.
22. Marcus, p44.
23. Marcus, p43.
24. Davie, p29.
25. Marcus, p43.
26. Behe, p1.
27. Evening Chronicle, 16 April 1912.
28. New York Times, 16 April 1912.
29. Marcus, p46.
30. *Ibid.*

Chapter 9
1. Beesley, p15.
2. Lee, BI, day 4.
3. Marcus, pp48–49.
4. Marcus, p48.
5. Symons, BI, day 10.
6. Davie, p39.
7. *Ibid.*
8. Hogg, BI, day 15.
9. Ismay, BI, day 16.
10. E&H, p93.
11. E&H, p94.
12. E&H, p92.
13. *Ibid.*
14. E&H, p93.
15. Marcus, p52.
16. E&H, p283.
17. New York Times, 16 April 1912.

18. Coleman, p67.
19. Marcus, p19.
20. E&H, p93.
21. Marcus, p64.
22. Bride, BI, day 14.
23. E&H DD, p11.
24. Gracie, p17.
25. E&H, p100.
26. E&H, p100.
27. E&H, p100.
28. *Ibid.*
29. Lord, p65.
30. Lord, p65; Oldham, p187.
31. E&H DD, p91.
32. E&H, p111.
33. Marcus, p57.
34. E&H, p100.
35. E&H, p101.

Chapter 10
1. Lightoller, BI, day 12.
2. Marcus, pp102–103.
3. Reade, p19.
4. Oldham, p254.
5. BI, p25.
6. Lord, p135.
7. Ismay, BI, day 16.
8. Davie, pp128–129.
9. Davie, p129.
10. Davie, p112.
11. O'Connor, p20.
12. Oldham, p188.
13. Behe, p4.
14. Marcus, pp104–105.
15. Ismay, BI, day 16.
16. Davie, p136.
17. Ismay, BI, day 17.
18. Turnbull, BI, day 14.
19. Ismay, BI, day 16.
20. Gracie, pp2–3.
21. Marcus, p104; Davie, p127.
22. Davie, p164.
23. Ismay, BI, day 16; Barrett, BI, day 4.
24. Cavell, BI, day 5.
25. Behe, p5.

26. Ismay, BI, day 16.
27. Lightoller, BI, day 12.
28. Sanderson, BI, day 17.
29. Bartlett, BI, day 21.
30. Lightoller, BI, day 11.
31. *Ibid.*
32. Gracie, p9.
33. Oldham, p38.
34. Oldham, p39.
35. Davie, p29.
36. *Ibid.*
37. Reade, p24.
38. Rowe, BI, day 15.
39. Ismay, BI, day 16.
40. Rowe, BI, day 15.
41. Pitman, BI, day 13.
42. Marcus, p119.
43. Boxhall, BI, day 13.
44. E&H, p114.
45. Barrett, BI, day 4.
46. *Ibid.*
47. BI, p18.
48. Lightoller, BI, day 11.
49. *Ibid.*
50. Behe, p3.
51. Ismay, BI, day 16.
52. Behe, p3.
53. Bride, BI, day 14.
54. Pitman, BI, day 13.
55. E&H, p115.
56. Lightoller, BI, day 11.
57. *Ibid.*
58. BI, p28.
59. Lightoller, BI, day 11.

Chapter 11
1. Marcus, p118.
2. Marcus, p88.
3. Marcus, p100.
4. Marcus, p118.
5. Boxhall, BI, day 13.
6. Reade, p115.
7. Boxhall, BI, day 13.
8. Pitman, BI, day 13.
9. Marcus, p119.
10. Jewell, BI, day 2.

11. Marcus, p124.
12. Gracie, pp250–251.
13. Symons, BI, day 10.
14. Reade, p24.
15. Marcus, p119.
16. Marcus, p100.
17. Marcus, p119.
18. Lightoller, BI, day 14.
19. Lightoller, BI, day 11.
20. Marcus, p256.
21. Davie, p39.
22. Marcus, p123; E&H, p115; Wade, p117.
23. Marcus, p256; Lightoller, BI, day 12.
24. Marcus, p265.
25. Marcus, p123.
26. Lightoller, BI, day 11.
27. *Ibid.*
28. Gracie, pp12–13.
29. Hart, BI, day 9.
30. Reade, p80.
31. Boxhall, BI, day 13.
32. Lightoller, BI, day 11.
33. Hitchens, BI, day 3; Behe, p3.
34. Behe, p23, note a.
35. Gracie, pp250–251; Lee, BI, day 4.
36. Marcus, p78.
37. Marcus, p114.
38. Reade, p28.
39. BI, Lightoller, days 11 & 14; Boxhall, day 14; Lowe, day 14.
40. Pitman, BI, day 13.
41. Reade, pp24–25.
42. Fleet, BI, day 15.
43. Poigndestre, BI, day 4.
44. Lee, BI, day 4.
45. Lightoller, BI, day 12.
46. Fleet, BI, day 15.
47. Behe, pp8–12.
48. Behe, p13.
49. Behe, p16.
50. Behe, p11.
51. Behe, p32, note b; Reade, p25.
52. Lightoller, BI, day 12.

53. Behe, p17.
54. Hitchens, BI, day 3.

Chapter 12
1. Lee, BI, day 4.
2. Gracie, p101.
3. Harrison, p224.
4. Lord, p12.
5. Harrison, p104.
6. Harrison, pp104–105.
7. Gracie, p17.
8. Lord, p12.
9. Davie, p35.
10. Symons, BI, day 10.
11. Davie, pp136–137.
12. Marcus, p134.
13. Harrison, p167.
14. Davie, pp51–54.
15. Reade, p28.
16. Davie, p56.
17. Lord, p13.
18. Davie, p166.
19. Oldham, p194.
20. Poigndestre, BI, day 4.
21. Lord, p16.
22. Barrett, BI, day 3.
23. Beauchamp, BI, day 3.
24. Dillon, BI, day 5.
25. Barrett, BI, day 3.
26. Wilding, BI, day 19.
27. *Ibid.*
28. Lord, p24.
29. Cavell, BI, day 5.
30. Barrett, BI, day 4.
31. Wilding, BI, day 19.
32. Wade, p166.
33. Lord, pp14–15.
34. Marcus, p113.
35. Lord, p16.
36. *Ibid.*
37. Gracie, p293.
38. Gracie, p292.
39. Gracie, p14.
40. Lord, p22.
41. Marcus, p137.
42. Gracie, p16.
43. Gracie, pp15–16.

44. Harrison, p223
45. Gracie, p16.
46. Davie, pp159–160.
47. Gracie, p143.
48. Gracie, p127.
49. Wade, pp158–159.
50. Wade, p159.
51. Buley, BI, day 16.
52. Lord, p22.
53. Davie, p5.
54. Shiers, BI, day 5.
55. Lord, p13.
56. Scarrott, BI, day 2.
57. *Ibid.*
58. Lord, p27.
59. Lord, p13.
60. Lord, p18.
61. Davie, p71.
62. Gracie, p268.
63. Lord, p12.
64. Lord, p13.
65. Wheat, BI, day 9.
66. Lord, p19.
67. Lord, p13.
68. Symons, BI, day 10.
69. Lord, p29.
70. Lord, p27.
71. Lord, p22.
72. Hemmings, BI, day 15; Lord, pp33–34.
73. Shipbuilder, Fig 14.

Chapter 13
1. Gracie, p228.
2. Lord, p14.
3. *Ibid.*
4. Mauge, BI, day 19.
5. Davie, p127.
6. *Ibid.*
7. Lord, p22.
8. Lord, p33.
9. Pearcy, BI, day 9.
10. Rule, BI, day 7.
11. Hart, BI, day 9.
12. Oldham, p192.
13. Gracie, p94; American Inquiry, 1142.

14. MacKay, BI, day 9.
15. Lord, p28.
16. Hendricksen, BI, day 5.
17. Joughin, BI, day 6.
18. Lord. P24.
19. Wheat, BI, day 9.
20. Lord, p23.
21. Lord, p28.
22. Lord, p19.
23. Lord, pp18–19.
24. Gracie, p14.
25. Lord, p18.
26. Lord, p19.
27. Lord, p33.
28. Marcus, p131; Gracie, pp62–63; Symons, BI, day 10.
29. Lord, p23.
30. Hendricksen, BI, day 5.
31. Lord, p23.
32. E&H, inside back cover.
33. Lord, p22.

Chapter 14
1. Dillon, BI, day 5.
2. Hitchens, BI, day 3.
3. Wade, pp157 to 167.
4. Lightoller, BI, day 12.
5. Dillon, BI, day 5.
6. *Ibid.*
7. *Ibid.*
8. Scott, BI, day 6.
9. *Ibid.*
10. *Ibid.*
11. BI, day 18.
12. Boxhall, BI, day 13.
13. Marcus, p129; Lord, p16; Boxhall, BI, day 13.
14. Reade, p26.
15. Hitchens, BI, day 3.
16. *Ibid.*
17. *Ibid.*
18. Pearcy, BI, day 9.
19. Scott, BI, day 6.
20. Lightoller, BI, day 12.
21. Boxhall, BI, day 13.
22. Lord, p19.
23. Marcus, p136.

24. Lord, p22.
25. Lord, p40.
26. Lord, pp29–30.
27. Symons, BI, day 10.
28. Lightoller, BI, day 12.
29. Marcus, p145.
30. Lightoller, day 12.
31. Marcus, p131.
32. Oldham, p194; Lord, p26; Ismay, BI, day 17.
33. Lord, p21.
34. Lord, p28.
35. Lord, p21.
36. Reade, pp115–116.
37. *Ibid.*
38. Lord, pp30–31.
39. Davie, p137.
40. Marcus, p134; Lord, pp30–31; Davie, p137.
41. Bride, BI, day 14.
42. Davie, p138.
43. Durrant, BI, day 15.
44. Harrison, p227.
45. Barrett, BI, day 3.
46. Lord, p24.
47. Lord, pp24–25.
48. Marcus, p161.
49. Wilding, BI, day 19.
50. Lord, p29.
51. Lord, p42.
52. Wynne, BI, day 11.

Chapter 15
1. Lord, p89.
2. Pelegrino, pp32–33.
3. Gracie, p145.
4. Davie, p193.
5. Robinson, BI, day 11.
6. Lord, p54.
7. Joughin, BI, day 6.
8. Lord, p53.
9. Gracie, p26.
10. Gracie, pp40–41.
11. Lord, p70.
12. Harrison, p167.
13. Rowe, BI, day 15.
14. Davie, p62.

15. Gracie, pp20 & 178–179.
16. Lord, p67.
17. Lightoller, BI, day 12.
18. Lord, p42.
19. Lightoller, BI, day 12.
20. Wheat, BI, day 11.
21. Rule, BI, day 6.
22. Gracie, p26.
23. Marcus, p146.
24. Lightoller, BI, day 12; Reade, p47.
25. Reade, p47.
26. Harrison, p168.
27. Reade, p35.
28. Hitchens, BI, day 3.
29. Crawford, BI, day 16.
30. Reade, p59.
31. Symons, BI, day 10.
32. Gracie, p300.
33. Boxhall, BI, day 13.
34. Harrison, p102; Boxhall, BI, day 13.
35. Boxhall, BI, day 13.
36. Reade, p35.
37. Wynne, BI, day 11.
38. Crawford, BI, day 16.
39. Rowe, BI, day 15; Gracie, p301.
40. MacKay, BI, day 9.
41. Boxhall, BI, day 13.
42. Gracie, p21.
43. Lightoller, BI, day 12; Reade, p307.
44. Pitman, BI, day 13.
45. Reade, p55.
46. Lowe, BI, day 13.
47. Ismay, BI, day 17.
48. Reade, p33.
49. Boxhall, BI, day 13; Harrison, p116.
50. Harrison, pp146–147.
51. Davie, p52.
52. Davie, p51.

Chapter 16

1. Gracie, p247.
2. Gracie, p245.
3. *Ibid.*
4. Gracie, p285.
5. Johnson BI, day 4.
6. *Ibid.*
7. Wheat, BI, day 9.
8. Finlay, BI, day 12.
9. Pescett, BI, day 20.
10. Lord, p53.
11. *Ibid.*
12. Gracie, p79.
13. Hogg, BI, day 15.
14. Gracie, pp228–229.
15. Jewell, BI, day 2.
16. *Ibid.*
17. Bebe, pp14–15.
18. Oldham, P194.
19. Fleet, BI day 15.
20. Lightoller, BI, day 12.
21. *Ibid.*
22. *Ibid.*
23. Lord, p42.
24. Hitchens, BI, day 3.
25. Gracie, p129.
26. Hitchens, BI, day 3.
27. *Ibid.*
28. Davie, p166.
29. Lord, p56.
30. Gracie, p42.
31. Gracie, p126.
32. Davie, p166.
33. Shiers, BI, day 5.
34. Gracie, pp235, 240 & 243.
35. Pitman, BI, day 13.
36. *Ibid.*
37. Gracie, p234.
38. Gracie, p149.
39. Gracie, p249; Rule, BI, day 6.
40. Gracie, p249.
41. Rule, BI, day 6.
42. *Ibid.*
43. Duff-Gordon, BI, day 11.
44. Davie, p82.
45. Gracie, p262.
46. Collins, BI, day 11.
47. Duff-Gordon, BI, day 11.
48. Gracie, p272.

49. Lowe, BI, day 13; Symons, BI, day 10.
50. Lady Duff-Gordon, BI, day 11; Davie, p90.
51. Rule, BI, day 7.
52. Davie, p90.
53. Symons, BI, day 10.
54. *Ibid.*
55. Symons, BI, day 10; Gracie, p262.
56. Lowe, BI, day 13.
57. Symons, BI, day 10.
58. Gracie, p236.
59. Lightoller, BI, day 12.
60. Davie, p161.
61. Gracie, p298.
62. Hart, BI, day 9; Gracie, p299.
63. Harrison, p97; Crawford, BI, day 16.
64. Harrison, p99.
65. Davie, p162.
66. Crawford BI, day 16.
67. Gracie, p142.
68. Davie, p161; Gracie, p141.
69. Davie, p164.
70. Davie, p160.

Chapter 17
1. Oldham, p194.
2. Davie, p62.
3. E&H, p152.
4. Gracie, p280.
5. Gracie, p282.
6. Gracie, p26.
7. Wilding, BI, day 20.
8. Rowe, BI, day 15.
9. Wynne, BI, day 11; Gracie, pp279–283.
10. Gracie, p281.
11. Wheat, BI, day 11; MacKay, BI, day 9.
12. Wheat, BI, day 11; Gracie, p284.
13. Gracie, p285.
14. Robinson, BI, day 11.
15. Gracie, p292.
16. Gracie, p293.
17. Scott, BI, day 6; Hart, BI, day 9.
18. Scott, BI, day 6.
19. Joughin, BI, day 6.
20. Buley, BI, day 16.
21. Lord, p105.
22. Gracie, p150.
23. Joughin, BI, day 6.
24. *Ibid.*
25. Gracie, p148.
26. Joughin, BI, day 6.
27. Gracie, p147.
28. Wade, p195.
29. Hendricksen BI, day 5.
30. Gracie, p153.
31. Poigndestre, BI, day 4.
32. *Ibid.*
33. Gracie, p153.
34. Gracie, p283.
35. Gracie, p285.
36. Joughin, BI, day 6.
37. Scarrott, BI, day 2.
38. *Ibid.*
39. Lord, p90.
40. Gracie, p155.
41. Morris, BI, day 6.
42. Scarrott, BI, day 2.
43. Gracie, p155.
44. Lowe, BI, day 13; Lord, p64.
45. Gracie, p33.
46. Lowe, BI, day 13.
47. Archer, BI, day 16.
48. Gracie, pp170–171.
49. Leather, BI, day 11.
50. Gracie, p290.
51. Gracie, p294.
52. Gracie, p290.
53. Gracie, p291.
54. Gracie, p294.
55. Gracie, p290.
56. Harrison, p219.
57. Harrison, p211.
58. Gracie, p295; Beesley, pp92–94.
59. Beauchamp, BI, day 3.
60. Lee, BI, day 4.
61. Rev Pat Thomas.
62. Gracie, p291.

63. Gracie, p297.
64. *Ibid.*
65. Rule, BI, day 6.
66. Wilding, BI, day 20.
67. Lucas, BI, day 3.
68. Hart, BI, day 9.
69. Gracie, p298.
70. Hart, BI, day 9; Joughin, BI, day 6.
71. Lord, pp85–86; Hart, BI, day 9.
72. Rule, BI, day 9.
73. Joughin, BI, day 6.
74. Wilding, BI, day 18.
75. Shiers, BI, day 5.
76. Hart, BI, day 9; Gracie, pp298–299.
77. Hart, BI, day 9.
78. Gracie, p299.
79. Hart, BI, day 9.
80. Rule, BI, day 6.
81. Cavell, BI, day 5.
82. Rule, BI, day 6.
83. Lord, pp85–86.
84. Marcus, p147.
85. Rule, BI, day 6.
86. *Ibid.*
87. Gracie, p297.
88. Barrett, BI, day 4.
89. Davie, p62.
90. Gracie, p291.

Chapter 18
1. BI, p38.
2. *Ibid.*
3. Gracie, p221.
4. Gracie, p193.
5. Gracie, p227.
6. Sanderson, BI, day 17.
7. Rowe, BI, day 15.
8. Wilding, BI, day 19.
9. Sanderson, BI, day 17.
10. Pearcy, BI, day 9.
11. Davie, p128.
12. Lord, p130.
13. Davie, p127.
14. Pearcy, BI, day 9.
15. *Ibid.*
16. Symons, BI, day 10.
17. Hemmings, BI, day 15.
18. Mauge, BI, day 19.
19. *Ibid.*
20. Ismay, BI, day 16.
21. Johnson, BI, day 5.
22. Davie, p113.
23. Ismay, BI, day 17; Gracie, p308.
24. Rowe, BI, day 15.
25. Davie, p112.
26. Gracie, p314.
27. Brown, BI, day 9.
28. Davie, p118.
29. Davie, p125.
30. Ismay, BI, day 16.
31. Oldham, p195; Davie, p122.
32. Marcus, p214.
33. Rowe, BI day 15; Gracie, p300.
34. Pearcy, BI, day 9.
35. Pearcy, BI, day 9; Gracie, pp301–304.
36. Lord, p65.
37. Peacock, BI, day 25.
38. Wade, p201.
39. Gracie, pp172–173.
40. Gracie, p178.
41. Gracie, pp172–173.
42. Johnson, BI, day 5.
43. Boxhall, BI, day 13.
44. Gracie, pp172–173.
45. Gracie, p173.
46. Gracie, p30.
47. Gracie, p38.
48. Lord, pp68–69.
49. Gracie, pp68–69.
50. Lightoller, BI, day 12.
51. Gracie, p31.
52. Gracie, p194.
53. Gracie, p181.
54. *Ibid.*
55. Granger, BI, day 5.
56. Lucas, BI, day 3.
57. Gracie, p201.
58. *Ibid.*
59. Gracie, p204.

60. Lucas, BI, day 3.
61. *Ibid.*
62. Gracie, p206.
63. Gracie, p20.
64. Gracie, p205.
65. Gracie, p204.
66. Gracie, p202.
67. Lucas, BI, day 3.
68. Gracie, p304.
69. Gracie, pp200–201.
70. Lucas, BI, day 3.
71. Gracie, p199.
72. Lord, p73.
73. Davie, p67.
74. Wilding, BI, day 20.
75. Davie, p126.
76. Rev Pat Thomas.
77. Davie, p127.

Chapter 19
1. Mrs Ryerson, Gracie, p189.
2. Davie, p139.
3. Lord, p71.
4. Gracie, p65.
5. Lord, p76.
6. Marcus, p155.
7. Lord, p71.
8. Davie, p139.
9. Bride, BI, day 14.
10. Marcus, p156.
11. Davie, p140.
12. Lord, p77.
13. Lightoller, Whitely, Gracie, p64.
14. Gracie, p314.
15. Brown, BI day 9.
16. Lord, p73.
17. Gracie, p312.
18. Gracie, p317.
19. Wade, pp218–219.
20. Gracie, pp215–216.
21. Lightoller, BI, day 12.
22. Gracie, p210.
23. Lightoller, BI, day 12.
24. Gracie, p47.
25. Gracie, p39.
26. Gracie, p70.

27. Gracie, p79.
28. Gracie, p76.
29. Gracie, p77.
30. Davie, p73.
31. Joughin, BI, day 6.
32. Gracie, p54.
33. Pitman, BI, day 13.
34. Davie, pp73–75; Gracie, p288.
35. Gracie, p288.
36. Lee, BI, day 4.
37. Dillon, BI, day 5; Rule, BI, day 6.
38. Hendricksen, BI, day 10.
39. Lightoller, BI, day 12.
40. Davie, p73.
41. Gracie, p219.
42. Lowe, BI, day 13; Pitman, BI, day 13.
43. Scarrott, BI, day 2.
44. Scott, BI, day 6.
45. Poigndestre, BI, day 4.
46. Granger, BI, day 5.
47. Symons, BI, day 10.

Chapter 20
1. Davie, p139.
2. Davie, pp139 & 148.
3. Gracie, p65.
4. Gracie, p45.
5. Lord, p77.
6. Gracie, pp80 & 149.
7. BI, p41; E&H, p167.
8. Rev Pat Thomas.
9. Pearcy, BI, day 9.

Chapter 21
1. Davie, p91.
2. Harrison, p26.
3. Harrison, p32.
4. *Ibid.*
5. Harrison, pp35–36.
6. Harrison, p37.
7. Davie, p26.
8. Reade, p18.
9. *Ibid.*
10. *Ibid.*
11. Reade, p117.
12. Reade, p19.

13. Reade, p117.
14. Lord, BI, day 7; Harrison, p17.
15. Harrison, pp18–19.
16. Harrison, p20.
17. Harrison, p88.
18. Lord, BI, day 7; Davie, p96; Harrison, p20; Reade, p20.
19. Reade, pp124–125.
20. Lord, BI, day 7.
21. Harrison, p22.
22. Harrison, p20.
23. Groves, BI, day 8.
24. Reade, p37.
25. Harrison, p86.
26. Harrison, p85; Reade, p20.
27. Harrison, p17.
28. Reade, p199.
29. Lord, BI, day 7.
30. Harrison, p62.
31. Evans, BI, day 8; Reade, p220.
32. Reade, p221.
33. Harrison, p250.
34. Harrison, p23.
35. Lord, BI, day 7.
36. Harrison, p128.
37. Reade, p28.
38. Davie, p97; Harrison, pp85–86.
39. Lord, BI, day 7.
40. Groves, BI, day 8.
41. Davie, p95; Reade, p210.
42. Davie, p96.
43. Reade, p150.
44. Harrison, p97.
45. Harrison, p109.
46. Reade, pp156–157.

Chapter 22
1. Lord, BI, day 7.
2. Reade, p19.
3. Harrison, p68.
4. Harrison, p116.
5. Groves, BI, day 8.
6. Harrison, p79.
7. Stone, BI, day 8; Harrison, p251.
8. Davie, p92.

9. Stone, BI, day 7.
10. Harrison, p88.
11. Harrison, p61.
12. Davie, p92.
13. Gibson, BI, day 7.
14. Harrison, p48.
15. Gibson, BI, day 7.
16. *Ibid.*
17. Gibson, BI, day 7; Reade, p79; Harrison, pp78–79.
18. Harrison, p117.
19. Davie, p92.
20. *Ibid.*
21. Stone, BI, day 7.
22. Reade, p65.
23. Davie, p97.
24. Gibson, BI, day 7.
25. Reade, p59.
26. Reade, p73.
27. Harrison, pp24–25.
28. Harrison, p172; Reade, p73.
29. Lord, BI, day 7.
30. *Ibid.*
31. Harrison, p45.
32. *Ibid.*
33. Harrison, p55.
34. Reade, pp81–82; Groves, BI, day 8.
35. Reade, p84.
36. Reade, p85.
37. Davie, p98.
38. Groves, BI, day 8.
39. Groves, BI, day 8. Harrison p87.
40. Davie, p92.
41. Lord, pp31–32; Marcus, p177.
42. Reade, p244.
43. Reade, pp86–88.
44. Harrison, p81.
45. Davie, p93; Reade, p89.
46. Gibson, BI, day 7.
47. Reade, p90.
48. Harrison, p79.
49. *Ibid.*
50. Harrison, p80.
51. *Ibid.*
52. Stewart, BI, day 8.

53. *Ibid.*
54. Reade, p95.
55. Stewart, BI, day 8.
56. Davie, p93.
57. Lord, BI, day 7.
58. Davie, p93.
59. Harrison, p39.
60. Harrison, p92.
61. Evans, BI, day 8.
62. Reade, p99.
63. Reade, p199.
64. Reade, p103.
65. Reade, p101.
66. Harrison, p174.
67. Reade, p107.
68. Harrison, p58.
69. Reade, p108.
70. Lord, BI, day 7.
71. Lord, BI, day 7; Reade, p106.
72. Groves, BI, day 8.
73. Reade, p108.
74. Harrison, p87.
75. Harrison, pp132–133.
76. Harrison, pp42–43 & 133.
77. Evans, BI, day 8.
78. Reade, p112.
79. Harrison, p122.
80. Reade, p88.
81. Marcus, p229.
82. Harrison, p128.
83. Lord, BI, day 7.
84. *Ibid.*
85. Harrison, p129.

Chapter 23
1. Gracie, pp228–229.
2. Jewell, BI, day 2.
3. Gracie, p231.
4. Lord, p98.
5. Jewell, BI, day 2.
6. Gracie, pp242 & 247.
7. Davie, p167.
8. Gracie, pp139–140.
9. Hitchens, BI, day 3.
10. Lord, p102.
11. Lord, pp102–103.
12. Gracie, p132.
13. Davie, p167.
14. Hitchens, BI, day 3.
15. Davie, p167.
16. Hitchens, BI, day 3.
17. Marcus, p172.
18. Gracie, pp140–141.
19. Gracie, p249.
20. Gracie, p248.
21. E&H, p151.
22. Gracie, pp250 & 254.
23. Gracie, p249.
24. Rule, BI, day 6.
25. Gracie, p268; Horswill, BI, day 10.
26. Davie, pp82–83.
27. Horswill, BI, day 10.
28. Collins, BI, day 11.
29. Gracie, p271.
30. Davie, p75.
31. Marcus, p245.
32. Hendricksen, BI, day 5.
33. Marcus, p245.
34. Shee, BI, day 11.
35. Collins, BI, day 11.
36. Taylor, BI, day 10.
37. Taylor, BI, day 10.
38. Gracie, p271.
39. Davie, p87; Lady Duff-Gordon, BI, day 11.
40. Symons, BI, day 10.
41. Marcus, p215.
42. Symons, BI, day 10.
43. Pusey, BI, day 11.
44. Gracie, p271; Duff-Gordon, BI, day 10.
45. Taylor, BI, day 10.
46. Wade, p92.
47. Davie, p162.
48. Harrison, p100.
49. Davie, pp163–164.
50. Crawford, BI, day 16.
51. Gracie, p281.
52. Wynne, BI day 11.
53. Gracie, p150.
54. Buley, BI, day 16.

55. Gracie, p160; Marcus, p167; Oldham, p194; Davie, p168.
56. Lord, p97.
57. Gracie, p150.
58. Lord, p125.
59. Gracie, p155.
60. Gracie, p166.
61. Gracie, p154.
62. Joughin, BI, day 6.
63. Lord, p120.
64. Marcus, p193.

Chapter 24
1. Gracie, p163.
2. Gracie, p169.
3. *Ibid.*
4. Gracie, p170.
5. Gracie, p155.
6. Gracie, p166.
7. Gracie, p72.
8. Gracie, p164.
9. Lord, p95.
10. Gracie, p158; Lowe, BI, day 13.
11. Lowe, BI, day 13.
12. Scarrott, BI, day 2.
13. Lord, p120.
14. Gracie, p162.
15. Scarrott, BI, day 2.
16. Lord, p124.
17. Marcus, p171.
18. Gracie, p158.
19. Lowe, BI, day 13.
20. *Ibid.*
21. E&H, p182.
22. Marcus, p152.
23. Gracie, p296.
24. Davie, p71.
25. Beauchamp. BI, day 3.
26. Beesley, p102.
27. Hart, BI, day 9.
28. Gracie, p297.
29. Rule, BI, days 6 & 9.
30. Rule, BI, day 9.
31. Rule, BI, day 6.
32. Gracie, p172.
33. Gracie, p301.

34. Ismay, BI, day 16.
35. *Ibid.*
36. *Ibid.*
37. Gracie, p175.
38. Boxhall, BI, day 13.
39. Gracie, p176.
40. Boxhall, BI, day 13.
41. *Ibid.*
42. Gracie, p175.
43. Gracie, pp174–175.
44. Marcus, p186.
45. Marcus, p194.
46. Gracie, p183; Davie, p76.
47. Dillon, BI, day 5.
48. Davie, p53.
49. Gracie, p192.
50. *Ibid.*
51. Lord, p97.
52. Gracie, p191.
53. Gracie, p320.

Chapter 25
1. Gracie, p29.
2. Gracie, p81.
3. Gracie, p46.
4. Gracie, p65.
5. Gracie, p29.
6. Gracie, pp218–219.
7. Brown, BI, day 9.
8. Lord, p92; Gracie, p315.
9. Gracie, pp315–316.
10. Gracie, p318.
11. Gracie, p311.
12. Gracie, p318.
13. Lord, p121.
14. Lord, p103.
15. Bride, BI, day 14.
16. Davie, p140.
17. *Ibid.*
18. Gracie, p96.
19. Gracie, p216.
20. Gracie, p97.
21. Marcus, p214.
22. Gracie, pp98 & 215.
23. Gracie, p218.
24. Gracie, pp85–86.
25. Gracie, p83.

26. Gracie, pp74–75.
27. Lord, p103.
28. Gracie, p103.
29. Gracie, p97.
30. Lord, p93.
31. Gracie, p88.
32. Gracie, p95.
33. *Ibid.*
34. Lord, p104.
35. Gracie, p105.
36. Gracie, p88.
37. Gracie, p191.
38. Gracie, pp95 & 98.
39. Gracie, p94.
40. Joughin, BI, day 6.
41. Lord, p106; Joughin, BI, day 6.
42. Joughin, BI, day 6.
43. Gracie, p98.
44. Gracie, p95.
45. Gracie, p78.
46. Gracie, p108.
47. Davie, p141.
48. Gracie, p109.
49. Gracie, p111.
50. Gracie, p213.
51. Gracie, p110.

Chapter 26
1. Reade, p306.
2. Rostron, BI, day 28.
3. *Ibid.*
4. Lord, p110.
5. Lord, p113; Marcus, p183.
6. Marcus, p184.
7. Cottam, BI, day 15.
8. *Ibid.*
9. Lord. p113.
10. Marcus, pp184–185; Rostron, BI, day 28.
11. Harrison, p173.
12. Rostron, BI, day 28.
13. *Ibid.*
14. *Ibid.*
15. Rostron, BI, day 28.
16. Rostron, BI, day 28; Lord, p114; Marcus, p185.
17. Rostron, BI, day 28.

18. Reade, p120.
19. Reade, p123.
20. Reade, p117.
21. Reade, p116.
22. Reade, p159.
23. Marcus, p196.
24. Rostron, BI, day 28.
25. *Ibid.*
26. Rostron, BI, day 28; Marcus, p186; Gracie, p180.
27. Marcus, pp198–199.
28. Hendricksen, BI, day 10; Gracie, p270.
29. Hitchens, BI, day 3.
30. Beesley, p277.
31. Rostron, BI, day 28; Lord, 126.
32. Davie, p141.
33. Rostron, BI, day 28.
34. Harrison, p229.
35. Davie, p167; Harrison, pp229–230.
36. Carruthers, BI, day 25.

Chapter 27
1. Rostron, BI, day 28.
2. *Ibid.*
3. Harrison, p44.
4. Reade, p348.
5. Harrison, p121.
6. Lord, p125.
7. Lord, pp121–122.
8. Davie, p144.
9. Davie, p135.
10. Lord, p128.
11. Davie, pp143–144.
12. Davie, pp115–116.
13. Davie, p117.
14. Lord, pp90–91.
15. Lord, p127.
16. Oldham, p196.
17. Davie, p146.
18. Davie, p136.
19. Davie, p145.
20. *Ibid.*
21. Davie, p134.
22. Oldham, p200.
23. Davie, p147.

24. *Ibid.*
25. *Ibid.*
26. Davie, p148.
27. Davie, p135.
28. Davie, p149.
29. Davie, p146.
30. Davie, p145.
31. Davie, p149.
32. Oldham, pp199–200.
33. Harrison, p244.
34. Lord, p130.

Chapter 28
1. Davie, p154.
2. *Ibid.*
3. Davie, p156.
4. *Ibid.*
5. Oldham, p198.
6. *Ibid.*
7. Davie, p94.
8. Reade, pp195–196.
9. Gracie, p265.
10. Reade, pp217–218.
11. Reade, p218.
12. Reade, p105.
13. Reade, p224.
14. Reade, pp257–258.
15. Harrison, p95.
16. Davie, p146.
17. Davie, p147.
18. Davie, p145.
19. Davie, p146.
20. Harrison, p175.
21. Marcus, p275.
22. Davie, p169.
23. *Ibid.*
24. Davie, p147.
25. Davie, p171.

Chapter 29
1. James Fenton, 1971.
2. Ismay, BI, day 16.
3. Davie, p172.
4. *Ibid.*
5. Reade, pp234–235.
6. Davie, p172.
7. Davie, p175.

8. Davie, p180.
9. Reade, pp228–229.
10. Reade, pp230–231.
11. Reade, pp232–234.
12. Reade, p232.
13. *Ibid.*

Chapter 30
1. Davie, p176.
2. Reade, p232.
3. Davie, p178.
4. Reade, p232.
5. Marcus, p223.
6. Reade, p234.
7. Marcus, p209; Davie, p185.
8. Davie, p186.
9. Davie, p187.
10. *Ibid.*
11. Davie, p188.
12. Davie, p187.
13. Harrison, pp108–109.
14. Harrison, p254.
15. Harrison, p68.
16. Reade, p233.
17. Scarrott/Scanlen/Mersey, BI, day 2.
18. Scarrott, BI, day 2.
19. Fleet, BI, day 15.
20. Harrison, p116.
21. Lord, p108.
22. Marcus, p234.
23. Stone, BI, day 7.
24. Laing, BI, day 7.
25. Harrison, p69.
26. Harrison, p86.
27. Harrison, p89.
28. Harrison, p90.
29. Harrison, p92.
30. Harrison, p261.
31. Davie, p96; Marcus, p275.
32. Marcus, p246.
33. Symons, BI, day 10.
34. BI, day 10.
35. Duke, BI, day 10.
36. Symons, BI, day 10.
37. Gracie, pp277–278.

38. Taylor, BI, day 10.
39. Marcus, p254.
40. Lightoller, BI, days 11 & 12.
41. Shackleton, BI, day 26.
42. Mersey, BI, day 18.
43. Davie, p182.
44. Boxhall, BI, day 13.

Chapter 31
1. Turnbull, BI, day 13.
2. Mersey, BI, day 14.
3. Lightoller, BI, day 12.
4. Harrison, p101.
5. Harrison, p100.
6. Mersey, BI, day 16.
7. Harrison, p70.
8. Davie, p96.
9. Harrison, p96.
10. Mersey, BI, day 16.
11. Ismay, BI, day 16; Davie, p11.
12. Ismay, BI, day 17; Gracie, pp307–308.
13. Ismay, BI, day 16.
14. Davie, p123.
15. Hays, BI, day 21.
16. Davie, p123.
17. Ismay, BI, day 16.
18. Gracie, p249.
19. Ismay, BI, day 16.
20. *Ibid.*
21. Mersey, BI, day 20.
22. Carlisle, BI, day 20.
23. Ismay, BI, day 16.
24. Sanderson, BI, day 17.
25. Passow, BI, day 21.
26. Steel, BI, day 21.
27. Reade, p249.
28. *Ibid.*
29. Harrison, p110.
30. Harrison, p106.
31. Harrison, p273.
32. Lightoller, BI, day 12.
33. Gibbs, p32.
34. Marcus, p222.
35. Davie, p173.
36. *Ibid.*

37. Reade, p228.
38. Hays, BI, day 21.

Chapter 32
None.

Chapter 33
None.

Bibliography

Newspapers
Daily Express; London 17 September 1993.
Evening Chronicle (Newcastle) 15, 16, 17, 18, 19, 20, 22 and 25 April 1912. Henceforward known as *Evening Chronicle*.
Independent on Sunday; 15 July 1990
Lloyd's Weekly News; **Gibbs, P.**; 'The Deathless Story of the *Titanic*', 1912. Henceforward referred to as Gibbs.
New York Times, 16 April 1912. Henceforward referred to as NYT.
Oxford Mail; 2 April 1992.
*The Daily Telegrap*h; 3 April 1992, 10 March 1993.
The Guardian; London, 21 September 1993; 31 January 1994 and 23 March 1994.
*The Independen*t; 10 July 1990.
The Oxford Times; 20 April 1912.
*The Time*s; London, 17 September 1993.

Magazines
'Reader's Digest; Great Mysteries Of The Past'; New York, 1992.
Journal of Commerce, 'Report of British Official Inquiry into the Circumstances Attending the Loss of the RMS *Titanic*'; London, 1912. Henceforward referred to as (Name), BI, day (number).
Journal of Commerce; **Oldham, W. J.**; 'The Ismay Line'; Henceforward referred to as Oldham.
National Geographic; April 1986, December 1986 and October 1987.
Oxford Journal Illustrated; 17 and 24 April 1912.
Proceedings; **Institute of Mechanical Engineers**, July 1895.
The Sunday Mirror Magazine; 11 October 1987, 22 November 1987.

Books
Angelucci & Cucari; *Ship*s; MacDonald & Jane's, London, 1975. Henceforward referred to as Angelucci & Cucari.
Ballard, R. D.; *The Discovery of the* Titanic; Guild, Hodder & Stoughton, London, 1987. Henceforward referred to as Ballard.
Beesley, L.; *The Loss of the SS* Titanic; Heinemann, 1912. Henceforward referred to as Beesley.
Boyd-Smith, P.; Titanic: *from Rare Historical Reports*; Brooks Books, Southampton, 1992.

Cahill, R. A.; *Disasters At Sea:* Titanic *to* Exxon Valdez; Century, 1990. Henceforward referred to as Cahill.

Coleman, T.; *The Liners*; Penguin, Harmondsworth, 1976. Henceforward referred to as Coleman.

Davie, M.; *The* Titanic*: The Full Story of a Tragedy*; 1986. Henceforward referred to as Davie.

Eaton, John P. & Haas, Charles A.; Falling Star: Misadventures of White Star Line Ships; Patrick Stephens, Sparkford, 1989. Henceforward referred to as E&H FS.

Eaton, John P. & Haas, Charles A.; Titanic: *Destination Disaster*; Patrick Stephens, Sparkford, 1987. Henceforward referred to as E&H DD.

Eaton, John P. & Haas, Charles A.; Titanic: *Triumph and Tragedy*; Patrick Stephens, Sparkford, 1986. Henceforward referred to as E&H.

Encyclopaedia Britannica, 1957.

Garrett, R.; Atlantic Disaster: *The* Titanic *and Other Victims of the North Atlantic*; Buchan & Enright, London, 1986. Henceforward referred to as Garrett.

Gracie, A.; *The Truth About The* Titanic; 1913 reprinted 1985. Henceforward referred to as Gracie.

Harrison, L.; *A* Titanic *Myth: The* 'Californian' *Incident*; William Kimber, 1986. Henceforward referred to as Harrison.

Hobson, D.; *The Pride of Lucifer*; Hamish Hamilton, 1990.

Hutchings, D. F.; *RMS* Titanic*: A Modern Legend*; Waterfront Publications, Blandford Forum, 1993. Henceforward referred to as Hutchings.

Jackson, S.; *J. P. Morgan*; Heinemann, 1984. Henceforward referred to as Jackson.

Lord, W.; *A Night To Remember*; Corgi, London, 1956. Henceforward referred to as Lord.

Lord, W.; *The Night Lives On*; 1987.

Lynch, D. & Marschall, K.; Titanic: *An Illustrated History*; Hodder & Stoughton, 1992. Henceforward referred to as Lynch.

Marcus, G.; *The Maiden Voyage*; Manor Books, New York, 1978. Henceforward referred to as Marcus.

Mills, S.; *RMS* Olympic: *The Old Reliable*; Waterfront Publications, Blandford Forum, 1993. Henceforward referred to as Mills.

O'Connor, R.; *Down To Eternity; Gold Medal Books*, Fawcett Publications. Henceforward referred to as O'Connor.

Pellegrino, C.; *Her Name* Titanic: *The Untold Story of the Sinking and Finding of the Unsinkable Ship*; 1990. Henceforward referred to as Pellegrino.

Preston, A.; *History Of The Royal Navy*; Hamlyn Bison, London, 1983. Henceforward known as Preston.

Reade, L.; *The Ship That Stood Still*; Patrick Stephens, Sparkford, 1993. Henceforward referred to as Reade.

Report on the *Loss of the SS* Titanic; The Official Government Inquiry, HMSO, 1912. Henceforward referred to as Brit Inq.

Rostron, A.; *The Loss Of The* Titanic; *Titanic* Signals Archive, Westbury, Wilts, 1991. Henceforward referred to as Rostron.

Shipbuilder; *Ocean Liners of the Past*; *White Star Triple Screw Atlantic Liners* Olympic & Titanic; Patrick Stephens, Sparkford, 1988. Henceforward referred to as Shipbuilder.

Shipbuilders to the World: 125 years of Harland & Wolff; Belfast, 1861–1986.

Stenson, P.; Lights: *The Odyssey of C. H. Lightoller*; Bodley Head, 1984.

Titanic *Signals News*; White Star Publications, Winter/Spring, 1994.

Titanic — *Reappraisal of Evidence Relating to SS* Californian; Marine Accidents Investigation Board, HMSO, 1992. Henceforward referred to as Brit Inq 2.

Wade, W. C.; *The* Titanic: *End of a Dream*; Weidenfeld & Nicolson, London, 1979. Henceforward referred to as Wade.

Woodroffe & MacDonald; *Titanic*; MacDonald & Co, London, 1989.

Videos

Secrets of The *Titanic*; National Geographic, 1986.

Titanic; W H Smith, 1993.

Titanic; The Way We Were.

Lusitania; Network First.

Index